# RACIAL
# THOUGHT
# IN AMERICA

*From the Puritans to Abraham Lincoln*

# RACIAL THOUGHT IN AMERICA

## Volume I

*From the Puritans to Abraham Lincoln*

A Documentary History

Edited and with an Introduction and Notes by
LOUIS RUCHAMES

The University of Massachusetts Press  1969

TO
FLORENCE, DENNIS,
KENNETH, ALLEN, *and* MICHAEL

# *Preface*

The purpose of this work is to provide a panoramic view of the development of racial thought in the United States from Colonial times to the beginning of the Civil War. The second volume will depict racial thought from the Civil War to the present. In order to keep the manuscript within manageable proportions, I have emphasized racial thought relating to whites and Negroes. Documents involving the Indian are included primarily to throw light upon racial thought relating to Negroes and whites.

I wish to express my gratitude to a number of colleagues who have read the manuscript, in whole or in part, and offered very helpful suggestions: Professors Sidney Kaplan, Department of English, and Milton Cantor, Department of History, University of Massachusetts in Amherst; Professor Peter Rose, Department of Sociology, Smith College; Professor Clement Eaton, Department of History, University of Kentucky; and Dr. Staughton Lynd. Professor Louis Cohn-Haft, Department of History, Smith College, was very helpful in providing certain translations from the Latin as well as additional explanatory material. I am also grateful to Joseph Greene, editor of Grosset & Dunlap, for his helpfulness at all stages of the publication of this volume, to Miss Paula Cohn, of Grosset & Dunlap, for her superb editorial assistance, and Mrs. Leone Stein, Director of the University of

Massachusetts Press, for her interest in the manuscript and her attention to numerous details involved in the arrangements for publication.

Regrettably, Winthrop D. Jordan's erudite *White Over Black: American Attitudes Toward the Negro, 1550–1812,* and Herbert S. Klein's *Slavery in the Americas: A Comparative Study of Cuba and Virginia,* came to hand too late to be of use.

Mrs. Dorothy Koval has been exceedingly helpful as research assistant, typist and proofreader. She has also compiled the Index.

To Miriam, whose understanding and devotion have helped smooth many an obstacle, I can offer in return only my appreciation and love.

## A NOTE ON THE SELECTIONS

To illustrate the diverse conflicts and problems at stake in American race relations and racial thought, the selections seek to present a balance of historical views on the subject. No consideration of racial thought in the United States can skirt the ugly but crucial institution of Negro slavery; hence a number of documents dealing with the pros and cons of slavery have been included when they throw light upon racial attitudes. Brought to the fore by the rise of the anti-slavery movement, such evaluations of slavery represent a substantial attempt to analyze hereditary and environmental factors in racial differentiation.

Wherever feasible, original spelling and usage have been retained, and introductory passages have been kept brief, to permit the inclusion of as much firsthand source material as possible and let the participants speak directly for themselves. Beneath the sometimes archaic expressions, behind the occasional devices of rhetoric, lie vital beliefs and fundamental issues—morality and science, economics and legislation, life and death—which influenced and were affected by racial thought in the United States.

# Contents

# Introduction

## THE SOURCES OF RACIAL THOUGHT
## IN COLONIAL AMERICA

Racial thought is as old as civilized man. It had its origin in man's first awareness of physical, cultural, religious or economic differences between groups. Explanation of these differences in terms of durable and hereditary group characteristics, physical or mental, constitutes racial thinking.

The racial attitudes, distinctions and prejudices brought to the American continent by the earliest colonists were those prevailing in Europe in their day. Racial thought had been a part of European and Oriental culture since antiquity. Its elements existed in India, China, Egypt, Palestine and Greece. "We find modern race theories sketched in outline"[1] in the thought of Aristotle, notes Friedrich Hertz. Aristotle propounded the view that nature destines some men to be masters and others to be slaves, giving each those qualities appropriate to his position in society. In Aristotle's view, the relationship of master and slave is for their mutual benefit. As he notes in the *Politics*, "It is clear, then, that some men are by nature free, and others slaves, and that for these latter slavery is both expedient and right."[2]

During the Middle Ages and extending into the early modern

1

period, racial thought was used to explain differences between economic and social classes, especially between the peasantry and the nobility. Some thinkers regarded the peasants as descended from Ham, the accursed son of Noah, and the knights from the Trojan heroes, who had presumably settled in England, Germany and France after their defeat. In the seventeenth century, Count de Boulainvilliers, a spokesman for the French nobility, declared the nobles to be descended from their Germanic conquerors and the masses of the people from the subject Celts and Normans.[3]

Ethnocentrism and slavery were additional elements of the cultural heritage which the early colonists brought to the American continent. Slavery had existed in Europe since antiquity.[4] It prevailed in England during Saxon and Norman times. While it declined in Western Europe from about 900 to 1300, giving place to serfdom,[5] it increased again at the end of the Middle Ages and during the early modern period. Venetian and Genoese slave traders bought Armenians, Bulgarians, Circassians and Serbs from the Turks and sold them in Mediterranean countries. Spanish Christians sold Moors into slavery as they conquered all of Spain. Moslem traders in Africa brought Sudanese Negroes across the Sahara to North African ports and sold them to Mediterranean towns as house slaves.[6] After the fall of Constantinople in 1453, at least 50,000 of its citizens were sold into slavery. As the Portuguese made their discoveries of land and Negroes along the African coast in the fifteenth century, the trade in slaves rose.[7] John Hawkins's voyage to Guinea in 1562, where he acquired three hundred Negroes, which he then sold in Hispaniola,[8] meant the entrance of England into the slave trade and the beginning of what ultimately became a vast increase in the number of Africans sold as slaves.

Ethnocentrism provided the rationale and the apology for slavery and the slave trade among Christians. If Christianity was the only true religion, and Christians the new "chosen people," they could do as they saw fit with the earth and its non-Christian populations. Heathens, Jews, Moslems and others were fair game; witness Pope Nicholas V's order in 1452 empowering the King of Portugal "to despoil and sell into slavery all Moslems, heathen and other foes of Christ."[9] The Church itself held slaves.

Moorish slaves sent to Pope Innocent VIII in 1488 by Ferdinand the Catholic were distributed among the Cardinals and other dignitaries.[10] Although, as early as about A.D. 600, Pope Gregory the Great had expressed the opinion that manumission was a great good and had freed two church slaves, the accepted interpretation was that it applied primarily to those who accepted Christianity and even in these instances "manumission was not the right of the slave but a pious and commendable act on the part of the master."[11]

Nor is there any doubt that slavery was accepted as a necessary social institution by most European thinkers. Two men as different as Sir Thomas More and Martin Luther argued the need for slavery. More included slavery in his Utopia and Luther used the Bible to justify slavery and the sale of slaves.[12] In his discussion of Columbus's attitude toward the enslavement of American Indians, Samuel Eliot Morison writes: "There never crossed the mind of Columbus, or his fellow discoverers and conquistadors, any other notion of relations between Spaniard and American Indian save that of master and slave. It was a conception founded on the Spanish enslavement of Guanches in the Canaries, and on the Portuguese enslavement of Negroes in Africa, which Columbus had observed and taken for granted, and which the Church condoned. It never occurred to him that there was anything wrong in this pattern of race relations, begun and sanctioned by that devout Christian prince, D. Henrique of Portugal."[13]

Slavery and the slave trade received their greatest impetus with the discovery of America and the subsequent effort to exploit its resources of men and materials. The Indians were enslaved on plantations and in mines. Though such humanitarians as the Spanish priest Bartolomé de Las Casas protested against Spanish enslavement of the Indians,[14] and the institution itself was prohibited by royal decree in the famous New Laws of 1542, the prohibition was not always observed by the colonists, and where it was observed, other forms of forced labor took the place of outright slavery.[15] As the Indians of South America were decimated by overwork and disease, Negroes were imported from Africa to take their place.[16] Because of the expensiveness of such importation, the African slave trade did not reach its full stride until the end of the sixteenth century when sugar consumption "skyrocketed," sugar became "the most valuable agricultural commodity in international trade,"[17] and the vast profits from sugar production justified the high cost of the African slave trade. The result was the importation of an estimated 900,000 Africans into the New World in the sixteenth century and 2,750,-000 in the seventeenth.[18]

With the increase in slavery and the slave trade, and more numerous encounters of Europeans with Indians and Negroes, European scholars began to give greater attention to race and racial differences. It is interesting to note that it was only during the modern period that the term "race" came into use. The English term was first used at the beginning of the sixteenth century, the Italian *razza* first appeared in the fourteenth century, while the Spanish *raza,* the Portuguese *raca* and the French *race* were first used in the fifteenth century.[19]

Questions of a racial nature began to interest Europeans—such questions as whether or not Negroes and Indians were to be regarded as human beings whose souls could be saved by conversion to Christianity; the origin of racial differences, especially skin color; whether or not other races were inferior to whites; and so forth. At a very early date, "a favorite Spanish theory was to look upon them [the Indians] as descendants of the lost ten tribes of Israel."[20] A Scottish professor in Paris, John Major, first applied the Aristotelian doctrine of natural slavery to the Indians in a book published in Paris in 1510.[21] Antonio de Montesinos, a Spanish Dominican friar, preached a sermon in Hispaniola in 1511, in which he protested against Spanish mistreatment of the Indians and asked: "Are these Indians not men? Do they not have rational souls? Are you not obliged to love them as you love yourselves?"[22]

In 1537, as a result of the efforts of Las Casas and others, who opposed enslavement of the Indians no less than their extermination, Pope Paul III issued a bull entitled "Sublimis Deus."[23] In it he condemned the view that the Indians "should be treated as dumb brutes created for our service . . . incapable of receiving the catholic faith," and affirmed that "the Indians are truly men and that they are not only capable of understanding the catholic faith but, according to our information, they desire exceedingly to receive it." At the same time, he decreed that the Indians "are by no means to be deprived of their liberty or the possession of their property, even though they be outside the faith of Jesus Christ; and that they may and should . . . enjoy their liberty and the possession of their property; nor should they be in any way enslaved. . . ."[24]

One of the important events in the history of racial thought took place in 1550 and 1551 at Valladolid, Spain, in a debate between Juan Genés de Sepulveda and Las Casas on the question of whether the Aristotelian theory, that some men are slaves by nature, could be applied to the Indians. Sepulveda argued that the Indians were rude and inferior beings by nature, with no capacity for political life, whose inferiority required that the superior Spaniards rule over them.[25] Las Casas argued that the Indians were rational beings, superior to many ancient peoples, even the Greeks and Romans, and therefore worthy of freedom.[26] Neither contestant gained a clear-cut victory. Although Lewis Hanke argues that Las Casas' publicly stated views strengthened those who believed "that all the people of the world are human beings" and represented "one more painful and faltering step . . . along the road of justice for all races,"[27] he admits that during the seventeenth century, the Aristotelian view of race "reigned almost supreme in Europe and America."[28]

Other thinkers too were speculating about the nature of races. In 1520, Paracelsus declared that Negroes and other peoples were not descended from Adam, and in 1591, Giordano Bruno maintained that "No sound thinking person will refer the Ethiopians to the same protoplast as the Jewish one."[29] During the same century, Montaigne, who believed in the equality of all men, remarked concerning the Brazilian Indian: "There is nothing savage or barbarous about his nature save for the fact that each of us labels whatever is not among the customs of his own people as barbarism."[30]

During the sixteenth and seventeenth centuries, English opinion on the slave trade and slavery, as well as on Negroes and Indians, was not very different from that of most Spaniards and Portuguese. Most Englishmen approved of slavery and despised Negroes and Indians. To some extent, theory was better than practice. Many Englishmen who had read Las Casas' writings, beginning with an English edition in 1583 entitled *The Spanish Colonie, or Briefe Chronicle of the Acts and Gestes of the Spaniards in the West Indies,* were horrified by Spanish cruelty. A pamphlet on America by William Lightfoote, *The Complaint of England,* published in 1587, had a section on Spanish cruelty to the Indians, probably based on Las Casas. There were Englishmen who believed that if placed in a similar situation, they would have treated the natives better than had the Spaniards. The English preacher George Benson, in a sermon at Paul's Cross on May 7, 1609, urged the colonization of Virginia and expressed the hope that Englishmen "would be more humane" than the Spaniards who were depicted in the writings of Las Casas.[31]

The attitudes of most Englishmen, however, were probably quite similar to that of Queen Elizabeth when she heard of Sir John Hawkins's first slavery venture in 1562–63. Her first comment was that "it was detestable and would call down vengeance from heaven upon the undertakers." But when Hawkins came to see her and showed her his profit sheet, "not only did she forgive him but she became a shareholder in his second slaving voyage."[32] James A. Froude writes that when it was established in the sixteenth century, the slave traffic "had the sanction of the church, and no objection had been raised to it anywhere on the score of morality. . . . One regrets that a famous Englishman should have been connected with the slave trade; but we have no right to heap violent censures upon him because he was no more enlightened than the wisest of his contemporaries. . . . Hawkins on his return to England [after his first voyage] formed an African Company out of the leading citizens of London."[33]

Slavery, too, was condoned in England.[34] As has been noted, Sir Thomas More approved it for his Utopia. Hanke points out that "during all the time English-speaking peoples were allowing their blood to be chilled by Las Casas' revelations of Spanish cruelty, almost no one arose among them to denounce slavery as he had done. In the Church of England one lone clergyman criticized Negro slavery in the seventeenth century, and even the Quakers in eighteenth-century America 'groped their way slowly, with heart searching, toward the conviction that slavery could not be truly reconciled with the Christian faith.' "[35] Finally, Henry S. Burrage, the editor of "Early English and French Voyages, 1534–1600," writes that "neither in the relation of the second voyage by Sparke, nor in this by Hawkins, is there any intimation whatever that at that time the slightest disgrace attached to slave-stealing and slave-selling."[36]

H. N. Brailsford, describing the second Civil War in England (1648), refers to "the systematic sale of the prisoners, Welshmen, Scots and Englishmen, to serve as slaves in all but name in the plantations of Barbados and Virginia." Thousands of prisoners were involved. "One lot of 2,000 Scots was offered in succession first to the Most Catholic and then to the Most Christian King, but the Spaniards had no ready cash and the French bid too little.

"In those days the slave trade worked in both directions, with white merchandise as well as black. After the battle of Worcester 1,500 Scottish prisoners were granted to the Guinea merchants and set to work in the mines of Africa. . . . It is to the credit of Sir Harry Vane's humanity that after the royalist rising round Salisbury in 1655 he protested, though in vain, against the barbarity of sending political opponents as slaves to the Caribbean islands."[37] And elsewhere in his volume, commenting on the Negro slave trade, Brailsford notes that in all the writings of the Puritan Revolution, "One brief passage, but only one, condemns the slave trade, which was already the source of some great families' fortunes." The writer of the passage was the Leveller, William Walwyn.[38]

African Negroes were known to Englishmen primarily through the African slave trade and West Indian plantations. As might be expected, the result was that Negroes were regarded as inferior beings who were fit only for slavery or a "savage" existence in Africa. The same may be said of English attitudes toward the Indians, which, despite an occasional protesting voice, were best expressed by William Cunningham in 1559, when he spoke of Indians as "comparable to brute beasts."[39]

It was but a short step to the opinion which finally prevailed— that the English as civilized and superior human beings, who were Christians and therefore the elect of God, had the right to possess themselves of the territories of the savage Indians, as the Israelites took the lands of the Canaanites.[40] The recompense to the Indians was the opportunity to convert to Christianity and thus achieve salvation. Indeed, as was true also of the Spanish

settlers, the Christianization of the Indians was regarded as a
serious responsibility of the settlers by many clergymen as well as
laymen; it thus became one of the chief rationalizations of the
colonization enterprise. Louis B. Wright remarks that "even
Raleigh, least religious of the great Elizabethan adventurers,
seems to have been convinced of the value of evangelizing the
heathen," although he warned "that the refusal of the infidels to
accept Christianity immediately should not be made an excuse
for laying waste their land with the sword."[41] Many, if not most,
of Raleigh's contemporaries were convinced, however, of "the
right of followers of the true Jehovah to take by force the lands
of the Canaanites."[42] The most popular arguments for colonization were those that united the saving of heathen souls with the
material advancement of the colonists. Wright cites Edward
Hayes, captain of one of Sir Humphrey Gilbert's vessels, who
wrote an account of the expedition, as using both arguments.
Hayes first demonstrates England's claim to North America with
the assertion that God intended the English to colonize and
Christianize it. To achieve success, the adventurers "must be
stirred by a zeal to save 'poore infidels captivated by the devill,'
as well as by a desire to relieve the poor of England and advance
the interest of the nation." In addition to the "harvest of
heathen souls," as a reward of colonization, "he adroitly suggested that *rich mines might also be found*—and fat lands that
would bring wealth to their owners. The happy union of material prosperity and spiritual benefits made an argument believed to be irresistible."[43]

A sermon preached at Whitechapel in 1609 to an audience
many of whose members were about to depart for Virginia fore-
shadowed the colonists' attitudes toward the Indians and Negroes. Using as a text Genesis 12:1–3, it urged that "Abrams
posteritie [must] keepe to themselves. They may not marry nor
give in marriage to the heathen, that are uncircumcised. . . . The
breaking of this rule may breake the necks of all good successe of
this voyage, whereas by keeping the feare of God, the planters in
shorte time, by the blessing of God, may grow into a nation
formidable to all the enemies of Christ."[44]

In his *Notes on the History of Slavery in Massachusetts*, G. H.
Moore emphasizes that "the colonists of Massachusetts assumed

to themselves 'a right to treat the Indians on the footing of Canaanites or Amalekites,' and practically regarded them from the first as forlorn and wretched heathen, possessing few rights which were entitled to respect."[45] This helps to explain the well known if apocryphal story of a meeting of the settlers of Milford, Conn., at which the problem of taking Indian lands was discussed. The settlers came to a decision which was inscribed in the minutes of their meeting and which took the form of a syllogism.

"1. The earth is the Lord's and the fullness thereof. Voted.

"2. The Lord can dispose of the earth to his saints. Voted.

"3. We are his saints. Voted."[46]

That conversion to Christianity made little difference in the Puritan treatment of Indians, is suggested by Theodore Parker, the great Unitarian scholar: "A sharp distinction was always made," he writes, "between converted Indians and other Christians; they were treated, in every respect, as an inferior race; restricted to villages of their own, and cut off by opinion, as well as law, from intermarriage and intercourse with the whites. No one was allowed to sell them horses or boats. It was proposed to exterminate them, as being of the 'cursed seed of Ham.' "[47]

As Parker suggests, segregation was widespread among the colonists. Its prevalence is indicated by the editors of Judge Samuel Sewall's *Diary*. In a note to an entry in his *Diary*, dated January 30, 1708, they write as follows:

It is illustrative of the strong antipathy felt by all those of English blood here, at that time, against coming into any close relation with the Indians on terms of social equality. The feeling of repulsion, which the first settlers brought with them, regarding the natives as heathens, was strongly intensified by subsequent relations with them, whether peaceful or hostile, till it generally resulted in contempt or disgust. Those who are well versed in our history are familiar with the many evidences of this antipathy, presenting themselves as long as any of the native race survived in this neighborhood. It was quite otherwise with the French, who came into terms of very free association and intimacy with the Indians, and never manifested, even if they felt, this antipathy of race. But "English stomachs" revolted from such fellowship. The same strong repugnance was indulged by them against social intimacy with the Indians, with which we are more familiar as felt toward Negroes. The Jesuit Father and the French Bushranger freely shared the loathsome lodging and food of the Indian, and came into hearty fellowship with him. Roger Williams, more than any other Englishman, struggled against this race antipathy. He says that he forced himself to lodge "in the filthy, smokey holes" of savages, that he "might win their language." But the wife of the good John Eliot, apostle as he was, carefully prepared some food for him to take with him when he mounted his horse to visit his red flock at Natick, and he tells us that he had partitioned off a lodging place and a bed in the loft of the Indian meeting-house for his private use.[48] He reserved the closest fellowship with his converts till they should meet in heavenly regions, and would "all be changed," appearing in "celestial bodies." Judge Sewall, in his gentle kindness of spirit and his humanity of righteousness, proved himself far in advance of his contemporaries in his sympathy with Negroes and Indians. Yet, as we read the above entry in his journal, we present to ourselves his evident embarrassment. An approved Indian convert and preacher, on his way to professional service at Natick, calls on Sewall with letters from his friend Reverend Roland Cotton, of Sandwich, also a friend of the Indians, and a preacher to them. Sewall shifts off the intended lodger upon the keeper of a tavern open to very promiscuous guests. "They could not do it," writes the good Judge, "so I was fain to lodge him in my study." The hospitable guest chamber in the house was reserved for another class of lodgers. However, most of the citizens of Boston, at that time, would, if compelled to entertain an Indian, have given him a couch of straw and horse blankets in a barn.[49]

Theodore Parker, in the previously cited essay, underscores the sharp racial consciousness of the early settlers. "In New England more pains were taken than elsewhere in America to spare, to civilize, and to convert the sons of the wilderness; but yet here the distinction of race was always sharply observed. Even community of religion and liturgical rites, elsewhere so powerful a bond of union, was unable to soften the Englishman's repugnance to the Indian. The Puritan hoped to meet the Pequods in heaven, but wished to keep apart from them on earth, nay, to exterminate them from the land. Besides, the English met with no civilized tribe in America, and for them to unite in wedlock with such children of the forest as they found in North America would have been contrary, not only to the Anglo-Saxon prejudice, but to the general usage of the world—a usage to which even the French in Canada afford but a trifling exception. The Spaniards had less of this exclusiveness of race, perhaps none at all. They met with civilized tribes of red men, met and mingled in honorable and permanent connection. In Peru and Mexico, at this day, there are few men of pure Spanish blood."[50]

Parker's opinion that the English colonists showed much greater prejudice toward Indians and Negroes than did the Spanish and Portuguese, is shared by many observers, some of whom apply the distinction to English and French settlers as well. The English seem to have segregated the Indians and Negroes and passed far more laws prohibiting interracial marriages than did the Spanish, the Portuguese or the French.[51] It is also claimed that slavery in Latin America, under the Spanish and Portuguese, was far less severe than among the English in the Southern portion of the United States.

Several explanations have been given for such differing national attitudes toward racial segregation and slavery. These include differences between Catholic and Protestant theology, religious belief and practices, the influence of Roman law on Spanish and Portuguese slavery, and the longer contact of the Portuguese and the Spanish with colored peoples.[52] William C. MacLeod, in *The American Indian Frontier,* points out that those who contrast French and English reactions "make the cardinal error of comparing French traders not with British traders but with British agriculturalists." Actually, "French and British traders alike married Indian women and gave rise to numbers of half-breeds; and both groups were able to adapt themselves to Indian ways of life and the Indian manner of thinking." On the other hand, "the agricultural settlers, both French and British, did not want Indian women as wives. Farmers needed wives who knew the ways of European housekeeping and husbandry, who knew how to milk cows, fry eggs, and so on. Indian women would not do." With regard to the Spanish and Portuguese, the early settlers preferred to import European wives but it was the military "who initiated the development of an important half-breed stock which, because of the civilizing nature of the Indian policies pursued became of social, political and economic importance and served as a link between the wholly red and the wholly white elements of the population."[53]

Herbert Moller, too, denies any basic difference in attitude

toward the natives between English, French, Spanish and Portuguese colonists. He attributes differences in racial miscegenation
to the impact of a high sex ratio.[54] Thus, even among the English, "miscegenation was practiced wherever white women were
extremely rare and where current moral ideas were not yet influenced by the presence of a considerable number of white
women. Among the Puritans of New England such a condition
never existed. There a strong repugnance was prevalent from the
very beginning of the settlements." Those individuals who were
not opposed to social intercourse with the Indians "were found
particularly in the servant class which always had a higher sex
ratio than the upper strata." While accepting MacLeod's explanation for the avoidance of racial intermarriage in the British
colonies, i.e., the farmers' need for wives who understood European housekeeping and farming, Moller explains the very strong
racial repugnance as being due to "the presence and influence of
white women." "Aversion to so-called 'hypogamy' is considered a
normal trait of feminine psychology and its existence can be
taken for granted in any stratified society. Whereas in Europe
this feminine attitude prevented women from marrying beneath
their social status, it worked in America against their marrying
into culturally and socially inferior races. Moreover, through
their enhanced influence on family and community life, women
became more or less unintentionally the foremost agents in the
establishment of racial barriers. Thus the development of aversion to racial miscegenation in the thirteen colonies can be traced
to the invasion of feminine sentiments into colonial society."[55]

With the landing of twenty Negroes at Jamestown, Virginia,
in 1619, began the racial problem with which we are directly
concerned. By 1638, Negro slaves had been introduced into Massachusetts, and in 1641 the Massachusetts "Body of Liberties"
gave sanction to slavery by providing that there was not to be
bond slavery in the colony "unless it be lawfull Captives taken in
just warres, and such strangers as willingly sell themselves or are
sold to us." Virginia gave statutory recognition to slavery in 1661.
By the end of the century, Negro slavery was an accepted and
important part of colonial life.

Given the existence of Negro slaves in the colonies at an early
date,[56] what is the relation of slavery to prejudice against the

Negro—to the opinion of him as an inferior being, fit only for slavery? The accepted view regards racial prejudice as an outgrowth and rationalization of slavery. It is suggested by as early an observer as Tocqueville in his *Democracy in America*,[57] and by as recent a writer as Oscar Handlin, who remarks that "since slavery as an institution was not readily shaken off, it was necessary to justify the exploitation involved in it; and that led many earnest men along a line of thought few regarded with favor yet not many could resist."[58] The line of thought he refers to is, of course, the belief in Negro inferiority.

This view of prejudice as an outgrowth of slavery has recently been challenged by Carl Degler.[59] He notes that slavery, as for instance in Brazil and Spanish America, has not always given rise to racial prejudice. He argues, too, that discrimination against the Negro existed before slavery, existed indeed from the very beginning of settlement. "Thus, legal slavery in the English colonies reinforced and helped to perpetuate the discrimination against the Negro which prevailed almost from the beginning of settlement."[60] Finally, this discrimination was due to a recognition by the English "of Negroes as different in race, religion, and culture." Racial prejudice, it appears, led to discrimination and discrimination to slavery. "In this sense," he concludes, "it might be proper to speak of slavery in the English colonies as the institutionalization of a folk prejudice."[61]

It should be noted, first, that Degler is not quite consistent in his point of view. Elsewhere in the same essay he remarks that "American race prejudice originated in the discriminatory social atmosphere of the seventeenth century. . . ."[62] The suggestion seems to be that prejudice was a result rather than a cause of discrimination. What, then, one may ask, was the cause of seventeenth century discrimination? Moreover, Degler offers two different explanations for the origin of prejudice or discrimination against the Negro. First is the fact that the Negro, born in Africa, "was a heathen at a time when 'Christian' was a title of import; moreover, he was black and culturally different." But this does not explain why Jews, Irishmen and others who were culturally different from English Christians were not placed in the category of the Negro and similarly discriminated against. If the answer is that they *were* discriminated against, the logical question then is, why did not such discrimination result in slavery as it did with the Negro?

His second explanation seems more reasonable but it vitiates his entire theory. "The fact that Negroes arrived in English America as the cargo of the international slave trade unquestionably fostered a sense of superiority among Englishmen. . . . It was to be anticipated that from the beginning a special inferior position would be assigned black men."[63] If, as Degler suggests, the arrival of Negroes to these shores as slaves led almost immediately to prejudice and discrimination against them, does not this mean that it was slavery that led to prejudice and discrimination and not the reverse? Thus, while Handlin is in error in attributing prejudice to the growth of slavery in the 1660's—for the former did exist from the very beginning of colonial settlement—Degler errs in assuming that prejudice did not result from slavery. True, it did not result from the American slavery of the 1660's, but it did arise with the slavery of the slave trade.[64] Thus, as one writer suggests, "the Negroes were not enslaved because the British colonists specifically despised dark-skinned people and regarded them alone as properly suited to slavery; the Negroes came to be the object of the virulent prejudices because they and they alone could be enslaved."[65]

The attitudes of Englishmen, their prejudices and practices toward the Negro, during the sixteenth, seventeenth and eighteenth centuries, were formed mainly through their experience with the slave trade, which, for Englishmen, began with the slaving voyage of Sir John Hawkins in the sixteenth century. It was the Negro as slave, torn from African soil and transported to the West Indies, or to England, and, from 1619 on, to the English colonies in North America, who provided the foundation for the English image of the Negro as an inferior creature in England and the colonies.

The role of the slave trade and slavery in forming colonial attitudes toward the Negro is alluded to by Chief Justice Taney in a very revealing statement in the Dred Scott decision. Though one need not accept the inferences concerning citizenship rights of Negroes in the United States in the 1850's which Justice Taney draws from his observations, the facts themselves are cor-

rect. He notes that in Europe in the seventeenth and eighteenth
centuries, Negroes had been regarded

as beings of an inferior order, and altogether unfit to associate with
the white race, either in social and political relations; and so far inferior, that they had no rights which the white man was bound to respect; and that the Negro might justly and lawfully be reduced to
slavery for his benefit. He was bought and sold, and treated as an ordinary article of merchandise and traffic, whenever a profit could be
made by it. . . .

And in no nation was this opinion more firmly fixed or more uniformly acted upon than by the English government and English people. They not only seized them on the coast of Africa, and sold them
or held them in slavery for their own use; but they took them as ordinary articles of merchandise to every country where they could make a
profit on them, and were far more extensively engaged in this commerce than any other nation in the world.

The opinion thus entertained and acted upon in England was naturally impressed upon the colonies they founded on this side of the
Atlantic.

The white man's enslavement of the African Negro, as a being
obviously different from himself, and his ability to continue to
do so with impunity, were the basic factors in the origin of
prejudice and discrimination toward the black man.[66]

## NOTES

1. Friedrich Hertz, *Race and Civilization*, tr. by A. S. Levetus and W. Entz
(New York, 1928), p. 4. For examples of racial thought in antiquity, see
Thomas F. Gossett, *Race: The History of an Idea* (Dallas, 1963), p. 3 ff.
In one instance, Gossett's treatment is tendentious. In delineating the
views of the early Hebrews he fails to mention those opposed to racial
or religious superiority, as, for example, the books of Ruth and Jonah.
The most recent and best study of Jewish racial attitudes in the Bible
is by Maurice Samuel, *Race, Nation, and People in the Jewish Bible*
(The B. G. Rudolph Lectures in Judaic Studies, Syracuse University,
March 1967).

2. I, 5. See also Hans Kohn, "Race Conflict," *Encyclopedia of the Social
Sciences*, XIII, 36, and Hertz, *Race and Civilization*, p. 4, for discussions of
Aristotle's views on race. William L. Westermann argues against the
existence of racial prejudice in Roman slavery. *The Slave Systems of
Greek and Roman Antiquity* (Philadelphia, 1955), p. 104. M. I. Finley
differentiates between the racial feelings of ancient Greece and Rome and

those of the American South. Thus, "though the Greeks tried to denigrate the majority of their slaves with the 'barbarian' label and though Roman writers . . . are full of contemptuous references to 'Orientals' among their slaves and freedmen, the weaknesses of this simple classification were apparent enough even to them. The decisive fact is that widespread manumission and the absence of strict endogamy together destroy all grounds for useful comparison with the American South on this score." "Between Slavery and Freedom," *Comparative Studies in Society and History*, VI (April 1964) , 246. See also his "Race Prejudice in the Ancient World," *The Listener*, Feb. 1, 1968, pp. 146, 147.

3. See Hertz, *Race and Civilization*, p. 5; Henri, Comte de Boulainvilliers, *Histoire de l'Ancien Gouvernement de la France*, 3 vols. (1727, published posthumously) , cited in Hertz, p. 5; Kohn, "Race Conflict," pp. 36–41.

4. M. I. Finley notes that freedom "is a concept which had no meaning and no existence for most of European history." "Between Slavery and Freedom," p. 237. Elsewhere in the same essay, Finley remarks that "not even the ancient believers in the brotherhood of men were opponents of slavery; the best that Seneca the Stoic and St. Paul the Christian could offer was some variation on the theme, 'status doesn't matter.' " P. 244.

5. Melvin Knight, "Medieval Slavery," *Encyclopedia of the Social Sciences*, XIII, 77–80.

6. Sir Arthur Helps, *The Spanish Conquest of America* (London and New York, 1900) , p. 5n.

7. Their first voyage brought back 200 kidnapped Negroes; thereafter, between 1444 and 1460, seven to eight hundred African slaves were brought to Portugal and Spain each year. See Helps, *The Spanish Conquest*, p. 36. See also Elizabeth Donnan, *Documents Illustrative of the History of the Slave Trade to America* (Washington, D.C., 1930) , I, 1. For the most recent emphasis on the continuity of slavery and the slave trade in European society, see David Brion Davis, *The Problem of Slavery in Western Culture* (Ithaca, 1966) , pp. 31, 42–44.

8. See Daniel P. Mannix, in collaboration with Malcolm Cowley, *Black Cargoes: A History of the Atlantic Slave Trade, 1518–1865* (New York, 1962) , pp. 21–22. Contrary to accepted opinion, Hawkins was not the first Englishman to engage in the African slave trade. The first was a certain John Lok who carried off five Negroes from the Guinea Coast under the justification that the Negroes "were a people of beastly living, without God, law, religion or commonwealth." However, the consequence of his action was a disruption of the trade in gold and ivory which English merchants had been carrying on for some time with the African tribes. The merchants of London forced him to return his booty in order to help then re-establish their trade. See O. A. Sherrard, *Freedom from Fear: The Slave and His Emancipation* (New York, 1959) , pp. 36–37.

9. Knight, "Medieval Slavery," pp. 77–80.

10. *Ibid.*

11. *Ibid.*

12. John Howard Lawson, *The Hidden Heritage* (New York, 1950), pp. 102, 116–117, 172, discusses the views of both men regarding slavery. See also Davis, *The Problem of Slavery*, pp. 107–8.

13. *Admiral of the Ocean Sea, A Life of Christopher Columbus* (Boston, 1942), p. 291.

14. For further information about Las Casas see Lewis Hanke, *Bartolomé de Las Casas* (Philadelphia, 1952); Marcel Brion, *Bartolomé de Las Casas* (New York, 1929); Sir Arthur Helps, *Life of Las Casas* (London, 1868). Originally Las Casas favored the introduction of Negro slaves to replace the Indians, believing the former better able to withstand the heavy work demanded by the Spaniards. He later changed his opinion and opposed Negro enslavement as well. See Lewis Hanke, *The Spanish Struggle for Justice in the Conquest of America* (Philadelphia, 1949), p. 60.

15. For a brilliant discussion of the causes of the New Laws and their ultimate effect, see Marvin Harris, *Patterns of Race in the Americas* (New York, 1964), pp. 16–20.

16. It may be argued that Europeans treated Negroes more severely or at least with fewer pangs of conscience than they did Indians. See Lewis Hanke, *Aristotle and the American Indians: A Study of Race Prejudice in the Modern World* (Chicago, 1959), p. 9; Davis, *The Problem of Slavery*, p. 10.

17. Harris, *Patterns of Race*, p. 13.

18. John Hope Franklin, *From Slavery to Freedom: A History of American Negroes* (New York, 1963), p. 58.

19. See Jack Carrick Trevor, "Race," *Chamber's Encyclopedia* (New York, 1950), XI, 428; also "Race," in Sir James Murray (ed.), *A New English Dictionary on Historical Principles*, VIII (Oxford, 1910), Part I; Ashley Montagu, *Man's Most Dangerous Myth*, 4th ed. (New York and Cleveland, 1964), p. 47n.

20. Woodbury Lowery, *The Spanish Settlements Within the Present Limits of the United States, 1513–1561* (New York and London, 1901), p. 56.

21. Hanke, *Aristotle and the American Indians*, p. 14.

22. *Ibid.*, p. 15; also Hanke, *The Spanish Struggle for Justice*, pp. 17–19.

23. For the complete text see Francis Augustus McNutt, *Bartholomew de Las Casas* (New York and London), pp. 427–431.

24. In *Aristotle and the American Indians*, pp. 106–7, Hanke notes that this attitude toward the Indians was far milder than that shown toward the Jews of Spain at the end of the 15th century, when they were given the alternatives of assimilation or expulsion.

25. Another opponent of Las Casas, Gonzalo Fernandez de Oviedo, is said to have written that the Indians were "naturally lazy and vicious, melancholic, cowardly, and in general a lying, shiftless people." See Hanke, *The Spanish Struggle for Justice*, p. 11.

26. *Ibid.*, p. 123.

27. *Ibid.*, p. 132.

28. *Aristotle and the American Indians*, p. 56.

29. I. Bendyshe, "The History of Anthropology," *Memoirs of the Anthropological Society of London* (1865), I, 353–5, quoted in T. K. Penniman, *A Hundred Years of Anthropology* (New York, 1936), pp. 41–42.

30. Quoted in Juan Comas, "Racial Myths," in *The Race Question in Modern Science* (UNESCO, 1956), p. 13.

31. Lewis Hanke, *Bartolomé de Las Casas,* pp. 52–58; also Louis B. Wright, *Religion and Empire: The Alliance between Piety and Commerce in English Expansion, 1558–1625* (Chapel Hill, 1943), pp. 47–97.

32. Mannix and Cowley, *Black Cargoes,* p. 22. John A. Williamson, in *Sir John Hawkins, the Time and the Man* (Oxford, 1927), pp. 79–80, notes that the 16th-century French "had ethical objections to slavery. Jacques de Sores refused to countenance it, and a French legal decision of the period anticipated by two centuries the Mansfield judgment of 1772."

33. James Anthony Froude, *English Seamen in the Sixteenth Century* (New York, 1895), pp. 38–40.

34. Sidney Mintz, in a review of Stanley Elkins' *Slavery,* quotes a remarkable passage from a 19th-century Jamaican writer, who emphasizes the close relationship between white slavery in England and Negro slavery in the West Indies during the 16th century. "Not seventy years prior to the settlement of Barbadoes, a remarkable badge of servitude had been imposed on British subjects, by the statute against vagabonds, which adjudged them, expressly and absolutely, to positive slavery; inflicting violent punishments on the disobedient, stigmatising runaways by branding, and, for the second offense, decreeing death. The same law empowered the master to rivet an iron ring around the neck of his slave, affixing the penalty of ten pounds upon the person removing it; and it repeats the word '*slave*,' so odious to British ears, no less than thirty-eight times.

"Such remained the effective law of England in the year 1553; and it was only thirty years after that period that Barbadoes fell into the possession of the Lord High Treasurer. The enactments regarding Negro slaves in the colonies were therefore, naturally enough, transcribed from these late precedents at home, where the name and character of slavery was thus familiar. (I:507–508, *The Annals of Jamaica*, London, John Murray, 1827)." The writer was the Rev. G. W. Bridges. Mintz, *American Anthropologist*, LXIII (June 1961), 582.

35. Hanke, *Bartolomé de Las Casas,* p. 58, quotes Thomas E. Drake, *Quakers and Slavery in America* (New Haven, 1950), pp. 2–4. The clergyman referred to was Morgan Godwyn.

36. In the series entitled *Original Narratives of Early American History,* Vol. III, J. Franklin Jameson, ed. (New York, 1906), p. 135.

37. *The Levellers and the English Revolution* (London, 1961), pp. 333–4. I am indebted to Staughton Lynd for this reference.

38. *Ibid.,* pp. 282, 287n.

39. *The Cosmological Glosse* (London, 1559), fols. 200–201, quoted in Hanke, *Aristotle and the American Indians,* p. 99. Almon W. Lauber, *Indian Slavery in Colonial Times Within the Present Limits of the United States*

(New York, 1913), p. 159n, quotes Samuel G. Drake, *The Old Indian Chronicle* (edition of 1867), p. 7, to the effect that Englishmen regarded the Indians as a "degraded, inferior and faithless race, and no more to be regarded than the Africans."

40. Louis B. Wright, *Religion and Empire*, p. 157, notes that "the pioneers of New England were convinced that they were the children of God, another Chosen People. Their sense of election operated to their material advantage and gave them a valuable assurance of right in all their endeavors." The right of Englishmen to displace the Indians from their lands left some pangs of conscience among many apologists, as is shown by the efforts of clergymen and others to justify that right. One such effort was by Samuel Purchase in 1625 in the concluding Chapter XX of the "Ninth Booke" of *Hakluytus Posthumus or Purchas His Pilgrimes*, Vol. XIX (Glasgow, 1906). In this chapter, which he entitles "Virginia Verger; or a Discourse shewing the benefits which may grow to this Kingdome from American English Plantations, and specially those of Virginia and Summer Islands," he bases the English right to New World lands upon a "commission" from God, "naturall right," and economic progress and profit. Wright has an excellent evaluation of "Samuel Purchas and the Heathen," in *Religion and Empire*, pp. 115–133.

41. *Religion and Empire*, pp. 28–29.

42. *Ibid.*

43. *Ibid.*, pp. 24–26.

44. Quoted in Arthur W. Calhoun, *A Social History of the American Family* (Cleveland, 1917), I, 323.

45. New York, 1866, p. 30. George E. Ellis, "The Indians of Eastern Massachusetts," in Justin Winsor, *Memorial History of Boston* (1800), I, 242, says: "It was of the very fibre and texture, of the very vigor and essence of the faith of the Puritan exile, that, in coming to occupy these wild realms where the imbruted savages roamed, they were fortified by the same Divine rights, and held to the same solemn obligations as were the chosen people of old, of whom they read so trustfully in their Bibles. . . . They, too, were to dispossess and drive out the heathen, and to put them to the sword, to form no truce with them, and to exterminate even their offspring." For similar views of Virginia colonists, see Wright, *Religion and Empire*, pp. 90–93.

46. Wright, *Religion and Empire*, pp. 157–8.

47. "Prescott's Conquest of Mexico," in *Theodore Parker's Works*, ed. Frances Power Cobbe (London, 1865), X, 121.

48. See also "Gookin's Historical Collections of the Indians in New England," *Massachusetts Historical Society Collections*, 1st Series, I, 181; Ellis, "The Indians of Eastern Massachusetts," *op. cit.*, I, 264; Lauber, *Indian Slavery in Colonial Times*, p. 252.

49. Samuel Sewall's *Diary*, *Massachusetts Historical Society Collections*, 5th Series, VI, 212–213n.

50. "Prescott's Conquest of Mexico," *Works*, X, 121.

51. Charles H. Lincoln (ed.), *Narratives of the Indian Wars*, Vol. XIV of the

*Original Narratives of Early American History* (New York, 1913), writes:
"From his arrival on the St. Lawrence the Frenchman regarded the Indian
as a possible friend, and joined with him in his wars as well as in all
hunting expeditions. . . . Very different was the behavior of the New
Englander toward the Indian. Nothing could induce him to regard the
red man as an equal, although in no English colony save Pennsylvania
was the Indian better treated. Massachusetts tried to educate the Indian,
and endeavored to convert him to Christianity, traded with him, and
fought with him, but neither people felt at home in the presence of the
other." See also Lauber, *Indian Slavery in Colonial Times*, p. 171; and
Alexis de Tocqueville, *Democracy in America*, ed. Phillips Bradley (New
York, 1958), I, 359n, 388–9.

52. See Frank Tannenbaum, *Slave and Citizen: The Negro in the Americas*
(New York, 1946), pp. 43 ff. Stanley Elkins accepts Tannenbaum's analysis
and conclusions and expands upon them. Elkins, *Slavery, A Problem in
American Institutional and Intellectual Life* (New York, 1963), pp. 37 ff.;
also, Carl N. Degler, *Out of Our Past: The Forces That Shaped Modern
America* (New York and Evanston, 1959), pp. 28 ff. For a trenchant attack
upon Tannenbaum's thesis that race prejudice and slavery were more
severe among the English than among the Spanish and Portuguese, see
Harris, *Patterns of Race*, pp. 65–94. Harris denies that Spanish-Portuguese
slavery, in practice, was less harsh than the English variety, or that the
former were less prejudiced toward Negroes and Indians than the latter.
He does find a difference in the treatment of the freed slave, which he
traces to the different economic and social roles of the freed slave in the
two societies.

David B. Davis also takes a critical view of the Tannenbaum-Elkins
thesis. While repeating some of Harris's arguments, he is strangely un-
aware of Harris's work. He suggests that the medieval and early modern
legal codes of Spain were far more severe toward the slave than is
realized. Latin American slaveholders, more often than not, disregarded
whatever legal rights the mother country sought to confer upon Negro
slaves. Their treatment of their slaves was frequently harsh and cruel,
except where economic and political conditions dictated otherwise, and
racial prejudice was widespread. For instance, in areas of Brazil in the
18th and 19th centuries, Negroes were regarded as inferior beings, not
true men, and were subjected to "harsh chattel slavery and racial prejudice." He concludes that "the subject is too complex and the evidence
too contradictory for us to assume that the treatment of slaves was
substantially better in Latin America than in the British colonies, taken
as a whole." *The Problem of Slavery*, pp. 224–243.

Arnold A. Sio, in a recent examination of the subject, concludes that
"a much greater similarity existed between slavery in the United States
and Latin America than heretofore suspected," a similarity which, as he
notes, included a strong component of racial prejudice. "Interpretations of
Slavery: The Slave Status in the Americas," *Comparative Studies in
Society and History*, VII (April 1965), 298–308. The most recent defender

of the Tannenbaum-Elkins thesis is Herbert S. Klein, "Anglicanism, Catholicism and the Negro Slave," *Comparative Studies in Society and History,* VIII (April 1966), 295–327. His evidence and conclusions are questioned by Elsa V. Goveia, "Comment on 'Anglicanism, Catholicism and the Negro Slave,'" *ibid.,* 328–330. An excellent critical review of Elkins's book is by Sidney Mintz, *American Anthropologist,* LXIII (June 1961), 579–87. Gilberto Freyre, in *New World in the Tropics: The Culture of Modern Brazil* (New York, 1963), emphasizes that there was far less racial prejudice toward Indians and Negroes among the Portuguese in Brazil than in the English colonies. See pp. 8–11. The 1945 edition of this volume and other writings by Freyre are among the sources cited by Tannenbaum and Degler.

53. New York, 1928, pp. 359–361.

54. Davis writes that sexual relations between white men and Negro slave-women were "more common and acceptable in regions where there were relatively few white women." Yet, after noting the prevalence of racial prejudice in the Spanish and Portuguese colonies, he concludes that "for all their racial consciousness, the Spanish and Portuguese were distinctive in their final acceptance of the inevitability of intermixture." He attributes the change to the acceptance of concubinage by Latin American society and the view that each infusion of white blood was an advance in status. See *The Problem of Slavery,* pp. 273–5.

55. Herbert Moller, "Sex Composition and Correlated Culture Patterns of Colonial America," *The William and Mary College Quarterly,* II (April 1945), 131–137. Winthrop Jordan has recently sought to relate miscegenation to sex ratio and the proportion of Negroes in a total population. "American Chiaroscuro: The Status and Definition of Mulattoes in the British Colonies," *William and Mary Quarterly,* 2nd Series, XIX (April 1962), 183–200. Davis suggests that "Jordan tends to underestimate the importance of racial discrimination even in Jamaica," yet admits the validity of much of his evidence. Davis, *The Problem of Slavery,* p. 273n. It is curious that neither Davis nor Jordan is aware of the work of either Moller or MacLeod.

56. It should be noted that American historians differ on the date of the origin of slavery as an institution in the colonies. Oscar Handlin believes that it did not develop until the 1660's. "The status of Negroes was that of servants, and so they were identified and treated down to the 1660's." *Race and Nationality in American Life* (New York, 1957), p. 7. Ulrich Bonnell Phillips believes that legal slavery was slow in appearing. *American Negro Slavery* (New York, 1933), pp. 74–77. So does J. C. Ballagh, *History of Slavery in Virginia* (Baltimore, 1902), pp. 28–35. Historians who believe that slavery may have existed from the very first arrival of the Negro are Susie Ames, *Studies of the Virginia Eastern Shore in the Seventeenth Century* (Richmond, 1940), pp. 101–110; and W. F. Craven, *Southern Colonies in the Seventeenth Century, 1607–1689* (Baton Rouge, 1949), pp. 217–9. George H. Moore, the pioneer historian of slavery in Massachusetts, asserts its early origin in fact and in legislation. *Notes on*

*the History of Slavery in Massachusetts* (New York, 1860) , pp. 1–19. Carl N. Degler seems undecided: in one part of an essay he writes concerning legal slavery that "the first mention does not occur until after 1660"; but then he notes that "the first legal code of Massachusetts, the Body of Liberties of 1641, . . . clearly permitted enslavement of those who are 'sold to us,' which would include Negroes brought in by the international slave trade." "Slavery and the Genesis of American Race Prejudice," *Comparative Studies in Society and History,* II (October 1959) , 50, 62–63. Elkins reviews the debate in *Slavery,* pp. 39–40n. Phillips remarks with some justification that "the first comers were slaves in the hands of their maritime sellers; but they were not fully slaves in the hands of their Virginia buyers, for there was neither law nor custom then establishing the institution of slavery in the colony." *American Negro Slavery,* p. 75.

57. New York, 1948, I, 358–360.

58. *Race and Nationality,* p. 22.

59. *Out of Our Past,* pp. 26–42; "Slavery and the Genesis of American Race Prejudice," *op. cit.,* pp. 49–66.

60. *Out of Our Past,* p. 30.

61. *Ibid.,* p. 38.

62. *Ibid.,* p. 30.

63. *Ibid.,* p. 31.

64. Elkins's statement that "the British colonists . . . brought with them no legal categories comparable to that of 'slave' as the term would be understood by the end of the seventeenth century" (*Slavery,* pp. 37–38) is highly dubious. Whether or not "slave" existed as a legal category in English law, the relationship between the English slave trade and the captured African slave had all the essential elements of later American slavery. A knowledge of this relationship was certainly a part of early English colonial experience.

65. Harris, *Patterns of Race,* p. 70. Davis believes that "the mainland colonists adopted from Barbados the view that Negroes were especially suited for perpetual slavery; and that while the early status of some Negroes was close to that of white servants, an increasingly degraded position was both a source and result of racial prejudice." (*The Problem of Slavery,* p. 245.)

66. For a recent discussion of the history of the controversy over the relationship between slavery and prejudice, see Winthrop D. Jordan, "Modern Tensions and the Origins of American Slavery," *Journal of Southern History,* XXVIII (February 1962) , 18–30. Jordan shares Degler's and Handlin's failure to evaluate the impact of more than half a century of the English slave trade and Negro slavery in England upon the attitudes of the English colonists toward the Negro. Yet, in an earlier essay, Jordan does seem to understand the relationship, at least in part. After discussing the rise of Negro slavery in the English West Indies, he suggests that "Negro slavery in New England depended on a perception of the Negro as a peculiar kind of social being, a creature whom it was fitting and proper to enslave for life. This perception may well have been borrowed from an area, the West Indies, where economic conditions provided a fertile soil for the growth of

such a view. New England itself seems to have lacked the soil but appropriated the harvest." See "The Influence of the West Indies on the Origins of New England Slavery," *William and Mary Quarterly*, XVIII (April 1961) , 250.

*Part One*

# THE COLONIAL AGE

# CHAPTER 1

## Indians and Colonists in the Seventeenth Century

It has been suggested the the earliest English colonists regarded the Indians as inferior creatures whose lands and lives were best utilized when put to the service of Christian Englishmen. With the onset of conflict between the colonists and the Indians during the Pequot War in 1637 and King Philip's War in 1675 and 1676, the settlers' attitudes hardened and increasing numbers favored the enslavement or extermination of the Indians. Those who were seriously concerned about Indian welfare were generally few in number and decreased during the latter part of the seventeenth century. Only isolated voices were raised in the Indians' behalf, and even these were limited in their demands. Two such voices were those of Daniel Gookin and John Eliot.

The first of the following selections is an example of early Puritan thought about the Indians' origins; the second is a protest against the practice of selling Indians into slavery. Both throw valuable light on existing racial attitudes toward the Indians and anticipate subsequent reactions to Negroes in the American colonies.

### DANIEL GOOKIN

#### HISTORICAL COLLECTIONS OF THE INDIANS IN NEW ENGLAND

Daniel Gookin (1612—March 19, 1687), born either in Kent, England, or County Cork, Ireland, spent most of his life in Virginia, Maryland and, after 1644, Massachusetts. A landowner, officeholder and soldier, possessed of a scholarly mind and a deep interest in the welfare of the Indians, Gookin became unpopular during King Philip's War by the protection which, as a magistrate, he extended to the Indians; in 1681 he became major-general of Massachusetts. In the following essay he brings together and evaluates the theories of his day concerning Indian origins. Frequent references to the Indians as "savages" and "heathen" indicate the extent to which even humanitarian settlers regarded the Indians as inferiors. This selection is from Gookin's book, "Historical Collections of the Indians in New England: Of the Several Nations, Numbers, Customs, Manners, Religion and Government, Before the English Planted There." Though written in 1674, it was not published until a century after Gookin's death, in the *Collections of the Massachusetts Historical Society*, Vol. I (Boston, 1792).

## Chap. 1. *Several Conjectures of Their Original*

1. Concerning the original of the Savages, or Indians, in New-England, there is nothing of certainty to be concluded. But yet, as I conceive, it may rationally be made out, that all the Indians of America, from the straits of Magellan and its adjacent islands on the south, unto the most northerly part yet discovered, are originally of the same nations or sort of people. Whatever I have read or seen to this purpose, I am the more confirmed therein. I have seen of this people, along the sea coasts and within land, from the degrees of 34 unto 44 of north latitude; and have read of the Indians of Magellanica, Peru, Brasilia, and Florida, and have also seen some of them; and unto my best apprehension, they are all of the same sort of people.

The colour of their skins, the form and shape of their bodies, hair, and eyes, demonstrate this. Their skins are of a tawny colour, not unlike the tawny Moors in Africa; the proportion of their limbs, well formed; it is rare to see a crooked person among them. Their hair is black and harsh, not curling; their eyes, black and dull; though I have seen, but very rarely, a grey-eyed person among them, with brownish hair. But still the difficulty yet remains, whence all these Americans had their first original, and from which of the sons of Noah they descended, and how they

came first into these parts; which is separated so very far from
Europe and Africa by the Atlantick Ocean, and from a great part
of Asia, by Mar del Zur, or the South sea; in which sea Sir
Francis Drake, that noble hero, in his famous voyage about the
world, sailed on the west of America, from the straits of Magellan, lying about 52 degrees of south latitude, unto 38 degrees of
north latitude: where he possessed a part of the country, and
received subjection from those very tractable Indians, in the
right of the English nation, and his sovereign prince, the famous
queen Elizabeth, then reigning, and her successors, and gave it
the name of New Albion; which country lies west northerly of
Massachusetts in New England; for Boston lies in 42° 30'. and
New Albion in 48° of north latitude, which is near six degrees
more northerly.

There are divers opinions about this matter.

2. First, some conceive that this people are of the race of the
ten tribes of Israel, that Salmanasser carried captive out of their
own country, A. M. 3277, of which we read in II. Kings, xviii.
9–12; and that God hath, by some means or other, not yet discovered, brought them into America; and herein fulfilled his just
threatening against them, of which we may read, II. Kings, xvii.
from 6. to the 19 verses; and hath reduced them into such woful
blindness and barbarism, as all those Americans are in; yet hath
reserved their posterity there: and in his own best time, will fulfil
and accomplish his promise, that those *dry bones shall live,* of
which we read Ezek. xxxvii. 1–24. A reason given for this is taken
from the practice of sundry Americans, especially of those inhabiting Peru and Mexico, who were most populous, and had
great cities and wealth; and hence are probably apprehended to
be the first possessors of America. Now of these the historians
write, that they used circumcision and sacrifices, though often-
times of human flesh; so did the Israelites sacrifice their sons unto
Moloch. II. Kings, xvii. 17. But this opinion, that these people
are of the race of the Israelites, doth not greatly obtain. But
surely it is not impossible, and perhaps not so improbable, as
many learned men think.[1]

3. Secondly, another apprehension is, that the original of these
Americans is from the Tartars, or Scythians, that live in the
northeast parts of Asia; which some good geographers conceive **is**

nearly joined unto the north west parts of America, and possibly are one continent, or at least, separated, but by some narrow gulf; and from this beginning have spread themselves into the several parts of North and South America; and because the southern parts were more fertile, and free from the cold winters incident to the northern regions, hence the southern parts became first planted, and most populous and rich. This opinion gained more credit than the former, because the people of America are not altogether unlike in colour, shape, and manners, unto the Scythian people, and in regard that such a land travel is more feasible and probable, than a voyage by sea so great a distance as is before expressed, from other inhabited places, either in Europe, Asia, or Africa; especially so long since, when we hear of no sailing out of sight of land, before the use of the loadstone and compass was found. But if this people be sprung from the Tartarian or Scythian people, as this notion asserts, then it is to me a question, why they did not attend the known practice of that people; who, in all their removes and plantations, take with them their kine, sheep, horses, and camels, and the like tame beasts; which that people keep in great numbers, and drive with them in all their removes. But of these sorts and kinds of beasts used by the Tartars, none were found in America among the Indians. This question or objection is answered by some thus. First, possibly the first people were banished for some notorious offences; and so not permitted to take with them of these tame beasts. Or, secondly, possibly, the gulf, or passage, between Asia and America, though narrow, comparatively, is yet too broad to waft over any of those sort of creatures; and yet possibly men and women might pass over it in canoes made of hollow trees, or with barks of trees, wherein, it is known, the Indians will transport themselves, wives and children, over lakes and gulfs, very considerable for breadth. I have known some to pass with like vessels forty miles across an arm of the sea.

4. But before I pass to another thing, suppose it should be so, that the origination of the Americans came from Asia, by the northwest of America, where the continents are conceived to meet very near, which indeed is an opinion very probable; yet this doth not hinder the truth of the first conjecture, that this people may be of the race of the ten tribes of Israel: for the king

of Assyria who led them captive, as we heard before, transported them into Asia, and placed them in several provinces and cities, as in II. Kings, xvii. 6. Now possibly, in process of time, this people, or at least, some considerable number of them, whose custom and manner it was to keep themselves distinct from the other nations they lived amongst; and did commonly intermarry only with their own people; and also their religion being so different from the heathen, unto whom they were generally an abomination, as they were to the Egyptians; and also partly from God's judgment following them for their sins: I say, it is not impossible but a considerable number of them might withdraw themselves; and so pass gradually into the extreme parts of the continent of Asia; and where-ever they came, being disrelished by the heathen, might for their own security, pass further and further, till they found America; which being unpeopled, there they found some rest; and so, in many hundreds of years, spread themselves in America in that thin manner, as they were found there, especially in the northern parts of it; which country is able to contain and accommodate millions of mankind more than were found in it. And for their speech, which is not only different among themselves, but from the Hebrew, that might easily be lost by their often removes, or God's judgment.

5. A third conjecture of the original of these Indians, is, that some of the tawny Moors of Africa, inhabiting upon the sea coasts, in times of war and contention among themselves, have put off to sea, and been transported over, in such small vessels as those times afforded, unto the south part of America, where the two continents of Africa and America are nearest; and they could not have opportunity or advantage to carry with the small vessels of those times any tame beasts, such as were in that country. Some reasons are given for this notion. First, because the Americans are much like the Moors of Africa. Secondly, the seas between the tropicks are easy to pass, and safe for small vessels; the winds in those parts blowing from the east to the west, and the current setting the same course. Thirdly, because it is most probable, that the inhabitants of America first came into the south parts; where were found the greatest numbers of people, and the most considerable cities and riches.

6. But these, or any other notions, can amount to no more

than rational conjecture; for a certainty of their first extraction cannot be attained: for they being ignorant of letters and records of antiquity, as the Europeans, Africans, and sundry of the Asians, are and have been, hence any true knowledge of their ancestors is utterly lost among them. I have discoursed and questioned about this matter with some of the most judicious of the Indians, but their answers are divers and fabulous. Some of the inland Indians say, that they came from such as inhabit the sea coasts. Others say, that there were two young squaws, or women, being at first either swimming or wading in the water: The froth or foam of the water touched their bodies, from whence they became with child; and one of them brought forth a male; and the other, a female child; and then the two women died and left the earth: So their son and daughter were their first progenitors. Other fables and figments are among them touching this thing, which are not worthy to be inserted. These only may suffice to give a taste of their great ignorance touching their original; the full determination whereof must be left until the day, wherein all secret and hidden things shall be manifested to the glory of God.

7. But this may upon sure grounds be asserted, that they are Adam's posterity, and consequently children of wrath; and hence are not only objects of all Christians' pity and compassion, but subjects upon which our faith, prayers, and best endeavours should be put forth to reduce them from barbarism to civility; but especially to rescue them out of the bondage of Satan, and bring them to salvation by our Lord Jesus Christ; which is the main scope and design of this tractate.

## NOTE

1. For an interesting bibliographical essay on the literature dealing with the relationship between the Indians and the ten tribes of Israel, see Lewis Hanke, *The First Social Experiments in America, A Study in the Development of Spanish Indian Policy in the Sixteenth Century* (Gloucester, Mass., 1964), pp. 72–3.

# JOHN ELIOT

## A Protest

John Eliot (1604—May 21, 1690), an Englishman who came to Massachusetts in 1631, was pastor of a Puritan church at Roxbury for more than forty years. He is perhaps best known for his missionary efforts among the Indians as well as for his attempts to mitigate the harsh treatment meted out to the Indians by the colonists. He was no less interested in the welfare of the Negro slaves. Cotton Mather writes of Eliot's effort to secure Christian instruction for them in *Magnalia Christi Americana* (Hartford, 1855, p. 576); and George H. Moore, in *Slavery in Massachusetts* (New York, 1866, p. 37n), states that he was the "first in America to lift up his voice against the treatment which Negroes received in New England." He was a prolific writer whose works included translations of the Old and New Testaments into the Indian language. The following selection protests the cruel treatment of the Indians in the wake of King Philip's War. It was originally printed in Justin Winsor's *The Memorial History of Boston*, Vol. I (Boston, 1880), p. 322. See also Convers Francis, *Life of John Eliot, the Apostle to the Indians* (Boston and London, 1836); Cotton Mather, *The Life of the Rev. John Eliot, the First Missionary to the Indians in North America* (London, 1820); E. H. Byington, "John Eliot, the Puritan Missionary to the Indians," *Papers Am. Soc. Ch. Hist.*, VIII (1897), 109–145. For a remarkable account of white attitudes toward Indians, from 1609 to 1851, see Roy Harvey Pearce, *The Savages of America* (Baltimore, 1953). A useful account of the relations between Indians and whites, from colonial times to the present, is William T. Hagan, *American Indians* (Chicago and London, 1961).

To the Honorable Council sitting at Boston this 13th 6th 1675:—

The humble petition of John Eliot showeth that the terror of selling away such Indians into the islands for perpetual slavery,

who shall yield up themselves to your mercy, is like to be an
effectual prolongation of the war. Such an exasperation of them
as it may produce we know not what evil consequence upon all
the land. Christ hath said: 'Blessed are the merciful, for they
shall obtain mercy.' This usage of them is worse than death. To
put to death men that have deserved to die is an ordinance of
God, and a blessing is promised for it. It may be done in faith.
The design of Christ in these last days is not to extirpate nations,
but to gospelize them. He will spread the gospel round the world
about. Rev. xi. 15: 'The kingdoms of the world are become the
kingdoms of our Lord and of his Christ.' His sovereign hand and
grace hath brought the gospel into these dark places of the earth.
When we came we declared to the world, and it is recorded, yea,
we are engaged by our Letters Patent from the King's Majesty,
that the endeavor for the Indians' conversion, not their extirpation, were one great end of our enterprise in coming to these
ends of the earth. The Lord hath so succeeded the work as that
(by his grace) they have the Holy Scriptures, and sundry of
themselves able to teach their countrymen the good knowledge of
God. The light of the gospel is risen among those that sat in
darkness and in the region of the shadow of death. And however
some of them have refused to receive the gospel, and now are
incensed in their spirits into a war against the English, yet by
that good promise,—Psalm ii. 1,2,3,4,5,6,7,—I doubt not but the
morning of Christ is to open a door for the free passage of the
gospel among them, and that the Lord will publish the word.
Ver. 6: 'Yet have I set my king, my anointed, upon the holy hill
of Zion, though some rage at it.'

My humble request is that you would follow Christ his de-
signs in this matter to foster[?] the passages of religion among
them, and not to destroy them. To send into a place a slave away
from spiritual direction, to the eternal ruin of their souls, is as I
apprehend to act contrary to the mind of Christ. Christ's command is we should enlarge the kingdom of Jesus Christ. Isa.
liv. 2: 'Enlarge the place of thy tent.'

It seemeth to me that to sell them away as slaves is to hinder
the enlargement of his kingdom. How can a Christian sell [ex-
cept?] to act in casting away their souls for which Christ hath in
an eminent hand provided an offer of the gospel? To sell souls

for money seemeth to me a dangerous merchandise. If they deserve to die, it is far better to be put to death under godly persons who will take religious care that means may be used that they may die penitently. To sell them away from all means of grace when Christ hath provided means of grace for them is the way for us to be active in destroying their souls, when we are highly obliged to seek their conversion and salvation, and have opportunity in our hand so to do. Deut. xxiii. 15, 16. A fugitive servant from a Pagan master might not be delivered to this master, but be kept in Israel for the good of his soul. How much less lawful is it to sell away souls from under the light of the gospel into a condition where their souls shall be utterly lost so far as appeareth unto men! All men (of reading) condemn the Spaniard for cruelty upon this point in destroying men and depopulating the land. The country is large enough. Here is land enough for them and us too.

In the multitude of people is the King's honor. It will be more to the glory of Christ to have many brought in to worship his great name.

I beseech the honorable Council to pardon my boldness, and let the case of conscience be discussed orderly before the thing be acted. Pardon my weakness, and leave to reason and religion their liberty in this great case of conscience.

# CHAPTER 2

# *Quakers, Negroes and Slaves in the Seventeenth Century*

Writing about Negro slavery in the New World during the seventeenth century, Thomas E. Drake, author of *Quakers and Slavery in America,* notes that "hardly anyone questioned the prevailing belief in the economic necessity of slaveholding, and the morality of slavery seemed justified by its necessity."[1] Since Negroes were believed to be a cursed and heathen people, enslavement would serve the additional purpose of leading them to salvation.[2] By the end of the seventeenth century, Negro slavery was an approved and securely established institution in American life, North and South.[3]

The one protest against Negro slavery prior to 1688 was an act passed by the Commissioners of Providence and Warwicke, in Rhode Island, on May 19, 1652, which read:

> Whereas, there is a common course practised among Englishmen to buy Negers, to that end they may have them for service or slaves for ever; for the preventinge of such practices among us, let it be ordered, that no blacke mankind or white being forced by covenant bond, or otherwise, to serve any man or his assighnes longer than ten yeares, or untill they come to be twentiefour years of age; if they bee taken in under fourteen, from this time of their cominge within the liberties of this Collonie. And at the end or terms of ten yeares to sett them free, as is the manner with the English servants. And that man that will not let them goe free, or shall sell them away elsewhere, to that end that they may be enslaved to others for a long time, hee or they shall forfeit to the Collonie forty pounds.[4]

Apparently, however, it was not enforced.[5]

Because of the lack of opposition to slavery—and, therefore, of any need to defend it—the two most important sources of racial thought in this country prior to the Civil War were missing in the seventeenth century. Hence the absence of significant speculation regarding the nature of the Negro, his relationship to other human beings and his fitness or unfitness for slavery. Yet such thought is not entirely lacking. It is present in the anti-slavery statement of the Germantown Quakers, who remark that "though they are black, we cannot conceive there is more liberty to have them slaves, as [than] it is to have other white ones." It is present even more elaborately in George Keith's remarks.

## NOTES

1. New Haven, 1950, p. 1.
2. John Hope Franklin, *From Slavery to Freedom, A History of American Negroes,* 2nd ed. (New York, 1956), p. 104.
3. George H. Moore, after mentioning that Roger Williams and John Eliot of New England sought to mitigate the horrors of slavery but did not oppose the institution itself, notes: "In their time there was no public opinion against slavery, and probably very little exercise of judgment against it. Even among the Quakers the inner light had not yet disclosed its enormity, or awakened tender consciences to its utter wretchedness." *Slavery in Massachusetts,* p. 72.
4. R. I. *Records,* I, 248, quoted in Moore, *Slavery in Massachusetts,* p. 73.
5. Moore, *ibid.,* pp. 73–74.

# THE GERMANTOWN QUAKERS

## THE FIRST PROTEST AGAINST SLAVERY (1688)

This statement by four Quakers, submitted to their Monthly Meeting at Germantown, Pennsylvania, was at that period a unique and isolated instance of anti-slavery opinion. Essentially it argued that it was as wrong to enslave blacks as to enslave whites. It was not approved by the Monthly Meeting nor by the Quarterly Meeting at Philadelphia or the Yearly Meeting at Burlington, New Jersey.

Although in the ensuing years other isolated Quaker voices were raised against slavery, the vast majority, until the middle of the eighteenth century, "did not see any inconsistency in buying and keeping slaves—they had the same economic interest as all the colonists in employing slave labor."[1]

The Germantown Quakers were not Englishmen but Rhineland artisans—German, Swiss and Dutch—who founded Germantown in 1684. Their protest was not printed and was more or less forgotten until discovered by Nathan Kite in 1844, in the Records of Philadelphia Yearly Meeting (Orthodox). He published it in the *Friend*, XVII (Philadelphia, 1844), 125.[2] It was later reprinted in George H. Moore, *Notes on the History of Slavery in Massachusetts*, pp. 74–78, and elsewhere.

This is to the monthly meeting held at Richard Worrell's:

These are the reasons why we are against the traffic of menbody, as followeth: Is there any that would be done or handled at this manner? viz., to be sold or made a slave for all the time of his life? How fearful and faint-hearted are many at sea, when they see a strange vessel, being afraid it should be a Turk, and they should be taken, and sold for slaves into Turkey. Now, what is *this* better done, than Turks do? Yea, rather it is worse for them, which say they are Christians; for we hear that the most part of such negers are brought hither against their will and consent, and that many of them are stolen. Now, though they are black, we cannot conceive there is more liberty to have them slaves, as [than] it is to have other white ones. There is a saying, that we should do to all men like as we will be done ourselves;

making no difference of what generation, descent, or colour they are. And those who steal or rob men, and those who buy or purchase them, are they not all alike? Here is liberty of conscience, which is right and reasonable; here ought to be likewise liberty of the body, except of evil-doers, which is another case. But to bring men hither, or to rob and sell them against their will, we stand against. In Europe, there are many oppressed for conscience-sake; and here there are those oppressed which are of a black colour. And we who know that men must not commit adultery—some do commit adultery *in* others, separating wives from their husbands, and giving them to others: and some sell the children of these poor creatures to other men. Ah! do consider well this thing, you who do it, if you would be done at this manner—and if it is done according to Christianity! You surpass Holland and Germany in this thing. This makes an ill report in all those countries of Europe, where they hear of [it,] that the Quakers do here handel men as they handel there the cattle. And for that reason some have no mind or inclination to come hither. And who shall maintain this your cause, or plead for it? Truly, we cannot do so, except you shall inform us better hereof, viz.: that Christians have liberty to practise these things. Pray, what thing in the world can be done worse towards us, than if men should rob or steal us away, and sell us for slaves to strange countries; separating husbands from their wives and children. Being now this is not done in the manner we would be done at, [by]; therefore, we contradict, and are against this traffic of menbody. And we who profess that it is not lawful to steal, must, likewise, avoid to purchase such things as are stolen, but rather help to stop this robbing and stealing, if possible. And such men ought to be delivered out of the hands of the robbers, and set free as in Europe. Then is Pennsylvania to have a good report, instead, it hath now a bad one, for this sake, in other countries: Especially whereas the Europeans are desirous to know in what manner *the Quakers* do rule in *their* province; and most of them do look upon us with an envious eye. But if this is done well, what shall we say is done evil?

If once these slaves (which they say are so wicked and stubborn men,) should join themselves—fight for their freedom, and handel their masters and mistresses, as they did handel them before; will these masters and mistresses take the sword at hand

and war against these poor slaves, like, as we are able to believe, some will not refuse to do? Or, have these poor negers not as much right to fight for their freedom, as you have to keep them slaves?

Now consider well this thing, if it is good or bad. And in case you find it to be good to handel these blacks in that manner, we desire and require you hereby lovingly, that you may inform us herein, which at this time never was done, viz., that Christians have such a liberty to do so. To the end we shall be satisfied on this point, and satisfy likewise our good friends and acquaintances in our native country, to whom it is a terror, or fearful thing, that men should be handelled so in Pennsylvania.

This is from our meeting at Germantown, held yͤ 18th of the 2d month, 1688, to be delivered to the monthly meeting at Richard Worrell's.

GARRET HENDERICH,
DERICK OP DE GRAEFF,
FRANCIS DANIEL PASTORIUS,
ABRAM OP DE GRAEFF.

At our monthly meeting, at Dublin, yͤ 30th 2d mo., 1688, we having inspected yͤ matter, above mentioned, and considered of it, we find it so weighty that we think it not expedient for us to meddle with it *here,* but do rather commit it to yͤ consideration of yͤ quarterly meeting; yͤ tenor of it being related to yͤ truth.

On behalf of yͤ monthly meeting,

JO. HART.

This abovementioned, was read in our quarterly meeting, at Philadelphia, the 4th of yͤ 4th mo., '88, and was from thence recommended to the yearly meeting, and the above said Derrick, and the other two mentioned therein, to present the same to yͤ above said meeting, it being a thing of too great weight for this meeting to determine.

Signed by order of yͤ meeting.

ANTHONY MORRIS.

## NOTES

1. Drake, *Quakers and Slavery in America,* p. 4.
2. Drake, *ibid.,* p. 12n.

## GEORGE KEITH

### THE FIRST PRINTED PROTEST AGAINST SLAVERY (1693)

George Keith (1638–1716) was born in Scotland and lived in America from about 1685 to 1704. He had an important impact upon American Quakerism, although, following years of conflict with the Friends, he joined the Anglican Church in 1700. Keith was then already regarded as an apostate by the Friends; those of Philadelphia had disowned him in 1692. The following statement was adopted by the Keithian Friends' Monthly Meeting in 1693 and was printed by William Bradford, a follower of Keith.[1] It represented the opinion of a tiny minority among the Friends. As Keith's biographer remarks, "nearly a century was to elapse before the Quakers definitely disavowed slavery."[2]

The statement affirms the humanity of Negroes and their right to salvation through Christianity. It condemns the slave trade and the cruel treatment of Negro slaves, urging Friends "not to buy any Negroes, unless it were on purpose to set them free." In modern terms, Keith may be called a gradualist, for he suggests that those who have bought Negroes "may set them at liberty . . . after some reasonable time of moderate service." George H. Moore argues that some of Keith's opinions are taken directly from George Fox, the Quaker pioneer.[3]

### An Exhortation & Caution To Friends Concerning buying or keeping of Negroes

S[e]eing our Lord Jesus Christ hath tasted Death for every Man, and given himself a Ransom for all, to be testified in due time, and that his Gospel of Peace, Liberty and Redemption from Sin, Bondage and all Oppression, is freely to be preached unto all, without Exception, and that *Negroes, Blacks* and *Taunies* are a real part of Mankind, for whom Christ hath shed his precious Blood, and are capable of Salvation, as well as *White Men;* and Christ the Light of the World hath (in measure) enlightened them, and every Man that cometh into the World, and that all such who are sincere *Christians* and true Believers in

Christ Jesus, and Followers of him, bear his Image, and are made conformable unto him in Love, Mercy, Goodness and Compassion, who came not to destroy mens Lives, but to save them, nor to bring any part of Mankind into outward Bondage, Slavery or Misery, nor yet to detain them, or hold them therein, but to ease and deliver the Oppressed and Distressed, and bring into Liberty both inward and outward.

Therefore we judge it necessary that all faithful Friends should discover themselves to be true *Christians* by having the Fruits of the Spirit of Christ, which are *Love, Mercy, Goodness, and Compassion* towards all in Misery, and that [further (?)] Oppression and severe Usage, so far as in them is possible to ease and relieve them, and set them free of their hard Bondage, whereby it may be hoped, that many of them will be gained by their beholding these good Works of sincere *Christians,* and prepared thereby, through the Preaching the Gospel of Christ, to imbrace the true Faith of Christ. And for this cause it is, as we judge, that in some places in *Europe* Negroes cannot be bought and sold for Money, or detained to be Slaves, because it suits not with the Mercy, Love & Clemency that is essential to *Christianity,* nor to the Doctrine of Christ, nor to the Liberty the Gospel calleth all men unto, to whom it is preached. And to buy Souls and Bodies of men for Money, to enslave them and their Posterity to the end of the World, we judge is a great hinderance to the spreading of the Gospel, and is occasion of much War, Violence, Cruelty and Oppression, and Theft & Robery of the highest Nature; for commonly the Negroes that are sold to white Men, are either stollen away or robbed from their Kindred, and to buy such is the way to continue these evil Practices of Man-stealing, and transgresseth that Golden Rule and Law, *To do to others what we would have others do to us.*

Therefore, in true *Christian Love,* we earnestly recommend it to all our Friends and Brethren, Not to buy any Negroes, unless it were on purpose to set them free, and that such who have bought any, and have them at present, after some reasonable time of moderate Service they have had of them, or may have of them, that may reasonably answer to the Charge of what they have laid out, especially in keeping Negroes Children born in their House, or taken into their House when under Age, that after a reasonable time of service to answer that Charge, they may set them at Liberty, and during the time they have them, to teach them to read, and give them a Christian Education.

### Some Reasons and Causes of our being against keeping of Negroes for Term of Life.

*First,* Because it is contrary to the Principles and Practice of the *Christian Quakers* to buy Prize or stollen Goods, which we bore a faithful Testimony against in our Native Country; and therefore it is our Duty to come forth in a Testimony against stollen Slaves, it being accounted a far greater Crime under *Moses's* Law than the stealing of Goods; for such were only to restore four fold, *but he that stealeth a Man and selleth him, if he be found in his hand, he shall surely be put to Death, Exod.* 21. 16. Therefore as we are not to buy stollen Goods, (but if at unawares it should happen through Ignorance, we are to restore them to the Owners, and seek our Remedy of the Thief) no more are we to buy stollen Slaves; neither should such as have them keep them and their Posterity in perpetual Bondage and Slavery, as is usually done, to the great scandal of the *Christian Profession.*

*Secondly,* Because Christ commanded, saying, *All things whatsoever ye would that men should do unto you, do ye even so to them.* Therefore as we and our Children would not be kept in perpetual Bondage and Slavery against our Consent, neither should we keep them in perpetual Bondage and Slavery against their Consent, it being such intollerable Punishment to their Bodies and Minds, that none but notorious Criminal Offendors deserve the same. But these have done us no harme; therefore how inhumane is it in us so grievously to oppress them and their Children from one Generation to another.

*Thirdly,* Because the Lord hath commanded, saying, *Thou shalt not deliver unto his Master the Servant that is escaped from his Master unto thee, he shall dwell with thee, even amongst you in that place which he shall chuse in one of thy Gates, where it liketh him best; thou shalt not oppress him, Deut.* 23. 15, 16. By which it appeareth, that those which are at Liberty and freed from their Bondage, should not by us be delivered into Bondage again, neither by us should they be oppressed, but being escaped from his Master, should have the Liberty to dwell amongst us, where it liketh him best. Therefore, if God extend such Mercy under the legal Ministration and Dispensation to poor Servants, he doth and will extend much more of his Grace and Mercy to them under the clear Gospel Ministration; so that instead of punishing them and their Posterity with cruel Bondage and perpetual Slavery, he will cause the Everlasting Gospel to be preached effectually to all Nations, to them as well as others; *And the Lord will extend Peace to his People like a River, and the Glory of the* Gentiles *like a flowing Stream; And it shall come to pass, saith the Lord, that I will gather all Nations and Tongues, and they shall come and see my Glory, and I will set a sign among them, and I will send those that escape of them unto the Nations, to Tarshish, Pull and Lud that draw the Bow, to Tuball and Javan, to the Isles afar off that have not heard my Fame, neither have seen my Glory, and they shall declare my Glory among the* Gentiles, *Isa.* 66. 12–18.

*Fourthly,* Because the Lord hath commanded, saying, *Thou shalt not oppress an hired Servant that is poor and needy, whether he be of thy Brethren, or of the Strangers that are in thy Land within thy Gates, least he cry against thee unto the Lord, and it be sin unto thee; Thou shalt neither vex a stranger nor oppress him, for ye were strangers in the Land of* Egypt, *Deut.* 24. 14, 15. *Exod.* 12. 21. But what greater Oppression can there be inflicted upon our Fellow Creatures, than is inflicted on the poor Negroes! they being brought from their own Country against their Wills, some of them being stollen, others taken for payment of Debt owing by their Parents, and others taken Captive in War, and sold to Merchants, who bring them to the *American* Plantations, and sell them for Bond-Slaves to them that will give most for them; the Husband from the Wife, and the Children from the Parents; and many that buy them do exceedingly afflict them and oppress them, not only by continual hard Labour, but by cruel Whippings, and other cruel Punishments, and by short allowance of Food, some Planters in *Barbadoes* and *Jamaica,* 'tis said, keeping one hundred of them, and some more, and some less, and giving them hardly any thing more than they raise on a little piece of Ground appointed them, on which they work for themselves the seventh days of the Week in the after-noon, and on the first days, to raise their own Provisions, to wit, Corn and Potatoes, and other Roots, etc. the remainder of their time being spent in their Masters service; which doubtless is far worse usage than is practiced by the *Turks* and *Moors* upon their Slaves. Which tends to the great Reproach of the *Christian Profession;* therefore it would be better for all such as fall short of the Practice of those *Infidels,* to refuse the Name of a *Christian,* that those *Heathen* and *Infidels* may not be provoked to blaspheme against the blessed Name of Christ, by reason of the unparallel'd Cruelty of these cruel and hard hearted pretended *Christians.* Surely the Lord doth behold their Oppressions & Afflictions, and will further visit for the same by his righteous and just Judgments, except they break off their sins by Repentance, and their Iniquity by shewing Mercy to these poor afflicted, tormented miserable Slaves!

*Fifthly,* Because Slaves and Souls of Men are some of the *Merchandize of Babylon* by which the Merchants of the Earth are made Rich; but those Riches which they have heaped together, through the cruel Oppression of these miserable Creatures, will be a means to draw Gods Judgments upon them; therefore, *Brethren,* let us hearken to the Voice of the Lord, who saith, *Come out of* Babylon, *my People, that ye be not partakers of her Sins, and that ye receive not her Plagues; for her Sins have reached unto Heaven, and God hath remembred her Iniquities; for he that leads into Captivity shall go into Captivity, Rev.* 18. 4, 5. & 13. 10.

*Given forth by our Monethly Meeting in* Philadelphia, *the* 13th *day of the* 8th *Moneth,* 1693. *and recommended to all our Friends and Brethren, who are one with us in our Testimony for the Lord Jesus Christ, and to all others professing Christianity.*

## NOTES

1. Drake, *Quakers and Slavery,* p. 14.
2. Ethyn Williams Kirby, *George Keith, 1638–1716* (New York and London, 1942) , p. 89.
3. *Slavery in Massachusetts,* pp. 79–80.

# CHAPTER 3

# *A Trio of Puritans on the Black Man and Slavery*

Samuel Sewall, John Saffin and Cotton Mather represented the variety of Puritan thought concerning the Negro and slavery. Sewall was the most liberal of the three in his attack on slavery, yet he believed the Negro to be inferior. Saffin was an outright defender of slavery. Mather, though somewhat uncomfortable with the institution, never condemned it but did seek to ameliorate the condition of the slave under it.

## SAMUEL SEWALL

### A Puritan Condemns Slavery

Successful merchant, distinguished political figure and jurist of Massachusetts, Samuel Sewall (1652–1730) stands out for his integrity and humanity. The story of his confession of error and guilt in the Salem witchcraft trials and executions of August–September 1692 is well known. He is justly famous for his diary, which has been characterized by James Truslow Adams as "an incomparable picture of the mind and life of a Puritan of the Transition period." "The Selling of Joseph," printed in Boston on June 12, 1700, is one of the earliest anti-slavery tracts and the first by an American Puritan. Although Sewall condemns slavery, he shares the contemporary prejudice which regarded Negroes as inferior, foreign beings who could never be integrated into New England society. The essay is reprinted from the *Proceedings of the Massachusetts Historical Society, 1863–1864*, Vol. VII (Boston, 1864), pp. 161–5. Professor Louis

Cohn-Haft of the Department of History at Smith College has provided translations from the Latin and some information in the Notes.

## The Selling of Joseph

### A Memorial

FORASMUCH *as* LIBERTY *is in real value next unto* LIFE: *None ought to part with it themselves, or deprive others of it, but upon most mature Consideration.*

The Numerousness of Slaves at this day in the Province, and the Uneasiness of them under their Slavery, hath put many upon thinking whether the Foundation of it be firmly and well laid; so as to sustain the Vast Weight that is built upon it. It is most certain that all Men, as they are the Sons of *Adam,* are Coheirs; and have equal Right unto Liberty, and all other outward Comforts of Life. GOD *hath given the Earth* [with all its Commodities] *unto the Sons of* Adam, *Psal* 115.16. *And hath made of One Blood, all Nations of Men, for to dwell on all the face of the Earth, and hath determined the Times before appointed, and the bounds of their habitation: That they should seek the Lord. Forasmuch then as we are the Offspring of* GOD *&c. Act* 17.26, 27, 29. Now although the Title given by the last ADAM, doth infinitely better Mens Estates, respecting GOD and themselves; and grants them a most beneficial and inviolable Lease under the Broad Seal of Heaven, who were before only Tenants at Will: Yet through the Indulgence of GOD to our First Parents after the Fall, the outward Estate of all and every of their Children, remains the same, as to one another. So that Originally, and Naturally, there is no such thing as Slavery. *Joseph* was rightfully no more a Slave to his Brethren, than they were to him: and they had no more Authority to *Sell* him, than they had to *Slay* him. And if *they* had nothing to do to Sell him; the *Ishmaelites* bargaining with them, and paying down Twenty pieces of Silver, could not make a Title. Neither could *Potiphar* have any better Interest in him than the *Ishmaelites* had. *Gen.* 37.20, 27, 28. For he that shall in this case plead *Alteration of Property,* seems to have forfeited a great part of his own claim to Humanity. There is no proportion between Twenty Pieces of Silver, and LIBERTY. The Commodity it self is the Claimer. If *Arabian* Gold be imported in any quantities,[1] most are afraid to meddle with it, though they might have it at easy rates; lest if it should have been wrongfully taken from the Owners, it should kindle a fire to the Consumption of their whole Estate. 'Tis pity there should be more Caution used in buying a Horse, or a little lifeless dust; than there is in purchasing Men and Women: Whenas they are the Offspring of GOD, and their Liberty is,

. . . . . . . . *Auro pretiosior Omni.*[2]

And seeing GOD hath said, *He that Stealeth a Man and Selleth him, or if he be found in his hand, he shall surely be put to Death. Exod.* 21.16. This Law being of Everlasting Equity, wherein Man Stealing is ranked amongst the most atrocious of Capital Crimes: What louder Cry can there be made of that Celebrated Warning,    *Caveat Emptor!*[3]

And all things considered, it would conduce more to the Welfare of the Province, to have White Servants for a Term of Years, than to have Slaves for Life.[4] Few can endure to hear of a Negro's being made free; and indeed they can seldom use their freedom well; yet their continual aspiring after their forbidden Liberty, renders them Unwilling Servants. And there is such a disparity in their Conditions, Colour & Hair, that they can never embody with us, and grow up into orderly Families, to the Peopling of the Land: but still remain in our Body Politick as a kind of extravasat Blood. As many Negro men as there are among us, so many empty places there are in our Train Bands, and the places taken up of Men that might make Husbands for our Daughters. And the Sons and Daughters of *New England* would become more like *Jacob,* and *Rachel,* if this Slavery were thrust quite out of doors. Moreover it is too well known what Temptations Masters are under, to connive at the Fornication of their Slaves; lest they should be obligated to find them Wives, or pay their Fines. It seems to be practically pleaded that they might be Lawless; 'tis thought much of, that the Law should have Satisfaction for their Thefts, and other Immoralities; by which means, *Holiness to the Lord,* is more rarely engraven upon this sort of Servitude. It is likewise most lamentable to think, how in taking Negros out of *Africa*, and Selling of them here, That which GOD ha's joyned together men do boldly rend asunder; Men from their Country, Husbands from their Wives, Parents from their Children. How horrible is the Uncleanness, Mortality, if not Murder, that the Ships are guilty of that bring great Crouds of these miserable Men, and Women. Methinks, when we are bemoaning the barbarous usage of our Friends and Kinsfolk in *Africa*:[5] it might not be unseasonable to enquire whether we are not culpable in forcing the *Africans* to become Slaves amongst our selves. And it may be a question whether all the Benefit received by *Negro* Slaves, will balance the Accompt of Cash laid out upon them; and for the Redemption of our own enslaved Friends out of *Africa*. Besides all the Persons and Estates that have perished there.

Obj. 1. *These Blackamores are of the Posterity of* Cham, *and therefore are under the Curse of Slavery. Gen.* 9.25, 26, 27.

*Answ.* Of all Offices, one would not begg this; *viz.* Uncall'd for, to be an Executioner of the Vindictive Wrath of God; the extent and duration of which is to us uncertain. If this ever was a Commission; How do we know but that it is long since out of Date? Many have found it to their Cost, that a Prophetical Denunciation of Judgment against a Person or People, would not warrant them to inflict that evil. If it would, *Hazael* might justify himself in all he did against his Master, and the *Israelites,* from 2 *Kings* 8.10, 12.

But it is possible that by cursory reading, this Text may have been mistaken. For *Canaan* is the Person Cursed three times over, without the mentioning of *Cham*. Good Expositors suppose the Curse entaild on him, and that this Prophesie was accomplished in the Extirpation of the *Canaanites,* and in the Servitude of the *Gibeonites. Vide Pareum.*[6] Whereas the Blackmores are not descended of *Canaan*, but of Cush. *Psal.* 68.31. *Princes shall come out of Egypt* [Mizraim] *Ethiopia* [Cush] *shall soon stretch out her hands unto God.* Under which Names, all *Africa* may be comprehended; and their Promised Conversion ought to be prayed for. *Jer.* 13.23. *Can the Ethiopian change his skin?* This shows that Black Men are the Posterity of *Cush:* Who time

out of mind have been distinguished by their Colour. And for
want of the true, *Ovid* assigns a fabulous cause of it.

> *Sanguine Tum Credunt in corpora summa vocato*
> *Æthiopum populos nigrum traxisse colorem.*[7]
>
> Metamorph. lib. 2.

Obj. 2. *The* Nigers *are brought out of a Pagan Country, into
places where the Gospel is Preached.*

*Answ.* Evil must not be done, that good may come of it. The
extraordinary and comprehensive Benefit accruing to the Church
of God, and to *Joseph* personally, did not rectify his brethrens
Sale of him.

Obj. 3. *The* Africans *have Wars one with another; Our Ships
bring lawful Captives taken in those Wars.*

*Answ.* For ought is known, their Wars are much such as were
between *Jacob's* Sons and their Brother *Joseph*. If they be
between Town and Town; Provincial, or National: Every War is
upon one side unjust. An Unlawful War can't make lawful
Captives. And by Receiving, we are in danger to promote, and
partake in their Barbarous Cruelties. I am sure, if some Gentlemen should go down to the *Brewsters* to take the Air, and Fish:
and a stronger party from *Hull* should Surprise them, and Sell
them for Slaves to a Ship outward bound: they would think
themselves unjustly dealt with; both by Sellers and Buyers. And
yet 'tis to be feared, we have no other kind of Title to our *Nigers.*
*Therefore all things whatsoever ye would that men should do to
you, do ye even so to them: for this is the Law and the Prophets.*
*Matt.* 7.12.

Obj. 4. Abraham *had Servants bought with his Money, and
born in his House.*

*Answ.* Until the Circumstances of *Abraham's* purchase be
recorded, no Argument can be drawn from it. In the mean time,
Charity obliges us to conclude, that He knew it was lawful and
good.

It is Observable that the *Israelites* were strictly forbidden the
buying, or selling one another for Slaves. *Levit.* 25.39, 46. *Jer.*
34.8. . . . 22. And God gaged His Blessing in lieu of any loss they
might conceit they suffered thereby. *Deut.* 15.18. And since the
partition Wall is broken down, inordinate Self love should
likewise be demolished. God expects that Christians should be of

a more Ingenuous and benign frame of spirit. Christians should carry it to all the World, as the *Israelites* were to carry it one towards another. And for men obstinately to persist in holding their Neighbours and Brethren under the Rigor of perpetual Bondage, seems to be no proper way of gaining Assurance that God ha's given them Spiritual Freedom. Our Blessed Saviour ha's altered the Measures of the ancient Love-Song, and set it to a most Excellent New Tune, which all ought to be ambitious of Learning. *Matt.* 5.43, 44. *John* 13.34. These *Ethiopians,* as black as they are; seeing they are the Sons and Daughters of the First *Adam,* the Brethren and Sisters of the Last ADAM, and the Offspring of GOD; They ought to be treated with a Respect agreeable.

*Servitus perfecta voluntaria, inter Christianum & Christianum, ex parte servi patientis soepe est licita, quia est necessaria: sed ex parte domini agentis, & procurando & exercendo, vix potest esse licita: quia non convenit reguloe illi generali: Quoecunque volueritis ut faciant vobis homines, ita & vos facite eis. Matt. 7.12.*

*Perfecta servitus poenoe, non potest jure locum habere, nisi ex delicto gravi quod ultimum supplicium aliquo modo meretur: quia Libertas ex naturali oestimatione proxime accedit ad vitam ipsam, & eidem a multis proeferri solet.*

Ames Cas. Consc. Lib. 5. Cap. 23. Thes. 2,3.[8]

BOSTON of the Massachusets;

Printed by Bartholomew Green, and John Allen,

June, 24th. 1700.

## NOTES

1. A reference to Captain Kidd's treasure, part of which was under Sewall's charge. See Lawrence W. Towner, "The Sewall-Saffin Dialogue on Slavery," *William and Mary Quarterly,* XXI (January 1964) , 42.
2. "To every man more precious than gold."
3. "Let the buyer beware."
4. Herbert Aptheker, who has edited this document, points out that in the 17th century, white indentured servants, who were required to serve for a limited period, usually seven years, were more common than Negro slaves. *And Why Not Every Man?* Seven Seas Publishers, Berlin, 1961, p. 33n.
5. A reference to white New Englanders enslaved in Africa; Sewall had been involved in negotiations for their freedom.

6. "See Pareus." The reference is probably to Philippe Pareus, also known as Philippe Waengler (1576–1648), a German philologist and classical scholar, who in 1647 published the exegetical works of his father, David Pareus, Professor of Theology at the (Protestant) University of Heidelberg.

7. "Then it was, it is believed, when the blood was [caused by the heat to be] drawn to the outer surface of the body, that the Ethiopians assumed a black color. *Metamorphoses,* Book 2." Sewall's quotation from Ovid is here used to illustrate the silliness of some traditional explanations of human skin color—in this case, that a sudden, intense heat wave caused the Ethiopians to turn black.

8. The quotation is from a book by the early 17th-century Puritan divine, William Ames, entitled *De Conscientia, ejus Jure et Casibus* (On Conscience and Its Law, With Examples), Book 5, Chapter 23, Thesis 2, 3 (1632). The translation, by Professor Cohn-Haft, is interpretive rather than literal:

"Institutionalized slavery between Christian and Christian is frequently without sin on the part of the slave, the passive participant, because he has no choice; but on the part of the master, the active participant both in acquiring and commanding [the slave], it can hardly be without sin, for it does not conform to the general rule: Whatsoever ye would that men should do to you, do you even so to them. *Matt.* 7.12.

"Slavery as punishment cannot lawfully exist, except for a crime so serious that it merits the worst torment contrivable, for Liberty is by nature evaluated as being next to life itself, and by many is customarily given priority even over life."

# JOHN SAFFIN

## REPLY TO JUDGE SEWALL

John Saffin was a merchant, slave-dealer, officeholder and, in 1701, at the time of the writing of his reply, a member of the same court as Judge Sewall. Judge Saffin had been involved in litigation over a slave of his by the name of Adam; he refused to disqualify himself when the case came before the court. Judge Sewall was highly critical of Saffin's conduct and had advised him to free Adam. Stung by Sewall's private remarks and by the printed *Memorial,* Saffin replied publicly in the following statement, which was the earliest printed defense of slavery in Colonial America. It had been lost until George H. Moore discovered a copy and published it in an appendix to *Notes on the History of Slavery in Massachusetts,* pp. 251–6. The most comprehensive and most recent account of the controversy is in Lawrence W. Towner's "The Sewall-Saffin Dialogue on Slavery," *William and Mary Quarterly,* XXI (January 1964), 40–52.

### *A Brief and Candid Answer to a late Printed Sheet, Entituled,* The Selling of Joseph

That Honourable and Learned Gentleman, the Author of a Sheet, Entituled, *The Selling of Joseph,* A Memorial, seems from thence to draw this conclusion, that because the Sons of *Jacob* did very ill in selling their Brother *Joseph* to the *Ishmaelites,* who were Heathens, therefore it is utterly unlawful to Buy and Sell Negroes, though among Christians; which Conclusion I presume is not well drawn from the Premises, nor is the case parallel; for it was unlawful for the *Israelites* to sell their Brethren upon any account, or pretence whatsoever during life. But it was not unlawful for the Seed of *Abraham* to have Bond men, and Bond women either born in their House, or bought with their Money, as it is written of *Abraham, Gen.* 14.14 & 21.10 & *Exod.* 21.16. & *Levit.* 25.44, 45, 46 *v.* After the giving of the Law: And in *Josh.* 9.23. That famous Example of the *Gibeonites* is a sufficient proof where there [is] no other.

To speak a little to the Gentlemans first Assertion: *That none ought to part with their Liberty themselves, or deprive others of it but upon mature consideration;* a prudent exception, in which he grants, that upon some consideration a man may be deprived of his Liberty. And then presently in his next Position or Assertion he denies it, *viz.: It is most certain, that all men as they are the Sons of* Adam *are Coheirs, and have equal right to Liberty, and all other Comforts of Life,* which he would prove out of *Psal.* 115.16. *The Earth hath he given to the Children of Men.* True, but what is all this to the purpose, to prove that all men have equal right to Liberty, and all outward comforts of this life; which Position seems to invert the Order that God hath set in the World, who hath Ordained different degrees and orders of men, some to be High and Honourable, some to be Low and Despicable; some to be Monarchs, Kings, Princes and Governours, Masters and Commanders, others to be Subjects, and to be Commanded; Servants of sundry sorts and degrees, bound to obey; yea, some to be born Slaves, and so to remain during their lives, as hath been proved. Otherwise there would be a meer parity among men, contrary to that of the Apostle, I *Cor.* 12 *from the* 13 *to the* 26 *verse,* where he sets forth (by way of comparison) the different sorts and offices of the Members of the Body, indigitating that they are all of use, but not equal, and of like dignity. So God hath set different Orders and Degrees of Men in the World, both in Church and Common weal. Now, if this Position of parity should be true, it would then follow that the ordinary Course of Divine Providence of God in the World should be wrong, and unjust, (which we must not dare to think, much less to affirm) and all the sacred Rules, Precepts and Commands of the Almighty which he hath given the Son of Men to observe and keep in their respective Places, Orders and Degrees, would be to no purpose; which unaccountably derogate from the Divine Wisdom of the most High, who hath made nothing in vain, but hath Holy Ends in all his Dispensations to the Children of men.

In the next place, this worthy Gentleman makes a large Discourse concerning the Utility and Conveniency to keep the one, and inconveniency of the other; respecting white and black Servants, which conduceth most to the welfare and benefit of this Province: which he concludes to be white men, who are in many respects to be preferred before Blacks; who doubts that? doth it therefore follow, that it is altogether unlawful for Christians to buy and keep Negro Servants (for this is the Thesis) but that those that have them ought in Conscience to set them free, and so lose all the money they cost (for we must not live in any known sin) this seems to be his opinion; but it is a Question whether it ever was the Gentleman's practice? But if he could perswade the General Assembly to make an Act, That all that have Negroes, and do set them free, shall be Re imbursed out of the Publick Treasury, and that there shall be no more Negroes brought into the Country; 'tis probable there would be more of his opinion; yet he would find it a hard task to bring the Country to consent thereto; for then the Negroes must be all sent out of the Country, or else the remedy would be worse than the Disease; and it is to be feared that those Negroes that are free, if there be not some strict course taken with them by Authority, they will be a plague to this Country.

*Again,* If it should be unlawful to deprive them that are lawful Captives, or Bondmen of their Liberty for Life being Heathens; it seems to be more unlawful to deprive our Brethren, of our own or other Christian Nations of the Liberty, (though but for a time) by binding them to Serve some Seven, Ten, Fifteen, and some Twenty Years, which oft times proves for their whole Life, as many have been; which in effect is the same in Nature, though different in the time, yet this was allow'd among the *Jews* by the Law of God; and is the constant practice of our own and other Christian Nations in the World: the which our Author by his Dogmatical Assertions doth condemn as Irreligious; which is Diametrically contrary to the Rules and Precepts which God hath given the diversity of men to observe in their respective Stations, Callings, and Conditions of Life, as hath been observed.

And to illustrate his Assertion our Author brings in by way of Comparison the Law of God against man Stealing, on pain of Death: Intimating thereby, that Buying and Selling of Negro's is a breach of that Law, and so deserves Death: A severe Sentence: But herein he begs the Question with a *Caveat Emptor.* For, in that very Chapter there is a Dispensation to the People of *Israel,* to have Bond men, Women and Children, even of their own Nation in some case; and Rules given therein to be observed concerning them; Verse the 4*th.* And in the before cited place,

*Levit.* 25.44, 45, 46. Though the *Israelites* were forbidden (ordinarily) to make Bond men and Women of their own Nation, but of Strangers they might: the words run thus, verse 44. *Both thy Bond men, and thy Bond maids which thou shalt have shall be of the Heathen, that are round about you: of them shall you Buy Bond men and Bond maids,* &c. See also, I *Cor.* 12.13. Whether we be Bond or Free, which shows that in the times of the New Testament, there were Bond men also, etc.

*In fine,* The sum of this long Haurange, is no other, than to compare the Buying and Selling of Negro's unto the Stealing of men, and the Selling of *Joseph* by his Brethren, which bears no proportion therewith, nor is there any congrueity therein, as appears by the foregoing Texts.

Our Author doth further proceed to answer some Objections of his own framing, which he supposes some might raise.

Object. 1. *That these Blackamores are of the Posterity of* Cham, *and therefore under the Curse of Slavery. Gen.* 9.25, 26, 27. The which the Gentleman seems to deny, saying, *they were the Seed of Canaan that were Cursed,* etc.

*Answ.* Whether they were so or not, we shall not dispute: this may suffice, that not only the seed of *Cham* or *Canaan,* but any lawful Captives of other Heathen Nations may be made Bond men as hath been proved.

Obj. 2. *That the Negroes are brought out of Pagan Countreys into places where the Gospel is Preached.* To which he Replies, *that we must not doe Evil that Good may come of it.*

*Ans.* To which we answer, That it is no Evil thing to bring them out of their own Heathenish Country, where they may have the Knowledge of the True God, be Converted and Eternally saved.

Obj. 3. *The* Africans *have Wars one with another;* our Ships bring lawful Captives taken in those Wars.

To which our Author answer Conjecturally, and Doubtfully, *for ought we know,* that which may or may not be; which is insignificant, and proves nothing. He also compares the Negroes Wars, one Nation with another, with the Wars between *Joseph* and his Brethren. But where doth he read of any such War? We read indeed of a Domestick Quarrel they had with him, they envyed and hated *Joseph;* but by what is Recorded, he meerly passive and meek as a Lamb. This Gentleman farther adds, *That there is not any War but is unjust on one side,* etc. Be it so, what doth that signify: We read of lawful Captives taken in the Wars, and lawful to be Bought and Sold without contracting the guilt of the *Agressors;* for which we have the example of *Abraham* before quoted; but if we must stay while both parties Warring are in the right, there would be no lawful Captives at all to be Bought; which seems to be rediculous to imagine, and contrary to the tenour of Scripture, and all Humane Histories on that subject.

Obj. 4. *Abraham had Servants bought with his Money, and born in his House. Gen.* 14.14. To which our worthy Author answers, *until the Circumstances of Abraham's purchase be recorded, no Argument can be drawn from it.*

*Ans.* To which we Reply, this is also Dogmatical, and proves nothing. He farther adds, *In the mean time Charity Obliges us to conclude, that he knew it was lawful and good.* Here the gentleman yields the case; for if we are in Charity bound to believe *Abrahams* practice, in buying and keeping *Slaves* in his house to be lawful and good: then it follows, that our Imitation of him in this his Moral Action, is as warrantable as that of his Faith; *who is the Father of all them that believe. Rom.* 4.16.

In the close of all, Our Author Quotes two more places of Scripture, *viz.; Levit.* 25.46, and *Jer.* 34, from the 8. to the 22. *v.* To prove that the people of Israel were strictly forbidden the Buying and Selling one another for *Slaves:* who questions that? and what is that to the case in hand? What a strange piece of Logick is this? Tis unlawful for Christians to Buy and Sell one another for slaves. *Ergo,* It is unlawful to Buy and Sell Negroes that are lawful Captiv'd Heathens.

And after a Serious Exhortation to us all to Love one another according to the Command of Christ. *Math.* 5.43, 44. This worthy Gentleman concludes with this Assertion, *That these Ethiopeans as Black as they are, seeing they are the Sons and Daughters of the first* Adam; *the Brethren and Sisters of the Second* Adam, *and the Offspring of God; we ought to treat them with a respect agreeable.*

*Ans.* We grant it for a certain and undeniable verity, That all Mankind are the Sons and Daughters of *Adam,* and the Creatures of God: But it doth not therefore follow that we are bound to love and respect all men alike; this under favour we must take leave to deny; we ought in charity, if we see our Neighbour in want, to relieve them in a regular way, but we are not bound to give them so much of our Estates, as to make them equal with our selves, because they are our Brethren, the Sons of *Adam,* no, not our own natural Kinsmen: We are Exhorted *to do good unto all, but especially to them who are of the Houshold of Faith, Gal.* 6.10. And we are to love, honour and respect all men according to the gift of God that is in them: I may love my Servant well, but my Son better; Charity begins at home, it would be a violation of common prudence, and a breach of good manners, to treat a Prince like a Peasant. And this worthy Gentleman would deem himself much neglected, if we should show him no more Defference than to an ordinary Porter: And therefore these florid expressions, the Sons and Daughters of the First *Adam,* the Brethren and Sisters of the Second *Adam,* and the Offspring of God, seem to be misapplied to import and insinuate, that we ought to tender Pagan Negroes with all love, kindness, and equal respect as to the best of men.

By all which it doth evidently appear both by Scripture and Reason, the practice of the People of God in all Ages, both before and after the giving of the Law, and in the times of the Gospel, that there were Bond men, Women and Children commonly kept by holy and good men, and improved in Service; and therefore by the Command of God, *Lev.* 25.44, and their venerable Example, we may keep Bond men, and use them in our Service still; yet with all candour, moderation and Christian prudence, according to their state and condition consonant to the Word of God.

### The Negroes Character.

*Cowardly and cruel are those* Blacks *Innate,*
*Prone to Revenge, Imp of inveterate hate.*
*He that exasperates them, soon espies*
*Mischief and Murder in their very eyes.*
*Libidinous, Deceitful, False and Rude,*
*The Spume Issue of Ingratitude.*
*The Premises consider'd, all may tell,*
*How near good* Joseph *they are parallel.*

## COTTON MATHER

### THE NEGRO CHRISTIANIZED

In *The Negro Christianized,* printed in Boston in 1706, Cotton Mather argues that a slave-owner has the obligation to save his slave's soul by leading him to Christianity. He assures the master that conversion to Christianity does not mean freedom for the slave, but that "Your Servants will be the *Better Servants,* for being *Christian Servants.*" In a recent, very valuable essay, Milton Cantor suggests that "Cotton Mather may have incidentally wished to inculcate piety among the Negroes of Massachusetts, but his primary motive was to increase their usefulness, and he assumed the Negro's inequality and incapacity for freedom." ("The Image of the Negro in Colonial Literature," *The New England Quarterly,* XXXVI, [Dec. 1963], 453.) This judgment may be a bit too severe. In his demand for conversion of the slaves and in his support of slavery, Mather is typical of early eighteenth-century religious opinion in New England. Yet, in his suggestion that the Negro may belong to the elect of God, in his reference to the Negro as the white man's "neighbor" and "brother," and in his concern for the plight of the black man, he differs markedly from Saffin and represents a far more liberal and humane position.

*An Essay to Excite and Assist that Good Work, The Instruction of Negro-Servants in Christianity*

*Josh.* 24.15. *As for me, and my House, we will Serve the Lord.*
*Psal.* 68.31. Ethiopia *shall soon Stretch out her Hands unto God.*

It is a *Golden Sentence,* that has been sometimes quoted from *Chrysostom;* That *for a man to know the Art of Alms, is more than for a man to be Crowned with the Diadem of Kings: But to Convert one Soul unto God, is more than to pour out Ten Thousand Talents into the Basket of the Poor.* Truly, to Raise a *Soul,* from a dark State of Ignorance and Wickedness, to the Knowledge of GOD, and the Belief of CHRIST, and the practice of our Holy and Lovely RELIGION; 'Tis the noblest Work, that ever was undertaken among the Children of men. . . . And such an opportunity there is in your Hands, O all you that have any NEGROES in your Houses; an Opportunity to try, Whether you may not be the Happy *Instruments,* of Converting, the *Blackest* Instances of *Blindness* and *Baseness,* into admirable *Candidates* of Eternal Blessedness. Let not this Opportunity be Lost; if you have any concern for *Souls,* your Own or Others; but, make a Trial, Whether by your Means, the most *Bruitish* of Creatures upon Earth may not come to be disposed, in some Degree, like the *Angels* of Heaven; and the *Vassals* of Satan, become the *Children* of God. Suppose these Wretched *Negroes,* to be the Offspring of *Cham* (which yet is not so very certain,) yet let us make a Trial, Whether the CHRIST who *dwelt in the Tents of Shem,* have not some of His Chosen among them; Let us make a Trial, Whether they that have been Scorched and Blacken'd by the Sun of *Africa,* may not come to have their Minds Healed by the more Benign *Beams* of the *Sun of Righteousness.*

It is come to pass by the *Providence* of God, without which there comes nothing to pass, that Poor NEGROES are cast under your Government and Protection. You take them into your *Families;* you look on them as part of your *Possessions;* and you Expect from their Service, a Support, and perhaps an Increase, of your other *Possessions.* How agreeable would it be, if a Religious Master or Mistress thus attended, would now think with themselves! *Who can tell but that this Poor Creature may belong to the Election of God! Who can tell, but that God may have sent this Poor Creature into my Hands, that so One of the Elect may by my means be Called; & by my Instruction be made Wise unto Salvation! The glorious God will put an unspeakable Glory upon me, if it may be so!* The Considerations that would move you, To Teach your *Negroes* the *Truths* of the Glorious Gospel, as far as you can, and bring them, if it may be, to Live according to those *Truths,* a *Sober,* and a *Righteous,* and a *Godly* Life; They are *Innumerable;* And, if you would after a *Reasonable* manner consider, the Pleas which we have to make on the behalf of *God,* and of the *Souls* which He has made, one would wonder that they should not be *Irresistible. Show yourselves Men,* and let *Rational Arguments* have their Force upon you, to make you treat, not as *Bruits* but as *Men,* those *Rational Creatures* whom God has made your *Servants.*

For,

First; the Great GOD *Commands* it, and *Requires* it of you, to do what you can that *Your Servants,* may also be *His.* It was an Admonition once given; Eph. 5.9. *Masters, Know that your Master is in Heaven.* You will confess, That the God of Heaven is your *Master.* If your *Negroes* do not comply with your *commands,* into what Anger, what Language, Perhaps into a mis-becoming *Fury,* are you transported? But you are now to attend unto the *Commands* of your more Absolute *Master;* and they are His *Commands* concerning your *Negroes* too. What can be more Expressive, than those words of the Christian Law? Col. 4.1. *Masters, give unto your Servants, that which is Just & Equal, knowing that ye also have a Master in Heaven.* Of what *Servants* is this Injunction to be understood? Verily, of *Slaves.* For *Servants* were generally such, at the time of Writing the New Testament. Wherefore, *Masters,* As it is *Just & Equal,* that your *Servants* be not *Over-wrought,* and that while they *Work* for you, you should *Feed* them, and *Cloath* them, and afford convenient *Rest* unto them, and make their Lives comfortable; So it is *Just* and *Equal,* that you should Acquaint them, as far as you can, with the way to Salvation by JESUS CHRIST. You deny your *Master in Heaven,* if you do nothing to bring your *Servants* unto the Knowledge and Service of that Glorious *Master.* One Table of the *Ten Commandments,* has this for the Sum of it; *Thou shalt Love thy Neighbor as thy self.* Man, Thy *Negro* is thy *Neighbour.* T'were an Ignorance, unworthy of a *Man,* to imag-ine otherwise. Yea, if thou dost grant, *That God hath made of one Blood, all Nations of men,* he is thy *Brother* too. Now canst thou *Love* thy *Negro,* and be willing to see him ly under the Rage of Sin, and the Wrath of God? Canst thou *Love* him, and yet refuse to do any thing, that his miserable Soul may be rescued from Eternal miseries? Oh! Let thy *Love* to that Poor *Soul,* appear in thy concern, to make it, if thou canst, as happy as thy own! We are Commanded, *Gal.* 6.10. *As we have opportunity let us Do Good unto all men, especially unto them, who are of the Household of Faith.* Certainly, we have *Opportunity,* to *do Good*

unto our *Servants,* who are of our *own Houshold;* certainly, we
may do something to *make them Good,* and bring them to be of
the *Houshold of Faith.* In a word, All the Commandments in the
Bible, which bespeak our *Charity* to the *Souls* of others, and our
*Endeavour* that the *Souls* of others may be delivered from the
Snares of Death; every one of these do oblige us, to do what we
can, for the *Souls* of our *Negroes.* They are more nearly *Related*
unto us, than many others are; we are more fully capable to do
for them, than for many others.

To deal yet more plainly with you; Secondly; With what Face
can you call yourselves *Christians,* if you do nothing that your
*Servants* also may become *Christians?*. . . . Are they Worthy to
be counted *Christians,* who are content tho' a part of their
*Families* remain *Heathen,* who do *not know God,* nor *call upon
His Name?*. . . . It is *Natural* for men, to promote their own
Religion. Shall *Christians* fall short of *Mahometans,* or of *Idol-
aters?*. . . . The *Christians* who have no concern upon their
Minds to have *Christianity Propagated,* never can justify themselves. *They say they are* Christians, *but they are not;* What they
are, we know not. . . . The greatest *Good* that we can do for
any, is to bring them unto the fullest Acquaintance with *Christianity.* Will *Christianity* allow him then to be, A *Good Man,* or,
which is the same thing, *A Christian,* who refuses to do this
*Good,* for the *Servants* that are under his influence?. . . . But
what shall we say of it, When *Masters* that would be thought
*Christians* already shall even refuse to have the *Servants* in their
*Families* duely *Christianized?* Pray, deal faithfully; Don't mince
the matter; say of it, as it is; It is a *Prodigy* of *Wickedness;* It is a
prodigious Inconsistency, with true *Christianity!* Housholder, art
thou a *Christian?* Then the *Glory* of a precious CHRIST is of such
Account with thee, that it afflicts thee to think, that any one
Person in the World should be without the Sight of it. And how
can it be, that thou shouldest be negligent about bringing to a
sight of the *Glory of God, in the Face of* JESUS CHRIST, the *Folks
of thy own House,* upon whom thou art able to do a great deal
more than upon the rest of the World? Art thou a *Christian?*
Then thou dost *Pray* for thy *Servants,* that they may become the
*Servants* of the Lord Jesus Christ, and the *Children* of God, and
not *fall short of entering into Rest.* What! *Pray* for this; and yet

never *do* any thing for it! It is impossible, or, such *Praying,* is but *Mocking* of God?. . . . Suppose that Language were heard from the mouth of a Master concerning a Servant; *If I can have the Labour of the Slave, that's all I care for: Let his Soul go and be damn'd for all me!* would not every Christian say, This were Language for the Mouth of a *Devil,* rather than for the Mouth of a *Christian!* Would not every Christian cry out, *Let him not be call'd a Master, but a Monster that shall speak so!* Consider, Syrs, whether *Deeds* have not a Language in them, as well as *Words;* a plainer Language than *Words.*

But we were saying; the *Condition* of the *Servants!* This invites us to say, Thirdly: The *condition* of your *Servants* does loudly sollicit your pains to *Christianize* them; and you cannot but hear the cry of it, if you have not put off all *Christian Compassion,* all Bowels of *Humanity.* When you see how laboriously, how obsequiously your *Negros* apply themselves, to serve you, to content you, to enrich you, What? have you abandoned all principles of Gratitude, or of Generosity? A generous Mind cannot but entertain such sentiments as these: *Well, what shall I do, to make this poor creature happy? What shall I do, that this poor creature may have cause, to bless God forever, for falling into my Hands!* The very *First Thought* which will arise in a Mind thus disposed, will form a Resolution, to get these poor *Negroes* well instructed in *the things of their Everlasting Peace;* It cannot be otherwise! The State of your *Negroes* in this World, must be low, and mean, and abject; a State of Servitude. No *Great Things* in this World, can be done for them. Something then, let there be done, towards their welfare in the *World to Come.* . . . *Every one of us shall give account of himself to God.* But then Remember, that one Article of your *Account* will be this: *You had poor* Negroes *under you, and you expected and exacted Revenues of profit from them. Did you do any thing to save them from their Blindness and Baseness, and that the Great God might have Revenues of glory from them.* Alas, if you have not thought and car'd and *Watch'd for the Souls* of your *Negroes,* as *they that must give an Account,* You will give up your *Account* with *Grief,* and not with *Joy;* very *Grievous* will be the consequences. A *Prophet* of God, might without putting any *Disguise* upon the matter, thus represent it; God has brought a

*Servant* unto thee, and said, *Keep that Soul, Teach it, and Help it, that it may not be lost; if thou use no means to save that Soul, thy soul shall certainly smart for it.* Vain Dreamer; canst thou suppose that the *Negroes* are made for nothing but only to serve thy Pleasures, or that they owe no Homage to their *Maker?* Do thy part, that they may become a *People of so much Understanding,* as to Understand who is their *Maker* and their *Saviour,* and what Homage they owe unto Him: Else, *He that made them will not have mercy on them.* Yea, but *Thy* claim to His *Mercy* will be less than *Theirs.* More *Stripes* will belong unto thee.

On the other side, Fourthly:. . . . *Christianity* does Marvellously befriend and enrich and advance Mankind. The greatest *Kindness* that can be done to any Man is to make a *Christian* of him. Your *Negroes* are immediately Raised unto an astonishing Felicity, when you have *Christianized* them. They are become amiable spectacles, & such as the *Angels* of God would gladly repair unto the Windows of Heaven to look upon. Tho' they remain your *Servants,* yet they are become the *Children* of God. Tho' they are to enjoy no *Earthly Goods,* but the small Allowance that your Justice and Bounty shall see proper for them, yet they are become *Heirs* of God, and *Joint-Heirs* with the Lord Jesus Christ. Tho' they are your *Vassals,* and must with a profound subjection wait upon you, yet the *Angels* of God now take them under their Guardianship and vouchsafe to tend upon them. Oh! what have you done for them!. . . .

Yea, the pious *Masters,* that have instituted their *Servants* in Christian Piety, will even in this Life have a sensible *Recompence.* The more *Serviceable,* and Obedient and obliging Behaviour [of] their Servants unto them, will be a sensible & a notable *Recompence.* Be assured, Syrs; Your *Servants* will be the *Better Servants,* for being made *Christian Servants.* To *Christianize* them aright, will be to *fill them with all Goodness. Christianity* is nothing but a very Mass of Universal *Goodness.* Were your *Servants* well tinged with the spirit of *Christianity,* it would render them exceeding *Dutiful* unto their *Masters,* exceeding *Patient* under their *Masters,* exceeding faithful in their Business, and afraid of speaking or doing any thing that may justly displease you. It has been observed, that those *Masters,* who have used their *Negroes* with most of *Humanity,* in allowing them all the Comforts of Life, that are necessary and *Convenient* for them, (Who have remembered, that by the Law of God, even an Ass was to be relieved, When *Sinking under his Burden,* and an Ox might not be *Muzzled* when *Treading out the Corn;* and that if a *Just man will regard the Life of his Beast,* he will much more allow the comforts of life to and not hide himself *from his own flesh:*) have been better *Serv'd,* had more work done for them, and better done, then those *Inhumane Masters,* who have used their *Negroes* worse than their *Horses.* And those *Masters* doubtless, who use their *Negroes* with most of *Christianity,* and use most pains to inform them in, and conform them to, *Christianity,* will find themselves no losers by it. *Onesimus* was doubtless a *Slave:* but this poor *Slave,* on whose behalf a great Apostle of God was more than a little concerned; yea, one Book in our Bible was Written on his behalf! When he was *Christianized,* it was presently said unto his *Master,* Philem. II. *In time past he was unprofitable to thee, but now he will be profitable.* But many *Masters* whose *Negroes* have greatly vexed them, with miscarriages, may do well to examine, Whether Heaven be not chastising of them, for their failing in their Duty about their *Negroes.* Had they done more, to make their *Negroes* the knowing and willing *Servants* of God, it may be, God would have made their *Negroes* better *Servants* to them. Syrs, you may Read your *Sin* in the *Punishment.*

And now, what *Objection* can any Man Living have, to refund the force of these *Considerations?* Produce *thy cause,* O Impiety, *Bring forth thy strong reasons,* and let all men see what Idle and silly cavils, are thy best *Reasons* against this Work of God.

It has been cavilled, by some, that it is questionable Whether the *Negroes* have *Rational Souls,* or no. But let that *Bruitish* insinuation be never Whispered any more. Certainly, their *Discourse,* will abundantly prove, that they have *Reason. Reason* showes it self in the *Design* which they daily act upon. The vast improvement that *Education* has made upon *some* of them, argues that there is a *Reasonable Soul* in *all* of them. An old Roman, and Pagan, would call upon the Owner of such Servants, *Homines tamen esse memento.*[1] They are *Men,* and not *Beasts* that you have bought, and they must be used accordingly. 'Tis true; They are Barbarous. But so were our own *Ancestors.* The

*Britons* were in many things as *Barbarous,* but a little before our Saviours Nativity, as the Negroes are at this time if there be any Credit in *Caesars Commentaries. Christianity* will be best cure for this *Barbarity.* Their *Complexion* sometimes is made an Argument, why nothing should be done for them. A *Gay* sort of argument! As if the great God went by the *Complexion* of Men, in His Favours to them! As if none but *Whites* might hope to be Favoured and Accepted with God! Whereas it is well known, That the *Whites,* are the least part of Mankind. The biggest part of Mankind, perhaps, are *Copper-Coloured;* a sort of *Tawnies.* And our *English* that inhabit some Climates, do seem growing apace to be not much unlike unto them. As if, because a people, from the long force of the African *Sun* & *Soyl* upon them, (improved perhaps, to further Degrees by maternal imaginations, and other accidents,) are come at length to have the small *Fibres* of their *Veins,* and the Blood in them, a little more Interspersed thro their Skin than other People, this must render them less valuable to Heaven than the rest of Mankind? Away with such Trifles! The God who *looks on the heart,* is not moved by the colour of the *Skin;* is not more propitious to one *Colour* than another. Say rather, with the Apostle; *Acts* 10.34, 35. *Of a truth I perceive, that God is no respecter of persons; but in every Nation, he that feareth Him and worketh Righteousness, is accepted with Him.* Indeed their *Stupidity* is a *Discouragement.* It may seem, unto as little purpose, to *Teach,* as to *wash an Æthopian.* But the greater their *Stupidity,* the greater must be our *Application.* If we can't learn them so much as we *Would,* let us learn them as much as we *Can.* A little divine *Light* and *Grace* infused into them, will be of great account. And the more *Difficult* it is, to fetch such *forlorn things* up out of the perdition whereinto they are fallen, the more *Laudable* is the undertaking: There will be the more of a *Triumph,* if we prosper in the undertaking. Let us encourage ourselves from that word; *Mat.* 3.9. *God is able of these Stones, to raise up Children unto Abraham.*

Well; But if the *Negroes* are *Christianized,* they will be *Baptised;* and their *Baptism* will presently entitle them to their *Freedom;* so our *Money* is thrown away.

Man, if this were true; that a *Slave* bought with the *Money,* were by thy means brought unto the *Things that accompany Salvation,* and thou shouldest from this time have no more service from him, yet the *Money* were not thrown away. That Mans *Money will perish with him,* who had rather the *Souls* in his Family should *Perish,* than that he should lose a little *Money.* And suppose it were so, that *Baptism* gave a legal Title to *Freedom.* Is there no guarding against this Inconvenience? You may by sufficient *Indentures,* keep off the things, which you reckon so Inconvenient. But it is all a Mistake. There is no such thing. What *Law* is it, that Sets the *Baptised Slave* at *Liberty?* Not the *Law of Christianity:* that allows of *Slavery;* Only it wonderfully Dulcifies, and Mollifies, and Moderates the Circumstances of it. *Christianity* directs a *Slave,* upon his embracing the *Law of the Redeemer,* to satisfy himself, *That he is the Lords Free-man,* tho' he continues a *Slave.* It supposes, *(Col.* 3.11.) That there are *Bond* as well as *Free,* among those that have been *Renewed in the Knowledge and Image of Jesus Christ.* Will the *Canon-Law* do it? No; The *Canons* of Numberless *Councils,* mention, the *Slaves* of *Christians,* without any contradiction. Will the *Civil Law* do it? No: Tell, if you can, any part of *Christendom,* wherein *Slaves* are not frequently to be met withal. But is not *Freedom* to be claim'd for a *Baptised Slave,* by the *English* Constitution? The English *Laws,* about *Villians,* or, *Slaves,* will not say so; for by those *Laws,* they may be granted *for Life,* like a *Lease,* and passed over with a *Mannor,* like other *Goods* or *Chattels.* And by those *Laws,* the Lords may sieze the Bodies of their *Slaves* even while a Writt, *De libertate probanda,*[2] is depending. These English *Laws* were made when the *Lords* & the *Slaves,* were both of them *Christians;* and they stand still unrepealed. If there are not now such *Slaves* in *England* as formerly, it is from the *Lords,* more than from the *Laws.* The *Baptised* then are not thereby entitled unto their *Liberty.* Howbeit, if they have arrived unto such a measure of *Christianity,* that *none can forbid Water for the Baptising of them,* it is fit, that they should enjoy those *comfortable circumstances* with us, which are due to them, not only as the *Children* of *Adam,* but also as our *Brethren,* on the same level with us in the expectations of a blessed Immortality, thro' the *Second Adam.* Whatever Slaughter the Assertion may make among the pretensions which are made unto *Christianity,* yet while the *sixteenth* Chapter of *Matthew* is in the Bible, it must be asserted; the *Christian,* who cannot so far *Deny himself,* can be no *Disciple* of the Lord JESUS CHRIST. But, O Christian, thy *Slave* will not Serve thee one jot the worse for that *Self-denial.*

The way is now cleared, for the work that is proposed: that excellent WORK, THE INSTRUCTION OF THE NEGROES IN THE CHRISTIAN RELIGION.

A CATECHISM shall be got ready for them; first a *Shorter,* then a *Larger;* Suited to their poor Capacities.

They who cannot themselves *Personally* so well attend the *Instruction* of the *Negroes,* may employ and reward those that shall do it for them. In many *Families,* the *Children* may help the *Negroes,* to Learn the *Catechism,* or their well-instructed and well-disposed *English Servants* may do it: And they should be *Rewarded* by the *Masters,* when they do it.

In a Plantation of many *Negroes,* why should not a *Teacher* be hired on purpose, to instil into them the principles of the *Catechism?*

Or, if the *Overseers* are once *Catechised* themselves, they may soon do the Office of *Catechisers* unto those that are under them.

However, Tis fit for the *Master* also *Personally* to enquire into the progress which his *Negroes* make in *Christianity,* and not leave it *Entirely* to the management of others.

There must be *Time* allow'd for the *Work.* And why not THE LORDS-DAY? The precept of God concerning the *Sabbath,* is very positive; *Remember the* SABBATH-DAY, *to keep it Holy. Thou shalt not then do any work, thou nor thy Son, nor thy daughter, thy Man-Servant, nor thy Maid-Servant.* By virtue of this precept, we do even demand, THE LORDS-DAY, for the *Negroes:* that they may be permitted the Freedom of THE LORDS-DAY, and not be than unnecessarily diverted from attending on such *means of Instruction,* as may be afforded unto them.

To quicken them unto the learning of the *Catechism,* it would be very well to propose unto the *Negroes, Agreeable Recompences, & Priviledges,* to be receiv'd and enjoy'd by them, when they shall have made a good progress in it. Syrs, A *Mahometan* will do as much as this comes to, for any one that will embrace his *Alcoran.* Oh, Christians, will not you do more for *your*

*Generation,* than the *Children of this World* for theirs. And it is to be desired, that the *Negroes* may not learn to say their *Catechism* only by rote, like *Parrots;* but that their Instructors, may put unto them such other, *Questions* relating to the points of the *Catechism,* that by their *Answers,* (at least of YES, or NO,) it may be perceived, that they *Know* what they Say.

But it will be also needful and useful, to uphold a more particular *Conference* often with the *Negroes;* and in conferring with them, to inculcate on them such *Admonitions of Piety;* as may have a special tendency to *Form* & *Mould* their Souls for the Kingdom of God.

Having told them, *Who Made* them, and *Why* He made them, and that they have *Souls,* which will be *Wretched* or *Happy* forever, according as they mind *Religion;* then tell them;

*That by their sin against God, they are fallen into a dreadful condition.*

Show them, That the Almighty *God is Angry* with them, and that, if they Dy under the *Anger of God,* they will after *Death,* be cast among *Devils;* and that all the *Stripes,* and all the *Wants,* and all the sad things they ever suffered in this World, are nothing, to the *many Sorrows,* which they shall suffer among the Damned, in the *Dungeon of Hell.*

Tell them; *That* JESUS CHRIST *is a Saviour for them as well as others, and as willing to save them out of their dreadful condition, as any others.*

Show them, That JESUS CHRIST, who is both *God* and *Man* in One Person, came, and Kept the *Law* of God, and then Offer'd up His *Life* to God, on the *Cross,* to make amends for our Sin; and that JESUS CHRIST invites *Them* as well as others, to *Look* to Him, and *Hope* in Him, for Everlasting Life; and that if they come to JESUS CHRIST, they shall be as Welcome to Him, as any People; Tho' He be the *King of Kings,* and *Lord of Lords,* yet He will cast a Kind Look upon Sorry *Slaves* and *Blacks* that Believe on Him, and will prepare a *Mansion* in *Heaven* for them.

Tell them; *That if they Serve God patiently and cheerfully in the Condition which he orders for them, their condition will very quickly be infinitely mended, in Eternal Happiness.*

Show them, That it is GOD who has caused them to be *Ser-*

*vants;* and that they Serve JESUS CHRIST, while they are at Work for their *Masters,* if they are *Faithful* and *Honest Servants,* and if they do cheerfully what they do, because the Lord JESUS CHRIST has bid them to do it; and that, if they give themselves up to JESUS CHRIST and keep always afraid of Sinning Against Him, it won't be *Long* before they shall be in a most *Glorious Condition;* It can't be *Long* before they Dy, and *then!* they shall *Rest* from all their Labours, and all their Troubles, and they shall be Companions of *Angels* in the Glories of a *Paradise.*

[The remainder of the essay consists in great part of a suggested cate-chism for slaves.]

## NOTES

1. "Remember, nevertheless, that they are human."
2. "Proof of personal freedom."

# CHAPTER 4

# A Virginia Planter on Racial Intermarriage and Slavery

## WILLIAM BYRD

Virginia planter, colonial official and author, William Byrd (1674–1744) differed from other Virginia officials of his time in his sense of humor, his love of ladies, and his unorthodox views on the race question. Byrd's opinion of the wisdom of interracial sexual relations and marriage was certainly not dominant in Virginia or the other English colonies. Indeed, as early as 1630 a white Virginian was ordered whipped for lying with a Negro woman, and in 1691 a Virginia law forbade intermarriage between the English, on the one hand, and Negroes, mulattoes and Indians on the other. In 1661, a Maryland law referred to the "disgrace" of intermarriage between white women and Negro slaves and placed strong penalties upon white women who entered such marriages. In 1705, Massachusetts forbade fornication and intermarriage between Negroes and whites and then extended the prohibition to include Indians as well.

In 1728, Byrd was one of the commissioners appointed to run the dividing line between Virginia and North Carolina. The result was his manuscript, *History of the Dividing Line*, which, together with his *A Journey to the Lands of Eden* and *Progress to the Mines*, were first published in 1841 as *The Westover Manuscripts*. The following selection consists of pp. 8–10 and 101–103 of the *History of the Dividing Line*, which is included in *The Writings of "Colonel William Byrd of Westover in Virginia Esqr."* (New York, 1901), edited by John Spencer Bassett.

### History of the Dividing Line: Run in the Year 1728

They had now made peace with the Indians, but there was one thing wanting to make that peace lasting. The Natives coud, by no means, perswade themselves that the English were heartily their Friends, so long as they disdained to intermarry with them. And, in earnest, had the English consulted their own Security and the good of the Colony—Had they intended either to Civilize or Convert these Gentiles, they would have brought their Stomachs to embrace this prudent Alliance.

The Indians are generally tall and well-proportion'd, which may make full Amends for the Darkness of their Complexions. Add to this, that they are healthy & Strong, with Constitutions untainted by Lewdness, and not enfeebled by Luxury. Besides, Morals and all considered, I cant think the Indians were much greater Heathens than the first Adventurers, who, had they been good Christians, would have had the Charity to take this only method of converting the Natives to Christianity. For, after all that can be said, a sprightly Lover is the most prevailing Missionary that can be sent amongst these, or any other Infidels.

Besides, the poor Indians would have had less reason to Complain that the English took away their Land, if they had received it by way of Portion with their Daughters. Had such Affinities been contracted in the Beginning, how much Bloodshed had been prevented, and how populous would the Country have been, and, consequently, how considerable? Nor wou'd the Shade of the Skin have been any reproach at this day; for if a Moor may be washt white in 3 Generations, Surely an Indian might have been blancht in two.

The French, for their Parts, have not been so Squeamish in Canada, who upon Trial find abundance of Attraction in the Indians. Their late Grand Monarch thought it not below even the Dignity of a Frenchman to become one flesh with this People, and therefore Ordered 100 Livres for any of his Subjects, Man or Woman, that woud intermarry with a Native.

By this piece of Policy we find the French Interest very much Strengthen'd amongst the Savages, and their Religion, such as it is, propagated just as far as their Love. And I heartily wish this well-concerted Scheme don't hereafter give the French an Advantage over his Majesty's good Subjects on the Northern Continent of America.

. . . For my Part, I must be of Opinion, as I hinted before, that there is but one way of Converting these poor Infidels, and reclaiming them from Barbarity, and that is, Charitably to intermarry with them, according to the Modern Policy of the most Christian King in Canada and Louisiana.

Had the English done this at the first Settlement of the Colony, the Infidelity of the Indians had been worn out at this Day, with their Dark Complexions, and the Country had swarm'd with People more than it does with Insects.

It was certainly an unreasonable Nicety, that prevented their entering into so good-Natur'd an Alliance. All Nations of men have the same Natural Dignity, and we all know that very bright Talents may be lodg'd under a very dark Skin. The principal Difference between one People and another proceeds only from the Different Opportunities of Improvement.

The Indians by no means want understanding, and are in their Figure tall and well-proportion'd. Even their Copper-colour'd Complexion wou'd admit of Blanching, if not in the first, at the farthest in the Second Generation.

I may safely venture to say, the Indian Women would have made altogether as Honest Wives for the first Planters, as the Damsels they us'd to purchase from aboard the Ships. It is Strange, therefore, that any good Christian Shou'd have refused a wholesome, Straight Bed-fellow, when he might have had so fair a Portion with her, as the Merit of saving her Soul.

8. We rested on our clean Mats very comfortably, tho' alone, and the next Morning went to the Toilet of some of the Indian Ladys, where, what with the Charms of their Persons and the Smoak of their Apartments, we were almost blinded. They offer'd to give us Silk-Grass Baskets of their own making, which we Modestly refused, knowing that an Indian present, like that of a Nun, is a Liberality put out to Interest, and a Bribe plac'd to the greatest Advantage.

Our Chaplain observ'd with concern, that the Ruffles of Some of our Fellow Travellers were a little discolour'd with pochoon, wherewith the good Man had been told those Ladies us'd to improve their invisible charms.

About 10 a Clock we marched out of Town in good order, & the War Captains saluted us with a Volley of Small-Arms. From thence we proceeded over Black-water Bridge to colo' Henry Harrisons, where we congratulated each other upon our Return into Christendom. . . .

### On Negro Slavery

Byrd's liberal views on interracial mingling did not, however, extend to the Negro. He saw in the importation of Negro slaves a menace to the safety of white settlers and sought to prohibit it. Yet his views on slavery were probably more liberal than those of other Virginians. His reference to "this unchristian Traffick, of makeing Merchandise of our Fellow Creatures," indicates a hostility to the slave trade which hardly prevailed at the time. The following letter was originally published in the *Virginia Magazine of History and Biography,* XXXVI (July 1928) , 219–222.

### *To Lord Egremont*[1]

VIRGINIA 12th July 1736.

MY LORD. I had the honour of your Lordship's commands of the 9th Sep. & since that time have had the pleasure of conversing a great deal with yr picture. It is uncomparably well done & the Painter has not only hit your Ayr, but some of the Virtues too which usd to soften & enliven yr Features. So that every connoisseur, that sees it, can see T'was drawn for a generous benevolent & worthy Person. It is no wonder perhaps, that I cou'd discern so many good things in the Portrait, when I knew them so well in the original, just like those who pick out the meaning of the Bible altho in a strange language, because they were acquainted with the subject before. But I own I was pleased to find some strangers able to read your Lordship's character on the Canvas, as plain as if they had been Physiognomists by profession. Your

Lordship's opinion concerning Rum & negroes is certainly very just & your excluding both of them from your colony of Georgia will be very Happy: tho' with Respect to Rum, the Saints of New England, I fear will find out some trick, to evade your Act of Parliament. They have a great dexterity at palliating a perjury so well, as to leave no tast of it in the mouth, nor can any People like them slip through a Penal Statute. They will give some other name to their Rum which they may safely do, because it gos by that of Kill Devil in this Country, from its baneful qualitys. A watchfull eye, must be kept on these foul Traders, or all the precautions of the Trustees will be in vain. I wish we coud be blessed with the same Prohibition. They import so many negro's hither, that I fear this Colony will sometime or other be confounded by the name of New Guinea. I am sensible of many bad consequences of multiplying these Ethiopians amongst us. They blow up the pride, & ruin the Industry of our White People, who Seeing a Rank of poor Creatures below them, detest work for fear it shoud make them look like Slaves. Then that poverty which will ever attend upon Idleness, disposed them, as much to pilfer as it does the Portuguise, who account it much more like a gentleman to steal, than to dirty their hands with Labour of any kind. Another unhappy Effect of many Negroes is, the necessity of being severe. Numbers make them insolent and then foul Means must do what fair will not. We have however nothing like the Inhumanity here, that is practiced in the Islands & God forbid we ever shou'd. But these base Tempers require to be rid with a tort rein, or they will be apt to throw their Rider. Yet even this is terrible to a good natured Man, who must submit to be either a Fool or a Fury. And this will be more our unhappy case, the more the Negros are increast amongst us. But these private mischeifs are nothing, if compared to the publick danger. We have already at least 10,000 men of these descendants of Ham, fit to bear Arms, & these numbers increase every day, as well by birth, as by Importation. And in case there should arise a Man of desperate courage amongst us, exasperated by a desperate fortune, he might with more advantage than Cataline kindle a Servile War. Such a man might be dreadfully mischeivous before any opposition coud be formed against him, & tinge our Rivers as wide as they are with blood, besides the Calamitys which wou'd be brought upon us by such an attempt, it wou'd cost our Mother Country many a fair Million, to make us as profitable, as we are at present. It were there-fore, worth the consideration, of a British Parliament, My Lord, to put an end, to this unchristian Traffick, of makeing Merchandise of our Fellow Creatures. At Least, the farther importation of them, into our Colonys, shoud be prohibited, lest they prove as troublesome, & dangerous every where, as they have been lately in Jamaica, where besides a vast expence of money, they have cost the lives of many of his Majesty's Subjects. We have mountains in Virginia too, to which they may retire, as Safely, & do as much mischief, as they do in Jamaica. All these matters, duly considered, I wonder the Legislature will Indulge a few ravenous Traders, to the danger of the Publick safety, & such Traders as woud freely sell their Fathers, their Elder Brothers, & even the Wives of their bosomes if they cou'd black their Faces & get anything for them. In intirely agree with your Lordship in the Detestation you seem to feel for that Diabolical Liquor Rum, which dos more mischief to Peoples Industry & morals, than any thing except Gin & the Pope. And if it were not a little too Poetical, I shoud fancy, as the Gods of old are said to quaff Nector, so the Devils are fobb'd off with Rumm. Tho my Dear Country-men, woud think this unsavory Spirit, much too good for Devils, because they are fonder of it, than Wives or Children, for they often sell the Bread, out of their mouths, to buy Rumm to put in their own. Thrice happy Georgia, if it be in the power of any Law to keep out so great an enimy to Health, Industry & Virtue!

## NOTE

1. John Perceval (1683–1748), 1st Earl of Egmont (not Egremont), was a partner with Oglethorpe in the founding of Georgia. He wrote much on biography and genealogy. His portrait was one of those in the collection of Col. Byrd's friends, placed first at Westover and then at Brandon.

# CHAPTER 5

# Six Quaker Voices Against Slavery

During the first half of the eighteenth century, slavery was well entrenched throughout the colonies, and those who questioned the institution were few and isolated. To condemn slavery meant incurring the odium of the wealthy and powerful, and not many were willing to make the sacrifice. Yet there were voices raised in protest, and these were primarily Quakers. Why this was so is not easily explained. That the cause could not have been Quaker theology is shown by the fact that many Quaker leaders, including theologians, were slaveholders and defenders of slavery. That the Quaker community did not gladly suffer anti-slavery rebels in its midst—with the exception of Elihu Coleman of Nantucket[1]— is shown by the persecution to which Ralph Sandiford and Benjamin Lay were subjected, both of whom were disowned by the Society of Friends. It was not until after the middle of the century that such Quakers as John Woolman and Anthony Benezet were able to preach without fear of Quaker displeasure. By then, of course, many others besides Quakers were beginning to see the evils of slavery.

As one studies the writings of the six men whose opinions are presented here, one notes an interesting progression. John Hepburn and Elihu Coleman rely primarily upon religious arguments. They stress slavery's denial of man's God-given right to free will, its repudiation of the Golden Rule, and the encouragement given to the Turkish enslavement of Christians by the Christian enslavement of Africans. These arguments are not neglected by Ralph Sandiford and Benjamin Lay, who also stress the great injustice involved in slavery and the slave trade while strongly attacking Quakers as slave-owners. Finally, John Woolman and Anthony Benezet place great reliance on the additional argument of the Negro's nature: they emphasize his humanity, his rationality and the essential equality of his mental capacity to that of whites. What differences they find between white masters and Negro slaves, they attribute to the effects of slavery, and they deny any inherent inferiority in the Negro.

## NOTE

1. It may be that the moderateness of his criticism of slavery coupled with the fact that he attacked "slavery on a remote island off the New England Coast" saved him from censure. (See Drake, *Quakers and Slavery*, pp. 38–9.)

# JOHN HEPBURN

## THE AMERICAN DEFENSE OF THE CHRISTIAN GOLDEN RULE

John Hepburn's *The American Defense of the Christian Golden Rule* appeared in 1715 as a 94-page octavo book. The title page does not reveal the place of publication, and scholarly opinion varies between New York,[1] Philadelphia[2] and England.[3] Born in England, and never himself a slave-owner, Hepburn lived in America for thirty years before speaking out against slavery. Henry J. Cadbury notes that "it is really only circumstantial evidence that makes us regard him as a Friend,"[4] but Drake does not express any doubts about Hepburn's being a Quaker.[5] In any event, Hepburn's statement seems to have gone unnoticed among Friends. The following selections include the Preface and pp. 1–10, 14–15 and 18.[6]

## *The Preface to the Reader*

CHRISTIAN READER;

It is not singularity or Ostentation that I appear in Print, but my Christian Duty, in Honour to God, and the Salvation and well being of the souls of men, in the Detection of the Anti-christian Practice in *making Slaves* of them who bear the Image of God, *viz.* their fellow, Creature, Man; A Practice so *cruel* and *inhumane,* that the more it is thought upon by judicious men, the more they do abhor it; It being so vile a contradiction to the Gospel of the blessed Messiah.

And if our Negro-Masters were put to it, to bring an Instance that a man denied the Christian Faith, I think they could not bring a stronger Instance, then that he was found in the Practice of making Slaves of men. And furthermore, I doubt not, but this may be to some a very unwelcome Theam, and they would wonder to find their beloved *Delilah,* the making Slaves of Negroes, and others rejected, although the more moderate Christians do full well know, that I have the Truth on my side. And if these Lines should come to the *Island of Great Britain* (my native Land) I hope the sincere Christians there of all Sects will commend my Christian care, in detecting so gross a corruption as this, crept in by reason of the Ease and Gains it brings to our *American Christians;* and I hope the *learned Christians* there will admonish their *American Brethren,* for putting such an Affront upon the ever blessed *Messiah,* and his glorious Gospel as this their Practice doth, in making Slaves of Men.

This Practice cannot but be very offensive to sincere and honest hearted Christians, that this Practi[c]e should be heard among the Heathen, to harden them in such *heathenish Practices.*

And now, *Reader,* I am going to shew thee a Wonder, and that is, this thirty years that *I* have been in *America,* this Practice has been carried on almost in profound silence, which it is like the Negro-Masters will take it the harder to be opposed now. It is true, *John Tillotson*[7] of *Canterbury* hath two Sermons in print concerning *Restitution,* and he tells them there, that *they cannot have Admittance into Heaven without making Restitution of the wrong done to there fellow Creatures.* And if this be applyed to the wrong done to Negroes, I have Bishop *Tillotson* on my side. This and many other excellent things have dropt from the Pen of that (in many things, no doubt, an) excellent man.

And *Cotton Mather* calls the Inslaving of Negroes, *A crying Sin in the Land.*[8]

*And George Fox* printed against this Practice, and sent it to the *Barbadoes-Quakers.*[9] Such was the early care of this excellent man above forty years ago; But his Christian Admonition was rejected. It is true, there are some excellent souls among them still, who came out of *Old England,* that have kept their Integrity, namely *John Saltkill* [Salkeld][10], *Thomas Chalkley,*[11] and others, who when they see this Abomination acted by their *American brethren,* they openly bear Testimony in their publick Assemblies, and declare against it (as I am credibly informed) There was another Paper Printed by (I think) *G. Keith*[12] his Party at *Philadelphia;* and half a Sheet was printed against this Practice at *London,* called *the Athenian Oracle,* But the most of all those writings I doubt are destroyed by *Negro-Masters,* that the Reader will find them almost as scarce to be found as the *Phenix Egg.* And last of all, I have appeared against this Practice, although I have lain dormant above this thirty years; for the which I acknowledge my Failure before God and man, and I desire forgiveness of God, and next I desire the forgiveness of man; for the reason that I was silent so long, because I waited for my betters to undertake the Work; and if any had appeared in this Work, it is like I had been silent still.

Now whether they will hear or forbear for the future, I hope to be clear of their Blood, and if they will not repent and make Restitution, I cannot help it; for I have faithfully warned them of their Danger; For I earnestly contended for the Truth, and honestly declared against this *Inriching Sin,* in making Slaves of Men. And now I think to end my Preface as I began it, and that is, I chiefly design the *Honour of God,* and next the *Welfare and Salvation* of Souls. If happily I might be instrumental to deter any one Soul from being catcht with this inriching Sin, or instrumental of the Repentance of Restitution made by one Soul that is and already guilty, then I desire they should give God the Glory, and I make no Question in having my Reward.

> *And now to find the Longitude,*
> *Many a Man hath gone about,*
> *But the Perpetual Motion,*
> *Our Negro Masters have found out.*

*New-Jersey,*
*1st Month,* 1714.

JOHN HEPBURN

## Argument the First

The more a Man becomes conformable to the Attributes of God, the more just and holy he is, and the more beloved of God, and consequently a more perfect Christian.

*First,* then, God hath given to man a Free-Will, so that he is Master of his own Choice (whether it be good or evil) and will in no way force and compel the Will of man; yea, not unto that part which is good, far less unto evil, notwithstanding his Attribute of Omnipotence. And seeing then, it is thus with God and his Creatures, we ought also to do so by our fellow mortals, and therefore we ought not to force and compel our fellow creatures, the Negroes, Nay, not although we judge it for them a better way of living; For when we force their will, this is a manifest Robbery of that noble Gift their bountiful Creator hath given them, and is a right down Contradiction to the aforesaid Attributes of God, and consequently an Anti-Christian Practice. And so, those that oppose God and his Attributes, they may expect to incur his Displeasure; So they may find a pregnant instance in *Pharaoh* and his Egyptian Task-Masters.

*2dly.* This Practice contradicts Christs command, who commanded us, *To do to all men as we would they should do to us,* or as we would be done by. Now the buying and selling of the *Bodies* and *Souls* of Men, was and is the Merchandize of the Babylonish Merchants spoken of in the *Revelations.* Now the Tyranizing over and making Slaves of our Fellow Creatures, the Negroes, every one knows, or may know, this is not the way they would be done unto.

Now, I have shown you, *first,* That this Practice opposes God and his Attributes, and *2dly,* That it opposes Christ and his Command; And what is this in Effect but to bid Defyance, and to live in Opposition to Christ and his Gospel? and if so, it is a high Degree of an Antichristian Life and Practice. . . .

*3ly,* I have shewed before, that GOD, who is no respecter of persons, hath given to all men a Freedom of their Wills, to pitch upon their own choice, for both Soul and Body, which are the only parts, next unto the Life, the free donation of our heavenly Father, in this terrestrial world; But it would seem by the Negro-Masters Practice and Arguments, that God did miss the matter, by his Wisdom, when he gave the Negros (his Creatures) the Freedom of their Wills; but our Negro-Masters have found out, by their Inginuity, how to mend this (seeming) Defect, in two respects, to wit, that is to rob them of their Freedom, and make them bond-Slaves and their Posterity forever. And in the next place, they can highly inrich themselves by the Bargain; by the unparallelled and never enough lamented Bondage and Slavery of those poor Creatures and handy work of God, And can afford to keep themselves with white hands, except at some Times they chance to be besparkled with the Blood of those poor Slaves, when they fall to beating them with their *twisted Hides* and *Horse-whips,* and other *Instruments of Cruelty,* too barbarous here to relate, all done in the name of their deservings and correction. And furthermore, they can afford (by their beloved *Diana,* their Slaves) to go with *fine powdered Perriwigs,* and great *bunched Coats;* and likewise keep their Wives idle (*Jezebel-like*) to *paint their Faces,* and *Puff,* and *powder their Hair,* and to bring up their Sons and Daughters in *Idleness* and *Wantonness,* and in all manner of *Pride* and *Prodigality,* in *decking* and *adorning* their *Carkasses* with pufft and powdered Hair, with *Ruffles* and *Top-knots, Ribbands* and *Lace,* and *gay Cloathing,* and what not; All, and much more, the miserable Effects produced by the Slavery of Negroes; and their Slaves in the *vilest Raggs,* much ado to cover their nakedness, and many of them not a *Shirt* upon their Backs, and some of them not a *Shoe* upon their Foot in *cold Frosts* and *Snow* in the Winter Time, that many of them have their Feet and other members *frozen off,* by reason of their Cruell Usage; and some of them must lie by the *Fire* among the *Ashes,* or be driven out to lie in *Huts* out of Doors among the worst of their *Dogs,* for some of the finest of their Dogs they permit to lie in the bed with themselves.

And they accomodate their Slaves which such Names as these, *Toby, Mando, Mingo, Jacko, Hector* and *Hagar,* and such like Names they give to their *Dogs* and *Horses.*

And when their Masters see fit they will *hang them up by their Thumbs,* and then command another Negro to beat him so long, as his Master sees fit; this he must not refuse to do, if it were his *own Father,* nay, further, they will force them to be very *Hangmen,* And notwithstanding of all this, some of them must go with a *hungry Belly,* and that which they do get to eat (ye need not doubt but it) is the *worst the House affords.*

Now all that fear God cannot but know that those men who use such Cruelty are not only void of the *Fear of God,* but are even destitute of *humane Civility,* and *Pity* and *Mercy;* Therefore their Example can be no more a Rule for keeping Slaves than it is for using such inhumane Cruelty, which all sober Men abhor; For it cannot be expected that men of such Cruelty have much regard to the lawfulness of what they do, and it is great Pity that men who are naturally more moderate and merciful should be led to the Practice of an unlawful thing by the Example of the *vilest of men.*

But to return to the Servants of such cruel masters; By this Description all may see that they are put under an unavoidable Necessity of sinning to maintain *Self-Preservation,* an Instinct of Nature belonging to all the Creatures of God; So self-preservation puts them to *steal, rob,* and *lye,* and many other sinfull Actions; nay, some of them when they see themselves surrounded and trappaned with all the Miseries aforesaid, and many more, then they go into Dispair, and miserably *murder themselves,* and some their *Masters,* to get rid of their Tortures and miserable Slavish Life. There was one of them (I think) within less then two years ago, shot himself with a Gun, near his Masters House, within a few miles off the place where I write this lamentable story.

Now for those heinous Sins, as Lying, Stealing, Robbing, and Self-Murder; they cannot escape Punishment, by the Justice of God. Now as I have said before, they being put under such necessity of sinning, and they themselves being but *Infidels,* I desire the Negro-Masters to inform me, who must answer for all these abominable Sins?

And now, *Reader,* I have given thee a small View of the Usage and Treatment of these poor miserable Slaves; for if I would enlarge upon their Usage, I need write nothing else to swell up a Book to I know not what bigness; The *parting of Man* and *Wife* being such a heinous sin committed by the Negro-Masters, I cannot pass by; The parting the Husband from the Wife, and the Wife from the Husband, and their Children from them both, to make up their Masters Gains, they force them thus to break the seventh Command, and commit Adultery with other strangers, or other mens Wives or Husbands. These and the like Usages, is enough to make them believe, there is no God at all, and harden them in Idolatrous Worship, and make them blaspheme against the holy God, that he takes not immediate Vengeance on such notorious Offenders. And here are the *first three* Commands broken, occasioned by their Masters. And the breaking the *fourth* is evident to all; for some, for want of Food and other necessaries, for all their hard weeks Labour to inrich their Master, for to maintain Self-preservation, puts them to work on the First Day of the Week, to supply their pure Necessities, and so break that which their Masters call the Christian Sabbath. And so, here is all the Commands of the first Table broken by them, occasioned by the *Cruelty* of their Masters. And their Children being sold from their Parents, they unavoidably cannot honour them; and here is the breach of the *fifth*. And to get rid of their miserable Tortures, many kill themselves and others; and here is the breach of the *Sixth*. The parting of Man and Wife makes them commit *Adultery* with others; and here is the breach of the *Seventh*. To maintain Self-preservation, they unavoidably must *Steal;* and here is the breach of the *Eight*. Then they run away to avoid their Tortures, and when they are catcht their Master will ask them, *Do you not deserve to be hung up and Beat?* and here they must bear False witness against themselves (which is worse than against their Neighbours) and say, *yes, I do, deserve to be hung up and Beat;* and here is the breach of the *ninth*. And when they are in great necessity of Food and Rayment, and have it not of their own, they unavoidably must covet it of their Neighbours, and here is the breach of the *Tenth*.

Now *Reader,* here are all the Ten Commands of God (occasioned by their Masters) broken by them. This is such a Charge, that I doubt it will be too hot or too heavy for the Negro-Masters to answer.

And now that those Christians who in their *Baptism* did engage to keep *all Gods holy commands,* should not keep them, but break them themselves and for their own Gains, do lay all manner of unavoidable Necessities upon their Slaves to break them also; This is a poor encouragement for Godfathers indeed.

I may truly say, as *Nesterius* did, who was Arch-Bishop of *Constantinople,* and was banished from them by the prevailing Party in his Time, to the outermost part of the *Roman Empire* among the *Barbarians,* because he said and taught, that *Mary* ought not to be called the *Mother of God,* but the *Mother of Christ,* and that it could not go down with him to say, that God was a year old, or a Month, or a Day old, etc. As we may read in that great Book called *Eusebius*.[13] And when he found great Kindness from those Barbarians he wrote a learned and eloquent letter to those Christians that banished him, to this Effect, that *For his Banishment he could undergo it patiently, but his Fear and Lamentation was, that their Actions should go unto the Heathen, that thereby they should be imboldened in* Heathenism, *and give them Advantage to blaspheme against Christ and the Christian Religion;* And so advised them not to be a stop and a Hinderance to that glorious Gospel that had cost so many Lives for the spreading and advancing of it.

Now, I can truly say, that this is my concern as it was the concern of *Nesterius,* that ever the Actions of our *American* Negro-Masters should go unto the *Turks* and other *Heathen* Nations, to harden them in *Mahumetanism* and other *Heathenism,* and to imbolden them to blaspheme against Christ and his Gospel, and the purest Christianity.

I wish this may come to be the concern of our Negro-Masters, That they be not hinderers, but Advancers of the glorious Gospel, and then I am sure they will be loath to do to any other Man what they would not be done by themselves.

Now, it is not unpossible but than an *American Negro Master* and a *Turk* should meet and discourse this Point betwixt them, And the *Turk* should say, "I am well pleased, Brother that you and we agree so well in this point, *viz.* in making Slaves of them we can have the Mastery over; And I doubt not but many of us have been at a stand whether it may not be a sin to use our fellow Creatures so cruelly: but now I think it is Time to give over such Doubts, when we see it so mightily practiced by the *Christians,* I mean the *American Christians;* I make this Distinction, because it is not practiced in *Europe.*

"And now, Brother, I would argue a little plainer with you, How comes it to pass, that you find Fault with us for making Slaves of Men, when you your selves do the same? How can that be an evil and a sin in us, which is a Christian Practice among your selves? And I hear, that when any of your Slaves turns Christian, and is baptized and receives the Christian Faith, you keep them in perpetual Slavery for all, and so they have no encouragement to turn Christian upon that score, which shews to me, that you have but a small Esteem for your Religion, or at least are very lukewarm for *Proselytes.*

"This is worse then *Turks;* for when any of our Slaves turn, and embraces the *Muhametan Faith,* they are no longer Slaves, but presently set free, and many Times preferred to Places of

*Trust* and *Dignity,* such zeal have we for Proselytes, and our Religion.

"And how comes it that you differ among your selves in this Practice? for there are some zealous men among you, that both dispute and write against you, and they declare it to be an Antichristian Practice; And the Christians in *Europe* do not practice it. And I have heard that the Gospel was, *Glory to God in the Highest,* and *Peace* and *Good Will to all Men upon Earth,* and that ye should do to all men as ye would they should do to you. And if this be the Gospel of the blessed Messiah, I will tell you plainly, I look upon you to be apostatized in this Point, and I would advise you either to embrace the rest of our Mahometan Practices (and then we would receive you) or otherwise to walk more closely to the Rules and Practice of *Christianity;* and not to content your selves with a Name, and to be a perpetual Scandal to the rest of Christians."

So far Mahometan. . . .

*Negro Master.* Hold! I think I have another Proof, which, according to your own Argument, I think will bind you. There is another numerous and famous sect of Christians, called *Quakers,* who by their Practice do show that they have all those aforesaid Marks which thou hast nominated, and therefore by consequence of your Argument the only *true* and *real Christians,* and yet there is no People more forward to make Slaves of Negroes than they are; And now, if they be infallibly guided in all the other Principles and Practices of *Christianity,* one would think they could not be erroneous in this, *viz.* in making Slaves of Negros. And now, although all my other Arguments should fail, yet this last, one would think, should silence you. . . .

*Christians Answer.* There is a good Body of People without the Bounds of your Instance, and that is the *German-Quakers,* who live in *German Town* near *Philadelphia,* Who (to their re-nowned Praise be it spoken) have above all other Sects in *America,* kept their Hands clean from that *vile Oppression* and *inriching Sin* of making Slaves of their fellow Creatures, the Negros, as I was credibly informed by one of themselves, and so have particular Men of all Sects kept themselves free from this inriching sin. . . .[14]

## NOTES

1. The American Antiquarian Society suggests New York.
2. Charles Evans, *American Bibliography*, Vol. I, No. 1678 (New York, 1941) suggests Philadelphia.
3. Henry J. Cadbury, "Quaker Bibliographical Notes," *Bulletin* of Friends Historical Association, XXVI (Spring 1937), 41, suggests England.
4. *Ibid.* In his essay, "John Hepburn and his Book against Slavery, 1715," *Proceedings of the American Antiquarian Society*, April 20, 1949, Vol. 59, pp. 101–2, Cadbury cites evidence that Hepburn was a Quaker.
5. Drake, *Quakers and Slavery*, pp. 34–36.
6. The entire text was reprinted with valuable introductory remarks by Cadbury in "John Hepburn . . . ," *op. cit.*, pp. 89 ff.
7. John Tillotson (1630–1694), Archbishop of Canterbury.
8. This is an exaggeration of Mather's anti-slavery opinions.
9. In London, in 1676, George Fox published an essay called *Gospel Family-Order*, in which he suggested to the Quaker slaveholders of Barbados that they ought to educate their slaves in Christianity and perhaps free them after a term of service.
10. John Salkeld (1672–1739), Quaker minister and traveler; after he came to America, his home for most of his life was in Chester, Pa. (I am indebted to Henry J. Cadbury for this information.)
11. Nantucket's earliest Quaker missionary; he wrote and published a *Journal*.
12. See the statement by George Keith on p.      .
13. Eusebius of Caesaria (*c.* A.D. 265–340), church father and historian, wrote the *Chronicle* (303), a compendium of universal history, and *Ecclesiastical History* (311, last edition 324). Hepburn is probably referring to the latter.
14. See the anti-slavery statement by the Germantown Quakers on p. 38.

## ELIHU COLEMAN

### The First Anti-Slavery Tract by a New England Quaker

Elihu Coleman (1699–1789), a Nantucket carpenter, wrote *A Testimony Against that Antichristian Practice of Making Slaves of Men* in 1729–30 and published it in Boston in 1733. The manuscript was approved by the Nantucket Friends. The Quarterly meeting in Newport, though preponderantly pro-slavery, nevertheless gave him permission to print. There is no evidence of any further anti-slavery effort on his part,[1] but he had the satisfaction, before he died, of seeing the New England Yearly Meeting of 1773 require its members to emancipate their Negroes or face disownment by the Society. By 1778, there were no slaves among New England Friends, except in Newport, and by the end of the Revolution "no Quaker in America owned slaves unless, as in North Carolina, he was prevented by law from giving them liberty."[2]

## To the Reader

Before I speak of the Unlawfulness of this Practice of making Slaves, it is in my Mind to give a Relation how, and after what Manner I came to understand it so; and why, and for what Reason I now speak against it. After I had arrived to the Years of a Man, I was very desirous that I might come to know the Lord for my self: For altho' I did believe I was educated or taught the right way, yet upon serious Consideration, I came to see that the Religion of a Man's Education, was not the Religion of his, but of them, that educated him: And therefore I was very desirous to know him for my self; for I read in Scripture, that when Destruction came upon the City, that if *Daniel, Noah* and *Job* were in it, they by their Righteousness could save none but their own Souls. And altho' I might live in the midst of a righteous People, I saw that it would not avail any thing to me. And as I was thus concern'd, it pleased the Lord in his own Time to manifest himself to me, in some small Degree and Measure, so that then I could discern Things aright in some degree; and after I had considered the Principles of those my Friends called *Quakers,* I did, and now do believe that they are undeniably good, and that those that keep close to them, I do believe that there can never any Weapon be formed that shall prevail against them. And as I consider'd thereon, I found a Necessity in my self to join with those People, whose principles were so good: Yet notwithstanding I must confess, (and for that Reason I now write) that as I knew a Necessity to join with them in that which was good; the same Necessity I now find to speak against that which is evil, altho' it may be in some of them. For the Lord made me sensible in that convincing Day, that he would not allow of Sin, altho' it might be in *Jacob,* and that Transgression in *Israel* should not go unpunished, and that he would yet again search *Jerusalem* as with Candles, and bring to Light the hidden things of Dishonesty.

And now, altho' some may think it hard to have this Practice spoken against, that has been carried on so long pretty much in Silence; I may let such know, that I have found it hard to write against it; yet nevertheless believing it to be my Duty so to do, I have written according to the Understanding I have had thereof. And altho' I have written but little, and in a very plain Way, yet I hope that those Remarks I have made thereon, may serve as a Text for some to preach to themselves upon. I am not unthoughtful of the Ferment or Stir that such Discourses as this may make among some, who (like *Demetrius* of old) may say, By this Craft have we our Wealth, which caused the People to cry out with one Voice, saying, Great is *Diana* of the *Ephesians,* whom all *Asia* and the World worship. Therefore leaving such to worship what they will, I will also say, that there is many sober Men that has spoken against this Practice, both by Writing and in their publick Assemblies, whom I could Name, but chusing to be brief, I will only observe to the Reader, what I my self have observed, and that is, that those People that dwell nearest the Truth, and are most engaged in it, and are more concern'd for the spreading of it, than for any thing in this World beside, cannot allow of this Practice, they seeing it to be Oppression and Cruelty.

Now I have spoken something of the Reason why I have wrote this, I will conclude this my Preface, wishing the Reader an impartial Judgment.

## A Testimony Against that Antichristian Practice of Making Slaves of Men

Such hath been the Love and Goodness of God to Men, that in all Ages of the World he has had a People, Family or Church whom he hath called and also chosen, to bear a Testimony to his Name and Truth: Yet it may be observed by them that read the holy Scriptures, that those People whom he had called, and favoured above all the Families of the Earth, and had wrought Signs and Wonders for them, and had exalted them in the Sight of their Enemies; that those People in Times of Liberty and Ease, grew forgetful of God. . . . It may be also observed by them who read the Book of Martyrs or Sufferings of the People of God, from the Time our Lord was crucified, down to the Reign of the bloody Queen *Mary,* (which History I do believe is believed to be true by most Protestants) that in all that Length of Time, God had a People whom he had called out of the Worship, Ways and Customs of the World, who were a suffering People, and that in the midst of their greatest Sufferings, they were the most immediately upheld by the Divine Power of God; so that they could even Rejoice in the Flames. But when it pleased God that a good King or Emperor came to Rule, so that they were not persecuted or oppressed, that they grew forgetful of God, and some of them became Oppressors themselves. Now I do believe that God sometimes afflicteth outwardly, and sometimes inwardly, who best knows the Rod that is suitable to chastize with. We may observe also how it hath been with our elder Friends, who were a harmless and suffering People, who did not only bear Testimony in Word, but in Practice also, against all outward and carnal Weapons; which our Friend *Robert Barclay*[3] observing, said, that it was their innocent Lives and Conversations that convinced him, before ever he inspected into their Principles. He did not see them in this Practice of making Slaves of their Fellow Creatures, which Practice is upheld by the carnal Sword only, but he bore a Testimony against the carnal Sword, and would not allow of it to be used, altho' it were in Self-Preservation. Such Innocency was in that worthy Man, as well as many others in that Day, that they would not allow of this Practice, having more regard to that Command of Christ's, (to do to others as we would they should do to us) than to any outward Advantage in this World. And after our Friend *George Fox* had travelled in the Island of *Barbadoes* in the *West Indies,* where he saw this Practice of making Slaves, even to that degree, that their Houses were black with them, that he bore open Testimony against it, when he got home he wrote a little Book to them, wherein I find these Words, *'And if thy Brother, an Hebrew Man, or an Hebrew Woman, be sold unto thee, and serve thee six Years, then in the seventh Year thou shalt let him go free from thee. And when thou sendest him out free from thee, thou shalt not let him go away empty: Thou shalt furnish him liberally out of thy Flock, and out of thy Floor, and out of thy Winepress, of that wherewith the Lord thy God hath blessed thee, thou shalt give it to him. And remember that thou was a Bond man in the Land of* Egypt, *and the Lord thy God redeemed thee: Therefore I command thee this Thing to day.* Deut. 15.12, 13, 14, 15. See here this was to be done by the *Jews* to such as were of their own People; and indeed this will very well become Christians, Masters, Governors and Rulers of Families here in this Island or elsewhere, who should outstrip the *Jews* to deal so (as the Lord commanded) with their Servants and Apprentices, that were of their own Nation or People: And to close up all, let me tell you, it will doubtless be very acceptable to the Lord, if so be that Masters of Families here would deal so with their Servants the Negroes and Blacks whom they have bought with their Money, to let them go free after a considerable Term of Years, if they have served them faithfully: And when they go and are made free, let them not go away empty handed. This I say will be very acceptable to the Lord, whose Servants we are, and who rewards us plentifully for our Service done him, not suffering us to go away empty. . . . And let not your Families of Whites and Blacks be like *Sodom* and *Gomorrah,* like *Zeboim, Zepharuim,* and the rest of the Cities of the Plain, or like the Canaanites; lest sudden Destruction come upon you, and the Lord root you out, as he did them. Let not I say, your Servants under your Command, and such as are born in your Houses, and bred up in your Families, and such as you have bought with Money, suffer them not (I say) to take Husbands and Wives at their Pleasure, and then leave them again when they please, and then take others again as fast and suddenly as they will, and then leave them, this is not well, this may bring the Judgments of God upon you; yea, this manifests your Families to be unclean and adulterated Families.'

Now by these Words (tho' but a small part of what he wrote) we may see that he was against making Slaves of Men. Now I do believe if Men were ingenuous to acknowledge to the Truth, even as their Consciences bear them Witness, I need not go any farther for a Proof against this Practice: But because they be not, I will turn also to the holy Scriptures, that so they that are in this Practice may be condemned by both.

*First,* we may observe, when God had created Man, that he gave him a free Will, and would not compel the Will of Man, no not to that which was Good, much less to that which was Evil; therefore we ought not to compel our Fellow Creatures.

*Objection,* But had not God's People Bond-Servants in all Ages of the World, bought with their Money? To which I Answer, that in the Time of the Law they had Bond-Servants bought with their Money; but the Apostle saith, *The Servant abideth not in the House ever.* Now the Word *Servant* I understand to be but for a Time, but the Word *Slave* for ever. And those that merchandiz'd in Slaves we may find were *Babilon's* Merchants, *Rev.* 18. 13. And those that had Bond Servants under the Law, were commanded to let them go free after some Time of Service, and they were not to let them go empty handed neither, which some of them not observing, the Lord complained by the Prophet *Jeremiah,* that they *have not hearkened unto me, in proclaiming Liberty every one to his Brother, and every Man to his Neighbour: Behold, I proclaim a Liberty for you, saith the Lord, to the Sword, to the Pestilence, and to the Famine, and I will make you to be removed into all the Kingdoms of the Earth. Jer.* 34. 17.

*Objection,* But they were of their own Nation that the Command was against; now these Negroes are not of our own Nation, but are mere Infidels and Strangers. To which Objection I'll Answer as it is written in *Exod.* 22. 21. *Ye shall neither vex a Stranger, nor oppress him, for ye were Strangers in the Land of Egypt.* And *Exod.* 23. 9. *Also thou shalt not oppress a Stranger, for ye know the Heart of a Stranger, seeing ye were Strangers in the Land of* Egypt. Now I do not find that it is any more allowable to make a Slave of an Unbeliever, than a Believer, seeing we are commanded, *Mat.* 7. 12. *Therefore all things whatsoever ye would that Men should do to you, do ye even so to them, for this is the Law and the Prophets.* Now we may see that this was not only a Command of Christ's, but was the Law and the Prophets also; and those that comes to observe that Command, even fulfil both Tables at once. Now I have often considered how earnestly some Men will search into the Etemology or Original of some Things that may be but small, and in the mean while omit the greater. Now in my Judgment every thing ought to be looked upon according to the Importance, Weight or Value of the Thing; for to be very zealous in a small Thing, and to pass lightly over a greater, that Zeal may be properer called Superstition than good Zeal, which should be grounded upon Knowledge. Now I would have all to consider of this Practice of making Slaves of Negroes, or others that we can get the Mastery over, to see upon what Foundation it stands, or to see what's⁴ the Original of it, whether or no Pride and Idleness was not the first rise of it, that they might go with white Hands, and that their Wives might (*Jezebel* like) paint and adorn themselves, and their Sons and Daughters be brought up in Idleness, which may be very well termed the Mother of all Vice; for it is generally the richest sort of People that have them, that could do best without them, for the Poor are not so able to get them.

But some may object, as I my self have heard them, that there was a Mark set upon *Cain,* and they do believe that these Negroes are the Posterity of *Cain,* because of their Hair, and their being so black, differing from all others, and that *Canaan* was to be a Servant of Servants to his Brethren, whom they take to be of the same Linage: But if we do but observe, and read in the Genealogy of *Cain,* we may find that they were all drowned in the old World, and that *Canaan* was of the Line of *Seth.* And altho' it was the Will of God that the World was drowned, because of their great Wickedness; yet we may observe also, that there was unclean Beasts went into the Ark, as well as clean, and that it was the Will or Permission of God, that there should be a *Ham,* as well as a *Shem* and *Japhet:* By which we may see that

God suffers wicked Men to live as well as Righteous, and we find that the Sun shineth on the Evil as well as on the Good, and that the Rain falleth on the Unjust as well as the Just, and that Christ forbids his Followers to meddle with the Tares lest they hurt the Wheat; therefore none can have any Plea for making of them Slaves, for their being either ignorant or wicked; for if that Plea would do, I do believe they need not go so far for Slaves as now they do.

And altho' *Canaan* was to be a Servant of Servants to his Brethren, yet the Lord afterwards spake by the Prophets, that the Son should not bear the Iniquity of the Father, nor the Father should not bear the iniquity of the Son, but the Soul that sinneth should die. Then the Posterity of *Canaan*, or of *Ham*, do not bear their Sins: And the Apostle *Peter* saith, *Now I perceive of a Truth that God is no respecter of Persons, but in every Nation he that feareth God and worketh Righteousness, is accepted of him*. Now altho' the Negroes might not have the Understanding that some other Nations have, then I do believe there is the less required, and if they do but as well as they know, I do believe it is well with them. For *John* the Divine saith in the *Revelations*, that he saw them that were *sealed in their Foreheads, of the Tribes of Israel, of each Tribe Twelve Thousand, which made an Hundred and Forty and Four Thousand: And after this I beheld* (said he) *and lo a great Multitude which no Man could Number, of all Nations, and Kindreds, and People, and Tongues, stood before the Throne, and before the Lamb, clothed with white Robes, and Palms in their Hands, and they cried with a loud Voice, saying, Salvation to our God, which sitteth upon the Throne, and unto the Lamb, Rev. 7. 9,10.* Now if there was of all Nations, Kindreds, Tongues and People, then there was some of the Negroes.

Now altho' the *Turks* make Slaves of those they can catch, that are not of their Religion, yet (as History relates) as soon as any embraces the Mahomitan Religion, they are no longer kept Slaves, but are quickly set free, and for the most part put to some place of Preferment; so zealous are they for Proselites and their own Religion. Now if many among those called *Christians*, would but consider how far they fall short of the *Turks* in this Particular, it would be well; for they tell the Negroes that they must believe in Christ, and receive the Christian Faith, and that they must receive the Sacrament, and be baptized, and so they do; but still they keep them Slaves for all this. Now how partial are those that can judge a Negro that should run away from his Master to deserve beating, and if one called a Christian (altho' it may be no better Christian than the other) should run away from the *Turks*, they can judge him to be a good Fellow, and to have done well. Now I look upon this Practice of making Slaves to be so great a Sin, that even Men whose Principles will allow of killing Men in their own Defence, will not allow of making Slaves; for they counting it better to deprive them of Life that rise up against them, than to deprive those of Liberty that have done them no Harm.

Now if any one should ask one of the Negroes Masters that had a Negro Child and a Child of his own, what Harm the one had done, that it should be made a Slave more than the other? that they would not I believe be able to answer it; and if they have done us no Harm, (as it is evident they have not) then it is very contrary to Scripture, and even to Nature, to make them suffer. Now if we will but look back into the Original of this Practice, which ought to be most looked into, and spoken against; for until the Cause is removed, I know not how the Effect should cease; we shall find that they were stollen in the first place either by them that fetched them, or they carrying such Goods as induced some of their own Nation to steal them; and they standing ready to receive them, which is as bad as if they had stollen them themselves.

Now we may find that Man-stealing and Man-slaying were joined together, and there was the same Punishment for the one as for the other. See *Exod.* 21. 12,13,14,15,16. *And he that smiteth a Man, so that he die, shall surely be put to Death. And he that stealeth a Man, and selleth him, or if he be found in his Hands, he shall surely be put to Death.* We may find it also in the New Testament joined with the worst of Murderers, as such as were Murderers of Fathers and Murderers of Mothers, and Man-stealers, I *Tim.* 1. 9,10. The Prohibition is general, he that stealeth away Man, a Brother or a Stranger, or Heathen, or any Man, the Punishment is Capital; for he that killed was to be put to Death, because it was the Image of God, *Gen.* 9. 6. So he that robbeth a Man of his Freedom, which only maketh Knowledge useful, seems to deface the Image of God, and therefore is punished with Death.

*Objection,* But how can this Practice of making Slaves be so great a Sin, when it is so generally practiced among all the Societies of People? For let them differ about what they will else, they pretty generally agree about this. To which Objection I Answer, That if they did but as well agree about all other Points as they do about this, they might almost if not altogether be termed one Community, yet I cannot find this to be a Proof: For I take it for a Maxim, that in a general way, the Negroes are cruelly us'd; and therefore I do not find, that their Agreement in making Slaves can be an Example for us, any more than their using them cruelly. Therefore if we would but consider the Thing rightly, we shall not find that to be a Proof, because it is so general a Practice. For we may observe how it was when our Lord was crucified, that there was divers Sects of People, and of very differing Minds, yet in putting him to Death they could generally agree; and tho' they were so much at Variance, that as the Proverb is, they were at Daggers drawing, yet the Text has it, *that the same Day Pilate and Herod were made Friends.* Yet some that have Annotated thereon, have not scrupled to call that a cursed Friendship, that was contracted by putting to Death our Lord, that came in Love to their Souls. But I have a further Reply to make to what I have said before, of the general Agreement of making Slaves, *namely,* That there is some of all Perswasions, I do believe, that cannot allow of this Practice: For they seeing it to be contrary to Christ's Command, and even to Nature: For I have made this Observation my self, (tho' but young in Years) that those that dwell nearest the Truth, and contend most for it, cannot allow of this Practice, for they see it to be Oppression and Cruelty. But it may be objected, that there hath some spoken against this Practice, and they have come to nothing, or have not prospered in it. To which I Answer, That a good Cause may be badly managed, and by sad Experience we often see it is so. Now I do believe by what hath already been said, that all that have not concluded beforehand that they would not see, may see this Practice of making Slaves to be Antichristian; for it cannot be of Christ, because contrary to his Command; therefore of Antichrist.

Now I have heard some Men say, that they believe they did wrong in getting Negroes, but that they did not know what to do with them now they had got them; for if they let them go free after some Time, if any Mishap befel them, their Estates were obliged to maintain them. And tho' they seem to acknowledge the Wrong done to them, yet they seem to be very much afraid lest they should be forc'd to help them a little, and so seem to rest contented.

Now, suppose that to give the Negroes their Times, or let them go free here in this Country, was wrong, which I do not believe would be wrong, after they had served them some time; but if it were wrong to let them go free, whether or no those that see they did wrong in getting them, ought not to bear a Testimony against it? For their keeping them and being silent, encourages others to get them. . . .

Now I can truly say, that this Practice of making Slaves of Men, appears to be so great an Evil to me, that for all the Riches and Glory of this World, I would not be guilty of so great a Sin as this seems to be. And I do believe many would see it so, were they not blinded by Self-Interest. Now as I said in the beginning, how apt Men were to forget God in a Time of Liberty, as we now seem to have, which if rightly considered, we ought the more to remember him, and to prise his Favour therein. For I do believe if Persecution was on Foot again, and People were haled to Prisons, as they have been in Times past, that many would have more regard to their own Practices than now they have. For this Practice of making Slaves tends to many Evils, as parting Man and Wife, and Children from them both, and thereby causing them to commit Adultery with others, and so their Children cannot come to honour them. And all this is done by Violence, which is forbidden in the Scriptures; for there we are commanded to do Violence to no Man. And lastly, it is a hinderance to the spreading of the Gospel among those poor Creatures, for whom (as well as others) our Lord came and laid down his Life, and also hath said, that his Gospel should be preached unto all Nations. But some may object, as I have heard them, that by this

Means they come to hear the Gospel preached, and they believed this was the Way our Lord intended that Nation should have the Gospel preached to them, *viz.* to be brought Slaves here. To which I'll say, the Reader may quickly suppose what People these are, for it must be them that buy the Gospel pretty dear themselves, or else they would not think that the Negroes should be Bond Slaves, and their Children after them, for the Knowledge of the Gospel. But I do not find that the Gospel was either bought or sold for Money; neither do we find that God compelled any to receive it, but only intreated them or advised them to chuse Life, and live. Now by this Practice they hate the Name of a Christian; for all of us they can get (say they) they make Slaves of, and even Nature it self tells them that it is wrong. . . .

Now I having shewn by Scripture the Unlawfulness of this Practice, as it is now in Use, both in the Old Testament and in the New. And now, I would have all to turn their Minds inward, to that Divine Monitor or Counsellor, placed in the Heart of Man, which is as agreeable to the holy Scriptures (I do believe) as any internal Thing can be to an external one; to which I'll leave my Reader, even to that ever blessed Spirit, One with the Father.

*Nantucket,* the 20th of the
11th Mo. 1729–30.

ELIHU COLEMAN

## NOTES

1. Thomas E. Drake, "Elihu Coleman, Quaker Antislavery Pioneer of Nantucket," in Howard H. Brinton (ed.), *Byways in Quaker History* (Wallingford, Pa., 1944), pp. 111–136; see also Drake, *Quakers and Slavery,* pp. 37–39.
2. Drake, "Elihu Coleman," *op. cit.,* p. 129.
3. Robert Barclay (1648–1690), Quaker apologist and author, published in England as well as in America. His best known and greatest work is *An Apology for the True Christian Divinity Held by the Quakers,* published in 1678.
4. The text has "what's" but the " 's" seems a later insertion.

## RALPH SANDIFORD

### A PHILADELPHIA QUAKER INDICTS SLAVERY

Born in Liverpool, England, in 1693, Ralph Sandiford joined the Society of Friends early in life and came to Philadelphia as a youth. Earning his living as a merchant and trader, he was outraged by the sight of slave auctions in Philadelphia. In 1729 he published his little book, *A Brief Examination of the Practices of the Times*. Printed without official Quaker Approval, the book brought him ostracism, the enmity of wealthy Philadelphia Friends, and finally exclusion from the Society. He returned to the fray with a second edition, published, with small additions, under the title, *The Mystery of Iniquity in a Brief Examination of the Practice of the Times*. Neither edition carried the name of the printer. Almost sixty years later, Benjamin Franklin, in a letter to John Wright, a London Quaker Abolitionist, revealed that he had printed both editions of the book. Sandiford, faced with intense Quaker hostility, left Philadelphia in 1731 and moved to a farm several miles from the city, where he died at the age of forty.[1] The following selections are from *A Brief Examination of the Practices of the Times*, pp. 4–5 and 6–7 of the first edition.

## The Practices of the Times

IV. Neither can these Negroes be proved, by any Genealogy, the Seed of *Ham*, whom *Noah* cursed not, saith *Josephus*,[2] as being too nigh of Blood: But *Noah's* Curse on *Canaan* the youngest Son of *Ham*, is thought a suitable original for the Negro Trade: But the Curse is not so extensive, as you would have it, but is thus expressed, *Cursed be* Canaan, *a Servant of Servants shall he be, unto his Brethren*. So that he was to Serve the meanest of the Offspring of *Shem* and *Japheth*; but the Time came that the *Canaanites* were destroyed with a Mighty Destruction, according to the Promise of the Lord, *D*. vii. 23. and *Josephus*, Lib. 4. Chap. 8. and other places. And their Land given unto the Seed of *Abraham*, as the Lord shewed him in a

Vision, when he sojourned therein amongst the *Canaanites,* that then had Possession of it, *Genesis* xii. 6, 7. also *Judges* the v. *Deborah* in her Song, rejoyces that the very Stars in their Courses fought against *Sisera,* which is more fully expressed by *Josephus,* Lib. 5. Chap. I. & 6. that the Lord fought against the *Canaanites,* with Hosts of Judgments, until they were destroyed: So that their Race is ended, as well as that Dispensation; how then can these Negroes or Indians be Slaves to Christians, who are the Lord's Freemen? But if these Negroes are Slaves of Slaves, according to the Curse; Whose Slaves then must their Masters be? . . .

VI. And what greater Unjustice can be Acted, than to Rob a Man of his Liberty, which is more Valuable than Life; and especially after such a manner as this, to take a Man from his Native Country, his Parents and Brethren, and other natural Enjoyments, and that by Stealth, or by way of Purchase from them that have no Right to sell them, whereby thou receivest the Theft, which is as bad. And take them amongst a People of a strange Language, and unnatural Climates, which is hard for them to bear whose Constitutions are tendered by the Heat of their Native Country; for God that made the World, and all Men of one Blood, that dwell upon the Face of the Earth, has appointed them Bounds of their Habitations, *Acts,* 17. 26. Shall we then undertake to remove them, wheresoever Interest shall lead us, to sell them for Slaves, Husband from Wife, and Children from both, like Beasts, with all their Increase, to the vilest of Men, and their Offspring after them, to all Eternity: Oh! hard Lot! Oh! Eternal sinking in Iniquity; without Bottom or Bounds, as to the Will of Man. . . .

## NOTES

1. For information about Sandiford and Lay, the little book by Roberts Vaux, *Memoirs of the Lives of Benjamin Lay and Ralph Sandiford; Two of the Earliest Public Advocates for the Emancipation of the Enslaved Africans* (Philadelphia, 1815), is invaluable. Drake's *Quakers and Slavery,* pp. 39–47, is helpful.
2. A Jewish general and historian, Josephus (A.D. 37 or 38–100) lived in Palestine and, after the destruction of Jerusalem in A.D. 70, in Rome. The most important of his works was *The Antiquities of the Jews,* written in A.D. 93.

# BENJAMIN LAY

## ON QUAKERS AND SLAVERY

Benjamin Lay (1677[1]–1759), born of Quaker parents in Colchester, England, had settled in Barbados at the age of 41, where his outspoken opinions and vigorous efforts against slavery soon gained him the enmity of the inhabitants. After thirteen years there he moved to Philadelphia in 1731 and visited Ralph Sandiford shortly before the latter's death. Believing his friend to have been hounded to death for his anti-slavery views, Lay determined to continue the struggle against slavery.

His appearance was singular enough to be commented on by the slaves of Barbados: four feet seven inches in height, his head proportionately too large, his legs spindly, in later years he wore a huge white beard; his wife Sarah, about the same size, was also hunchbacked. Because of the hostility excited by his anti-slavery activities, Lay moved in 1732 to a cave-like cottage which he built several miles outside of Philadelphia, where he devoted most of his time to anti-slavery teaching. Though excluded by the Quakers, he considered himself one of them and directed most of his efforts to converting them to anti-slavery.

In 1737, Benjamin Franklin printed Lay's book, *All Slave-Keepers, that Keep the Innocent in Bondage, Apostates.* In this instance, too, Franklin discreetly kept his own name off the title page. A year later, the Philadelphia Friends publicly denounced and disowned Lay both because of his attacks against them and his statement in the book that he was publishing it at their request. Before his death, Lay learned that the Yearly Meeting of 1758 had voted to disown those members who continued to hold or import slaves. He exclaimed, "Thanksgiving and praise be rendered unto the Lord God," adding, "I can now die in peace."

The following selections from his book are from pp. 64, 67–70, 74–78, 88–94.

## All Slave-Keepers, That Keep the Innocent in
## Bondage, Apostates

. . . But some that have not, and will not keep Negroe Slaves of their own, may say, we must not be too censorious, for we are often at their[2] Houses, and Eat and Drink bravely, and have their Negroes to wait on us, our Horses, Wives and Children.

Beside all these Things, we buy, sell, Trade, get Gain by and with them, we must be careful how we offend our Benefactors, and Dear Friends. But here is yet a stronger Bond than the other, Pleasure and Profit, we love to Sleep with their Off-spring, so they be but Rich; for many of us have joyned Affinity with these *Ahabs* (O that hard Word) and *Jezabels* for Gains, by marrying with their rich Children, and if we become Prophets, and can prophesy such things as they like, we shall be highly favoured, and fed at *Jezabel*'s Table, though we should be twice 4500 of us. . . .

Upon a time when I was reasoning with an eminent Preacher R. J.[3] at his House in *Philadelphia*, concerning that great *Goliah*[th], Negroe or Slave-keeping, which hath defied the little Army of the living God so many Years, and still continues so to do.

He the said R. J. was pleased then and there to tell me, that I loved the Negroes better than I did my Friends; and accused me at *Stephen Jenkin's* House, before many Witnesses, of being the Death of my Dear Wife,[4] and a Persecutor of the Church; but before that I charged him with being instrumental of separating my Dear Wife from me by Death, in Writing for a separate Certificate for my Wife, to a Meeting to which we never did belong, as if he and two or three more had a mind to separate us; which is now brought to pass.[5]

I shall leave them to the great Judge of Heaven and Earth, if he will be pleased to forgive them, I hope I shall in time. But these things must be borne with I suppose, and more; when I have said to some Friends, Negroe-Keepers and their Adherents, that it seemed a little strange or novel, that a Friend should be hurried out of Meetings so constantly and roughly, before he be disowned, or some way dealt with for some Disorder or other, contrary to the known and acknowledged discipline of Friends as a People.

If thy Brother is overtaken in a Fault, go to him and tell him his fault, between him and thee; if he hears thee thou hast gained thy Brother; if he will not hear thee, then take two or three with thee; if he will not hear them, then take him to the Church; and if he will not hear the Church, then, not till then, cast him forth. My Dear Friends, have any of these things been done to B. L.[6] and yet still continue to cast him out, cast him out, cast him out, he is a troublesome Fellow, and has been so for many Years. Did our dear and well beloved Friends in *Boston* 60 or 70 Years ago, think this a just way of Proceeding, to be taken into Custody, put into *Bridewell,*[7] Whipt severely, and Banished the Town, time after time, without any legal Proceedings, only for being obstinate Quakers, as they were pleased to call them; dare to come again when they had Whipt them out of the Town so often. When I have put some Friends in mind of this, concerning our Dear Tender Friends great Suffering in *New-England,* in a Book called *New-England Judged,* some Friends have been pleased to tell me that *George Keith* used to say so, or talk after that manner. What he said I cannot tell, but by report, which is not always true; but this of Friends Suffering in *Boston* is true, for I have been upon the Spot or Lot of Ground, where the Dear Lambs were put to Death; for the Word of God and the Testimony of Jesus Christ, the Truth.

As to G. K.[8] he was an extraordinary Man, while he kept to the Testimony of Truth in his own Heart; I do firmly believe, according to the Account of him by Friends; and a great Sufferer for Truth, by Imprisonment, and other ways, and an excellent Writer, and Minister in Defence of Truth's Principles for about 30 Years, as I remember; as many of his Books manifest, to Judgment of Men that have read them, of right mind and good understanding in Things relating to God's Kingdom; as his *Revelation not ceased,* his *Way to the City of God,* very excellent indeed, and many more; while he dwelt in the Truth and walked in Truth, he did well; but when he went from that, he was like the *unsavory Salt, good for neither Land nor Dunghill,* and so it is now with some, or I am mistaken. And so it hath been with the very best of Men and Instruments that ever were in the World, though they had been never so much inlightened or illuminated from on High; they grow dark again, as they go from the Light, from God, from Truth, which are one in Nature and Essence, although three Names, for Men as Men do know that have good Natural Eyes, that the further they go from the Light outwardly, the more they go into Darkness until at length they cannot see any thing clearly, or at last not at all; and this comes upon Men because they love Darkness, which is Sin, and they live in Darkness, and walk in Darkness, and at last Darkness in Sin seems to be Light unto them. This is a dreadful State indeed: O that it may appear so before it be too late, to some poor Souls, is my true Desire for their eternal Welfare. Which I desire, as for my own Soul.

B. L.

*The 27th of the 9th Mo.* 1736.

This is Written in pure Love, concerning the Pure in Heart, of all Colours and Countries in the whole World; these are the Dwellers in the Rock of Ages.

ABINGTON, *The 7th Month,* 1736.

My Dear and Well-beloved Friends; my Joy and the Crown of all my sweet Delights in this World, I can truly say, is the true Unity with my true Brethren, which are the true Church in God the Father, and he in them, ever reigning in his own Blessed Kingdom, Body, House, Tabernacle, *New-Jerusalem,* or a Tent, synonimous Terms; while Israel abode here, no Divination could prevail, or inchantments against 'em; but when *Israel,* our Dear Friends, went out of their Tent to look at, and long after the Pleasures, Pride, Profit and Friendship of this World, then they came to be snared with this cursed Sin, Negroe-Trading, as well as some other gross Sins, of which this is Chief, considering the Hellish Train of Filthiness, which has, does, and ever will attend it, and is inseparable from it; for it is granted by all sober wise Men that truly fear God, and dearly love the Truth in Sincerity, and are well acquainted with this foul Trade from the beginning, and in all its progressions to this Day; I say such as have had a true Account, do know that those that are employed in this Trade, are some of the worst of Men, and withal some of the worst of Thieves, Pyrates and Murtherers, from whence our lesser Pyrates have proceeded. And many of these lesser Pyrates have been punished with Death, and some other ways; but the much greater Villains by far, not only go free but are encouraged, and have been near 50 Years, if not more, by us as a People, by buying of their cursed Hellish-gotten Ware, at a very great Price. And all this Time pretending to the most holy pure Religion in the whole World, to do unto all, as we would they should do unto us, and as *James* writes, *to Visit the Fatherless, and Widow, in their Afflictions, and keep ourselves unspotted from the World;* but I know no worse Engine the Devil has to make Widows and Fatherless Children, and to bring into Affliction and Bondage, and sore Captivity indeed, than this Hellish practice in *Pennsylvania*, Negroe-Keeping.

But these Hellish Miscreants, these Men-Stealers, pretend they fetch away these poor Creatures, that they may not kill one the other, when they are the Murtherers which sets 'em to the Work, (a cursed work it is) for as I have had an Account, near 35 Years ago, when 10 or 12 Sail of Vessels come on the Coast of *Guinea,* and they cannot catch Negroes enough to Freight their Vessels by the Sea side, and in Rivers where they send their Boats in Search and Pursuit of them, where they are acquainted; for they being us'd to the Business know where to go; and to find out some old Negroes that they have been used to trade with, which will bring off in Canoes, their Wives or Children, or their Neighbours Wives, and Children if they can catch 'em in Woods, or any where else, so bring 'em and sell them to our brave Christians, which come there with Ships for that purpose.—O brave! give 30s. for a Negroe and sell him for 30£. or 40, 50 or 60, 70, 80, 90, 100£. or more: Who would but be a Trader in Slaves and Souls of Men, altho' he goes to Hell for it, and in the mean time intail an Iniquity on his own, and his Neighbour's Posterity to their Destruction and the Ruin of the whole Country beside.

Above 30 Years ago, when I was a common Sailor, I had this Account, and likewise by some Sailors on Board. Capt. *Reeves,* coming this Voyage to *Philadelphia,* who had been at *Guinea,* and I suppose had been Pyrates, they did acknowledge they had been taken by them.

These vile Fellows on Board Capt. *Reeves,* in their Drink used to tell what cursed Work their former Captain and Salors made with the poor Negroes in their Passage, for their Lusts; the Captain 6 or 10 of 'em in the Cabbin, and the Sailors as many as they pleased; with much more too foul for me to mention, or for chaste Ears to hear.

But I pray, I beg, and beseech you my Friends, in the pure Love and Fear of God; consider what part have true Believers with such Infidels, or Christ with such *Belials,* or our Holy pure God with such unholy impure Devils, until we can join these together; now we can never reconcile Slave-Keeping with our Principles; we may as well say as *Solomon* of an Harlot, *their Steps go down to Death and their Feet take hold on Hell.* . . .

*The 30th of the 10th Mo.* 1736.

I did not know but I had done Scribling about Slave-Keeping, but this Day calling to see our Friend J. R. at his House in *Philadelphia,* who was newly arrived from *Bristol,* in *Old-England;* and he speaking of the Negroe, or *Guinea* Trade, said, while he was in *Bristol* four of five Weeks, there was fitted out for that Trade nine Sail; and he told me according to Account he had there, that there goes from Bristol about 50 Sail in a Year for Negroes: And I suppose some plain Coat-Men are concerned in it there as well as at *Leverpoole, Barbadoes,* and elsewhere; now if each of these 50 Vessels carries 300, some carry many more, it comes to 15000 Souls Yearly, Stolen by *Bristol*-Men; and if there should be four times as many Stolen by Vessels from *London, Leverpoole, North-Britain, Ireland, Barbadoes, Jamaica* and some other Places, as I suppose there may, it comes to 75,000 Yearly, Stolen and kept in Iron Furnaces; so that in 50 years and more since Friends have been concerned in this practice, beside what has been increased by Generation, comes to 3825000. Is not this ten times worse than the Sins of *Sodom* and *Egypt, Turk, Jew* or *Infidel?*

So I inquired of the Friend what they did with this or such vast Numbers of Slaves; he said, they carried them to *Jamaica* generally, and sold them to the *Spaniard* for the Mines, or any Body else, I suppose, that will give most for them, although they keep them and their Posterity, in their cursed Hellish Iron-Furnace for evermore.

O Brave Christians for the Devil, and Protestants too! is this the way to convince *Papists, Turks, Jews,* and *Infidels* of their notorious Wickedness and inhumanity, when we encourage them in it all we can, by supplying of them with Slaves, for our cursed Gain.

Several eminent Friends amongst us of great Note, have boasted in my hearing of having Servants or Slaves born in their House, alluding to *Abraham,* for keeping Slaves; but I cannot find in all the Scriptures that *Abraham* ever had any Slaves; Servants he might have born in his House, and bought with Money for a time; but I do not believe that righteous, perfect good Man would keep his fellow Creatures in Bondage, them and their Off-spring, for evermore. I have a better Opinion of that tender hearted, good vertuous Man, that was stiled the Father of the faithful, by the Lip of Truth, and that rightly too, for so he was; but the unfaithful hypocritical *Pharisees,* would, for a Cloak to their Wickedness, have him to their Father; but Truth told them, if they were *Abraham*'s Children they would do the Works of *Abraham;* but now ye are of your Father the Devil, and his Works ye will do. May not Truth say the same thing now, of our Preachers and Elders, Keepers and Traders in Slaves for nothing but their ungodly Gain. But what will our wicked Slave-Keepers get by flying beyond Gospel and Law, to *Abraham,* to patronise their cursed infernal practice; but what Truth said to the *Jews,* it will say to them, *Ye are of your Father the Devil.*

Now Friends, you that are Slave-Keepers, I pray and beseech ye, examine your own Hearts, and see and feel too, if you have not the same answer from Truth now within; while you Preach and exhort others to Equity, and to do Justice and love Mercy, and to walk humbly before the Lord and his People, and you yourselves live and act quite contrary, behave proudly, do unjustly and unmercifully, and live in and encourage the grossest Iniquity in the whole World. For I say, you are got beyond Gospel, Law, *Abraham,* Prophets, Patriarchs, to *Cain* the Murtherer, and beyond him too, to the Devil himself, beyond *Cain,* for he Murthered but one, that we know of, but you have many Thousands, or caused 'em to be so, and for ought I know many

Hundreds of Thousands, within 50 Years. What do you think of these Things, you brave Gospel Ministers? that keep poor Slaves to Work for you to maintain you and yours in Pride, Pride and much Idleness or Laziness, and Fulness of Bread, the Sins of *Sodom:* How do these Things become your plain Dress, Demure Appearance, feigned Humility, all but Hypocrisy, which according to Truth's Testimony, must have the hottest Place in Hell; to keep those miserable Creatures at hard Labour continually, unto their old Age, in Bondage and sore Captivity, working out their Blood and Sweat, and Bowels, youthful strength and vigour, then you drop into your Graves, go to your Places ordained or appointed for you; so leave these poor unhappy Creatures in their worn-out old Age, to your proud, Dainty, Lazy, Scornful, Tyrannical, and often beggerly Children, for them to Domineer and Tyrannize over, cursing them and you in your Graves, for working out their youthful Blood and strength for you, and then leave 'em to be a Plague to us; and then of the abuses, miseries and Cruelties these miserable old worn out Slaves go through, no Tongue can express, starved with Hunger, perish with Cold, rot as they go, for want of every thing that is necessary for an Humane Creature; so that Dogs and Cats are much better taken care for, and yet some have had the Confidence, or rather Impudence, to say their Slaves or Negroes live as well as themselves. I could almost wish such hardened, unthinking Sinful devilish Lyars were put into their Places, at least for a time, in a very hard Service, that they might feel a little in themselves, of what they make so light of in other People; and it would be but just upon 'em, and indeed why should they be against it, if the Negroes live as well and better than they; but such notorious Lies will never go down well, with any Sober right tender-hearted People truly fearing God, and that love the Truth above all; for such I believe firmly, when they come to see, and rightly consider the vileness of this practice in all its parts, and the cursed Fruit it brings forth, they will never enter into it; and if they are in, will endeavour to get out as soon as they can; for I do believe if all the Wickedness Tyrany, oppressions and abominable Barbarities were written concerning this Hellish Trade, it would fill a large Volume in Folio.

Many has said, they do not see it so great an Evil or Sin, that is, Negroe Keeping; who so Blind as them that will not see; but them that are willing to see, I think it my duty to inform them what I can by Word and Writing, and then leave it to the Lord.

## NOTES

1. The date is given by Vaux, *Memoirs of . . . Lay and . . . Sandiford*, p. 13; Drake cites 1681 as the date of birth, *Quakers and Slavery*, p. 44.
2. The slave-owners.
3. Drake suggests "Robert Jordan?" *Quakers and Slavery*, p. 45.
4. Sarah Lay died in 1735.
5. Lay replies that the Friends who had given Sarah a certificate of membership to the Abington monthly meeting but had refused him were ultimately responsible for her death.
6. Benjamin Lay.
7. A house of correction for vagrants and other misdemeanants.
8. George Keith.

# JOHN WOOLMAN

## SOME CONSIDERATIONS ON THE KEEPING OF NEGROES

John Woolman (1720–72) has been characterized as "the greatest Quaker of the eighteenth century and perhaps the most Christlike individual that Quakerism has ever produced."[1] His biographer, Janet Whitney, has called him "the saint American."[2] Born of Quaker parents, near Mt. Holly, New Jersey, in 1720, Woolman worked variously as a baker, tailor and scribe, and in 1743 was appointed minister of the Mt. Holly Friends Meeting. By 1746, he had become convinced of the sinfulness of slavery and determined to lend his voice to its elimination. The manuscript of his book on slavery, *Some Considerations on the Keeping of Negroes: Recommended to the Professors of Christianity of Every Denomination,* was complete by 1747, but it was not until 1754 that he felt confident enough of the validity of his opinions to put it into print. It was approved by the Overseers of the Press of Philadelphia Yearly Meeting, among whom was the great anti-slavery Quaker, Anthony Benezet. It was published in a small octavo volume in 1754 and distributed by the Overseers to every Yearly Meeting in America. Drake remarks that "no other anti-slavery document had hitherto received such extensive circulation in any language anywhere."[3]

In 1762, Benjamin Franklin and David Hall published the second part of the *Considerations on the Keeping of Negroes.*

Through his writing and travels—he covered thousands of miles in the South and in the North—Woolman proved to be one of the most effective agitators against slavery. The following selections are from the first and second parts of *Some Considerations. . . .*

> *Forasmuch as ye did it to the least of these my Brethren, ye did it unto me,* Matt. xxv. 40.

As Many Times there are different Motives to the same Actions; and one does that from a generous Heart, which another does for selfish Ends:—The like may be said in this Case.

There are various Circumstances amongst them that keep *Negroes,* and different Ways by which they fall under their Care; and, I doubt not, there are many well disposed Persons amongst them who desire rather to manage wisely and justly in this difficult Matter, than to make Gain of it.

But the general Disadvantage which these poor *Africans* lie under in an enlight'ned Christian Country, having often fill'd me with real Sadness, and been like undigested Matter on my Mind, I now think it my Duty, through Divine Aid, to offer some Thoughts thereon to the Consideration of others.

When we remember that all Nations are of one Blood, *Gen.* iii. 20. that in this World we are but Sojourners, that we are subject to the like Afflictions and Infirmities of Body, the like Disorders and Frailties in Mind, the like Temptations, the same Death, and the same Judgment, and, that the Alwise Being is Judge and Lord over us all, it seems to raise an Idea of a general Brotherhood, and a Disposition easy to be touched with a Feeling of each others Afflictions: But when we forget those Things, and look chiefly at our outward Circumstances, in this and some Ages past, constantly retaining in our Minds the Distinction betwixt us and them, with respect to our Knowledge and Improvement in Things divine, natural and artificial, our Breasts being apt to be filled with fond Notions of Superiority; there is Danger of erring in our Conduct toward them.

We allow them to be of the same Species with ourselves, the Odds is, we are in a higher Station, and enjoy greater Favours than they: And when it is thus, that our heavenly Father endoweth some of his Children with distinguished Gifts, they are intended for good Ends; but if those thus gifted are thereby lifted up above their Brethren, not considering themselves as Debtors to the Weak, nor behaving themselves as faithful Stewards, none who judge impartially can suppose them free from Ingratitude.

When a People dwell under the liberal Distribution of Favours from Heaven, it behoves them carefully to inspect their Ways, and consider the Purposes for which those Favours were bestowed, lest, through Forgetfulness of God, and Misusing his Gifts, they incur his heavy Displeasure, whose Judgments are just and equal, who exalteth and humbleth to the Dust as he seeth meet. . . .

To consider Mankind otherwise than Brethren, to think Favours are peculiar to one Nation, and exclude others, plainly supposes a Darkness in the Understanding: For as God's Love is universal, so where the Mind is sufficiently influenced by it, it begets a Likeness of itself, and the Heart is enlarged towards all Men. Again, to conclude a People froward, perverse, and worse by Nature than others (who ungratefully receive Favours, and apply them to bad Ends) this will excite a Behaviour toward them unbecoming the Excellence of true Religion.

To prevent such Error, let us calmly consider their Circumstance; and, the better to do it, make their Case ours. Suppose, then, that our Ancestors and we had been exposed to constant Servitude in the more servile and inferior Employments of Life; that we had been destitute of the Help of Reading and good Company; that amongst ourselves we had had few wise and pious Instructors; that the Religious amongst our Superiors seldom took Notice of us, that while others, in Ease, have plentifully heap'd up the Fruit of our Labour, we had receiv'd barely enough to relieve Nature, and being wholly at the Command of others, had generally been treated as a contemptible, ignorant Part of Mankind: Should we, in that Case, be less abject than they now are? Again, If Oppression be so hard to bear, that a wise Man is made mad by it, *Eccl.* vii. 7. then a Series of those Things altering the Behaviour and Manners of a People, is what may reasonably be expected.

When our Property is taken contrary to our Mind, by Means appearing to us unjust, it is only through divine Influence, and the Enlargement of Heart from thence proceeding, that we can love our reputed Oppressors: If the *Negroes* fall short in this, an uneasy, if not a disconsolate Disposition, will be awak'ned, and remain like Seeds in their Minds, producing Sloth and many other Habits appearing odious to us, with which being free Men, they, perhaps, had not been chargeable. These, and other Circumstances, rightly considered, will lessen that too great Disparity, which some make between us and them.

Integrity of Heart hath appeared in some of them; so that if we continue in the Word of Christ (previous to Discipleship, *John* viii. 31.) and our Conduct towards them be seasoned with his Love, we may hope to see the good Effect of it: The which, in a good Degree, is the Case with some into whose Hands they have fallen: But that too many treat them otherwise, not seeming conscious of any Neglect, is, alas! too evident.

When *Self-love* presides in our Minds, our Opinions are bias'd in our own Favour; in this Condition, being concerned with a People so situated, that they have no Voice to plead their own Cause, there's Danger of using ourselves to an undisturbed Partiality, till, by long Custom, the Mind becomes reconciled with it, and the Judgment itself infected.

To humbly apply to God for Wisdom, that we may thereby be enabled to see Things as they are, and ought to be, is very needful; hereby the hidden Things of Darkness may be brought to light, and the Judgment made clear: We shall then consider Mankind as Brethren: Though different Degrees and a Variety of Qualifications and Abilities, one dependant on another, be admitted, yet high Thoughts will be laid aside, and all Men treated as becometh the Sons of one Father, agreeable to the Doctrine of Christ Jesus. . . .

This Doctrine being of a moral unchangeable Nature, hath been likewise inculcated in the former Dispensation; *If a Stranger sojourn with thee in your Land, ye shall not vex him; but the Stranger that dwelleth with you, shall be as One born amongst you, and thou shalt love him as thyself. Lev.* xix. 33,34. Had these People come voluntarily and dwelt amongst us, to have called them Strangers would be proper; and their being brought by Force, with Regret, and a languishing Mind, may well raise Compassion in a Heart rightly disposed: But there is Nothing in such Treatment, which upon a wise and judicious Consideration, will any Ways lessen their Right of being treated as Strangers. If the Treatment which many of them meet with, be rightly examined and compared with those Precepts, *Thou shalt not vex him nor oppress him; he shall be as one born amongst you, and thou shalt love him as thyself, Lev.* xix. 33. *Deut.* xxvii. 19. there will appear an important Difference betwixt them.

It may be objected there is Cost of Purchase, and Risque of their Lives to them who possess 'em, and therefore needful that they make the best Use of their Time: In a Practice just and reasonable, such Objections may have Weight; but if the Work be wrong from the Beginning, there's little or no Force in them. If I purchase a Man who hath never forfeited his Liberty, the natural Right of Freedom is in him; and shall I keep him and his Posterity in Servitude and Ignorance? "How should I approve of this Conduct, were I in his Circumstances, and he in mine?" It may be thought, that to treat them as we would willingly be treated, our Gain by them would be inconsiderable: And it were, in divers Respects, better that there were none in our Country.

We may further consider, that they are now amongst us, and those of our Nation the Cause of their being here; that whatsoever Difficulty accrues thereon, we are justly chargeable with, and to bear all Inconveniencies attending it, with a serious and weighty Concern of Mind to do our Duty by them, is the best we can do. To seek a Remedy by continuing the Oppression, because we have Power to do it, and see others do it, will, I apprehend, not be doing as we would be done by. . . .

A Supply to Nature's lawful Wants, joined with a peaceful, humble Mind, is the truest Happiness in this Life; and if here we arrive to this, and remain to walk in the Path of the Just, our Case will be truly happy: And though herein we may part with, or miss of some glaring Shews of Riches, and leave our Children little else but wise Instructions, a good Example, and the Knowledge of some honest Employment, these, with the Blessing of Providence, are sufficient for their Happiness, and are more likely to prove so, than laying up Treasures for them, which are often rather a Snare, than any real Benefit; especially to them, who, instead of being exampled to Temperance, are in all Things taught to prefer the getting of Riches, and to eye the temporal Distinctions they give, as the principal Business of this Life. These readily overlook the true Happiness of Man, as it results from the Enjoyment of all Things in the Fear of God, and, miserably substituting an inferior Good, dangerous in the Acquiring, and uncertain in the Fruition, they are subject to many Disappointments, and every Sweet carries its Sting. . . .

It appears, by Experience, that where Children are educated in Fulness, Ease and Idleness, evil Habits are more prevalent, than is common amongst such who are prudently employed in the necessary Affairs of Life: And if Children are not only educated in the Way of so great Temptation, but have also the Opportunity of lording it over their Fellow Creatures, and being Masters of Men in their Childhood, how can we hope otherwise than that their tender Minds will be possessed with Thoughts too high for them? Which, by Continuance, gaining Strength, will prove, like a slow Current, gradually separating them from (or keeping from Acquaintance with) that Humility and Meekness in which alone lasting Happiness can be enjoyed.

Man is born to labour, and Experience abundantly sheweth, that it is for our Good: But where the Powerful lay the Burthen on the Inferior, without affording a Christian Education, and suitable Opportunity of Improving the Mind, and a Treatment which we, in their Case, should approve, that themselves may live at Ease, and fare sumptuously, and lay up Riches for their Posterity, this seems to contradict the Design of Providence, and, I doubt, is sometimes the Effect of a perverted Mind: For while the Life of one is made grievous by the Rigour of another, it entails Misery on both. . . .

If we call to Mind our Beginning, some of us may find a Time, wherein our Fathers were under Afflictions, Reproaches, and manifold Sufferings.

Respecting our Progress in this Land, the Time is short since our Beginning was small and Number few, compared with the native Inhabitants. He that sleeps not by Day nor Night, hath watched over us, and kept us as the Apple of his Eye. His Almighty Arm hath been round about us, and saved us from Dangers.

The Wilderness and solitary Desarts in which our Fathers passed the Days of their Pilgrimage, are now turned into pleasant Fields; the Natives are gone from before us, and we established peaceably in the Possession of the Land, enjoying our civil and religious Liberties; and, while many Parts of the World have groaned under the heavy Calamities of War, our Habitation remains quiet, and our Land fruitful.

When we trace back the Steps we have trodden, and see how the Lord hath opened a Way in the Wilderness for us, to the Wise it will easily appear, that all this was not done to be buried in Oblivion; but to prepare a People for more fruitful Returns, and the Remembrance thereof, ought to humble us in Prosperity, and excite in us a Christian Benevolence towards our Inferiors. . . .

To conclude, 'Tis a Truth most certain, that a Life guided by Wisdom from above, agreeable with Justice, Equity, and Mercy, is throughout consistent and amiable, and truly beneficial to Society; the Serenity and Calmness of Mind in it, afford an unparallel'd Comfort in this Life, and the End of it is blessed.

And, no less true, that they, who in the Midst of high Favours, remain ungrateful, and under all the Advantages that a Christian can desire, are selfish, earthly, and sensual, do miss the true Fountain of Happiness, and wander in a Maze of dark Anxiety, where all their Treasures are insufficient to quiet their Minds: Hence, from an insatiable Craving, they neglect doing Good with what they have acquired, and too often add Oppression to Vanity, that they may compass more.

*O that they were wise, that they understood this, that they would consider their latter End!* Deut. xxxii. 29.

## Some Considerations . . . Second Part

. . . Some *Negroes* in these Parts, who have had an agreeable Education, have manifested a Brightness of Understanding equal to many of us. A Remark of this Kind we find in Bosman,[4] Page 328. "The *Negroes* of *Fida,* saith he, are so accurately quick in their Merchandize Accounts, that they easily reckon as justly and quickly in their Heads only, as we with the Assistance of Pen and Ink, though the Sum amounts to several Thousands."

Through the Force of long Custom, it appears needful to speak in Relation to Colour.—Suppose a white Child, born of Parents of the meanest Sort, who died and left him an Infant, falls into the Hands of a Person, who endeavours to keep him a Slave, some Men would account him an unjust Man in doing so, who yet appear easy while many Black People, of honest Lives, and good Abilities, are enslaved, in a Manner more shocking than the Case here supposed. This is owing chiefly to the Idea of Slavery being connected with the Black Colour, and Liberty with the White:—And where false Ideas are twisted into our Minds, it is with Difficulty we get fairly disentangled.

A Traveller, in cloudy Weather, misseth his Way, makes many Turns while he is lost; still forms in his Mind the Bearing and Situation of Places, and though the Ideas are wrong, they fix as fast as if they were right. Finding how Things are, we see our Mistake; yet the Force of Reason, with repeated Observations on Places and Things, do not soon remove those false Notions, so fastened upon us, but it will seem in the Imagination as if the annual Course of the Sun was altered; and though, by Recollection, we are assured it is not, yet those Ideas do not suddenly leave us.

Selfishness being indulged, clouds the Understanding; and where selfish Men, for a long Time, proceed on their Way, without Opposition, the Deceiveableness of Unrighteousness gets so rooted in their Intellects, that a candid Examination of Things relating to Self-interest is prevented; and in this Circumstance, some who would not agree to make a Slave of a Person whose Colour is like their own, appear easy in making Slaves of others of a different Colour, though their Understandings and Morals are equal to the Generality of Men of their own Colour.

The Colour of a Man avails nothing, in Matters of Right and Equity. Consider Colour in Relation to Treaties; by such, Disputes betwixt Nations are sometimes settled. And should the Father of us all so dispose Things, that Treaties with black Men should sometimes be necessary, how then would it appear amongst the Princes and Ambassadors, to insist on the Prerogative of the white Colour?

Whence is it that Men, who believe in a righteous Omnipotent Being, to whom all Nations stand equally related, and are equally accountable, remain so easy in it; but for that the Ideas of *Negroes* and Slaves are so interwoven in the Mind, that they do not discuss this Matter with that Candour and Freedom of Thought, which the Case justly calls for?

To come at a right Feeling of their Condition, requires humble serious Thinking; for, in their present Situation, they have but little to engage our natural Affection in their Favour.

Had we a Son or a Daughter involved in the same Case, in which many of them are, it would alarm us, and make us feel their Condition without seeking for it. The adversity of an intimate Friend will incite our Compassion, while others, equally good, in the like Trouble, will but little affect us.

Again, the Man in worldly Honour, whom we consider as our Superior, treating us with Kindness and Generosity, begets a Return of Gratitude and Friendship toward him. We may receive as great Benefits from Men a Degree lower than ourselves, in the common Way of reckoning, and feel ourselves less engaged in Favour of them. Such is our Condition by Nature; and these Things being narrowly watched and examined, will be found to center in Self-love.

The Blacks seem far from being our Kinsfolks, and did we find an agreeable Disposition and sound Understanding in some of them, which appeared as a good Foundation for a true Friendship between us, the Disgrace arising from an open Friendship with a Person of so vile a Stock, in the common Esteem, would naturally tend to hinder it.—They have neither Honours, Riches, outward Magnificence nor Power; their Dress coarse, and often ragged; their Employ Drudgery, and much in the Dirt: They have little or nothing at Command; but must wait upon and work for others, to obtain the Necessaries of Life; so that, in their present Situation, there is not much to engage the Friendship, or move the Affection of selfish Men: But such who live in the Spirit of true Charity, to sympathise with the Afflicted in the lowest Stations of Life, is a Thing familiar to them. . . .

Though there were Wars and Desolations among the *Negroes,* before the *Europeans* began to trade there for Slaves, yet now the Calamities are greatly increased, so many Thousands being annually brought from thence; and we, by purchasing them, with Views of Self-interest, are become Parties with them, and accessary to that Increase.

In this Case, we are not joining against an Enemy who is fomenting Discords on our Continent, and using all possible Means to make Slaves of us and our Children; but against a People who have not injured us.

If those who were spoiled and wronged, should at length make Slaves of their Oppressors, and continue Slavery to their Posterity, it would look rigorous to candid Men: But to act that Part toward a People, when neither they nor their Fathers have injured us, hath something in it extraordinary, and requires our serious Attention.

Our Children breaking a Bone; getting so bruised, that a Leg or an Arm must be taken off; lost for a few Hours, so that we despair of their being found again; a Friend hurt, so that he dieth in a Day or two; these move us with Grief: And did we attend to these Scenes in *Africa*, in like Manner as if they were transacted in our Presence; and sympathise with the *Negroes*, in all their Afflictions and Miseries, as we do with our Children or Friends; we should be more careful to do nothing in any Degree helping forward a Trade productive of so many, and so great Calamities. Great Distance makes nothing in our Favour.—To willingly join with Unrighteousness, to the Injury of Men who live some Thousand Miles off, is the same in Substance, as joining with it to the Injury of our Neighbours.

In the Eye of pure Justice, Actions are regarded according to the Spirit and Disposition they arise from: Some Evils are accounted scandalous, and the Desire of Reputation may keep selfish Men from appearing openly in them; but he who is shy on that Account, and yet by indirect Means promotes that Evil, and shares in the Profit of it, cannot be innocent.

He who, with View to Self-interest, buys a Slave, made so by Violence, and only on the Strength of such Purchase holds him a Slave, thereby joins Hands with those who committed that Violence, and in the Nature of Things becomes chargeable with the Guilt.

Suppose a Man wants a Slave, and being in *Guiney*, goes and hides by the Path where Boys pass from one little Town to another, and there catches one the Day he expects to sail; and taking him on board, brings him home, without any aggravating Circumstances. Suppose another buys a Man, taken by them who live by Plunder and the Slave-Trade: They often steal them privately, and often shed much Blood in getting them. He who buys the Slave thus taken, pays those Men for their Wickedness, and makes himself Party with them.

Whatever Nicety of Distinction there may be, betwixt going in Person on Expeditions to catch Slaves, and buying those, with a View to Self-interest, which others have taken; it is clear and plain to an upright Mind, that such Distinction is in Words, not in Substance; for the Parties are concerned in the same Work, and have a necessary Connection with, and Dependance on, each other; for were there none to purchase Slaves, they who live by stealing and selling them, would of Consequence do less at it.

Some would buy a *Negroe* brought from *Guiney,* with a View to Self-interest, and keep him a Slave, who yet would seem to scruple to take Arms, and join with Men employed in taking Slaves.

Others have civil *Negroes,* who were born in our Country, capable and likely to manage well for themselves; whom they keep as Slaves, without ever trying them with Freedom, and take the Profit of their Labour as a Part of their Estates, and yet disapprove bringing them from their own Country.

If those *Negroes* had come here, as Merchants, with their Ivory and Gold Dust, in order to trade with us, and some powerful Person had took their Effects to himself, and then put them to hard Labour, and ever after considered them as Slaves, the Action would be looked upon as unrighteous.

Those *Negroe* Merchants having Children after their being among us, whose Endowments and Conduct were like other Peoples in common, who attaining to mature Age, and requesting to have their Liberty, should be told they were born in Slavery, and were lawful Slaves, and therefore their Request denied; the Conduct of such Persons toward them, would be looked upon as unfair and oppressive.

In the present Case, relating to Home-born *Negroes,* whose Understandings and Behaviour are as good as common among other People, if we have any Claim to them as Slaves, that Claim is grounded on their being the Children or Offspring of Slaves, who, in general, were made such through Means as unrighteous, and attended with more terrible Circumstances than the Case here supposed; so that when we trace our Claim to the Bottom, these Home-born *Negroes* having paid for their Education, and given reasonable Security to those who owned them, in case of their becoming chargeable, we have no more equitable Right to their Service, than we should if they were the Children of honest Merchants who came from *Guiney* in an *English* Vessel to trade with us.

If we claim any Right to them as the Children of Slaves, we

build on the Foundation laid by them, who made Slaves of their Ancestors; so that of Necessity we must either justify the Trade, or relinquish our Right to them, as being the Children of Slaves.

Why should it seem right to honest Men to make Advantage by these People more than by others? Others enjoy Freedom, receive Wages, equal to their Work, at, or near, such Time as they have discharged these equitable Obligations they are under to those who educated them.—These have made no Contract to serve; been no more expensive in raising up than others, and many of them appear as likely to make a right Use of Freedom as other People; which Way then can an honest Man withold from them that Liberty, which is the free Gift of the Most High to his rational Creatures?

The Upright in Heart cannot succeed the Wicked in their Wickedness; nor is it consonant to the Life they live, to hold fast an Advantage unjustly gained.

The *Negroes* who live by Plunder, and the Slave-Trade, steal poor innocent Children, invade their Neighbours Territories, and spill much Blood to get these Slaves: And can it be possible for an honest Man to think that, with View to Self-interest, we may continue Slavery to the Offspring of these unhappy Sufferers, merely because they are the Children of Slaves, and not have a Share of this Guilt. . . .

*Negroes* are our Fellow Creatures, and their present Condition amongst us requires our serious Consideration. We know not the Time when those Scales, in which Mountains are weighed, may turn. The Parent of Mankind is gracious: His Care is over his smallest Creatures; and a Multitude of Men escape not his Notice: And though many of them are trodden down, and despised, yet he remembers them: He seeth their Affliction, and looketh upon the spreading increasing Exaltation of the Oppressor. He turns the Channels of Power, humbles the most haughty People, and gives Deliverance to the Oppressed, at such Periods as are consistent with his infinite Justice and Goodness. And wherever Gain is preferred to Equity, and wrong Things publickly encouraged to that Degree, that Wickedness takes Root, and spreads wide amongst the Inhabitants of a Country, there is real Cause for Sorrow to all such, whose Love to Mankind stands on a true Principle, and wisely consider the End and Event of Things.

## NOTES

1. Drake, *Quakers and Slavery*, p. 51.
2. *John Woolman, American Quaker* (Boston, 1942) , p. 433.
3. *Quakers and Slavery*, p. 56.
4. A Dutch agent at the end of the 17th century at Elmina in modern Ghana, William Bosman was the author of *A New Accurate Description of the Coast of Guinea* (London, 1705) . See Daniel P. Mannix and Malcolm Cowley, *op. cit.,* p. 289 and *passim.*

# ANTHONY BENEZET

## ON THE NATURE OF THE AFRICAN

Born in France of a Huguenot family, Anthony Benezet (1713–84), "the foremost propagandist against the slave trade and slavery in the later eighteenth century,"[1] came to Philadelphia with his parents at the age of eighteen. He had joined the Society of Friends two years earlier. For several years, he pursued the vocation of merchant and from 1742 to 1754 he taught at the Friends' English Public School in Philadelphia. The remaining years of his life were devoted to teaching and writing. Benezet formed a close lifelong friendship with Woolman, seven years his junior, and was deeply influenced by Woolman to embark on his anti-slavery career. In 1759, he wrote a pamphlet entitled "Observations on the Inslaving, Importing and Purchasing of Negroes," which was issued in a second, slightly enlarged edition, during the following year. In 1762, there appeared his little book, *A Short Account of that Part of Africa Inhabited by the Negroes,* with second and third editions in 1763. In 1766, he published *A Caution and Warning to Great Britain and Her Colonies, in a Short Representation of the Calamitous State of the Enslaved Negroes in the British Dominions,* which is "perhaps his most important work."[2] It was followed by the *Historical Account of Guinea; Its Situation, Produce and the General Disposition of Its Inhabitants,* in 1771, a book which stirred Thomas Clarkson to begin his great anti-slavery work in England as it did John Wesley in his efforts.[3]

It ought to be noted that Benezet was also deeply aware of the great injustices inflicted upon the Indians. His last work, published anonymously in 1784, the year of his death, entitled *Some Observations on the Situation, Disposition, and Character of the Indian Natives of this Continent,* called attention to their plight.

The following selections are from *A Short Account . . . ,* second edition, pp. 4–8, 18–19, 65–68, 78–80.

# A Short Account of That Part of Africa Inhabited by the Negroes

A lamentable and shocking Instance of the Influence which the Love of Gain has upon the Minds of those who yield to its Allurements, even when contrary to the Dictates of Reason, and the common Feelings of Humanity, appears in the Prosecution of the *Negroe Trade,* in which the *English* Nation has long been deeply concerned, and some in this Province have lately engaged. An Evil of so deep a Dye, and attended with such dreadful Consequences, that no well-disposed Person (anxious for the Welfare of himself, his Country, or Posterity) who knows the Tyranny, Oppression and Cruelty with which this iniquitous Trade is carried on, can be a silent and innocent Spectator. How many Thousands of our harmless Fellow Creatures have, for a long Course of Years, fallen a Sacrifice to that selfish Avarice, which gives Life to this complicated Wickedness. The Iniquity of being engaged in a Trade, by which so great a Number of innocent People are yearly destroyed, in an untimely and miserable Manner, is greatly aggravated from the Consideration that we, as a People, have been peculiarly favoured with the Light of the Gospel; that Revelation of Divine Love, which the Angels introduced to the World, by a Declaration *of Peace on Earth, and Good Will to Men—of every Nation, Kindred, Tongue and People.* How miserable must be our Condition, if, for filthy Lucre, we should continue to act so contrary to the Nature of this Divine Call, the Purpose of which is to introduce an universal and affectionate Brotherhood in the whole human Species; by removing from the Heart of every Individual, who submits to its Operation, the Darkness and Corruption of Nature, and transforming the selfish, wrathful, proud Spirit, into Meekness, Purity and Love: For this End the Son of God became Man, suffered, and died; and the whole Tenor of the Gospel declares, that for those who refuse, or neglect the Offers of this great Salvation, the Son of God has suffered in vain.

The End proposed by this Essay, is to lay before the candid Reader the Depth of Evil attending this iniquitous Practice, in the Prosecution of which, our Duty to God, the common Father

of the Family of the whole Earth, and our Duty of Love to our
Fellow Creatures, is totally disregarded; all social Connection
and tender Ties of Nature being broken, Desolation and Bloodshed continually fomented in those unhappy People's Country. It
is also intended to invalidate the false Arguments, which are
frequently advanced, for the Palliation of this Trade, in Hopes it
may be some Inducement to those who are not defiled therewith
to keep themselves clear; and to lay before such as have unwarily
engaged in it, their Danger of totally losing that tender Sensibility to the Sufferings of their Fellow Creatures, the Want
whereof sets Men beneath the Brute Creation: A Trade by which
many Thousands of innocent People are brought under the
greatest Anxiety and Suffering, by being violently rent from their
Native Country, in the most cruel Manner, and brought to our
Colonies, to be employed in hard Labour, in Climates, unsuited
to their Nature, or in a State of the most abject and barbarous
Slavery, subject to the Humours and inhuman Lash of some of
the most hard hearted and inconsiderate of Mankind, without
any Hopes of ever returning to their Native Land, or seeing an
End to their Misery: Nor must we omit, in this dismal Account,
the Weight of Blood which lies on the Promoters of this Trade,
from the great Numbers that are yearly butchered in the Incur-
sions and Battles which happen between the *Negroes,* in order to
procure the Number delivered to the *Europeans;* and the many
of these poor Creatures whose Hearts are broken, and they perish
through Misery and Grief, on the Passage. May the Almighty
preserve the Inhabitants of *Pennsylvania* from being further
defiled by a Trade, which is entered upon from such sensual
Motives, and carried on by such devilish Means.

Persons whose Minds are engrossed by the Pleasures and Profits
of this Life, are generally so taken up with present Objects, that
they are but little affected with the distant Sufferings of their
Fellow Creatures, especially when their Wealth is thereby increased. Nevertheless every one who is in any respect concerned
in this wicked Trafique, if not so hardened by the Love of
Wealth, as to be void of Feeling, must upon a serious Recollection, be impressed with Surprize and Terror, from a Sense that
there is a Righteous God, and a State of Retribution which will
last for ever. It is frequently alledged, in excuse for this Trade,

that the *Negroes* sold in our Plantations, are mostly Persons who have been taken Prisoners in those Wars which arise amongst themselves, from their mutual Animosities; and that these Prisoners would be sacrificed to the Resentment of those who have taken them Captive, if they were not purchased and brought away by the *Europeans.* It is also represented, that the *Negroes* are generally a stupid, savage People, whose Situation in their own Country is necessitous and unhappy, which has induced many to believe, that the bringing them from their Native Land is rather a Kindness than an Injury.

To confute these false Representations, the following Extracts are proposed to the candid Reader's Consideration; they are taken from the Writings of the principal Officers, not only in the *English,* but in the *French* and *Dutch* Factories, or Settlements in *Guiney,* some of whome have lived many Years in those Countries, and have been Eye-witnesses to the Transactions they relate. By which it will appear, that the *Negroes* are generally a sensible humane and sociable People, and that their Capacity is as good, and as capable of Improvement as that of the Whites. That their Country, though unfriendly to the *Europeans,* yet appears peculiarly agreeable, and well adapted to the Nature of the *Blacks,* and so fruitful as to furnish its Inhabitants plentifully with the Necessaries of Life, with much less Labour than in our more northern Climates.

And as to the common Arguments alledged in Defence of the Trade. *viz.* That the *Slaves* sold to the *Europeans* are Captives taken in War, who would be destroyed by their Conquerors if not thus purchased; it is without Foundation: For altho' there were doubtless Wars amongst the *Negroes* before the *Europeans* began to trade with them, yet certain it is, that since that Time, those Calamities have prodigiously encreased, which is principally owing to the Solititications of the white People, who have instigated the poor *Africans* by every Method, even the most iniquitous and cruel, to procure Slaves to load their Vessels, which they freely and gladly purchase without any Regard to the Precepts of the Gospel; the Feelings of Humanity, or the common Dictates of Reason and Equity. . . .

Many more Accounts could be given of the good Disposition of the Generality of the *Negroes,* and of the Plenty their Country affords; but the Foregoing are sufficient to shew them to be entirely different from the stupified and malicious People, some would have them thought to be. They have Judgment and Industry sufficient to cultivate their Country, which in most Parts abounds in the Necessaries of Life, and are so far from being uncapable of Society, that they are generally a kind and well disposed People. Neither are they to be dispised, with respect to the Manner in which Justice is administred, in several of the *Negro* Governments, which from the Accounts given by divers Authors, appears to be done with so much Equity and Dispatch, as might well be worthy the Imitation of some more civilized People. . . .

Doubts may arise in the Minds of some, whether the foregoing Accounts, relating to the natural Capacity and good Disposition of many of the Inhabitants of *Guinea,* and of the violent Manner in which they appear to be torn from their native Land, is sufficiently founded on Truth, as the *Negroes* who are brought to us are seldom heard to complain, and do not manifest that Docility and Quickness of Parts which might be expected from this Account; Persons who may make such Objections, are desired impartially to consider whether this is not owing to the many Discouragements these poor *Africans* labour under, though in an enlightened Christian Country, and the little Opportunity they have of exerting and improving their natural Talents. They are constantly employed in servile Labour, and the abject Condition in which we see them, from our Childhood, has a natural Tendency to create in us an Idea of a Superiority and induces many to look upon them as an ignorant and contemptible Part of Mankind; add to this, that they have but little Opportunity of freely conversing with such of the Whites as might impart Instruction to them, the endeavouring of which would, indeed, by most, be accounted Folly, if not Presumption. A Fondness for Wealth, or for gaining Esteem and Honour, is what prompts most Men to the Desire of excelling others, but these Motives for the Exertion and Improvement of their Faculties can have but little or no Influence upon the Minds of the *Negroes,* few of them having Hopes of attaining to any Condition beyond that of Slavery; so that tho' the natural Capacity of many of them be ever so good, yet they have no Inducement or Opportunity of exerting it to any Advantage, which naturally tends to depress their Minds, and sink their Spirits into Habits of Idleness and Sloth, which they would, in all Likelihood, have been free from, had they stood upon an equal Footing with the white People: Nevertheless it may, with Truth, be said, that amongst those who have obtained their Freedom, as well as those who remain in Servitude, some have manifested as much Sagacity and Upright-ness of Heart as could have been expected from the Whites, under the like Circumstances; and if all the free *Negroes* have not done the same, is it a Matter of Surprize? Have we not Reason to make Complaint with Respect to many of our white Servants, when from under our Care, tho' most of them have had much greater Advantages than the Blacks; who, even when free, still labour under the Difficulties before-mentioned, having but little Access to, and Intercourse with, the white People; they yet remained confined within the former Limits of Conversation with those of their own Colour, and consequently have but little more Opportunity of Knowledge and Improvement than when in Slavery.

And if they seldom complain of the unjust and cruel Usage they have received, in being forced from their native Country, &c. it is not to be wondered at; as it is a considerable Time after their Arrival amongst us before they can speak our Language, and, by the Time they are able to express themselves, they cannot but observe, from the Behaviour of the Whites, that little or no Notice would be taken of their Complaints; yet let any Person enquire of those who had attained the Age of Reason, before they were brought from their native Land, and he shall hear such Relations as, if not lost to the common Feelings of Humanity, will sensibly affect his Heart. The Case of a poor *Negroe,* not long since brought from *Guinea,* is a recent Instance of this Kind. From his first Arrival he appeared thoughtful and dejected, the Cause of which was not known till he was able to speak *English,* when the Account he gave of himself was, that he had a Wife and Children in his own Country, that some of them being sick and thirsty, he went, in the Nighttime, to fetch Water at a Spring, where he was violently seized, and carried away by some Persons who lay in Wait to catch Men, whence he was transported to *America;* the Remembrance of his Family, Friends, and other Connections left behind, which he never expected to see any more, were the principal Causes of his Dejection and Grief. Can any compassionate Heart hear this Relation without being affected with Sympathy and Sorrow? And doubtless the Case of many of these unhappy People would, upon Enquiry, appear attended with Circumstances equally tragical and aggravating. Now, you that have studied the Book of Conscience, and those that are learned in the Law, what will you say to this deplorable Case? When, and how, has this Man forfeited his Liberty? Does not Justice loudly call for its being restored to him? Has he not the same Right to demand it as any of us should have, if we had been violently snatched by Pyrates from our native Land? Where Instances of this Kind frequently occur, and are neither enquired into, nor redressed by those whose Duty it is *to seek Judgment, and relieve the Oppressed,* what can be expected, but that the Groans and Cries of these Sufferers will reach Heaven; and *what shall ye do when* God *riseth up, and when he visiteth, what shall ye answer him? Did not he that made them make us, and did not one fashion us in the Womb?*

. . .

Upon the Whole, of what has been said, it must appear to every honest unprejudiced Reader, that the Negroes are equally intituled to the common Priviledges of Mankind with the Whites, that they have the same rational Powers; the same natural Affections, and are as susceptible of Pain and Grief as they, that therefore the bringing and keeping them in Bondage, is an Instance of Oppression and Injustice of the most grievous Nature, such as is scarcely to be parallelled by any Example in the present or former Ages. Many of its woful Effects have already been expressed, but those which more particularly calls for the Notice and Redress of the Government, arises from its inconsistancy with every Thing that is just and humane, whence the worst Effects naturally flow to the Religion and Morals of the People where it prevails. Its destructive Consequences to labouring People, and Tradesmen is no less worthy the Attention of those who have Inclination and Power to serve their Country. This Rank of People, as they are the chief Strength and Support of a Community; so their Situation and Welfare calls for the particular Care of every prudent Government; but where Slave-keeping prevails, their Places and Services being supplied by the Negroes, they find themselves slighted, disregarded, and robbed of the natural Oppertunities of Labour common in other Countries, whereby they are much discouraged and their Families often reduced to Want: To which may be added the Discouragement also given by this Trade to many poor People, that can scarce get Bread in our Mother Country, who, if not prevented, on Account of the great Number of Negroes, would be likely to come over into the Colonies where they might, with Ease, procure to themselves a more comfortable Living than at Home. Another direful Effect arises from the fearful Apprehensions and Terrors which often seize the Minds of the People, for the Suppression of which the most cruel Methods are pursued, such as are indeed a Reproach to Christianity, and will by Degrees harden the Hearts of those who are active therein, so as totally to exclude them from that Tenderness and Sympathy for the Sufferings of their Fellow Creatures, which constitutes the Happiness of Society, and is the Glory of intelligent Beings. As for the possessors of the Negroes themselves, though the Sumptuousness and Ease in which they live, and the Attendance and Obsequiousness of their Slaves, may raise in their Minds an imagined Apprehension of their being Persons more happy, and of greater Importance than other People, who do live in the like Affluence and State; yet happy would it be if they were sensible how great is their Mistake, and could be persuaded seriously to consider and apply the Parable of the rich Man and poor *Lazarus,* mentioned by our SAVIOUR, whereby they might plainly perceive that they have no Cause to exult, because of their Power and Plenty, but have rather Occasion to mourn over themselves, their Children, and their Country; the natural Effect of their Situation being such as has been repeatedly observed. *"To fill Men with Haughtiness, Tyranny, Luxury and Barbarity; corrupting the Minds, and debasing the Morals of their Children, to the unspeakable Prejudice of Religion and Virtue, and the Exclusion of that holy Spirit of universal Love, Meekness and Charity, which is the unchangeable Nature and Glory of true Christianity."*

## NOTES

1. Drake, *Quakers and Slavery*, p. 62. Mary Stoughton Locke, in *Anti-Slavery in America: 1609–1808* (Boston, 1901), p. 28, says that, during the period in which he lived, no other man "did so much for the anti-slavery movement in America as Anthony Benezet." Elbert Russell, *The History of Quakerism* (New York, 1942), p. 253, suggests that "in his influence on the anti-slavery movement in the Society, he was second only to John Woolman."

2. Amelia Mott Gunimere, *Dictionary of American Biography*, Vol. II, p. 178.

3. For this and much other information about Benezet, I am deeply indebted to George S. Brookes, *Friend Anthony Benezet* (Philadelphia, 1937), pp. 76–109 and *passim*.

*Part Two*

# REVOLUTION
# AND NATIONHOOD

# CHAPTER 6

# The Revolutionary Age

The struggle of the American colonists for freedom from English domination marks a watershed in the history of racial thought. The colonists' emphasis upon their natural rights and equal rights soon spilled over into the issue of Negro slavery and the nature and rights of the Negro.[1] Some of the earliest denunciations of English oppression, e.g., James Otis's argument against the Writs of Assistance in 1761, included a defense of Negro rights and freedom. The philosophy of Locke helped form the over-all climate of opinion, as did the writings of Montesquieu, which were much read in America, including his trenchant comments on Negro slavery. Of similar importance was the application of Scottish philosophy and law, which stressed every man's original, inalienable right to liberty.[2]

Slaveholders and non-slaveholders alike were influenced by the Revolutionary fervor. Slave-owners such as Jefferson, Washington and Patrick Henry looked forward to the ultimate extinction of the institution, although their personal involvement and economic interests seem to have overcome their ideological aversion, which was never great enough to cause them to free their own slaves. John Adams, on the other hand, never owned slaves, though others in Massachusetts did—and though he believed that their use would have brought him great profit.[3] Benjamin Franklin and John Jay were even more prominent in their advocacy of the anti-slavery cause and in their common insistence upon the humanity of the Negro.

Pro-slavery views were not lacking, however. These could be found in the writings of Richard Nisbet, who published two pamphlets defending slavery and Negro inferiority, the first in 1773 and the second in 1792. They are seen also in a pamphlet published in Philadelphia in 1773 by an anonymous author, under the title, *Personal Slavery Established, by the Suffrages of Custom and Reason. Being a Full Answer to the Gloomy and Visionary Reviries, of all the fanatical and Enthusiastical Writers on that Subject,* which admitted its indebtedness to Nisbet's pamphlet and emphasized the irrationality and intellectual inferiority of the Negro. These ideas were repeated once more in the address of a Harvard student delivered at the college's public commencement on July 21, 1773.

It is worthy of note that while scientific research and publication during the Revolution were curtailed by the requirements of war, the scientific activity that immediately followed the Revolution helped to spread racial equalitarian and anti-slavery thought. American scholars and scientists who wrote during the 1780's and 1790's were mostly sympathetic to the idea of racial equality and opposed to slavery. Among these were Benjamin Rush, the prominent physician, scientist and political figure who wrote *An Address to the Inhabitants of the British Settlements in America, Upon Slave Keeping* in 1773, and addressed the American Philosophical Society in 1792 on the origins of Negro skin color; Samuel Stanhope Smith, author of *An Essay on the Causes of the Variety of Complexion and Figure in the Human Species,* 1787, the first important study of the nature and origin of races by an American; Jedidiah Morse, "the father of American geography," who expressed his anti-slavery views in *The American Geography,* first published in 1789; and Noah Webster, the great lexicographer, who published his anti-slavery volume, *Effects of Slavery, on Morals and Industry,* in 1793. Webster, although opposed to slavery, did believe in the inferiority of the Negro, as did Jefferson, and was a colonizationist as well.

Of increasing importance during the final decades of the eighteenth century were the efforts of Negroes themselves, slave and free, to promote Negro freedom and equality and to bring about a better understanding of the true nature of the Negro. As early as the 1770's, Negro slaves in various New England states began to sue for their freedom and to seek an improvement in the conditions under which they lived. One such example was the petition of Negro slaves in 1773 addressed to Thomas Hutchinson, the Governor of Massachusetts, and to the House of Representatives. Negroes also began to write about themselves more vigorously in newspapers and periodicals, even analyzing the prejudices and stereotypes which characterized the whites of their day. One of the best of these by an anonymous Negro was entitled "Letter on Slavery" and was published in the *American Museum* in 1789. Equally worthy of note, in this respect, was Benjamin Banneker's letter of August 19, 1791, to Thomas Jefferson, which accompanied the presentation of his almanac for 1792 to the latter, and Jefferson's reply.

## NOTES

1. George Moore notes that the anti-slavery movement in Massachusetts did not really begin "until the cry of resistance to British tyranny began to resound through the colonies." *Slavery in Massachusetts,* p. 109.
2. Mary Stoughton Locke, *Anti-Slavery in America*, pp. 48–49.
3. John Adams, *Works,* X (1856) , 380.

# JAMES OTIS

## COLOR AND SLAVERY

James Otis (1725–1783) was perhaps the first to extend the principles of the Revolution to Negro freedom. In 1761, in a speech denouncing the *Writs of Assistance,* he affirmed the right of all men, including Negroes, to life, liberty and property. So strong were his remarks that John Adams "shuddered at the doctrine he taught" and at the "consequences that may be drawn from such premises."[1] Perhaps Adams's reaction is less indicative of the harshness of Otis's remarks on the issue of slavery, than of the prevailing acceptance of the institution, even in Massachusetts, at that date. For Adams remarks that in his earlier years "the best men in my vicinity thought slavery not inconsistent with their character."[2] Otis's remarks on the Negro were repeated by him in 1764 in *The Rights of the British Colonies Asserted and Proved,* from which the following is a selection.

The Colonists are by the law of nature free born, as indeed all men are, white or black. No better reason can be given for enslaving those of any color than such as baron Montesquieu has humorously given, as the foundation of that cruel slavery exercised over the poor Ethiopians; which threatens one day to reduce both Europe and America to the ignorance and barbarity of the darkest ages. Does it follow that tis right to enslave a man because he is black? Will short curl'd hair like wool, instead of christian hair, as tis called by those, whose hearts are as hard as the nether millstone, help the argument? Can any logical influence in favor of slavery be drawn from a flat nose, a long or a short face? Nothing better can be said in favor of a trade, that is the most shocking violation of the law of nature, has a direct tendency to diminish the idea of the inestimable value of liberty, and makes every dealer in it a tyrant from the director of an African company to the petty chapman in needles and pins on the unhappy coast. It is a clear truth, those who every day barter away other mens liberty will soon care little for their own. To this cause must be imputed that ferocity, cruelty and brutal barbarity that has long marked the general character of the sugar islands. . . .

## NOTES

1. John Adams, *Works*, X, 315.
2. *Ibid.*, 380.

## BENJAMIN RUSH

### The Negro's Abilities and Rights

Benjamin Rush (1745–1813) was one of the leaders of the Revolution, a member of the Continental Congress and a signer of the Declaration of Independence. As a leading physician of his day, he made outstanding contributions to the advancement of medical knowledge and education. A humanitarian and a friend of the Negro, he helped to organize the Pennsylvania Society for Promoting the Abolition of Slavery in 1774, and in 1803 became its president. In 1773 he published *An Address to the Inhabitants of the British Settlements in America, upon Slave-Keeping,* from which the following is a selection, with Rush's original notes. His views are characterized by a remarkable absence of either racial prejudice or any feelings of white superiority. See also Rush's essay on the origin of skin color, reprinted in this volume, pp. 218–225.

### *An Address . . . upon Slave-Keeping*

So much hath been said upon the subject of Slave-keeping, that an apology may be required for this address. The only one I shall offer is, that the evil still continues. This may in part be owing to the great attachment we have to our own interest, and in part to the subject not yet being fully exhausted. The design of the following address is to sum up the leading arguments against it, several of which have not been urged by any of those authors who have written upon it.

Without entering into the history of the facts which relate to the slave trade, I shall proceed immediately to combat the principal arguments which are used to support it.

And here I need hardly say any thing in favour of the intellects of the Negroes, or of their capacities for virtue and happiness, although these have been supposed by some to be inferior to those of the inhabitants of Europe. The accounts which travellers give us of their ingenuity, humanity, and strong attachment to their parents, relations, friends and country, show us that they are equal to the Europeans, when we allow for the diversity of temper and genius which is occasioned by climate. We have many well attested anecdotes of as sublime and disinterested virtue among them as ever adorned a Roman or a Christian character.[1] But we are to distinguish between an African in his own country, and an African in a state of slavery in America. Slavery is so foreign to the human mind, that the moral faculties, as well as those of the understanding are debased, and rendered torpid by it. All the vices which are charged upon the Negroes in the southern colonies and the West-Indies, such as Idleness, Treachery, Theft, and the like, are the genuine offspring of slavery, and serve as an argument to prove that they were not intended by Providence for it.

Nor let it be said, in the present age, that their black colour, (as it is commonly called) either subjects them to, or qualifies them for slavery.[2] The vulgar notion of their being descended from Cain, who was supposed to have been marked with this colour, is too absurd to need a refutation.—Without enquiring into the cause of this blackness, I shall only add upon this subject, that so far from being a curse, it subjects the Negroes to no inconveniences; but, on the contrary, qualifies them for that part of the globe in which Providence has placed them. The ravages of heat, diseases and time, appear less in their faces than in a white one; and when we exclude variety of colour from our ideas of beauty, they may be said to possess every thing necessary to constitute it in common with the white people.[3]

It has been urged by the inhabitants of the Sugar Islands and South Carolina, that it would be impossible to carry on the manufactories of sugar, rice, and indigo, without Negro slaves. No manufactory can ever be of consequence enough to society, to admit the least violation of the laws of justice or humanity. But I am far from thinking the arguments used in favour of employing Negroes for the cultivation of these articles, should have any weight. . . .

Now, if the plantations in the islands and the southern colonies were more limited, and free men only employed in working them, the general product would be greater, although the profits to individuals would be less,—a circumstance this, which by diminishing opulence in a few, would suppress luxury and vice, and promote that equal distribution of property, which appears best calculated to promote the welfare of society.[4]—I know it has been said by some, that none but the natives of warm climates could undergo the excessive heat and labour of the West-India islands. But this argument is founded upon an error; for the reverse of this is true. I have been informed by good authority, that one European who escapes the first or second year, will do twice the work, and live twice the number of years that an ordinary Negro man will do: nor need we be surprized at this, when we hear, that such is the natural fertility of soil, and so numerous the spontaneous fruits of the earth in the interior parts of Africa, that the natives live in plenty at the expense of little or no labour, which, in warm climates, has ever been found to be incompatible with long life and happiness. Future ages, therefore, when they read the accounts of the slave trade (if they do not regard them as fabulous) will be at a loss which to condemn most, our folly or our guilt, in abetting this direct violation of the laws of Nature and Religion.

But there are some who have gone so far as to say, that slavery is not repugnant to the genius of Christianity, and that it is not forbidden in any part of the Scriptures.[5] Natural and Revealed Religion always speak the same things, although the latter delivers its precepts with a louder, and more distinct voice than the former. If it could be proved that no testimony was to be found in the Bible against a practice so pregnant with evils of the most destructive tendency to society, it would be sufficient to overthrow its divine original. We read, it is true, of Abraham's having slaves born in his house; and we have reason to believe, that part of the riches of the Patriarchs consisted in them; but we can no more infer the lawfulness of the practice, from the short account which the Jewish historian gives us of these facts, than we can vindicate telling a lie, because Rahab is not condemned for it in the account which is given of her deceiving the King of Jericho. . . .

## NOTES [FROM THE ORIGINAL TEXT]

1. See *Spectator,* Vol. I. No. 11.

There is now in the town of Boston a free Negro Girl, about eighteen years of age, who has been but nine years in the country, whose singular genius and accomplishments are such as not only do honour to her sex, but to human nature. Several of her poems have been printed, and read with pleasure by the public.

2. Montesquieu, in his Spirit of Laws, treats this argument, with the ridicule it deserves:

"Were I to vindicate our right to make slaves of the Negroes, these should be my arguments.

"The Europeans having extirpated the Americans, were obliged to make slaves of the Africans, for clearing such vast tracts of land.

"Sugar would be too dear, if the plants which produce it were cultivated by any other than slaves.

"These creatures are all over black, and with such a flat nose, that they can scarcely be pitied.

"It is hardly to be believed that God, who is a wise being, should place a soul, especially a good soul, in such a black ugly body.

"The Negroes prefer a glass necklace to that gold, which polite nations so highly value: can there be a greater proof of their wanting common sense?

"It is impossible for us to suppose these creatures to be men, because, allowing them to be men, a suspicion would follow, that we ourselves are not Christians."

*Book XV. Chap. V.*

3. "Quamvis ille niger, quamvis tu candidus esses.
———— Nimium ne crede colori.
Alba Ligustra cadunt; Vaccinia nigra leguntur." *Virgil.*
"I am black,—but comely." *Song of Solomon.*

4. From this account of Le Poivre's, we may learn the futility of the argument, that the number of vessels in the sugar trade, serve as a nursery for seamen, and that the Negroes consume a large quantity of the manufactures of Great-Britain. If free men only were employed in the islands, a double quantity of sugar would be made, and of course twice the number of vessels and seamen would be made use of in the trade. One free man consumes yearly four times the quantity of British goods that a Negroe does. Slaves multiply in all countries slowly. Free men multiply in proportion as slavery is discouraged. It is to be hoped therefore, that motives of policy will at last induce Britons to give up a trade, which those of justice and humanity cannot prevail upon them to relinquish.

5. This opinion has been lately supported in a Treatise upon the Ranks of Society, by John Millar, L.L.D. Professor of Law in the University of Glasgow.

# RICHARD NISBET

## A Defense of Slavery

Benjamin Rush's pamphlet received a quick reply when Richard Nisbet, probably a former West-Indian planter, published a pamphlet entitled *Slavery Not Forbidden by Scripture. Or a Defence of the West-India Planters, from the Aspersions Thrown out against Them, by the Author of a Pamphlet, Entitled, "An Address to the Inhabitants of the British Settlements in America, upon Slave-Keeping."* Printed in Philadelphia in 1773, the tract emphasized the universality of slavery, as well as the inferiority of the Negro and his happiness when enslaved to whites. In 1792, in Baltimore, Nisbet published another pamphlet entitled *The Capacity of Negroes for Religious and Moral Improvement, Considered.* The selections which follow are from the earlier work, and consist of the preface and pp. 3, 21–26, with Nisbet's original notes.

## *Slavery Not Forbidden by Scripture*

### Preface

Conscious of a want of abilities, and having very little time to spare at present, it distresses me, not a little, to write any thing that has a chance of being perused by the publick.

I never should have attempted to contradict the author of the address, merely from being a native of the West Indies, for I hate national partiality; but as I have many valuable friends in that part of the world, I could not, patiently, hear them so unworthily traduced, without endeavouring to undeceive his readers.

I very well know, that slave keeping is thought inconsistent with religion, by great part of the people in this province, so that what I have said, concerning its legality, or the political necessity of admitting it, may be read with disgust by many.

I have not vanity enough to think, that any thing I have mentioned, will incline them to change their opinions, or to look upon it with a more favourable eye. But I flatter myself, that every honest man, whatever his religious or political principles may be, will favour every attempt to crush the most malevolent slander, especially when it is exaggerated beyond the most distant bounds of probability. The inhabitants of this city will please to recollect, that the West-Indies form a considerable branch of their commerce, and that they ought therefore to listen to every thing that can be said in favour of its inhabitants. They will, likewise, remember that they lately received a genteel sum of money from that quarter, for the use of their college, for which act of generosity I heard the West Indians highly commended, by the Provost of that seminary, on a late publick occasion. Every one must suppose that he, likewise, spoke the sentiments of the other professors, and surely those gentlemen, equally remarkable for their piety and learning, would not have bestowed praises where they were not due, nor deigned to receive any donations, if they thought they were granted by monsters and barbarians.

I trust to facts, and the goodness of my cause, rather than elegant language and flowery declamation; and I must observe, that, though I am infinitely inferior to the author of the address, in the qualifications of a writer, yet I have many advantages over him.

Abuse levelled at an entire body of people, seems so contrary to reason, and every charitable maxim, that a man who undertakes it, though of the first rate genius, lays himself open to be refuted by every school boy. Such performances, unless supported by the poetick fire of a Churchill, cannot bear a second reading, and must soon sink into utter oblivion.

. . . Slavery, like all other human institutions, may be attended with its particular abuses, but that is not sufficient totally to condemn it, and to reckon every one unworthy the society of men who owns a negro.

If precedent constitutes law, surely it can be defended, for it has existed in all ages. The scriptures, instead of forbidding it, declare it lawful. The divine legislator, Moses, says—"Both thy bond-men and thy bond-maids, which thou shalt have, shall be of the heathen that are round about you: of them shall ye buy bond-men and bond-maids. Moreover, of the children of the strangers that do sojourn among you, of them shall ye buy, and of their families that are with you, which they beget in your land: and they shall be your possession. And ye shall take them as an inheritance for your children after you, to inherit them for a possession, they shall be your bond-men for ever." . . .

Though one cannot talk with any degree of certainty, with regard to the situation of the Africans, in their own country, yet, very just notions can be formed concerning their dispositions, from the numbers which are brought to the West-Indies from every quarter of that extensive continent. It is impossible to determine, with accuracy, whether their intellects or ours are superior, as individuals, no doubt, have not the same opportunities of improving as we have: However, on the whole, it seems probable, that they are a much inferior race of men to the whites, in every respect.[1] We have no other method of judging, but by considering their genius, and government in their native country. Africa, except the small part of it inhabited by those of our own colour, is totally overrun with barbarism. There is not a kingdom of any eminence; it chiefly consisting of a number of petty monarchies, perpetually at war with each other; and the sovereigns, are said to have the lives and properties of their subjects at their absolute disposal. They are, in their own country, said to be utterly unacquainted with arts, letters, manufactures, and every thing which constitutes civilized life. I never could observe the Africans have the most distant idea of a supreme Being, or that they paid him the smallest worship. They have a confused notion of an evil spirit, called a *Fumbee*, who is able to do them mischief, and it is a custom among them, to hang a broken bottle, a bit of rag, or any thing else, by way of a charm, near their small spots of ground, which they name *Oby*. When their property is thus guarded, few negroes will have the boldness to steal any part of it. This, together with a few ceremonies, used at funerals, is all the religion they may be said to possess. They seem to be utterly unacquainted with friendship, gratitude, and every tie of the same kind. Great pains are taken to give a high colouring to the affecting scenes between relations when parted at a sale;[2] but I appeal to every one who has ever been present, at the disposal of a cargo, if he has not seen these creatures, separated from their nearest relations without looking after them or wishing them farewell. A few instances may be found, of

African negroes possessing virtues and becoming ingenious; but still, what I have said, with regard to their general character, I dare say, most people acquainted with them, will agree to.[3]

What is the reason that the vast continent of Africa remains in the same state of barbarism, as if it had been created yesterday? It must, in all probability, be owing to a want of genius in the people; for it has had more chances of improving than Europe, from its vast superiority in numbers of inhabitants. The stupidity of the natives cannot be attributed to *climate,* for the Moors, who are situated at no great distance from the blacks, have always made a figure in history, and the Egyptians were one of the first nations that became eminent for their progress in the arts. I might, likewise, mention the ingenious turn of many of the Asiaticks, in the same latitudes: And if we look at the Chinese, we may observe what improvements, a single nation of whites, can make in every thing that is useful and elegant.

It is no small disgrace to our ancestors, the ancient Britons, to be compared with the modern Africans. It is even probable, that they were not so barbarous as represented by the Roman authors, who, generally, gave an exaggerated picture, of the manners of the people with whom they were at war, that they might have an excuse for their lawless ambition. The Britons were remarkable for their intrepidity and warlike disposition, and it is likely, that if the different kingdoms had been united, Julius Caesar never could have conquered them. Their *Druids* are said to have possessed some share of learning; and the songs of the *bards* are, likewise, worthy of attention; The instances of magnanimity among their chiefs, attract our admiration. When did we ever hear of a *Caractarus* or a *Boadicea* existing in Africa?

Even the Aborigines of America, have shewn their superiority over the Africans. The vast empires of Mexico and Peru, their government, the magnificence of the emperors, the grandeur of the temples and publick buildings, the uncommon situation of the city of Mexico, built upon piles in the middle of a lake: These, and a variety of other circumstances, make us entertain a high opinion of their genius.

It is somewhat strange, that there is a great difference between the negroes imported from Africa, and those born in the West-Indies. The greatest part of the former are to the last degree stupid, lazy, and forbidding in their persons: The latter have much superior intellects, and are by far more inclinable to work. They may likewise, be distinguished at first sight, from the former, by the superior robustness of their persons, their vivacity of aspect, smoothness of skin, and regularity of features. When an estate is sold, they are appraised much higher than the natives of Africa; yet it is endeavoured to make us believe, that negroes pine and degenerate in our part of the world.

I am little acquainted with the method of carrying on the slave trade, and, therefore, shall say little on the subject. It appears plain, however, that slaves are bought in the fair course of trade, and that the Europeans have seldom, or never, an opportunity of carrying them off by stealth, though they were inclinable. It is, likewise, certain, that these creatures, by being sold to the Europeans, are often saved from the most cruel deaths, or more wretched slavery to their fellow barbarians.

I am at a loss to know, by what authority the Author of the address asserts, that wars were uncommon among the negroes, till their intercourse began with the whites. The conduct of savages in every other part of the world, and of several tribes of blacks, among whom there is no slave trade, convinces us, that all uncivilized nations are frequently fighting one another.

When negroes are exposed to sale, instead of being dispirited, they often shew signs of mirth. When individuals seem attached to their relations, they are seldom or never separated; as no person would be foolish enough to buy a negroe that appeared distressed, since he must run no small risque of losing him.

When a planter takes home a parcel of new slaves, it is not to be imagined that he will endanger the loss of great part of his fortune, by forcing them to work before they are able. They are attended with the same care as if they were infants, and many of them, who turn out well afterwards, will not be able to do the smallest service for above a twelvemonth. Others, though they may have no visible disorder, in spite of every care, can never be persuaded to work, and remain, for many years, a dead burthen to the proprietors. Many of these useless negroes have been purchased by masters of vessels, and carried to North America; by change of air they sometimes recover, and help to confirm the idle reports of cruel treatment in the West-Indies.

There is always abundance of easy work about a sugar planta-tion, for the weakly negroes, such as weeding and taking care of the live stock. The employment of the most robust is moderate, and not more severe than the labour of peasants in other countries.

## NOTES [FROM THE ORIGINAL TEXT]

1. I am apt to suspect the negroes, and in general, all the other species of man (for there are four or five different kinds) to be naturally inferior to the whites. There never was a civilized nation of any other complexion than white, nor any individual, eminent either in action or speculation. No ingenious manufactures among them, no arts, no sciences. On the other hand, the most rude and barbarous of the whites, such as the Ancient Germans, the present Tartars, have still something eminent about them, in their valour, form of government, or some other particular. Such a uniform and constant difference could not happen, in so many countries and ages, if nature had not made an original distinction, betwixt these breeds of men. Not to mention our colonies, there are negro slaves dispersed all over Europe, of which, none ever discovered any symptoms of ingenuity; though low people, without education, will start up among us, and dis-tinguish themselves in every profession. In Jamaica, indeed, they talk of one negro, as a man of parts and learning; but it is likely he is admired for very slender accomplishments, like a parrot, who speaks a few words plainly. HUME, vol. 1, p. 234, 8vo. edit.

2. A gentleman of my acquaintance assures me, that he attended most of the sales this year at Charlestown, and only saw two instances of a reluctance at parting; and another of my friends, who was a clerk two years in one of the first Guinea [houses?], in Granada, assures me, that he never saw a single influence of the kind.

3. The Author of the Address gives a single example of a negro girl writing a few silly poems, to prove that the blacks are not deficient to us in under-standing.

## NEGRO SLAVES DISCUSS THEIR CONDITION

In the following petition, a group of Negro slaves evaluate the nature of their condition and ask for help. It was printed in Boston in 1773, in a small pamphlet entitled *The Appendix: or, Some Observations on the Expediency of the Petition of the Africans, Living in Boston, &c. Lately Presented to the General Assembly of this Province.*

### *Petition of the Africans, Living in Boston*

Province of the MASSACHUSETTS-BAY.

To his Excellency THOMAS HUTCHINSON, Esq; Governor;
To the Honorable His Majesty's Council, and
To the Honorable House of REPRESENTATIVES in General Court assembled at BOSTON, the 6th Day of *January*, 1773.

The humble PETITION of many SLAVES, living in the Town of BOSTON, and other Towns in the Province is this, namely,

That your Excellency and Honors, and the Honorable the Representatives would be pleased to take their unhappy State and Condition under your wise and just Consideration.

We desire to bless GOD, who loves Mankind, who sent his Son to die for their Salvation, and who is no Respecter of Persons; that he hath lately put it into the Hearts of Multitudes on both Sides of the Water, to bear our Burthens, some of whom are Men of great Note and Influence; who have pleaded our Cause with Arguments which we hope will have their weight with this Honorable Court.

We presume not to dictate to your EXCELLENCY and Honors, being willing to rest our Cause on your Humanity and Justice; yet would beg Leave to say a Word or two on the Subject.

Although some of the Negroes are vicious, (who doubtless may be punished and restrained by the same Laws which are in Force against other of the King's Subjects) there are many others of a quite different Character, and who if made free, would soon be able as well as willing to bear a Part in the Public Charges; many of them of good natural Parts, are discreet, sober, honest, and industrious; and may it not be said of many, that they are virtu-ous and religious, although their Condition is in itself so un-friendly to Religion, and every moral Virtue except *Patience.* How many of that Number have there been, and now are in this Province, who have had every Day of their Lives imbittered with this most intollerable Reflection, That, let their Behaviour be what it will, neither they, nor their Children to all Generations, shall ever be able to do, or to possess and enjoy any Thing, no, not even *Life itself,* but in a Manner as the *Beasts that perish.*

We have no Property! We have no Wives! No Children! We have no City! No Country! But we have a Father in Heaven, and we are determined, as far as his Grace shall enable us, and as far as our degraded contemptuous Life will admit, to keep all his Commandments: Especially will we be obedient to our Masters, so long as GOD in his sovereign Providence shall *suffer* us to be holden in Bondage.

It would be impudent, if not presumptuous in us, to suggest to your Excellency and Honors any Law or Laws proper to be made, in relation to our unhappy State, which, although our greatest Unhappiness, is not our *Fault;* and this gives us great Encouragement to pray and hope for such Relief as is consistent with your Wisdom, Justice, and Goodness.

We think ourselves very happy, that we may thus address the Great and General Court of this Province, which great and good Court is to us, the best Judge, under GOD, of what is wise, just, and good.

We humbly beg Leave to add but this one Thing more: We pray for such Relief only, which by no Possibility can ever be productive of the least Wrong or Injury to our Masters; but to us will be as Life from the dead.

Signed, FELIX.


## A HARVARD STUDENT DEFENDS SLAVERY
## AND THE SLAVE TRADE

This statement was presented at a debate on slavery held at the public commencement of Harvard in Cambridge, Mass., on July 21, 1773. It justifies slavery as a natural rela-

tionship between the inferior African and the superior
white, a relationship similar to that between parent and
child. The text of the debate was printed as a pamphlet in
Boston that year with the title, *A Forensic Dispute on the
Legality of Enslaving the Africans, Held at the Public
Commencement in Cambridge, New England, July 21st,
1773.*

## On the Legality of Enslaving the Africans

B. My friend, I am no enemy to humour, but I think it rarely
serves to illustrate a logical conclusion. I confess my argument, as
you have represented it, appears ridiculous enough; but if you
had deferred your reply till I had made an application of the
principle to the point in hand, perhaps it had saved you this
needless expence of wit. I have not pretended, as a consequence
from my principles, that every degree of superiority in point of
discretion would warrant to any individual of a community a
right to exercise authority over his neighbour: I have only contended, that the notion of *equality*, in the strict sense, had no
foundation *in nature;* but as happiness is the only end of action,
so superiority in wisdom, goodness, &c. is in the nature of things
a proper foundation of authority. And as nature has made differences among creatures in these respects; so it is fit and proper,
and agreable to nature's law, that different degrees of authority
in point of direction of conduct should be exercised by them;
and that in some cases, even among the human species, this
difference is so important, as to render the exercise of authority
justifiable, even without the consent of the governed: For this I
have produced an example from fact, in the case of parents and
children. All this you have implicitly allowed. I now go on to say,
as a consequence from the same acknowledged principle, that
whenever such a connection of things takes place, that any
number of men cannot, consistently with the good of the whole,
have a residence in any community but in a state of involuntary
subordination, and that their residence in such community notwithstanding such subordination, be in fact best for the whole,
such subordination, though involuntary, is no violation of the
law of nature; but on the contrary to all intents and purposes

correspondent thereto. This is a true conclusion from premises incontestible, principles universally acknowledged, and which you yourself have but now admitted. Subordination in this case comes fully within the reason of the subordination of children, rests on precisely the same foundation, and is therefore justifiable on precisely the same principles. For whether the necessity of such subordination arises from natural incapacity, or from any other quarter, it matters not, if this is in fact the case; if the interest of the whole does require it; let the causes or reasons of such requirement be what they may, such subordination is equally justifiable as in any other case whatever; not only in the case of children, but even in the case of consent; for the obligation to submission arising from consent, is founded in the general obligation to fulfil contracts; which obligation is ultimately founded in the good of society.

Now fully within this predicament lies, as I conceive, the particular case of *Africans* in this country. That it is only in a state of limited subordination (I say *limited,* for it is to be remembered, that the authority of those to whom they are subordinate, is restricted by the superior authority of law, to which we are all subordinate, and which provides that they, as well as others, shall be treated according to the general principles of humanity) that these people can *consistently* enjoy a residence among us is, I suppose, acknowledged by all. And whether it is not better for them to reside here, notwithstanding such subordination, even regard being had to *their* interest only, than in their native country, no one can doubt, at least no one, who has a tolerably adequate conception of their misery, and wretchedness there. Figure to yourself my friend, you are not unacquainted with *African* history, figure to yourself the delightful situation of a natural inhabitant of *Africa.* View him necessarily destitute of every means of improvement in social virtue, of every advantage for the cultivation of those principles of humanity, in which alone consists the dignity of the rational nature, and from which only source springs all that pleasure, that happiness of life, by which the human species is distinguished from the other parts of the animal creation. Consider his situation as a candidate for an eternal existence; view him as necessarily ignorant of every principle of that religion, through the happy influence of which alone the degenerate race of Adam can rationally form the most distant expectation of future felicity. View him moreover in a state of the most abject slavery, a slavery of the worst kind, a slavery of all others most destructive of human happiness,—an entire subjection to the tyrannizing power of lust and passion,—wholly devoted to the governing influence of those irregular propensities, which are the genuine offspring of depraved nature, when unassisted by philosophy or religion. Behold him actually clothed in all that brutal stupidity, that savage barbarity which naturally springs from such a source. Add to this, his condition of perpetual insecurity, arising from the state of hostility and war that forever rages in those inhospitable climes; and consider the treatment he is to expect, whom the fortune of war has subjected to the power of his enraged foe, whose natural cruelty is perpetually sharpened, and whose desire of revenge is continually cherished, by a sense of his own danger. Reflect, I say, a moment upon the condition of a creature in human shape, (for in such a state of degradation one can hardly call him a man) the misery, the wretchedness of whose situation is by these expressions but faintly represented; and compare it with the condition of a slave in this country; and then see if you can hesitate one moment which of the two is most eligible. If peradventure a doubt should arise, if you will please to enquire, whether you would rather choose one, for whose prosperity you was tenderly concerned, should be educated in *Africa,* with all the immunities of a native *African,* or in this country, though in that state of subordination, to which *Africans* are here subjected, I will venture to warrant you of every such doubt a speedy resolution.

Here then I rest the argument, for upon this point the present question must infallibly determine. Notwithstanding all the uneasiness attending subordination, and all the miseries to which an *African* is exposed in his removal from his native country; while his condition here is so much more eligible than his condition there, his removal is to be esteemed a favor: And the constitution of our government, whereby such removal is countenanced and encouraged, is by no means to be esteemed reprehensible. It is in vain to alledge here the want of consent on his part. It is evident from the reasoning above, that consent, in order to subjection, is necessary in those cases only where the end of authority, the greatest possible good, cannot be promoted without it: But who I beseech you, ever thought the consent of a child, an ideot, or a madman necessary to his subordination? Every whit as immaterial is the consent of these miserable *Africans,* whose real character seems to be a compound of the three last mentioned. What can avail his consent, who through ignorance of the means necessary to promote his happiness, is rendered altogether incapable of choosing for himself? And as the consent of such a being could by no means involve subordination in a case where it would be otherwise improper, so the want of it can be no bar in a case where it would not. In all such cases it is undoubtedly the duty of those, whom providence has favored with the means of improvement in understanding, and the wisdom resulting from such improvement, to make use of their discretion in directing the conduct of those who want it.

I am sensible that I have already dwelt too long upon this argument; you will however in this connexion, permit me to add, that were involuntary subjection, in all cases, contrary to the law of nature, it is impossible to suppose, that the Governor of the universe, whose wisdom is infinite, and whose will is eternally and immutably coincident with, and *when revealed to us,* the *measure* of, this law, should ever have expressly tolerated it in any particular instance. I mention this in the present connexion, the rather because I suppose the authority, the Israelites, when under a government absolutely theocratical, were permitted to exercise over strangers, was founded in the same reason with the authority, for which I contend, viz: that it was better for them to reside among a people, where they might have some opportunity for improvement in knowledge and virtue, though in a state of subordination, than to remain amongst the barbarous and idolatrous nations, whence they originated.

Were it necessary or expedient, it would be easy to shew, by comparison, in a great variety of instances not mentioned, the superiority of a slave in this country, in point of condition, to a natural inhabitant of *Africa.* And though it be too true, that these unhappy creatures are, in many particular cases, cruelly treated, yet, while their importation is to them a redemption from a condition on the whole so much more miserable, we must, as I said before, justify the government in tolerating such importation; and with regard to the particular instances of abuse, we can only say *caveant qui sunt conscii*. ["Let the perpetrators beware."]

I have omitted the right, sometimes pretended to be derived from purchase, because I look upon the argument to be trifling. For though right of authority, if it be well founded, be possibly, in some cases, transferable, yet it is well known, that all the authority any one of these miserable creatures can pretend to over another, is founded merely in the fortune of a brutal, savage war, conducted without the le[a]st regard, on either side, to any principles of equity, justice, or national honor; and for the right of authority so founded I have no disposition to contend. But I think there is much more in their argument who contend that, by the purchase of these victims, their lives are preserved, which would otherwise undoubtedly be sacrificed to the cruelty of the captors. For though I am sensible, that to this is commonly replied, that the custom of purchasing captives is a perpetual source of war; yet if we consider that a people, so inhumanly savage as to dispose of their nearest relations for baubles, can never want matter of discord; and that, was it not for the advantages in this way made of them, the captives would generally perish, we shall have no reason to doubt whether the custom of purchasing may in this way be considered as a favor.

On the whole, since it is evident beyond all controversy, that the removal of the *Africans,* from the state of brutality, wretchedness, and misery, in which they are at home so deeply involved, to this land of light, humanity, and christian knowledge, is to them so great a blessing; however faulty any individuals may have been in point of unnecessary cruelty, practised in this business; yet, whether the general state of subordination here, which is a necessary consequence of their removal, be agreable to the law of nature, can by no means longer remain a question.

# ALEXANDER HAMILTON

## ON NEGROES AS SOLDIERS

At the time this letter was written, Alexander Hamilton, twenty-two years old, with the rank of lieutenant-colonel, was secretary and aide-de-camp to George Washington. John Jay was then President of the Continental Congress. The letter most probably represented the opinions of Washington as well as Hamilton. Benjamin Quarles suggests that "Hamilton presumably had secured the General's approval to the substance of this official letter."[1]

John Laurens (1754–1782), a native of South Carolina, who had joined Washington's staff as a volunteer aide in 1777 and had been subsequently commissioned a lieutenant-colonel by the Continental Congress, was the son of Henry Laurens, a planter, slaveholder, and president of the Continental Congress from November 1, 1777 to December 9, 1778. The elder Laurens and his son were far more liberal than most South Carolinians on the subject of slavery. In August 1775, the former had written to John that "I am devising means for manumitting many of them [his slaves] and for cutting off the entail of slavery."[2] As to John, since the beginning of the war he had urged the freeing of the slaves in exchange for their military service.

Congress responded to Hamilton's letter by unanimously recommending to South Carolina and Georgia the enlistment of slave soldiers. Despite this support, however, and young Laurens's very strenuous and devoted efforts, South Carolina refused to arm its slaves. John Laurens was slain in 1782, one of the last casualties of the Revolution.

This letter has been reprinted in Henry Cabot Lodge, ed., *The Works of Alexander Hamilton* (New York and London, 1886), Vol. VII, pp. 564–7; and Harold C. Syrett and Jacob E. Cooke, eds., *The Papers of Alexander Hamilton, 1768–1780*, Vol. II (New York and London, 1961), pp. 17–19. For further details concerning the letter, see Broadus Mitchell, *Alexander Hamilton, Youth to Maturity: 1755–1788* (New York, 1957), pp. 175–177.

*To John Jay*

HEADQUARTERS, March 14, 1779
[Middlebrook, New Jersey]

DEAR SIR:

Colonel Laurens, who will have the honor of delivering you this letter, is on his way to South Carolina, on a project which I think, in the present situation of affairs there, is a very good one and deserves every kind of support and encouragement. This is to raise two, three, or four battalions of negroes; with the assistance of the government of that state, by contributions from the owners, in proportion to the number they possess. If you should think proper to enter upon the subject with him, he will give you a detail of his plan. He wishes to have it recommended by Congress to the state; and, as an inducement, that they would engage to take those battalions into Continental pay.

It appears to me, that an expedient of this kind, in the present state of Southern affairs, is the most rational that can be adopted, and promises very important advantages. Indeed, I hardly see how a sufficient force can be collected in that quarter without it; and the enemy's operations there are growing infinitely serious and formidable. I have not the least doubt that the negroes will make very excellent soldiers, with proper management; and I will venture to pronounce, that they cannot be put in better hands than those of Mr. Laurens. He has all the zeal, intelligence, enterprise, and every other qualification requisite to succeed in such an undertaking. It is a maxim with some great military judges, that with sensible officers soldiers can hardly be too stupid; and on this principle it is thought that the Russians would make the best troops in the world, if they were under other officers than their own. The King of Prussia is among the number who maintain this doctrine; and has a very emphatical saying on the occasion, which I do not exactly recollect. I mention this, because I hear it frequently objected to the scheme of embodying negroes that they are too stupid to make soldiers. This is so far from appearing to me a valid objection that I think their want of cultivation (for their natural faculties are probably as good as ours) joined to that habit of subordination which they acquire from a life of servitude, will make them sooner become soldiers than our white inhabitants. Let officers be men of sense and sentiment, and the nearer the soldiers approach to machines, perhaps the better.

I foresee that this project will have to combat much opposition from prejudice and self-interest. The contempt we have been taught to entertain for the blacks, makes us fancy many things that are founded neither in reason nor experience; and an unwillingness to part with property of so valuable a kind will furnish a thousand arguments to show the impracticability or pernicious tendency of a scheme which requires such a sacrifice. But it should be considered, that if we do not make use of them in this way, the enemy probably will; and that the best way to counteract the temptations they will hold out will be to offer them ourselves. An essential part of the plan is to give them their freedom with their muskets. This will secure their fidelity, animate their courage, and I believe will have a good influence upon those who remain, by opening a door to their emancipation. This circumstance, I confess, has no small weight in inducing me to wish the success of the project; for the dictates of humanity and true policy equally interest me in favour of this unfortunate class of men. . . .

ALEX HAMILTON

## NOTES

1. *The Negro in the American Revolution* (Chapel Hill, 1961), p. 63.
2. Quoted in *ibid.*, p. 61.

# THOMAS PAINE

## EMANCIPATION IN PENNSYLVANIA

On March 1, 1780, the Pennsylvania Assembly passed an act for the emancipation of Negro slaves in that state, "the first legislative measure for the emancipation of Negro slaves in America."[1] The measure was introduced on November 2, 1779, the day that Paine became Clerk of the Assembly, and Paine helped significantly in putting it through the Assembly. The Preamble to the measure, which follows, was written by Paine, and expresses his intense sympathy for the oppressed Negro. Paine's first published anti-slavery essay was entitled "African Slavery in America," and appeared in the March 8, 1775, *Postscript to the Pennsylvania Journal and Weekly Advertiser*.

## *Preamble to the Act Passed by the Pennsylvania Assembly, March 1, 1780*

When we contemplate our abhorrence of that condition, to which the arms and tyranny of Great Britain were exerted to reduce us, when we look back on the variety of dangers to which we have been exposed, and how miraculously our wants in many instances have been supplied, and our deliverances wrought, when even hope and human fortitude have become unequal to the conflict, we are unavoidably led to a serious and grateful sense of the manifold blessings which we have undeservedly received from the hand of that Being, from whom every good and perfect gift cometh.

Impressed with these ideas, we conceive that it is our duty, and we rejoice that it is in our power, to extend a portion of that freedom to others, which has been extended to us, and release them from the state of thralldom, to which we ourselves were tyrannically doomed, and from which we have now every prospect of being delivered. It is not for us to inquire why, in the creation of mankind, the inhabitants of the several parts of the earth were distinguished by a difference in feature or complection. It is sufficient to know that all are the work of the Almighty

Hand. We find in the distribution of the human species, that the most fertile as well as the most barren parts of the earth are inhabited by men of complexions different from ours, and from each other; from whence we may reasonably as well as religiously infer, that He, who placed them in their various situations, has extended equally His care and protection to all, and that it becomes not us to counteract His mercies.

We esteem it a peculiar blessing granted to us, that we are enabled this day to add one more step to universal civilization, by removing, as much as possible, the sorrows of those who have lived in undeserved bondage, and from which, by the assumed authority of the kings of Great Britain, no effectual legal relief could be obtained. Weaned, by a long course of experience, from those narrow prejudices and partialities we had imbibed, we find our hearts enlarged with kindness and benevolence toward men of all conditions and nations; and we conceive ourselves at this particular period particularly called upon by the blessings which we have received, to manifest the sincerity of our profession, and to give a substantial proof of our gratitude.

2. And whereas the condition of those persons, who have heretofore been denominated Negro and mulatto slaves, has been attended with circumstances, which not only deprived them of the common blessings that they were by nature entitled to, but has cast them into the deepest afflictions, by an unnatural separation and sale of husband and wife from each other and from their children, an injury, the greatness of which can only be conceived by supposing that we were in the same unhappy case. In justice, therefore, to persons so unhappily circumstanced, and who, having no prospect before them whereon they may rest their sorrows and their hopes, have no reasonable inducement to render their services to society, which they otherwise might, and also in grateful commemoration of our own happy deliverance from that state of unconditional submission to which we were doomed by the tyranny of Britain.

3. *Be it enacted,* etc.

## NOTE

1. Philip Foner, *The Complete Writings of Thomas Paine* (New York, 1945), Vol. II, p. 21, where the Preamble is also reproduced.

# THOMAS JEFFERSON

## On Negro Ability

First printed in France in 1784–85, Jefferson's *Notes on the State of Virginia* went through many editions and helped create the author's reputation as a scholar and pioneer American scientist. In this book, Jefferson expressed his opposition to slavery, but suggested the desirability of joining colonization to Negro emancipation. He based his opinion upon what he believed to be the inherent antagonism of the races and the inferiority of the Negro. In the following selection from Query XIV of the *Notes,* reprinted from H. A. Washington, ed., *The Writings of Thomas Jefferson* (Washington, D.C., 1854), pp. 380–387, Jefferson presents his view of Negro ability and racial differences. (The footnotes are in the original.)

For an interesting discussion of Jefferson's thinking on this question, see Daniel J. Boorstin, *The Lost World of Thomas Jefferson* (Boston, 1948), especially the chapter on "Varieties of Mankind: the Indian and the Negro," pp. 81–98. See also Robert McColly, *Slavery and Jeffersonian Virginia* (Urbana, 1964), especially pp. 57–76 and 114–140. Additional documents representing Jefferson's racial thought appear in this volume on pp. 171–179 and page 216.

## Notes on Virginia

[In a preceding paragraph, Jefferson explains that "the first assembly which met after the establishment of the commonwealth appointed a committee to revise the whole code . . . and report it to the assembly. This work has been . . . reported; but probably will not be taken up till a restoration of peace shall leave to the legislature leisure to go through such a work." It was reported in the form of 126 new acts, one of which was a plan for slave emancipation. (L.R.)]

. . . To emancipate all slaves born after the passing the act. The bill reported by the revisers does not itself contain this proposition; but an amendment containing it was prepared, to be offered to the legislature whenever the bill should be taken up, and farther directing, that they should continue with their parents to a certain age, then to be brought up, at the public expense, to tillage, arts, or sciences, according to their geniuses, till the females should be eighteen, and the males twenty-one years of age, when they should be colonized to such place as the circumstances of the time should render most proper, sending them out with arms, implements of household and of the handicraft arts, seeds, pairs of the useful domestic animals, &c., to declare them a free and independent people, and extend to them our alliance and protection, till they have acquired strength; and to send vessels at the same time to other parts of the world for an equal number of white inhabitants; to induce them to migrate hither, proper encouragements were to be proposed. It will probably be asked, Why not retain and incorporate the blacks into the State, and thus save the expense of supplying by importation of white settlers, the vacancies they will leave? Deep-rooted prejudices entertained by the whites; ten thousand recollections, by the blacks, of the injuries they have sustained; new provocations; the real distinctions which nature has made; and many other circumstances, will divide us into parties, and produce convulsions, which will probably never end but in the extermination of the one or the other race. To these objections, which are political, may be added others, which are physical and moral. The first difference which strikes us is that of color. Whether the black of the negro resides in the reticular membrane between the skin and scarf-skin, or in the scarf-skin itself; whether it proceeds from the color of the blood, the color of the bile, or from that of some other secretion, the difference is fixed in nature, and is as real as if its seat and cause were better known to us. And is this difference of no importance? Is it not the foundation of a greater or less share of beauty in the two races? Are not the fine mixtures of red and white, the expressions of every passion by greater or less suffusions of color in the one, preferable to that eternal monotony, which reigns in the countenances, that immovable veil of black which covers the emotions of the other race? Add to these, flowing hair, a more elegant symmetry of form, their own judgment in favor of the whites, declared by their preference of them, as uniformly as is the preference of the Oranootan for the black woman over those of his own species. The circumstance of

superior beauty, is thought worthy attention in the propagation
of our horses, dogs, and other domestic animals; why not in that
of man? Besides those of color, figure, and hair, there are other
physical distinctions proving a difference of race. They have less
hair on the face and body. They secrete less by the kidneys, and
more by the glands of the skin, which gives them a very strong
and disagreeable odor. This greater degree of transpiration,
renders them more tolerant of heat, and less so of cold than the
whites. Perhaps, too, a difference of structure in the pulminary
apparatus, which a late ingenious[1] experimentalist has discovered to be the principal regulator of animal heat, may have
disabled them from extricating, in the act of inspiration, so much
of that fluid from the outer air, or obliged them in expiration, to
part with more of it. They seem to require less sleep. A black
after hard labor through the day, will be induced by the slightest
amusements to sit up till midnight, or later, though knowing he
must be out with the first dawn of the morning. They are at least
as brave, and more adventuresome. But this may perhaps proceed
from a want of forethought, which prevents their seeing a danger
till it be present. When present, they do not go through it with
more coolness or steadiness than the whites. They are more
ardent after their female; but love seems with them to be more
an eager desire, than a tender delicate mixture of sentiment and
sensation. Their griefs are transient. Those numberless afflictions, which render it doubtful whether heaven has given life to
us in mercy or in wrath, are less felt, and sooner forgotten with
them. In general, their existence appears to participate more of
sensation than reflection. To this must be ascribed their disposition to sleep when abstracted from their diversions, and unem-
ployed in labor. An animal whose body is at rest, and who does
not reflect, must be disposed to sleep of course. Comparing them
by their faculties of memory, reason, and imagination, it appears
to me that in memory they are equal to the whites; in reason
much inferior, as I think one could scarcely be found capable of
tracing and comprehending the investigations of Euclid; and
that in imagination they are dull, tasteless, and anomalous. It
would be unfair to follow them to Africa for this investigation.
We will consider them here, on the same stage with the whites,

and where the facts are not apochryphal on which a judgment is to be formed. It will be right to make great allowances for the difference of condition, of education, of conversation, of the sphere in which they move. Many millions of them have been brought to, and born in America. Most of them, indeed, have been confined to tillage, to their own homes, and their own society; yet many have been so situated, that they might have availed themselves of the conversation of their masters; many have been brought up to the handicraft arts, and from that circumstance have always been associated with the whites. Some have been liberally educated, and all have lived in countries where the arts and sciences are cultivated to a certain degree, and all have had before their eyes samples of the best works from abroad. The Indians, with no advantages of this kind, will often carve figures on their pipes not destitute of design and merit. They will crayon out an animal, a plant, or a country, so as to prove the existence of a germ in their minds which only wants cultivation. They astonish you with strokes of the most sublime oratory; such as prove their reason and sentiment strong, their imagination glowing and elevated. But never yet could I find that a black had uttered a thought above the level of plain narration; never saw even an elementary trait of painting or sculpture. In music they are more generally gifted than the whites with accurate ears for tune and time, and they have been found capable of imagining a small catch.[2] Whether they will be equal to the composition of a more extensive run of melody, or of complicated harmony, is yet to be proved. Misery is often the parent of the most affecting touches in poetry. Among the blacks is misery enough, God knows, but no poetry. Love is the peculiar oestrum of the poet. Their love is ardent, but it kindles the senses only, not the imagination. Religion, indeed, has produced a Phyllis Wheatly; but it could not produce a poet. The compositions published under her name are below the dignity of criticism. The heroes of the Dunciad are to her, as Hercules to the author of that poem. Ignatius Sancho has approached nearer to merit in composition; yet his letters do more honor to the heart than the head. They breathe the purest effusions of friendship and general philanthropy, and show how great a degree of the latter may be compounded with strong religious zeal. He is often happy in the turn of his compliments, and his style is easy and familiar, except when he affects a Shandean fabrication of words. But his imagination is wild and extravagant, escapes incessantly from every restraint of reason and taste, and, in the course of its vagaries, leaves a tract of thought as incoherent and eccentric, as is the course of a meteor through the sky. His subjects should often have led him to a process of sober reasoning; yet we find him always substituting sentiment for demonstration. Upon the whole, though we admit him to the first place among those of his own color who have presented themselves to the public judgment, yet when we compare him with the writers of the race among whom he lived and particularly with the epistolary class in which he has taken his own stand, we are compelled to enrol him at the bottom of the column. This criticism supposes the letters published under his name to be genuine, and to have received amendment from no other hand; points which would not be of easy investigation. The improvement of the blacks in body and mind, in the first instance of their mixture with the whites, has been observed by every one, and proves that their inferiority is not the effect merely of their condition of life. We know that among the Romans, about the Augustan age especially, the condition of their slaves was much more deplorable than that of the blacks on the continent of America. The two sexes were confined in separate apartments, because to raise a child cost the master more than to buy one. Cato, for a very restricted indulgence to his slaves in this particular,[3] took from them a certain price. But in this country the slaves multiply as fast as the free inhabitants. Their situation and manners place the commerce between the two sexes almost without restraint. The same Cato, on a principle of economy, always sold his sick and superannuated slaves. He gives it as a standing precept to a master visiting his farm, to sell his old oxen, old wagons, old tools, old and diseased servants, and everything else become useless. . . . The American slaves cannot enumerate this among the injuries and insults they receive. It was the common practice to expose in the island Æsculapius, in the Tyber, diseased slaves whose cure was like to become tedious.[4] The emperor Claudius, by an edict, gave freedom to such of them as should recover, and first declared that if any person chose to kill rather than to expose them, it should not be deemed homicide. The exposing them is a crime of which no instance has existed with us; and were it to be followed by death, it would be punished capitally. We are told of a certain Vedius Pollio, who, in the presence of Augustus, would have given a slave as food to his fish, for having broken a glass. With the Romans, the regular method of taking the evidence of their slaves was under torture. Here it has been thought better never to resort to their evidence. When a master was murdered, all his slaves, in the same house, or within hearing, were condemned to death. Here punishment falls on the guilty only, and as precise proof is required against him as against a freeman. Yet notwithstanding these and other discouraging circumstances among the Romans, their slaves were often their rarest artists. They excelled too in science, insomuch as to be usually employed as tutors to their master's children. Epictetus, Terence, and Phaedrus, were slaves. But they were of the race of whites. It is not their condition then, but nature, which has produced the distinction. Whether further observation will or will not verify the conjecture, that nature has been less bountiful to them in the endowments of the head, I believe that in those of the heart she will be found to have done them justice. That disposition to theft with which they have been branded, must be ascribed to their situation, and not to any depravity of the moral sense. The man in whose favor no laws of property exist, probably feels himself less bound to respect those made in favor of others. When arguing for ourselves, we lay it down as a fundamental, that laws, to be just, must give a reciprocation of right; that, without this, they are mere arbitrary rules of conduct, founded in force, and not in conscience; and it is a problem which I give to the master to solve, whether the religious precepts against the violation of property were not framed for him as well as his slave? And whether the slave may not as justifiably take a little from one who has taken all from him, as he may slay one who would slay him? That a change in the relations in which a man is placed should change his ideas of moral right or wrong, is neither new, nor peculiar to the color of the blacks. Homer tells us it was so two thousand six hundred years ago.

'Emisu, ger t' aretes apoainutai euruopa Zeus
Haneros, eut' an min kata doulion ema elesin.

Odd. 17, 323.

Jove fix'd it certain, that whatever day
Makes man a slave, takes half his worth away.

But the slaves of which Homer speaks were whites. Notwith-standing these considerations which must weaken their respect for the laws of property, we find among them numerous instances of the most rigid integrity, and as many as among their better instructed masters, of benevolence, gratitude, and unshaken fidelity. The opinion that they are inferior in the faculties of reason and imagination, must be hazarded with great diffidence. To justify a general conclusion, requires many observations, even where the subject may be submitted to the anatomical knife, to optical glasses, to analysis by fire or by solvents. How much more then where it is a faculty, not a substance, we are examining; where it eludes the research of all the senses; where the condi-tions of its existence are various and variously combined; where the effects of those which are present or absent bid defiance to calculation; let me add too, as a circumstance of great tender-ness, where our conclusion would degrade a whole race of men from the rank in the scale of beings which their Creator may perhaps have given them. To our reproach it must be said, that though for a century and a half we have had under our eyes the races of black and of red men, they have never yet been viewed by us as subjects of natural history. I advance it, therefore, as a suspicion only, that the blacks, whether originally a distinct race, or made distinct by time and circumstances, are inferior to the whites in the endowments both of body and mind. It is not against experience to suppose that different species of the same genus, or varieties of the same species, may possess different qualifications. Will not a lover of natural history then, one who views the gradations in all the races of animals with the eye of philosophy, excuse an effort to keep those in the department of man as distinct as nature has formed them? This unfortunate difference of color, and perhaps of faculty, is a powerful obstacle to the emancipation of these people. Many of their advocates, while they wish to vindicate the liberty of human nature, are anxious also to preserve its dignity and beauty. Some of these, embarrassed by the question, "What further is to be done with them?" join themselves in opposition with those who are actuated by sordid avarice only. Among the Romans emancipation required but one effort. The slave, when made free, might mix with, without staining the blood of his master. But with us a second is necessary, unknown to history. When freed, he is to be removed beyond the reach of mixture. . . .

## Notes [from the original text]

1. Crawford.
2. The instrument proper to them is the Banjar, which they brought hither from Africa, and which is the original of the guitar, its chords being precisely the four lower chords of the guitar.
3. Tous doulous etaxen orismenou nomesmatos homilein tais therapainsin. —Plutarch. Cato. ["He assigned slaves to cohabit with females at a fixed price."]
4. Suet. Claud. 25.

# GILBERT IMLAY

## An Assault Upon Jefferson's View of the Negro

Gilbert Imlay (1754–1828[?]), born probably in Monmouth County, N.J., served as captain in the American army during the Revolution, as land surveyor in Kentucky following the war, and apparently left the United States in 1786. In 1792 he published in London *A Topographical Description of the Western Territory of North America*. A novel, *The Emigrants,* appeared in 1793. That year he entered into a love affair with Mary Wollstonecraft, who bore him a daughter; the affair ended in 1796 with Imlay's disappearance. Nothing further is known of him except that in 1828 the parochial register of St. Brelade's in the Island of Jersey recorded the death of one Gilbert Imlay.

The selection which follows consists of pp. 221–231 of the 1797 edition of Imlay's book, published in London, bearing the following title: *A Topographical Description of the Western Territory of North America: Containing a Succinct Account of Its Soil, Climate, Natural History, Population, Agriculture, Manners, and Customs. With an Ample Description of the several Divisions into which that Country is Partitioned.* The letters give the impression of having been written in the United States.

## Letter IX

KENTUCKY

My Dear Friend,

I had the pleasure of receiving, within these two days, your favour, dated the 24th of August last, and admire the virtue and humanity of those of your citizens you mention to have left off the use of West India produce, in consequence of your parliament not having adopted any mode of effecting the abolition of the slave trade.

The little pamphlet you did me the favour to send with your packet, addressed to the people of Great Britain on that subject, with observations upon the situation of the unfortunate Africans enslaved, contains the purest sentiments of benevolence, and the most rational ideas, and it is written with a precision which does the highest honour to the author's head, as well as to his heart.

We have disgraced the fair face of humanity, and trampled upon the sacred privileges of man, at the very moment that we were exclaiming against the tyranny of your ministry; but in contending for the birthright of freedom, we have learned to feel for the bondage of others; and, in the libations we offer to the fair goddess of liberty, we contemplate an emancipation of the slaves of this country, as honourable to themselves, as it will be glorious to us.

I have been ashamed, in reading Mr. Jefferson's book, to see, from one of the most enlightened and benevolent of my countrymen, the disgraceful prejudices he entertains against the unfortunate negroes. But if he has given Europeans a flagrant proof of his prejudices, he has afforded common sense an opportunity of judging from his paradoxes, that such cannot be the general sentiments of the people of America.

In the revision of a code of laws proposed for the State of Virginia, it was recommended to emancipate all slaves born after passing the act, who were to be brought up, at the public expence, to different vocations, until females should be 18, and the males 21 years of age; when they should be colonized to such place as circumstances should render most proper, giving them arms, implements, &c. &c. to declare them a free and independent people, and extend to them their alliance and protection, until they should have acquired strength and power equal to self-protection.

Concerning which measure, Mr. Jefferson says, "It will probably be asked, Why not retain and incorporate the blacks?" He then attempts to give reasons to prove why it would be impolitic; by alleging that the deep-rooted prejudices of the whites, and the recollection of past injuries by the blacks, would be productive of continual feuds, which would probably never end but in the extermination of one or the other race.

To such objections, which he calls political, he says, "may be added others, which are moral and physical." I will observe upon his political opinions first. The great charge such a business would be to that state, would necessarily tend to procrastinate its execution, and perhaps render abortive the whole design, by making it necessary to relinquish an object which the finances of the government would not admit of being carried into execution; and thus a most odious tyranny would be prolonged. Besides, what could be so impolitic, in such a country as Virginia, as banishing a numerous class of men who might be made useful citizens, risking a depopulation of one colour, in order to supply their places with another? an undertaking which, independent of the great expence it would be attended with, would also prove surrounded by many other difficulties. From what country is the vacancy to be filled? Emigrations have been frequent from Europe to America: but it would require a length of time to recruit 250,000 inhabitants, which, I suppose, is nearly the amount of the slaves of Virginia.

There are in politics, as well as in physic, cases which require irregular prescriptions. There is no law in nature which binds one man to another; and laws, which are not founded in the principles of reason and truth, invalidate themselves. There is no statute which gives power to a white man to exercise despotism over a man because he is black. It is contrary to our bill of rights, as well as repugnant to the code of nature. But the mischief lies in the prejudices of the times. A complete emancipation, perhaps, would not be borne in Virginia; for which reason it must be gradual, as it has been in Pennsylvania. It would therefore be wise in that state to attach their slaves to the land of their respective masters for a certain term of years; after which they should be at liberty to change their situations, as their circumstances or pleasure would direct, the same as any other tenants.

Such a system, under salutary regulations, would not only afford the negro a considerable proportion of freedom, but would be highly advantageous to the state; as, by parcelling out their immense waste tracts of lands into little farms, the low country, which has been impoverished by the pernicious cultivation of tobacco, would become fertilized, and restored to its pristine fecundity.

Let us suppose the present slaves of Virginia placed in such a situation for their lives, and that all blacks, born after passing an act for this purpose, should be free at 25 years of age. This would afford time not only to put these little farms in order, but it would reclaim the exhausted land, and leave the proprietors in a better situation than they otherwise would have been in, from a system which encourages indolence, promotes ignorance, tyranny, and every radical vice; but the blacks, by liberal conditions upon such a plan, with industry, might be able to educate their children, and accumulate a small property to encourage and support their liberty and independence, and the state would have time to acquire white emigrants, if the blacks did not answer the purposes of cultivation, and the end of the civil polity of an enlightened government; to suppose which would be as uncharitable as the remarks of Mr. Jefferson.

It will, doubtless, require a length of time to generalize marriages between the whites and blacks; but that would not prove a material disadvantage to the state. There would always be some whites who would marry blacks for the sake of property; and, no doubt, when prejudices are worn away, they would unite from more tender and delicate sentiments.

A judicious author of this country, who has written on the complexion and figure in the human species, has said, "A nation which migrates to a different climate will, in time, be impressed with the characters of its new state. The dark colour of the natives of the West India islands is well known to approach very near to a dark copper. The descendants of the Spaniards in South America are already become copper-coloured. The Portuguese of Mitomobo, in Sierra Leone, on the coast of Africa, have, by intermarrying with the natives, and by adopting their manners, become, in a few generations, perfectly assimilated in aspect, figure, and complexion." And Lord Kaims,[1] who cannot be suspected of partiality on this subject, says of another Portuguese settlement on the coast of Congo, "That the descendants of those polished Europeans have become, both in their persons and in their manners, more like beasts than like men. These examples tend to strengthen the inference from the changes that have happened in the Anglo-Americans; and they shew how easily climate would assimilate foreigners to natives, in the course of time, if they would adopt the same manners, and equally expose themselves to its influence."

Whether the black of negroes resides in the reticular membrane between the skin and scarf-skin, or in the scarf-skin itself—whether it proceeds from the colour of the blood, the colour of the bile, or from that of some other secretion, the difference is not fixed in nature, but is the mere effect of climate, which is proved by the daily testimony of the most enlightened philosophers of the present age; who have for their support the observations and remarks of travellers upon the effects of climate in every part of the globe.

Mr. Jefferson says, it is fixed in nature; and asks, "if the difference is of no real importance?" I answer, that it is of no real importance, when compared with the object of rescuing some millions of miserable human beings from the odious prejudices which have degraded a whole race of men to the rank of beasts of burden, because they had the misfortune not to have the tinge of *red* and *white*.

Were a man, who, with all the ardour of a youthful passion, had just been gazing upon the fair bosom of a loved and beautiful mistress, and afterwards marked the contrast of that paradise of sublunary bliss, to the African or Indian hue, to exclaim in the terms which Mr. Jefferson has used, he might be judged excusable on account of the intoxication of his heated senses: but when a grave philosopher, who has passed the meridian of life, sits down to meliorate, by his writings and opinions, the condition of the slaves of his country, whose fetters have fixed an obliquity upon the virtue and humanity of the southern Americans, I confess it appears to me not a little inconsistent.

As to the whites being more elegantly formed, as asserted by Mr. Jefferson, I must confess that it has never appeared so to me. On the contrary, I have often observed, in families which have been remarkable for feeding their blacks well, and treating them in other respects with humanity, that their negroes have been as finely formed as any whites I ever saw.—Indeed my admiration has often been arrested in examining their proportion, muscular strength, and athletic powers.

If they secrete less by the kidneys, and more by the glands of the skin, which gives them a strong and disagreeable odour, it is also certain that white men, inhabiting southern climates, do the same, more than in northern latitudes: by which means an evaporation takes place from the whole surface of the body, which produces that degree of cold which is requisite to counter-act the heat of the climate. As there is always a flow of bile proportionate to the degree of heat, the perspirable matter will be more or less saturated with that fluid, which, from an antiseptic quality, produces that odour which is supposed to indicate an original difference; but which, in reality may be discovered in a degree in all black-haired people in all countries.

No doubt, too, much of that odour is owing to their difference of living from that of the whites: for it is certain, that those negroes who are cleanly, and live in the manner of their masters, have less of it.

However, there can be no doubt but that the animal system may be so materially affected by climate, as to require a length of time to restore it to its pristine state; and whether man was aboriginal to Asia, or whether every continent has had its Adam, is of no consequence to the argument:—it is certain we are essen-tially the same in shape and intellect.

"Comparing them by their faculties of memory, reason, and imagination, it appears to me," says Mr. Jefferson, "that in memory they are equal to the whites, in reason much inferior, as I think one could scarcely be found capable of tracing and comprehending the investigation of Euclid; and that in imagina-tion they are dull, tasteless, and anomalous. It would be unfair to follow them to Africa for this investigation; we will consider them here on the same stage of the whites, and where the facts are not apocryphal on which a judgment is to be formed."

Can any position be more puerile and inconsistent? "We will consider them on the same stage of the whites, and then a com-parison is not apocryphal." Now I beg to know what can be more uncertain and false than estimating or comparing the intellect or talents of two descriptions of men; *one enslaved, degraded, and fettered in all their acts of volition, without a vista through which the rays of light and science could be shot to illumine their ignorant minds*—the other free, independent, and with the ad-vantage of appropriating the reason and science which have been the result of the study and labors of the philosophers and sensible men for centuries back. If there have been some solitary instances where negroes have had the advantage of education, they have shown that they are in no degree inferior to whites, though they have always had in this country the very great disadvantage of associating only with their ignorant countrymen, which not only prevents that polish so essential to arrest admiration, but which imperceptibly leads to servility from the prevalence of manners.

Mr. Jefferson's own arguments invalidate themselves. Homer told us, he says, nearly 3000 years since,

> "Jove fix'd it certain, that whatever day
> Makes man a slave, takes half his worth away."

Now it is most certain that the negroes in America have not only been enslaved, but that they have existed under the most inhuman and nefarious tyranny, particularly in the southern States.

Baron de Tott, speaking of the ignorance of the Turks, who are also slaves, but whites, said, "that it was with difficulty that he could make them comprehend how two triangles could be equal to one right one." But it is only necessary, to prove the nullity of Mr. Jefferson's arguments, to copy his own reflection. He asks, "if the world has produced more than two poets acknowledged to be such by all nations; how many mathematicians, how many great inventors in arts and sciences had Europe, north of the Alps, when the Romans crossed those mountains?" and then he says, "it was sixteen centuries before a Newton could be formed." And after asking these questions, he absurdly expects that black poets and mathematicians are to spring up like mushrooms.

However, a black in New-England has composed an ephemeris, which I have seen, and which men, conversant in the science of astronomy, declare exhibits marks of acute reason and genius.

To contend, however, that the world has produced but two poets, is rather the assertion of a pedant than a philosopher; and to maintain that no persons read Milton and Shakespear with delight but Englishmen, is not strictly just! For every man of taste and judgment who understands the English language to perfection, must read them, and many other English poets with the most animated pleasure. And if the Jerusalem Delivered, the Henriade, and the Lusiad, have only been generally read by the countrymen of the respective authors, it is not because they have neither genius nor excellence, but because it has been more the system of education in Europe to study the classics than the modern languages, which has given a predominant preference among the literati in every country to the Greek and Latin poet.

"Religion has produced a Phyllis Wheatly; but it could not produce a poet," is another of Mr. Jefferson's dogmata. Phyllis was brought from Africa to America, between 7 and 8 years of age; and without any assistance from a school education, and before she was 15 years old, wrote many of her poems. This information is attested by her then master, John Wheatly, dated Boston, November 14, 1772. I will transcribe part of her poem on Imagination, and leave you to judge whether it is poetical or not. It will afford you an opportunity, if you have never met with it, of estimating her genius and Mr. Jefferson's judgment; and I think, without any disparagement to him, that, by comparison, Phyllis appears much the superior. Indeed, I should be glad to be informed what white upon this continent has written more beautiful lines.

> "Imagination! who can sing thy force?
> Or who describe the swiftness of thy course?
> Soaring through air to find the bright abode,
> Th' imperial palace of the thund'ring god,
> We on thy pinions can surpass the wind,
> And leave the rolling universe behind:
> From star to star the mental optics rove,
> Measure the skies, and range the realms above;
> There in one view we grasp the mighty whole,
> Or with new worlds amaze th' unbounded soul.
> Though winter frowns, to fancy's raptur'd eyes
> The fields may flourish, and gay scenes arise;
> The frozen deeps may burst their iron bands,
> And bid their waters murmur o'er the sands;
> Fair Flora may resume her fragrant reign,
> And with her flow'ry riches deck the plain;
> Sylvanus may diffuse his honours round,
> And all the forest may with leaves be crown'd;
> Show'rs may descend, and dews their gems disclose,
> And nectar sparkle on the blooming rose."

Mr. Jefferson has been equally severe upon Ignatius Sancho. But, as I have not the honour to be acquainted with Mr.

Sancho's writings, I shall conclude that that criticism is equally
marked with prejudice. His saying, "that Terence was a slave,
but not black," is in contradiction to the testimony of every other
authority; who all agree, that he was not only an African but a
Numidian, who are all known to be black.

But, to complete his paradoxes, Mr. Jefferson has remarked,
"that the Indian with no advantage of education, is eloquent
and ingenious," without recollecting that the savage is free while
the poor African is enslaved; though he allows that servitude
destroys half the worth of the human soul.

But to do justice to his candour and heart, I will give you his
conclusion upon this subject; "The whole commerce between
master and slave is a perpetual exercise of the most boisterous
passions, the most unremitting despotism on one part, and degrading submissions on the other. Our children see this, and
learn to imitate it. The parent storms, the child looks on, catches
the lineaments of wrath, puts on the same airs, gives a loose to his
worst of passions; and thus nursed, educated, and daily exercised
in tyranny, cannot be stamped with odious peculiarities."

After making several moral reflections upon the subject of
slavery, he finishes with these emphatical words: "Indeed, I
tremble for my country, when I reflect that God is just: that his
justice cannot sleep for ever: that, considering numbers, nature,
and natural means only, a revolution of the wheel of fortune, an
exchange of situation, is among possible events: that it may
become probable by supernatural interference! The ALMIGHTY
has no attribute which can take side with us in such a contest."

You see, my dear friend, how powerful is the effect of habit
and prejudice; that with ideas and principles founded in reason
and truth, sufficient to demonstrate that slavery destroys the
energy of the human mind, and with a heart which does honour
to Mr. Jefferson as a man, his mind is so warped by education
and the habit of thinking, that he has attempted to make it
appear that the African is a being between the human species
and the oran-outang; and ridiculously suffered his imagination
to be carried away with the idle tales of that animal's embracing
the negro women, in preference to the females of its own species.

GREAT GOD! how long is the world to be tantalized with such
paltry sophistry and nonsense! My pity and indignation has been

alternately excited since I have been writing this letter. But, I hope those dazzling rays of philanthrophy which gleam in the flattering account you have given me of the disposition of your countrymen, will give a stab to the principles of domestic tyranny, and fix an odium upon those leachers of human blood, as flagrant as they are contemptible. Farewell. In the libations of this night, and appropriate hours of love and social pleasure, the object of using my feeble powers in attempting to alleviate the oppressions of the miserable in every part of the world, shall not be forgotten.

I remain, most affectionately,
Yours, &c.

## NOTE

1. Lord Henry Home Kames (1696–1782), Scottish philosopher, jurist, and author of several books on law, farming education, and history, was elevated to the bench in 1752. His *Sketches of the History of Man,* from which the following quotation was probably taken, was published in Edinburgh and London in 1774.

# SAMUEL STANHOPE SMITH

## THE ORIGIN OF RACIAL DIFFERENCES

Samuel Stanhope Smith (1750–1819), Presbyterian clergy-man, teacher at the College of New Jersey (later Princeton), then its president, was an influential clergyman-scholar of his day. The three printed volumes of his sermons were widely read and his two-volume *Lectures . . . on the Subjects of Moral and Political Philosophy,* according to one writer, "have had a lasting influence."[1] In 1787, in Philadelphia, there appeared his volume, *An Essay on the Causes of the Variety of Complexion and Figure in the Human Species,* the substance of which had been delivered as an oration before the American Philosophical Society in Philadelphia, on February 28, 1787.[2] Daniel Boorstin has called it "probably the most ambitious American inquiry of the period into physical anthropology."[3] William Stanton notes that it was "the first ambitious American treatise on ethnology."[4] The essence of Smith's thesis was a denial of the theory of the separate creation of the various races of man. In explaining racial differences, he relied, primarily, upon climate and, secon-darily, upon the influence of society, the manner of living, diet and disease. In his views on race, Smith built upon the work of Linnaeus (1707–78), whose *Systemae Naturae* had been published in 1735; George Leclerc Buffon, whose 44-volume *Natural History* appeared between 1749 and 1804; Dr. John Hunter, an Englishman, whose *Dissertation,* pub-lished in 1775, stressed climate as the most important cause of race differences; and John Friedrich Blumenbach (1752–1840), of the University of Gottingen, a pioneer in the science of anthropology, who divided mankind into five races and ascribed racial differences to a combination of climate and other factors.

Dr. Smith published a second, expanded edition of his work in 1810 in which he developed his anti-slavery views and took strong issue with Jefferson's derogatory view of Negro intelligence. In 1965, the Harvard University Press published the 1810 edition, edited, with an excellent introduction, by Winthrop D. Jordan. The selection which follows consists of pp. 1–18 of the 1787 edition, and pp. 9–14 of the 1810 edition. Notes are from the original text.

## On the Causes of the Variety of Complexion and Figure in the Human Species

In the history and philosophy of human nature, one of the first objects that strikes an observer is the variety of complexion and of figure among mankind. To assign the causes of this phenomenon has been frequently a subject of curious speculation. Many philosophers have resolved the difficulties with which this enquiry is attended by having recourse to the arbitrary hypothesis that men are originally sprung from different flocks, and are therefore divided by nature into different species. But as we are not at liberty to make this supposition, so I hold it to be unphilosophical to recur to hypothesis, when the whole effect may, on proper investigation, be accounted for by the ordinary laws of nature.[5]

On this discussion I am now about to enter; and shall probably unfold, in its progress, some principles the full importance of which will not be obvious, at first view, to those who have not been accustomed to observe the operations of nature with minute and careful attention—principles, however, which, experience leads me to believe, will acquire additional evidence from time and observation.

Of the causes of these varieties among mankind I shall treat under the heads—

I. Of Climate
II. Of the State of Society

In treating this subject, I shall not espouse any peculiar system of medical principles which, in the continual revolutions of opinion, might be in hazard of being afterwards discarded. I shall, as much as possible, avoid using terms of art; or attempting to explain the *manner of operation* of the causes, where diversity of opinion among physicians, has left the subject in doubt.

And, in the beginning, permit me to make one general remark which must often have occurred to every judicious enquirer into the powers both of moral and physical causes—that every permanent and characteristic variety in human nature, is effected by slow and almost imperceptible gradations. Great and sudden changes are too violent for the delicate constitution of man, and always tend to destroy the system. But changes, that become incorporated, and that form a character of a climate or a nation, are progressively carried on through several generations, till the causes that produce them, have attained their utmost operation. In this way, the minutest causes, acting constantly, and long continued, will necessarily create great and conspicuous differences among mankind.

I. Of the first class of causes, I shall treat under the head of climate.

In tracing the globe from the pole to the equator, we observe a gradation in the complexion nearly in proportion to the latitude of the country. Immediately below the arctic circle a high and sanguine colour prevails. From this, you descend to the mixture of red in white: afterwards succeed the brown, the olive, the tawny, and, at length, the black, as you proceed to the line. The same distance from the sun, however, does not, in every region, indicate the same temperature of climate. Some secondary causes must be taken into consideration as correcting and limiting its influence. The elevation of the land, its vicinity to the sea, the nature of the soil, the state of cultivation, the course of winds, and many other circumstances, enter into this view. Elevated and mountainous countries are cool, in proportion to their altitude above the level of the sea—vicinity to the ocean produces opposite effects, in northern and southern latitudes; for the ocean, being of a more equal temperature than the land, in one case corrects the cold, in the other, moderates the heat. Ranges of mountains, such as the Appennines in Italy, and Taurus, Caucasus and Imaus in Asia, by interrupting the course of cold winds, render the protected countries below them warmer, and the countries above them colder, than is equivalent to the proportional difference of latitude. The frigid zone in Asia is much wider than it is in Europe; and that continent hardly knows a temperate zone. From the northern ocean to Caucasus, says Montesquieu, Asia may be considered as a flat mountain. Thence, to the ocean that washes Persia and India, it is a low and level country without seas, and protected by this immense range of hills from the polar winds. The Asiatic is, therefore, warmer than the European continent, below the fortieth degree of latitude; and, above that latitude, it is much more cold. Climate also receives some difference from the nature of the soil; and some from the degree of cultivation. Sand is susceptible of greater heat than clay; and an uncultivated region, shaded with forests, and covered with undrained marshes, is more frigid in northern, and more temperate in southern latitudes, than a country laid open to the direct and constant action of the sun. History informs us, that, when Germany and Scythis were buried in forests, the Romans often transported their armies across the frozen Danube; but, since the civilization of those barbarous regions, the Danube rarely freezes. Many other circumstances might be enumerated which modify the influence of climate. These will be sufficient to give a general idea of the subject: and by the intelligent reader they may be easily extended, and applied to the state of particular countries.

From the preceding observations we derive this conclusion, that there is a general ratio of heat and cold, which forms what we call climate, and a general resemblance of nations, according to the latitude from the equator; subject however, to innumerable varieties from the infinite combinations of the circumstances I have suggested. After having exhibited the general effect, I shall take up the capital deviations from it, that are found in the world, and endeavour to shew that they naturally result from certain concurrences of these modifying causes.

Our experience verifies the power of climate on the complexion. The heat of summer darkens the skin, the cold of winter chafes it, and excites a sanguine colour. These alternate effects, in the temperate zone, tend in some degree to correct each other. But when heat or cold predominates in any region, it impresses, in the same proportion, a permanent and characteristical complexion. The degree, in which it predominates, may be considered as a constant cause, to the action of which the human body is exposed. This cause will affect the nerves, by tension or relaxation, by dilatation or contraction—It will affect the fluids by increasing or lessening the perspiration, and by altering the proportions of all the secretions—It will peculiarly affect the skin by the immediate operation of the atmosphere, of the sun's rays, or of the principle of cold upon its delicate texture. Every sensible difference in the degree of the cause, will create a visible change in the human body. To suggest at present a single example.—A cold and piercing air chafes the countenance and exalts the complexion. An air that is warm and misty relaxes the constitution, and gives some tendency, in valetudinarians especially, to a bilious hue. These effects are transient, and interchangeable in countries where heat and cold alternately succeed in nearly equal proportions. But when the climate constantly repeats the one or the other of these effects in any degree, then, in proportion, an habitual colour begins to be formed. Colour and figure may be styled habits of the body. Like other habits, they are created, not by great and sudden impressions, but by continual and almost imperceptible touches. Of habits, both of mind and body, nations are susceptible, as well as individuals. They are transmitted to their offspring, and augmented by inheritance. Long in growing to maturity, national features, like national manners, become fixed, only after a succession of ages. They become, however, fixed at last. And if we can ascertain any effect produced by a given state of weather or of climate, it requires only repetition during a sufficient length of time, to augment and impress it with a permanent character. The sanguine countenance, will, for this reason, be perpetual in the highest latitudes of the temperate zone; and we shall forever find the swarthy, the olive, the tawny and the black, as we descend to the south.

The uniformity of the effect in the same climate, and on men in a similar state of society, proves the power and certainty of the cause. If the advocates of different human species suppose that the beneficent Deity created the inhabitants of the earth of different colours because these colours are best adapted to their respective zones, it surely places his benevolence in a more advantageous light, to say, he has given to human nature the power of accommodating itself to every zone. This pliancy of nature is favourable to the unions of the most distant nations, and facilitates the acquisition and the extension of science, which would otherwise be confined to few objects, and to a very limited range. It opens the way particularly to the knowledge of the globe which we inhabit—a subject so important and interesting to man.—It is verified by experience. Mankind are forever changing their habitations by conquest or by commerce. And we find them in all climates, not only able to endure the change, but so *assimilated* by time, that we cannot say with certainty whose ancestor was the native of the clime, and whose the intruding foreigner.

I will here propose a few principles on the change of colour, that are not liable to dispute, and that may tend to shed some light on this subject.

In the beginning, it may be proper to observe that the skin, though extremely delicate and easily susceptible of impression from external causes, is, from its structure, among the least mutable parts of the body.[6] Change of complexion does for this reason continue long, from whatever cause it may have arisen. And if the causes of colour have deeply penetrated the texture of the skin, it becomes perpetual. Figures, therefore, that are stained with paints inserted by punctures made in its surface, can never be effaced.[7] An ardent sun is able entirely to penetrate its texture. Even in our climate, the skin, when first exposed to the direct and continued action of the solar rays, is inflamed into blisters, and scorched through its whole substance. Such an operation not only changes its colour, but increases its thickness. The stimulus of heat exciting a greater flux of humours to the skin, tends to incrassate its substance, till it becomes dense enough to resist the action of the exciting cause.[8] On the same principle, friction excites blisters in the hand of the labourer, and thickens the skin till it becomes able to endure the continued operation of his instruments. The face or the hand, exposed uncovered during an entire summer, contracts a colour of the darkest brown. In a torrid climate, where the inhabitants are naked, the colour will be as much deeper, as the ardor of the sun is both more constant and more intense. And if we compare the dark hue that, among us, is sometimes formed by continual exposure, with the colour of the African, the difference is not greater than is proportioned to the augmented heat and constancy of the climate.[9]

The principle of colour is not, however, to be derived solely from the action of the sun upon the skin. Heat, especially, when united with putrid exhalations that copiously impregnate the atmosphere in warm and uncultivated regions, relaxes the nervous system. The bile in consequence is augmented, and shed through the whole mass of the body. This liquor tinges the complexion of a yellow colour, which assumes by time a darker hue. In many other instances, we see that relaxation, whether it be caused by the vapours of stagnant waters, or by sedentary occupations, or by loss of blood, or by indolence, subjects men to disorders of the bile, and discolours the skin. It has been proved, by physicians, that, in fervid climates, the bile is always augmented in proportion to the heat. Bile exposed to the sun and air, is known to change its colour to black—black is therefore the tropical hue. Men, who remove from northern to southern regions, are usually attacked by dangerous disorders, that leave the blood impoverished, and shed a yellow appearance over the skin. These disorders are perhaps the efforts of nature, in breaking down and changing the constitution, in order to accommodate it to the climate; or to give it that degree of relaxation, and to mingle with it that proportion of bile, which is necessary for its new situation.[10] On this dark ground the hue of the climate becomes, at length, deeply and permanently impressed.

On the subject of the physical causes of colour I shall reduce my principles to a few short propositions derived chiefly from experience and observation, and placed in such connexion as to illustrate and support one another. They may be enlarged and multiplied by men of leisure and talents who are disposed to pursue the inquiry farther.

1. It is a fact that the sun darkens the skin although there be no uncommon redundancy of the bile.

2. It is also a fact that a redundancy of bile darkens the skin, although there be no uncommon exposure to the sun.[11]

3. It is a fact equally certain that where both causes co-operate, the effect is much greater, and the colour much deeper.[12]

4. It is discovered by anatomists, that the skin consists of three lamellae, or folds,—the external, which in all nations, is an extremely fine and transparent integument,—the interior, which is also white,—and an intermediate, which is a cellular membrane filled with a mucous substance.

5. This substance, what ever it be, is altered in its appearance and colour with every change of the constitution—as appears in blushing, in fevers, or in consequence of exercise. A lax nerve, that does not propel the blood with vigour, leaves it pale and

sallow—it is instantly affected with the smallest surcharge of bile, and stained of a yellow colour.

6. The change of climate produces a proportionable alteration in the internal state and structure of the body, and in the quantity of the secretions.[13] In southern climates particularly, the bile, as has been remarked, is always augmented.

7. Bile, exposed to the sun and air, in a stagnant, or nearly in a stagnant state, tends in its colour towards black.

8. The secretions as they approach the extremities, become more languid in their motion, till at length they come almost to a fixed state in the skin.

9. The aqueous parts escaping easily by perspiration through the pores of the skin, those that are more dense and incrassated remain in a mucous or glutinous state, in that cellular membrane between the interior skin and the scars, and receive there, during a long time, the impressions of external and discolouring causes.

10. The bile is peculiarly liable to become mucous and incrassated;[14] and in this state, being unfit for perspiration, and attaching itself strongly to that spongy tissue of nerves, it is there detained for a length of time till it receives the repeated action of the sun and atmosphere.

11. From all the preceding principles taken together, it appears, that the complexion, in any climate, will be changed towards black, in proportion to the degree of heat in the atmosphere, and to the quantity of bile in the skin.

12. The vapours of stagnant waters, with which uncultivated regions abound; all great fatigues and hardships; poverty and nastiness, tend as well as heat, to augment the bile. Hence, no less than from their nakedness, savages will always be discoloured, even in cold climates. For though cold, when assisted by succulent nourishment, and by the comfortable lodging and clothing furnished in civilized society, propels the blood with force to the extremities, and clears the complexion; yet when hardships and bad living relax the system, and when poor and shivering savages, under the arctic cold, do not possess those conveniencies that, by opening the pores, and cherishing the body, assist the motion of the blood to the surface, the florid and sanguine principle is repelled, and the complexion is left to be formed by the dark coloured bile; which, in that state, becomes

the more dark, because the obstruction of the pores preserves it longer in a fixed state in the skin. Hence, perhaps, the deep Lapponian complexion which has been esteemed a phenomenon so difficult to be explained.

13. Cold, where it is not extreme,[15] is followed by a contrary effect. It corrects the bile, it braces the constitution, it propels the blood to the surface of the body with vigour, and renders the complexion clear and florid.[16]

Such are the observations which I propose concerning the proximate cause of colour in the human species. But I remark, with pleasure, that whether this theory be well founded or not, the fact may be perfectly ascertained, that climate has all that power to change the complexion which I suppose, and which is necessary to the present subject.—It appears from the whole state of the world—it appears from obvious and undeniable events within the memory of history, and from events even within our own view. . . .

### On the Variety of Complexion, Figure &c. in the Human Species

The unity of the human race, notwithstanding the diversity of colour, and form under which it appears in different portions of the globe, is a doctrine, independently of the authority of divine revelation, much more consistent with the principles of sound philosophy, than any of those numerous hypotheses which have referred its varieties to a radical and original diversity of species, adapted by the Creator, or by the necessary laws of the material world, to the respective climates which they were destined to inhabit. As there are several species of animals which seem to be confined by the physical laws of their constitution to a limited range of climate, and which either cannot exist, or do not attain the perfection of their nature, in regions either much farther to the North or to the South than those in which the Creator has planted them, superficial observers have been ready to conclude, from analogy, that different species of the human kind must have been originally circumscribed, by the forming hand of nature, within certain climatical limits, in which she has placed them, whence have sprung those varieties in external aspect, and in mental endowments, which distinguish the respective tribes of men from one another. But in contradiction to this principle, experience demonstrates that man is not exclusively confined in his range to any definite lines upon the earth. Although the fineness of texture, and delicacy of organization of the human constitution, renders it extremely susceptible of the impressions of climate, as well as of all other causes which act upon the animal frame, its peculiar flexibility, at the same time, enables it to adapt itself with wonderful facility, and without materially injuring the organs of life, to every degree of temperature from the extreme heats of the torrid, to the perpetual rigors of the frozen zone. We see commerce and war, ambition and avarice, transfer the same people to every clime upon the globe; and the American and European sailor reside equally at the pole, and under the equator. While the spirit of fanaticism carries the sun-burnt Saracen to the North, the love of war, and of plunder transplants the Tartar from the snows of Scythia to the burning plains of India.—Why then should we, without necessity, assume the hypothesis that originally there existed different species of the human kind? And not only without necessity, but contrary to the principles of true philosophy, since all its varieties may be accounted for, which I hope to demonstrate in the course of this essay, by the known operation of natural causes.

Different species must be subject to different laws both in the physical and moral constitution of their nature. The whole philosophy of man, therefore, is confounded by that hypothesis which divides the *kind* into various *species*, radically different from one another. The laws of morals designed to regulate the mutual intercourse of mankind, we derive from examining our own nature, or collecting the common sentiments of men in society, united together by a common system of feelings and ideas. But how shall we apply rules, derived from these sources, to different nations, and to different individuals whose moral principles, resulting, in like manner, from the constitution of their natures, respectively, may be as various as their several aspects. Can they, indeed, be universally applied to fix an in-variable moral code even for the same nation in different ages, after conquest, or commerce may have produced among them the most complicated mixture of species? *Varieties* may be created in the same species either in the animal or vegetable kingdom, by varying their culture, and, sometimes, by transferring them to a different soil, or climate; but to all these varieties, where there is no radical diversity of *kind,* the same general laws still apply. To man, in like manner, may be applied the same general principles of moral and physical action, if it be ascertained that all their differences indicate only one original species. But, destroy this unity, and no certain and universal principles of human nature remain. We have no general and infallible standard by which to judge of the moral ideas and habits of different nations, or even of different men.—Besides, if human nature actually embraces different species of men, by what criterion shall we distinguish them? What is their number? Where do they now exist pure and unmixed?—

Philosophers have never been able to give to these questions such precise and definite solutions as are sufficient to satisfy an inquisitive and discriminating mind. That criterion of identity of species first suggested by the English naturalist, Ray, and afterwards more largely insisted on by Buffon, has been, since his age, most generally received; that is, the power of procreating an offspring, that shall be itself endued with similar prolific powers. The horse and the ass can produce a mule; but the mule being barren, shews that the sire and dam are of different species. It is acknowledged, however, that experiments on the procreative virtue of animals, never have been, and probably never will be made, in sufficient number, or with sufficient accuracy, to establish the criterion of Ray and Buffon as a certain and universal fact. If it were entitled to the rank of an incontrovertible principle in natural science, there could no longer be any doubt concerning the unity of the human species under all the various forms and appearances in which it has existed in the different regions of the globe.

Dr. Blumenbach observes that "animals ought to be ranked in the same species when their general form and properties resemble one another, and the differences which subsist among them may be derived from some degenerating cause." According to this principle, if it be admitted, those only are to be esteemed of different species whose distinctive properties are so essential to each respectively, and so inherent in them, that they cannot be

changed, or their differences accounted for, by the known operation of any physical, or moral causes. If this, then, be received as
the acknowledged criterion of diversity of species, I doubt not
being able to demonstrate, in the progress of this essay, that all
the varieties of men may have sprung from the same original
stock. To whichever criterion, therefore, we appeal, the same
conclusion will result.

## NOTES

1. John E. Pomphret, *Dictionary of American Biography*, Vol. XVII, p. 345.
2. The work was reprinted in London in 1789. An edition with minor
   corrections by Smith and an introduction and notes by Benjamin Smith
   Barton was published in Edinburgh in 1788.
3. *The Lost World of Thomas Jefferson* (New York, 1948) , p. 66.
4. *The Leopard's Spots* (Chicago, 1960) , p. 4.
5. It is no small objection to this hypothesis, that these species can never be
   ascertained. We have no means of distinguishing, how many were
   originally formed, or where any of them are now to be found. And they
   must have been long since so mixed by the migrations of mankind, that
   the properties of each species can never be determined. Besides, this
   supposition unavoidably confounds the whole philosophy of human
   nature.—*See conclusion of this essay.* [This and following notes are from
   the original text.]
6. Anatomists inform us, that, like the bones, it has few or no vessels, and
   therefore is not liable to those changes of augmentation or diminution,
   and continual alteration of parts, to which the flesh, the blood, and the
   whole vascular system is subject.
7. It is well known what a length of time is required to efface the freckles
   contracted in a fair skin by the exposure of a single day. Freckles are seen
   of all shades of colour. They are known to be created by the sun; and
   become indelible by time. The sun has power equally to change every
   part of the skin, when equally exposed to its action. And it is, not
   improperly, observed by some writers, that colour may be justly considered
   as an universal freckle.
8. Anatomists know that all people of colour have their skin thicker than
   people of a fair complexion, in proportion to the darkness of the hue.
9. If the force of fire be sufficient at a given distance, to scorch the fuel,
   approach it as much nearer, as is proportional to the difference of heat
   between our climate and that of Africa, and it will burn it black.
10. Physicians differ in their opinions concerning the state of the bile in
    warm countries. Some suppose that it is thrown out to be a corrector of
    putridity. Others suppose, that in all relaxed habits, the bile is itself in a
    putrid state . . . will receive the action of the sun and atmosphere, and
    be, in proportion, changed towards black.

11. Redundancy of bile long continued, as in the case of the black jaundice, or of extreme melancholy, creates a colour almost perfectly black.

12. This we see verified in those persons, who have been long subject to bilious disorders, if they have been much exposed to the sun. Their complexion becomes in that case extremely dark.

13. This appears from the disorders, with which men are usually attacked, on changing their climate; and from the difference of figure and aspect, which takes place in consequence of such removals. This latter reflexion will hereafter be further illustrated.

14. In this state it is always copiously found, in the stomach and intestines, at least in consequence of a bilious habit of body.

15. Extreme cold is followed by an effect similar to that of extreme heat. It relaxes the constitution by overstraining it, and augments the bile. This, together with the fatigues, hardships and other evils of savage life, renders the complexion darker beneath the arctic circle, than it is in the middle regions of the temperate zone, even in a savage state of society.

16. Cold air is known to contain a considerable quantity of nitre; and this ingredient is known to be favourable to a clear and ruddy complexion.

# JOHN JAY

## THE UNITED STATES AND SLAVERY

John Jay was second to none of the "Founding Fathers" of this country in his dislike of slavery and the slave trade. At a time when hired servants were not easily available, he would buy Negro slaves and after a reasonable term of service would manumit them.[1] As Governor of New York, he signed the act for the abolition of slavery in that state and as president of the New York Society for Promoting the Manumission of Slaves he corresponded with the leaders of anti-slavery societies in other countries. The following letter reveals his ability to see the inconsistency between American professions of liberty and the existence of slavery, and indicates his efforts to increase the opportunities available to free Negroes. It is reprinted from Vol. III, pp. 340–344, of *The Correspondence and Public Papers of John Jay*, ed. Henry P. Johnson (New York, 1891).

## *Jay to the English Anti-Slavery Society*[2]

GENTLEMEN:

Our society has been favoured with your letter of the 1st of May last, and are happy that efforts so honourable to the nation are making in your country to promote the cause of justice and humanity relative to the Africans. That they who know the value of liberty, and are blessed with the enjoyment of it, ought not to subject others to slavery, is, like most other moral precepts, more generally admitted in theory than observed in practice. This will continue to be too much the case while men are impelled to action by their passions rather than their reason, and while they are more solicitous to acquire wealth than to do as they would be done by. Hence it is that India and Africa experience unmerited oppression from nations which have been long distinguished by their attachment to their civil and religious liberties, but who have expended not much less blood and treasure in violating the rights of others than in defending their own. The United States are far from being irreproachable in this respect. It undoubtedly is very inconsistent with their declarations on the subject of human rights to permit a single slave to be found within their jurisdiction, and we confess the justice of your strictures on that head.

Permit us, however, to observe, that although consequences ought not to deter us from doing what is right, yet that it is not easy to persuade men in general to act on that magnanimous and disinterested principle. It is well known that errors, either in opinion or practice, long entertained or indulged, are difficult to eradicate, and particularly so when they have become, as it were, incorporated in the civil institutions and domestic economy of a whole people.

Prior to the great revolution, the great majority or rather the great body of our people had been so long accustomed to the practice and convenience of having slaves, that very few among them even doubted the propriety and rectitude of it. Some liberal and conscientious men had, indeed, by their conduct and writings, drawn the lawfulness of slavery into question, and they made converts to that opinion; but the number of those converts compared with the people at large was then very inconsiderable. Their doctrines prevailed by almost insensible degrees, and was like the little lump of leaven which was put into three measures of meal: even at this day, the whole mass is far from being leavened, though we have good reason to hope and to believe that if the natural operations of truth are constantly watched and assisted, but not forced and precipitated, that end we all aim at will finally be attained in this country.

The Convention which formed and recommended the new Constitution had an arduous task to perform, especially as local interests, and in some measure local prejudices, were to be accommodated. Several of the States conceived that restraints on slavery might be too rapid to consist with their particular circumstances; and the importance of union rendered it necessary that their wishes on that head should, in some degree, be gratified.

It gives us pleasure to inform you, that a disposition favourable to our views and wishes prevails more and more, and that it has already had an influence on our laws. When it is considered how many of the legislators in the different States are proprietors of slaves, and what opinions and prejudices they have imbibed on the subject from their infancy, a sudden and total stop to this species of oppression is not to be expected.

We will cheerfully co-operate with you in endeavouring to procure advocates for the same cause in other countries, and perfectly approve and commend your establishing a correspondence in France. It appears to have produced the desired effect; for Mons. De Varville, the secretary of a society for the like benevolent purpose at Paris, is now here, and comes instructed to establish a correspondence with us, and to collect such information as may promote our common views. He delivered to our society an extract from the minutes of your proceedings, dated 8th of April last, recommending him to our attention, and upon that occasion they passed the resolutions of which the enclosed are copies.

We are much obliged by the pamphlets enclosed with your letter, and shall constantly make such communications to you as may appear to us interesting.

By a report of the committee for superintending the school we have established in this city for the education of negro children, we find that proper attention is paid to it, and that ———— scholars are now taught in it. By the laws of this State, masters may now liberate healthy slaves of a proper age without giving security that they shall not become a parish charge; and the exportation as well as importation of them is prohibited. The State has also manumitted such as became its property by confiscation; and we have reason to expect that the maxim, that every man, of whatever colour, is to be presumed to be free until the contrary be shown, will prevail in our courts of justice. Manumissions daily become more common among us; and the treatment which slaves in general meet with in this State is very little different from that of other servants.

I have the honour to be, gentlemen,

Your humble servant,

JOHN JAY,
*President of the Society for
Promoting the Manumission
of Slaves.*

# NOTES

1. See William Jay, *The Life of John Jay* (New York, 1833), I, 235; Bayard Tuckerman, *William Jay and the Constitutional Movement for the Abolition of Slavery* (New York, 1894). Louis Filler, in *The Crusade Against Slavery* (New York, 1960), p. 4, raises an eyebrow at Jay's practice of "slaveholding for humane' ends," but is perhaps overly cynical.
2. In 1788 a society in France, and another in England, formed for promoting the abolition of slavery, opened a correspondence with the New York society through its president. The above letter to the English society was from Jay's pen. See letter from Granville Sharp, May 1, 1788. [Editorial note by H. P. Johnson]

# JEDIDIAH MORSE

## SLAVERY AND THE WHITE MAN

Jedidiah Morse (1761–1826), a prominent Congregational clergyman in his day, achieved even greater eminence as the "father of American geography." His *Geography Made Easy* appeared in 1784, the first geography published in the United States. A larger work, *The American Geography; or a View of the Situation of the United States of America,* first published in 1789, passed through seven American and many European editions. The following selection is from pages 65–67 of *The American Geography* (Elizabethtown, 1789).

## From *The American Geography*

. . . A European writer has justly observed that 'If there be an object truly ridiculous in nature, it is an American patriot, signing resolutions of independency with the one hand, and with the other brandishing a whip over his affrighted slaves.'

Much has been written, of late, to shew the injustice and iniquity of enslaving the Africans; so much as to render it unnecessary here to say any thing on that part of the subject. We cannot, however, forbear introducing a few observations respecting the influence of slavery upon policy, morals and manners. From repeated and accurate calculations, it has been found, that the expence of maintaining a slave, especially if we include the purchase money, is much greater than that of maintaining a free man; and the labour of the freeman, influenced by the powerful motive of gain, is, at least, twice as profitable to the employer as that of the slave. Besides, slavery is the bane of industry. It renders labour, among the whites, not only unfashionable, but disreputable. Industry is the offspring of necessity rather than of choice. Slavery precludes this necessity; and indolence, which strikes at the root of all social and political happiness, is the unhappy consequence.

These observations, without adding any thing upon the injustice of the practice, shew that slavery is impolitic. Its influence on manners and morals is equally pernicious. The negro wenches in many, perhaps I may say in most instances, are nurses to their mistresses children. The infant babe, as soon as it is born, is delivered to its black nurse, and perhaps seldom or never tastes a drop of its mother's milk. The children, by being brought up, and constantly associating with the negroes, too often imbibe their low ideas, and vitiated manners and morals; and contract a *negroish* kind of accent and dialect, which they often carry with them through life. A mischief common, in a greater or less degree, in all the southern states, at which humanity and decency blush, is the criminal intercourse between the whites and blacks. 'The enjoyment of a negro or mulatto woman,' says a traveller of observation, 'is spoken of as quite a common thing. No reluctance, delicacy, or shame, appear about the matter.['] It is far from being uncommon to see a gentleman at dinner, and his reputed offspring a slave, waiting at the table. 'I myself,' says this writer, 'saw two instances of this kind; and the company would very facetiously trace the features of the father and mother in the child, and very accurately point out the more characteristic resemblances. The fathers neither of them blushed, nor seemed disconcerted. They were called men of worth, politeness, and humanity. Strange perversion of terms and language! The Africans are said to be inferior in point of sense, understanding, sentiment and feeling to white people: Hence the one infers a right to enslave the other. The African labours night and day to collect a small pittance to purchase the freedom of his child: The white man begets his likeness, and with much indifference and dignity of soul, sees his offspring in bondage and misery, and makes not one effort to redeem his own blood. Choice food for satire! wide field for burlesque! noble game for wit! sad cause for pity to bleed, and for humanity to weep! unless the enkindled blood inflame resentment, and vent itself in execrations! . . .

Under the Federal government which is now established, we have reason to believe that all slaves in the United States, will in time be emancipated, in a manner most consistent with their own happiness, and the true interest of their proprietors. Whether this will be effected by transporting them back to Africa; or by colonizing them in some part of our own territory, and extending to them our alliance and protection until they shall have acquired strength sufficient for their own defence; or by incorporation with the whites; or in some other way, remains to be determined. All these methods are attended with difficulties. The first would be cruel; the second dangerous; and the latter disagreeable and unnatural. Deep-rooted prejudices entertained by the whites; ten thousand recollections, by the blacks, of the injuries they have sustained; new provocations; the real distinction which nature has made; besides many other circumstances which would tend to divide them into parties, and produce convulsions,[1] are objections against retaining and incorporating the blacks with the citizens of the several states. But justice and humanity demand that these difficulties should be surmounted.

In the middle and northern States, there are comparatively but few slaves; and of course there is less difficulty in giving them their freedom. Societies for the manumission of slaves, have been instituted in Philadelphia and New-York; and laws have been enacted, and other measures taken in the New-England states to accomplish the same purpose. The FRIENDS, (commonly called Quakers,) have evinced the propriety of their name, by their goodness in originating, and their vigorous exertions in executing, this truly humane and benevolent design.

## NOTE

1. The preceding paragraph in Morse's text consists of a long quotation from Jefferson. The preceding lines in this paragraph are also quoted from Jefferson, but without quotation marks. Cf. *Notes on Virginia*, p. 162.

## A BLACK MAN EVALUATES WHITE PREJUDICES

The following essay appeared in the *American Museum* (Vol. VI, pp. 77–80) in 1789. Founded at Philadelphia in 1787 by Mathew Carey, "the greatest of eighteenth-century magazine editors,"[1] the *Museum* is indispensable to any study of the society and politics of its day. It includes many valuable writings about Negroes and slavery. The essay by an ex-slave reprinted here is perhaps the most thoughtful and best written by a Negro of that period. The letter was first printed in England and apparently reprinted in the *American Museum.*

### Letter on Slavery. By a Negro

I am one of that unfortunate race of men, who are distinguished from the rest of the human species, by a black skin and woolly hair—disadvantages of very little moment in themselves, but which prove to us a source of the greatest misery, because there are men, who will not be persuaded, that it is possible for a human soul to be lodged within a sable body. The West Indian planters could not, if they thought us men, so wantonly spill our blood; nor could the natives of this land of liberty, deeming us of the same species with themselves, submit to be instrumental in enslaving us, or think us proper subjects of a sordid commerce. Yet, strong as the prejudices against us are, it will not, I hope, on this side of the Atlantic, be considered as a crime, for a poor African not to confess himself a being of an inferior order to those, who happen to be of a different colour from himself; or be thought very presumptuous, in one who is but a negro, to offer to the happy subjects of this free government, some reflexions upon the wretched condition of his countrymen. They will not, I trust, think worse of my brethren, for being discontented with so hard a lot as that of slavery; nor disown me for their fellow creature, merely because I deeply feel the unmerited sufferings, which my countrymen endure.

It is neither the vanity of being an author, nor a sudden and capricious gust of humanity, which has prompted the present design. It has been long conceived, and long been the principal subject of my thoughts. Ever since an indulgent master rewarded my youthful services with freedom, and supplied me at a very early age with the means of acquiring knowledge, I have laboured to understand the true principles, on which the liberties of mankind are founded, and to possess myself of the language of this country, in order to plead the cause of those who were once my fellow slaves, and if possible to make my freedom, in some degree, the instrument of their deliverance.

The first thing then, which seems necessary, in order to remove those prejudices, which are so unjustly entertained against us, is to prove that we are men—a truth which is difficult of proof, only because it is difficult to imagine, by what arguments it can be combated. Can it be contended, that a difference of colour alone can constitute a difference of species?—if not, in what single circumstance are we different from the rest of mankind? what variety is there in our organization? what inferiority of art in the fashioning of our bodies? what imperfection in the faculties of our minds?—Has not a negro eyes?[2] has not a negro hands, organs, dimensions, senses, affections, passions?—fed with the same food; hurt with the same weapons; subject to the same diseases; healed by the same means; warmed and cooled by the same summer and winter, as a white man is? if you prick us, do we not bleed? if you poison us, do we not die? are we not exposed to all the same wants? do we not feel all the same sentiments— are we not capable of all the same exertions—and are we not entitled to all the same rights, as other men?

Yes—and it is said we are men, it is true; but that we are men, addicted to more and worse vices, than those of any other complexion; and such is the innate perverseness of our minds, that nature seems to have marked us out for slavery.—Such is the apology, perpetually made for our masters, and the justification offered for that universal proscription, under which we labour.

But I supplicate our enemies, to be, though for the first time, just in their proceedings towards us; and to establish the fact, before they attempt to draw any conclusion from it. Nor let them imagine, that this can be done, by merely asserting, that such is our universal character. It is the character, I grant, that our inhuman masters have agreed to give us, and which they have too industriously and too successfully propagated, in order to palliate their own guilt, by blackening the helpless victims of it, and to disguise their own cruelty under the semblance of justice. Let the natural depravity of our character be proved—not by appealing to declamatory invectives, and interested representations, but by shewing, that a greater proportion of crimes have been committed by the wronged slaves of the plantations, than by the luxurious inhabitants of Europe, who are happily strangers to those aggravated provocations, by which our passions are every day irritated and incensed. Shew us, that, of the multitude of negroes, who have, within a few years, transported themselves to this country[3] and who are abandoned to themselves; who are corrupted by example, prompted by penury, and instigated, by the memory of their wrongs, to the commission of every crime— shew us, I say, (and the demonstration, if it be possible, cannot be difficult) that a greater proportion of these, than of white men, have fallen under the animadversion of justice, and have been sacrificed to your laws. Though avarice may slander and insult our misery, and though poets heighten the horror of their fables, by representing us as monsters of vice—the fact is, that, if treated like other men, and admitted to a participation of their rights, we should differ from them in nothing, perhaps, but in our possessing stronger passions, nicer sensibility, and more enthusiastic virtue.

Before so harsh a decision was pronounced upon our nature, we might have expected—if sad experience had not taught us, to expect nothing but injustice from our adversaries—that some pains should have been taken, to ascertain, what our nature is, and that we should have been considered, as we are found in our native woods, and not as we now are—altered and perverted by an inhuman political institution. But, instead of this, we are examined, not by philosophers, but by interested traders: not as nature formed us, but as man has depraved us—and from such an enquiry, prosecuted under such circumstances, the perverseness of our dispositions is said to be established. Cruel that you are! you make us slaves; you implant in our minds all the vices, which are, in some degree, inseparable from that condition; and you then impiously impute to nature, and to God, the origin of those vices, to which you alone have given birth; and punish in us the crimes, of which you are yourselves the authors.

The condition of slavery is in nothing more deplorable, than in its being so unfavourable to the practice of every virtue. The surest foundation of virtue, is the love of our fellow-creatures; and that affection takes its birth, in the social relations of men to one another. But to a slave these are all denied. He never pays or receives the grateful duties of a son—he never knows or experiences the fond solicitude of a father—the tender names of husband, of brother, and of friend, are to him unknown. He has no country to defend and bleed for—he can relieve no sufferings—for he looks around in vain, to find a being more wretched than himself. He can indulge no generous sentiment—for, he sees himself every hour treated with contempt and ridicule, and distinguished from irrational brutes, by nothing, but the severity of punishment. Would it be surprising, if a slave, labouring under all these disadvantages—oppressed, insulted, scorned, and trampled on—should come at last to despise himself—to believe the calumnies of his oppressors—and to persuade himself, that it would be against his nature, to cherish any honourable sentiment, or to attempt any virtuous action? Before you boast of your superiority over us, place some of your own colour (if you have the heart to do it) in the same situation with us; and see, whether they have such innate virtue, and such unconquerable vigour of mind, as to be capable of surmounting such multiplied difficulties, and of keeping their minds free from the infection of every vice, even under the oppressive yoke of such a servitude.

But, not satisfied with denying us that indulgence, to which the misery of our condition gives us so just a claim, our enemies have laid down other and stricter rules of morality, to judge our actions by, than those by which the conduct of all other men is tried. Habits, which in all human beings, except ourselves, are thought innocent, are, in us, deemed criminal—and actions, which are even laudable in white men, become enormous crimes in negroes. In proportion to our weakness, the strictness of censure is increased upon us; and as resources are with-held from us, our duties are multiplied. The terror of punishment is perpetually before our eyes; but we know not, how to avert it, what rules to act by, or what guides to follow. We have written laws, indeed, composed in a language we do not understand, and never promulgated: but what avail written laws, when the supreme law, with us, is the capricious will of our overseers? To obey the dictates of our own hearts, and to yield to the strong propensities of nature, is often to incur severe punishment; and by emulating examples, which we find applauded and revered among Europeans, we risk inflaming the wildest wrath of our inhuman tyrants.

To judge of the truth of these assertions, consult even those milder and subordinate rules for our conduct, the various codes of your West India laws—those laws, which allow us to be men, whenever they consider us as victims of their vengeance, but treat us only like a species of living property, as often as we are to be the objects of their protection—those laws, by which (it may be truly said) that we are bound to suffer, and be miserable, under pain of death. To resent an injury, received from a white man, though of the lowest rank, and to dare to strike him, though upon the strongest and grossest provocation, is an enormous crime. To attempt an escape from the cruelties exercised over us, by flight, is punished with mutilation, and sometimes with death. To take arms against masters, whose cruelty no submission can mitigate, no patience exhaust, and from whom no other means of deliverance are left, is the most atrocious of all crimes; and is punished by a gradual death, lengthened out by torments, so exquisite, that none, but those who have been long familiarized, with West Indian barbarity, can hear the bare recital of them without horror. And yet I learn from writers, whom the Europeans hold in the highest esteem, that treason is a crime, which cannot be committed by a slave against his master; that a slave stands in no civil relation towards his master, and owes him no allegiance; that master and slave are in a state of war; and if the slave take up arms for his deliverance, he acts not only justifiably, but in obedience to a natural duty, the duty of self-preservation. I read in authors, whom I find venerated by our oppressors, that to deliver one's self and one's countrymen from tyranny, is an act of the sublimest heroism. I hear Europeans exalted, as the martyrs of public liberty, the saviours of their country, and the deliverers of mankind—I see their memories

honoured with statues, and their names immortalized in poetry
—and yet when a generous negro is animated by the same
passion, which ennobled them—when he feels the wrongs of his
countrymen as deeply, and attempts to revenge them as boldly—
I see him treated by those same Europeans, as the most exe-
crable of mankind, and led out, amidst curses and insults, to
undergo a painful, gradual, and ignominious death: and thus
the same Briton, who applauds his own ancestors, for attempting
to throw off the easy yoke, imposed on them by the Romans,
punishes us, as detested parricides, for seeking to get free from
the cruellest of all tyranies, and yielding to the irresistible
eloquence of an African Galgacus or Boadicea.

Are then the reason and the morality, for which Europeans so
highly value themselves, of a nature so variable and fluctuating,
as to change with the complexion of those, to whom they are
applied?—Do the rights of nature cease to be such, when a negro
is to enjoy them?—Or does patriotism, in the heart of an African,
rankle into treason?

                                                    A FREE NEGRO.


## NOTES

1. Frank Luther Mott, *A History of American Magazines, 1741–1850* (New
   York and London, 1930) , p. 30.
2. The ensuing lines parallel Shakespeare's *The Merchant of Venice,* Act III,
   Scene i, lines 64 ff., with "negro" substituted for "Jew" and "white" for
   "Christian."
3. This letter was originally published in England, where the number of
   negroes is considerably encreased, since the late war in America. [Editor's
   note in original]

## BENJAMIN FRANKLIN

### On Slavery and the Slave Trade

It was not until the last years of his life that Benjamin Franklin (1706–1790) became interested in the effort to abolish Negro slavery,[1] although in earlier years, as a printer, he had printed the anti-slavery writings of Ralph Sandiford, Benjamin Lay and John Woolman. In August 1772, in a letter to Anthony Benezet, Franklin first expressed the hope that the slave trade might be outlawed. In 1786 he became president of the Pennsylvania Society for Promoting the Abolition of Slavery, which had been formed shortly before the Revolution. He continued as president until his death. On February 3, 1790, he sent a memorial to Congress, on behalf of the Pennsylvania Abolition Society, in which he urged the abolition of slavery. Twenty-four days before he died, Franklin wrote a public letter which parodied the arguments of those who defended the slave trade. Both documents are reprinted here, the first from Joseph Gales, comp., *Annals of Congress* (Washington, 1834), Vol. I, cols. 1239–1240. This item is reprinted, with slight variations, in Matthew T. Mellon, *Early American Views on Negro Slavery* (Boston, 1934), pp. 30–32. Franklin's letter to the editor of the *Federal Gazette,* dated March 23, 1790, is taken from Albert Henry Smyth, *The Writings of Benjamin Franklin* (New York, 1907), X, 87–91.

### Anti-Slavery Memorial to Congress

The memorial respectfully showeth,—

That from a regard for the happiness of mankind, an association was formed several years since in this State, by a number of her citizens, of various religious denominations, for promoting the abolition of slavery, and for the relief of those unlawfully held in bondage. A just and acute conception of the true principles of liberty, as it spread through the land, produced accessions to their numbers, many friends to their cause, and a Legislative co-operation with their views, which, by the blessing of Divine Providence, have been successfully directed to the relieving from bondage a large number of their fellow-creatures of the African race. They have also the satisfaction to observe, that in consequence of that spirit of philanthropy and genuine liberty which is generally diffusing its beneficial influence, similar institutions are forming at home and abroad.

That mankind are all formed by the same Almighty Being, alike objects of his care, and equally designed for the enjoyment of happiness, the Christian religion teaches us to believe, and the political creed of Americans fully coincides with the position. Your memorialists, particularly engaged in attending to the distresses arising from slavery, believe it their indispensable duty to present this subject to your notice. They have observed, with real satisfaction, that many important and salutary powers are vested in you for 'promoting the welfare and securing the blessings of liberty to the people of the United States'; and as they conceive that these blessings ought rightfully to be administered, without distinction of color, to all descriptions of people, so they indulge themselves in the pleasing expectation, that nothing which can be done for the relief of the unhappy objects of their care, will be either omitted or delayed.

From a persuasion that equal liberty was originally the portion, and is still the birth-right of all men; and influenced by the strong ties of humanity, and the principles of their institution, your memorialists conceive themselves bound to use all justifiable endeavors to loosen the bands of slavery, and promote a general enjoyment of the blessings of freedom. Under these impressions, they earnestly entreat your serious attention to the subject of slavery; that you will be pleased to countenance the restoration of liberty to those unhappy men, who alone, in this land of freedom are degraded into perpetual bondage, and who, amidst the general joy of surrounding freemen, are groaning in servile subjection; that you will devise means for removing this inconsistency from the character of the American people; that you will promote mercy and justice towards this distressed race, and that you will step to the very verge of the power vested in you for discouraging every species of traffic in the persons of our fellow-men.

BENJ. FRANKLIN, *President.*

Philadelphia, February 3, 1790.

## To the Editor of the Federal Gazette

March 23d, 1790.

SIR,

Reading last night in your excellent Paper the speech of Mr. Jackson in Congress against their meddling with the Affair of Slavery, or attempting to mend the Condition of the Slaves, it put me in mind of a similar One made about 100 Years since by Sidi Mehemet Ibrahim, a member of the Divan of Algiers, which may be seen in Martin's Account of his Consulship, anno 1687. It was against granting the Petition of the Sect called *Erika*, or Purists, who pray'd for the Abolition of Piracy and Slavery as being unjust. Mr. Jackson does not quote it; perhaps he has not seen it. If, therefore, some of its Reasonings are to be found in his eloquent Speech, it may only show that men's Interests and Intellects operate and are operated on with surprising similarity in all Countries and Climates, when under similar Circumstances. The African's Speech, as translated, is as follows.

*"Allah Bismillah, &c. God is great, and Mahomet is his Prophet.*

"Have these *Erika* considered the Consequences of granting their Petition? If we cease our Cruises against the Christians, how shall we be furnished with the Commodities their Countries produce, and which are so necessary for us? If we forbear to make Slaves of their People, who in this hot Climate are to cultivate our Lands? Who are to perform the common Labours of our City, and in our Families? Must we not then be our own Slaves? And is there not more Compassion and more Favour due to us as Mussulmen, than to these Christian Dogs? We have now above 50,000 Slaves in and near Algiers. This Number, if not kept up by fresh Supplies, will soon diminish, and be gradually annihilated. If we then cease taking and plundering the Infidel Ships, and making Slaves of the Seamen and Passengers, our Lands will become of no Value for want of Cultivation; the Rents of Houses in the City will sink one half; and the Revenues of Government arising from its Share of Prizes be totally destroy'd! And for what? To gratify the whims of a whimsical Sect, who would have us, not only forbear making more Slaves, but even to manumit those we have.

"But who is to indemnify their Masters for the Loss? Will the State do it? Is our Treasury sufficient? Will the *Erika* do it? Can they do it? Or would they, to do what they think Justice to the Slaves, do a greater Injustice to the Owners? And if we set our Slaves free, what is to be done with them? Few of them will return to their Countries; they know too well the greater Hardships they must there be subject to; they will not embrace our holy Religion; they will not adopt our Manners; our People will not pollute themselves by intermarrying with them. Must we maintain them as Beggars in our Streets, or suffer our Properties to be the Prey of their Pillage? For Men long accustom'd to Slavery will not work for a Livelihood when not compell'd. And what is there so pitiable in their present Condition? Were they not Slaves in their own Countries?

"Are not Spain, Portugal, France, and the Italian states govern'd by Despots, who hold all their Subjects in Slavery, without Exception? Even England treats its Sailors as Slaves; for they are, whenever the Government pleases, seiz'd, and confin'd in Ships of War, condemn'd not only to work, but to fight, for small Wages, or a mere Subsistence, not better than our Slaves are allow'd by us. Is their Condition then made worse by their falling into our Hands? No; they have only exchanged one Slavery for another, and I may say a better; for here they are brought into a Land where the Sun of Islamism gives forth its Light, and shines in full Splendor, and they have an Opportunity of making themselves acquainted with the true Doctrine, and thereby saving their immortal Souls. Those who remain at home have not that Happiness. Sending the Slaves home then would be sending them out of Light into Darkness.

"I repeat the Question, What is to be done with them? I have heard it suggested, that they may be planted in the Wilderness, where there is plenty of Land for them to subsist on, and where they may flourish as a free State; but they are, I doubt, too little dispos'd to labour without Compulsion, as well as too ignorant to establish a good government, and the wild Arabs would soon molest and destroy or again enslave them. While serving us, we take care to provide them with every thing, and they are treated with Humanity. The Labourers in their own Country are, as I am well informed, worse fed, lodged, and cloathed. The Condition of most of them is therefore already mended, and requires no further Improvement. Here their Lives are in Safety. They are not liable to be impress'd for Soldiers, and forc'd to cut one another's Christian Throats, as in the Wars of their own Countries. If some of the religious mad Bigots, who now teaze us with their silly Petitions, have in a Fit of blind Zeal freed their Slaves, it was not Generosity, it was not Humanity, that mov'd them to the Action; it was from the conscious Burthen of a Load of Sins, and Hope, from the supposed Merits of so good a Work, to be excus'd Damnation.

"How grossly are they mistaken in imagining Slavery to be disallow'd by the Alcoran! Are not the two Precepts, to quote no more, *'Masters, treat your Slaves with kindness; Slaves, serve your Masters with Cheerfulness and Fidelity,'* clear Proofs to the contrary? Nor can the Plundering of Infidels be in that sacred Book forbidden, since it is well known from it, that God has given the World, and all that it contains, to his faithful Mussulmen, who are to enjoy it of Right as fast as they conquer it. Let us then hear no more of this detestable Proposition, the Manumission of Christian Slaves, the Adoption of which would, by depreciating our Lands and Houses, and thereby depriving so many good Citizens of their Properties, create universal Discontent, and provoke Insurrections, to the endangering of Government and producing general Confusion. I have therefore no doubt, but this wise Council will prefer the Comfort and Happiness of a whole Nation of true Believers to the Whim of a few *Erika,* and dismiss their Petition."

The Result was, as Martin tells us, that the Divan came to this Resolution; "The Doctrine, that Plundering and Enslaving the Christians is unjust, is at best *problematical;* but that it is the Interest of this State to continue the Practice, is clear; therefore let the Petition be rejected."

And it was rejected accordingly.

And since like Motives are apt to produce in the Minds of Men like Opinions and Resolutions, may we not, Mr. Brown, venture to predict, from this Account, that the Petitions to the Parliament of England for abolishing the Slave-Trade, to say nothing of other Legislatures, and the Debates upon them, will have a similar Conclusion? I am, Sir, your constant Reader and humble Servant,                                        HISTORICUS.

### NOTE

1. Matthew T. Mellon, *Early American Views on Negro Slavery* (Boston, 1934), p. 20.

# BENJAMIN BANNEKER

## ON THE NATURE OF THE NEGRO

Born in Maryland, the son of a free mother and slave father, Benjamin Banneker was a free Negro.[1] The first American to make a clock, his self-education and genius in mathematics and astronomy enabled him, in August 1791, to compile an almanac for the year 1792. Banneker sent a copy of the almanac to Jefferson, accompanied with the following letter.[2] Jefferson's reply is also printed here.

Nathan Schachner, in his biography of Jefferson, notes that Jefferson, who was then Secretary of State, took an active part in the transfer of the capital of the United States to Washington, D.C. On February 2, 1791, Major Andrew Ellicott was appointed to lay out and survey the city, and Banneker was chosen to assist him. The *Georgetown Weekly Ledger,* in its issue of March 12, 1791, reported the arrival in Washington D.C. of Major Ellicott, "attended by Benjamin Bannikar [sic], an Ethiopian, whose abilities as a Surveyor and Astronomer clearly prove that Mr. Jefferson's concluding that race of men void of mental endowments was without foundation."[3] Schachner observes that "the sarcastic reference was, of course, to Jefferson's animadversions in the *Notes on Virginia*."[4]

## To Thomas Jefferson

MARYLAND, Baltimore County, August 19, 1791.

SIR,

I am fully sensible of the greatness of that freedom, which I take with you on the present occasion; a liberty which seemed to me scarcely allowable, when I reflected on that distinguished and dignified station in which you stand, and the almost general prejudice and prepossession, which is so prevalent in the world against those of my complexion.

I suppose it is a truth too well attested to you, to need a proof here, that we are a race of beings, who have long laboured under the abuse and censure of the world; that we have long been looked upon with an eye of contempt; and that we have long been considered rather as brutish than human, and scarcely capable of mental endowments.

Sir, I hope I may safely admit, in consequence of that report which hath reached me, that you are a man far less inflexible in sentiments of this nature, than many others; that you are measurably friendly, and well disposed towards us; and that you are willing and ready to lend your aid and assistance to our relief, from those many distresses, and numerous calamities, to which we are reduced.

Now Sir, if this is founded in truth, I apprehend you will embrace every opportunity, to eradicate that train of absurd and false ideas and opinions, which so generally prevails with respect to us; and that your sentiments are concurrent with mine, which are, that one universal Father hath given being to us all; and that he hath not only made us all of one flesh, but that he hath also, without partiality, afforded us all the same sensations and endowed us all with the same faculties; and that however variable we may be in society or religion, however diversified in situation or colour, we are all of the same family, and stand in the same relation to him.

Sir, if these are sentiments of which you are fully persuaded, I hope you cannot but acknowledge, that it is the indispensable duty of those, who maintain for themselves the rights of human nature, and who possess the obligations of Christianity, to extend their power and influence to the relief of every part of the human race, from whatever burden or oppression they may unjustly labour under; and this, I apprehend, a full conviction of the truth and obligation of these principles should lead all to.

Sir, I have long been convinced, that if your love for yourselves, and for those inestimable laws, which preserved to you the rights of human nature, was founded on sincerity, you could not but be solicitous, that every individual, of whatever rank or distinction, might with you equally enjoy the blessings thereof; neither could you rest satisfied short of the most active effusion of your exertions, in order to their promotion from any state of degradation, to which the unjustifiable cruelty and barbarism of men may have reduced them.

Sir, I freely and cheerfully acknowledge, that I am of the

African race, and in that colour which is natural to them of the deepest dye; and it is under a sense of the most profound gratitude to the Supreme Ruler of the Universe, that I now confess to you, that I am not under that state of tyrannical thraldom, and inhuman captivity, to which too many of my brethren are doomed but that I have abundantly tasted of the fruition of those blessings, which proceed from that free and unequalled liberty with which you are favoured; and which, I hope, you will willingly allow you have mercifully received, from the immediate hand of that Being, from whom proceedeth every good and perfect gift.

Sir, suffer me to recall to your mind that time, in which the arms and tyranny of the British crown were exerted, with every powerful effort, in order to reduce you to a state of servitude: look back, I entreat you, on the variety of dangers to which you were exposed; reflect on that time, in which every human aid appeared unavailable, and in which even hope and fortitude wore the aspect of inability to the conflict, and you cannot but be led to a serious and grateful sense of your miraculous and providential preservation; you cannot but acknowledge, that the present freedom and tranquillity which you enjoy you have mercifully received, and that it is the peculiar blessing of heaven.

This, Sir, was a time when you clearly saw into the injustice of a state of slavery, and in which you had just apprehensions of the horrors of its condition. It was now that your abhorrence thereof was so excited, that you publicly held forth this true and invaluable doctrine, which is worthy to be recorded and remembered in all succeeding ages: "We hold these truths to be self-evident, that all men are created equal; that they are endowed by their Creator with certain unalienable rights, and that among these are, life, liberty, and the pursuit of happiness."

Here was a time, in which your tender feelings for yourselves had engaged you thus to declare, you were then impressed with proper ideas of the great violation of liberty, and the free possession of those blessings, to which you were entitled by nature; but, Sir, how pitiable is it to reflect, that although you were so fully convinced of the benevolence of the Father of Mankind, and of his equal and impartial distribution of these rights and privileges, which he hath conferred upon them, that you should at the same time counteract his mercies, in detaining by fraud and violence so numerous a part of my brethren, under groaning captivity and cruel oppression, that you should at the same time be found guilty of that most criminal act, which you professedly detested in others, with respect to yourselves.

I suppose that your knowledge of the situation of my brethren, is too extensive to need a recital here; neither shall I presume to prescribe methods by which they may be relieved, otherwise than by recommending to you and all others, to wean yourselves from those narrow prejudices which you have imbibed with respect to them, and as Job proposed to his friends, "put your soul in their souls' stead;" thus shall your hearts be enlarged with kindness and benevolence towards them; and thus shall you need neither the direction of myself or others, in what manner to proceed herein.

And now, Sir, although my sympathy and affection for my brethren hath caused my enlargement thus far, I ardently hope, that your candour and generosity will plead with you in my behalf, when I make known to you, that it was not originally my design; but having taken up my pen in order to direct to you, as a present, a copy of an Almanac, which I have calculated for the succeeding year, I was unexpectedly and unavoidably led thereto.

This calculation is the production of my arduous study, in this my advanced stage of life; for having long had unbounded desires to become acquainted with the secrets of nature, I have had to gratify my curiosity herein, through my own assiduous application to Astronomical study, in which I need not recount to you the many difficulties and disadvantages, which I have had to encounter.

And although I had almost declined to make my calculation for the ensuing year, in consequence of that time which I had allotted therefor, being taken up at the Federal Territory, by the request of Mr. Andrew Ellicott, yet finding myself under several engagements to Printers of this state, to whom I had communicated my design, on my return to my place of residence, I industriously applied myself thereto, which I hope I have accomplished with correctness and accuracy; a copy of which I have taken the liberty to direct to you, and which I humbly request you will favourably receive; and although you may have the opportunity of perusing it after its publication, yet I choose to send it to you in manuscript previous thereto, that thereby you might not only have an earlier inspection, but that you might also view it in my own hand writing.

And now, Sir, I shall conclude, and subscribe myself, with the most profound respect,

> Your most obedient humble servant,
>
> BENJAMIN BANNEKER.

## To Mr. Benjamin Banneker

PHILADELPHIA, August 30, 1791.

SIR,

I thank you, sincerely, for your letter of the 19th instant, and for the Almanac it contained. No body wishes more than I do, to see such proofs as you exhibit, that nature has given to our black brethren talents equal to those of the other colours of men; and that the appearance of the want of them, is owing merely to the degraded condition of their existence, both in Africa and America. I can add with truth, that nobody wishes more ardently to see a good system commenced, for raising the condition, both of their body and mind, to what it ought to be, as far as the imbecility of their present existence, and other circumstances, which cannot be neglected, will admit.

I have taken the liberty of sending your Almanac to Monsieur de Condozett,[5] Secretary of the Academy of Sciences at Paris, and Member of the Philanthropic Society, because I considered it as a document, to which your whole colour had a right for their justification, against the doubts which have been entertained of them.

> I am with great esteem, Sir,
>
> Your most obedient humble Servant,
>
> THOMAS JEFFERSON.

## NOTES

1. Carter G. Woodson and Charles H. Wesley, *The Negro in Our History*, 11th ed. (Washington, D.C., 1966), pp. 137 ff.

2. *Copy of a Letter from Benjamin Banneker to the Secretary of State,* Philadelphia, 1792. Jefferson's reply is reprinted from H. A. Washington, ed., *The Writings of Thomas Jefferson* (Washington, D.C., 1853), Vol. III, p. 291.

3. Quoted in Schachner, *Thomas Jefferson: A Biography* (New York and London, 1951), p. 447.

4. *Ibid.,* p. 447.

5. Condorcet.

## BENJAMIN RUSH
### ON THE ORIGIN OF BLACK COLOR

On July 14, 1792, at a meeting of the American Philosophical Society, Physician Benjamin Rush delivered an address in which he suggested that the black skin color of the Negro was a result of leprosy. The implication was that the cure of the disease, by eliminating the difference in color, and all oppression based thereon, would solve the race problem. The address is reprinted from the *Transactions* of the American Philosophical Society, 1799, Vol. IV, pp. 289–297. All notes are from the original text.

*Observations intended to favour a supposition that the Black Color (as it is called) of the Negroes is derived from the Leprosy*

Dr. Smith in his elegant and ingenious Essay upon the Variety of Color and Figure in the Human Species has derived it from four causes, viz. climate, diet, state of society, and diseases. I admit the Doctor's facts, and reasonings as far as he has extended them, in the fullest manner. I shall only add to them a few observations which are intended to prove that the color and figure of that part of our fellow creatures who are known by the epithet of negroes, are derived from a modification of that disease, which is known by the name of Leprosy.

Many facts recorded by historians, as well as physicians show the influence of unwholsome diet in having produced the leprosy in the middle and northern parts of Europe in the 13th and 14th centuries. The same cause, combined with greater heat, more savage manners, and bilious fevers, probably produced this disease in the skin among the natives of Africa. But I will not rest the proofs of the color and figure of the negroes being a leprosy simply upon its causes. Other circumstances make it much more probable. I shall briefly enumerate them.

The leprosy is accompanied in some instances with a black color of the skin. Of this I have met with a satisfactory proof in Dr. Theiry's account of the diseases of Asturia in Spain. I shall insert a translation of his own words upon this subject. "There are (says this excellent physician) above twenty hospitals for lepers in this province, and I have observed six species of the disorder. One of them, viz. the second, is called the *black albaras* of the Arabians. The skin becomes black, thick and greasey.— There are neither pustules, nor turbercles, nor scales, nor any thing out of the way on the skin. The body is not in the least emaciated. The breathing is a little difficult, and the countenance has some fierceness in it. They exhale perpetually a peculiar and disagreeable smell, which I can compare to nothing but the smell of a mortified limb."[1] This smell mentioned by Dr. Theiry continues with a small modification in the native African to this day.

2. The leprosy is described in the Old Testament, and by many ancient writers as imparting a preternatural whiteness to the skin. Persons thus marked, have lately received the name of *albanos*. Solitary instances of this disease are often met with it upon the Alps, but travellers tell us that it is one of the endemics of Java, Guinea and Panama where it is perpetuated through many generations. Mr. Hawkins in his travels into the interior parts of Africa has described the persons afflicted with this disease in the following words. "They go entirely naked; their skin is white, but has not that animated appearance so perceptible in Europeans. It has a dull deathlike whitish cast that conveys an idea more of sickness, than of health. Their hair is red, or ashes-coloured, yellowish wool, and their eyes are uniformly white, in that part by which others are distinguished into the black, grey and blue eyes. They are set deep in the head, and very commonly squint, for as their skin is deprived of the black mucous web, the distinguishing characteristic of these Africans, so their eyes are destitute of that black matter resembling a pigment, so universally found in people of all countries, and so useful in preventing the eye from being injured in cases of exposure to strong light."[2] This artless traveller does not stop here. The idea of this peculiarity in the color and features of these people being a disease, and even its specific nature did not escape him, hence he adds "These people rendered unfortunate by the prejudices of their countrymen, are born of black parents; they have all the features of other inhabitants, but differ from them only in the above

circumstances. The difference of color cannot arise from the intercourse of whites and blacks, for the whites are very rarely among them, and the result of this union is well known to be the yellow color, or mulatto. Many of the natives assert that they are produced by the women being debauched in the woods by the large baboon, ourang-outang, and by the species in particular called the guaga mooroos. No satisfactory discovery has been made to account for such singular, but not unfrequent phænomena in the species. It may perhaps be ascribed to *disease,* and that of the *leprous* kind, with more reason than to any other cause that has been yet assigned."[3] Mr. Bernardin concurs with Mr. Hawkins in ascribing this morbid whiteness in the skins of the Africans wholly to the leprosy.[4] However opposed it may be to their morbid blackness, it is in strict conformity to the operations of nature in other diseases. The same state of malignant fever is often marked by opposite colors in the stools, by an opposite temperature of the skin, and by opposite states of the alimentary canal.

The original connection of the black color of the negroes with the leprosy is further suggested by the following fact taken from Bougainville's voyage round the world.[5] He tells us that on an island in the Pacific Ocean which he visited, the inhabitants were composed of negroes and mulattoes. They had thick lips, woolly hair, and were sometimes of a yellowish color. They were short, ugly, ill proportioned, and most of them infected with the leprosy, a circumstance from which he called the island they inhabit, the Isle of Lepers.

3. The leprosy sometimes appears with white and black spots blended together in every part of the body. A picture of a negro man in Virginia in whom this mixture of white and black had taken place, has been happily preserved by Mr. Peale in his museum.

4. The leprosy induces a morbid insensibility in the nerves. In countries where the disease prevails, it is common to say that a person devoid of sensibility, has no more feeling than a leper. This insensibility belongs in a peculiar manner to the negroes. Dr. Moseley says, "they are void of sensibility to a surprizing degree. They sleep sound in every disease, nor does any mental disturbance ever keep them awake. They bear surgical operations

much better than white people, and what would be a cause of insupportable pain to a white man, a negro would almost disregard. I have amputated the legs of many negroes, who have held the upper part of the limb themselves."[6] This morbid insensibility in the negroes discovers itself further in the apathy with which they expose themselves to great heat, and the indifference with which they handle coals of fire.

5. Lepers are remarkable for having strong venereal desires. This is universal among the negroes, hence their uncommon fruitfulness when they are not depressed by slavery; but even slavery in its worst state does not always subdue the venereal appetite, for after whole days, spent in hard labor in a hot sun in the West Indies, the black men often walk five or six miles to comply with a venereal assignation.

6. The big lip, and flat nose so universal among the negroes, are symptoms of the leprosy. I have more than once seen them in the Pennsylvania hospital.

7. The woolly heads of the negroes cannot be accounted for from climate, diet, state of society, or bilious diseases, for all those circumstances, when combined have not produced it in the natives of Asia and America who inhabit similar latitudes. Wool is peculiar to the negro. Here the proofs of similarity in the symptoms of leprosy, and in the peculiarities of the negro body appear to fail, but there is a fact in the history of the leprosy which will probably throw some light upon this part of our subject. The Trichoma, or Plica Polonica of the Poles is a symptom of leprosy. This is evident not only from the causes which originally produced it, but from its symptoms as described in a late publication by F. L. De La Fontaine.[7] From this fact it would seem that the leprosy had found its way to the covering of the head, and from the variety of its effects upon the skin, I see no difficulty in admitting that it may as readily have produced wool upon the head of a negro, as matted hair upon the head of the Poles.

But how shall we account for the long duration of this color of the skin through so many generations and even ages?—I answer—1. That the leprosy is the most durable in its descent to posterity, and the most indestructable in its nature of any disease we are acquainted with. In Iceland Dr. Van Troil tells us, it often disappears in the second and third, and appears in the fourth generation.[8] 2dly. No more happens here than what happens to many nations who are distinguished by a peculiarity of figure, in any part of the body. Many of the inhabitants of the highlands of Scotland, have the same red hair, and the same high cheek bones which are ascribed to their ancestors by Tacitus after the invasion of Britain. Even the tumors in the throat in the Cretins who inhabit the Alps, are transmitted from father to son, through a long succession of generations. Madness, and consumption in like manner are hereditary in many families, both of which occupy parts of the body, much more liable to change in successive generations, than the skin.

Should it be objected to this theory that the leprosy is an infectious disorder, but that no infectious quality exists in the skin of the negro, I would reply to such objection by remarking in the first place, that the leprosy has in a great degree ceased to be infectious, more especially from contact, and secondly that there are instances in which something like an infectious quality has appeared in the skin of a negro. A white woman in North Carolina not only acquired a dark color, but several of the features of a negro, by marrying and living with a black husband. A similar instance of a change in the color and features of a woman in Buck's county in Pennsylvania has been observed and from a similar cause. In both these cases, the women bore children by their black husbands.

It is no objection to the theory I have attempted to establish, that the negroes are as healthy, and long lived as the white people. Local diseases of the skin seldom affect the general health of the body, or the duration of human life. Dr. Theiry remarks that the itch, and even the leprosy, did not impair longevity in those people who lived near the sea-shore in the healthy climate of Galicia.[9]

The facts and principles which I have delivered, lead to the following reflections.

1. That all the claims of superiority of the whites over the blacks, on account of their color, are founded alike in ignorance and inhumanity. If the color of the negroes be the effect of a disease, instead of inviting us to tyrannise over them, it should

entitle them to a double portion of our humanity, for disease all over the world has always been the signal for immediate and universal compassion.

2. The facts and principles which have been delivered, should teach white people the necessity of keeping up that prejudice against such connections with them, as would tend to infect posterity with any portion of their disorder. This may be done upon the ground I have mentioned without offering violence to humanity, or calling in question the sameness of descent, or natural equality of mankind.

3. Is the color of the negroes a disease? Then let science and humanity combine their efforts, and endeavour to discover a remedy for it. Nature has lately unfurled a banner upon this subject. She has begun spontaneous cures of this disease in several black people in this country. In a certain Henry Moss who lately travelled through this city, and was exhibited as a show for money, the cure was nearly complete. The change from black to a natural white flesh color began about five years ago at the ends of his fingers, and has extended gradually over the greatest part of his body. The wool which formerly perforated the cuticle has been changed into hair. No change in the diet, drinks, dress, employments, or situation of this man had taken place previously to this change in his skin. But this fact does not militate against artificial attempts to dislodge the color in negroes, any more than the spontaneous cures of many other diseases militate against the use of medicine in the practice of physic. To direct our experiments upon this subject I shall throw out the following facts.

1. In Henry Moss the color was first discharged from the skin in those places, on which there was most presssure from cloathing, and most attrition from labor, as on the trunk of his body, and on his fingers. The destruction of the black color was probably occasioned by the absorption of the coloring matter of the rete mucosum, or perhaps of the rete mucosum itself, for pressure and friction it is well known aid the absorbing action of the lymphatics in every part of the body. It is from the latter cause, that the palms of the hands of negro women who spend their lives at a washing tub, are generally as fair as the palms of the hands in labouring white people.

2. Depletion, whether by bleeding, purging, or abstinence has been often observed to lessen the black color in negroes. The effects of the above remedies in curing the common leprosy, satisfy me that they might be used with advantage in that state of leprosy which I conceive to exist in the skin of the negroes.

3. A similar change in the color of the negroes, though of a more temporary nature, has often been observed in them from the influence of fear.

4. Dr. Beddoes tells us that he has discharged the color in the black wool of a negro by infusing it in the oxygenated muriatic acid, and lessened it by the same means in the hand of a negro man. The land-cloud of Africa called by the Portuguese Ferrino Mr. Hawkins tells us has a peculiar action upon the negroes in changing the black color of their skins to a dusky grey.[10] Its action is accompanied, he says, with an itching and prickling sensation upon every part of the body which increases with the length of exposure to it so as to be almost intolerable. It is probably air of the carbonic kind, for it uniformly extinguishes fire.

5. A citizen of Philadelphia upon whose veracity I have perfect reliance,[11] assured me that he had once seen the skin of one side of the cheek inclining to the chin, and of part of the hand in a negro boy, changed to a white color by the juice of unripe peaches (of which he ate a large quantity every year) falling, and resting frequently upon those parts of his body.

To encourage attempts to cure this disease of the skin in negroes, let us recollect that by succeeding in them, we shall produce a large portion of happiness in the world. We shall in the first place destroy one of the arguments in favor of enslaving the negroes, for their color has been supposed by the ignorant to mark them as objects of divine judgments, and by the learned to qualify them for labor in hot, and unwholsome climates.

Secondly, We shall add greatly to *their* happiness, for however well they appear to be satisfied with their color, there are many proofs of their preferring that of the white people.

Thirdly, We shall render the belief of the whole human race being descended from one pair, easy, and universal, and thereby not only add weight to the Christian revelation, but remove a material obstacle to the exercise of that universal benevolence which is inculcated by it.

*June* 17, 1797.

## Notes [from the original text]

1. Observations de Physique et de Medecine faites en differens lieux de l'Espagne. Vol. ii. p. 130.
2. P. 116. 117.
3. P. 117. 118.
4. Studies of Nature, vol. ii. p. 2.
5. Page 294.
6. Treatise upon Tropical Diseases, p. 475.
7. Surgical and medical treatises upon various subjects respecting Poland.
8. Letters on Iceland, p. 122.
9. Vol. II. p. 171.
10. P. 120. 121.
11. Mr. Thomas Harrison.

# DAVID RICE

## RACIAL MIXTURE AND SLAVERY

Born and raised in Virginia, David Rice (1733–1816) was ordained a Presbyterian minister in Hanover, Virginia, in 1763. While in Virginia he helped found Hampden-Sydney College. In 1783 he moved to Kentucky, where he became known as the father of Presbyterianism. Elected a member of the convention which in 1792 framed the constitution of Kentucky, he sought to insert in the constitution an article which provided for the gradual emancipation of slaves, but failed. His convention address on behalf of emancipation was printed during the same year in Philadelphia under the title, *Slavery Inconsistent with Justice and Good Policy* (Phila., 1792). A selection from the address follows.

Another frightful objection to my doctrine is, that should we set our slaves free, it would lay a foundation for intermarriages and an unnatural mixture of blood, and our posterity at length would all be Mulattoes.

This effect, I grant, it would produce. I also grant, that this appears very unnatural to persons labouring under our prejudices of education. I acknowledge my own pride remonstrates against it; but it does not influence my judgment, nor affect my conscience.

To plead this, as a reason for the continuation of slavery, is to plead the fear that we should disgrace ourselves, as a reason why we should do injustice to others: to plead that we may continue in guilt, for fear the features and complexion of our posterity should be spoiled. We should recollect, that it is too late to prevent this great imaginary evil; the matter is already gone beyond recovery; for it may be proved, with mathematical certainty, that, if things go on in the present channel, the future inhabitants of America will inevitably be Mulattoes.

How often have men children by their own slaves, by their fathers' slaves, or the slaves of their neighbours? How fast is the number of Mulattoes increasing in every part of the land? Visit the little towns and villages to the Eastward; visit the seats of gentlemen, who abound in slaves; and see how they swarm on every hand? All the children of Mulattoes will be Mulattoes, and the whites are daily adding to the number; which will continually increase the proportion of Mulattoes. Thus this evil is coming upon us in a way much more disgraceful, and unnatural, than intermarriages. Fathers will have their own children for slaves, and leave them as an inheritance to their children. Men will possess their brothers and sisters as their property, leave them to their heirs, or sell them to strangers. Youth will have their grey headed uncles and aunts for slaves, call them their property, and transfer them to others. Men will humble their own sisters, or even their aunts, to gratify their lust. An hard-hearted master will not know, whether he has a blood relation, a brother or a sister, an uncle or an aunt, or a stranger of Africa, under his scourging hand. This is not the work of imagination; it has been frequently realized.

The worst that can be made of this objection, ugly as it is, is that it would be hastening an evil in an honest way which we are already bringing on ourselves in a way that is absolutely dishonest, perfectly shameful, and extremely criminal. This objection then can have no weight with a reasonable man, who can divest himself of his prejudices and his pride, and view the matter as really circumstanced. The evil is inevitable; but as it is a prejudice of education, it would be an evil only in its approach; as it drew near, it would decrease; when fully come, it would cease to exist.

# NOAH WEBSTER

## SLAVERY, EMANCIPATION AND COLONIZATION

One of the little-known works by the great lexicographer was a booklet, fifty-six pages in length, published in 1793 in Hartford, Connecticut, under the title, *Effects of Slavery, on Morals and Industry.*

The title page identifies the author as a counsellor at law and member of the Connecticut Society for the Promotion of Freedom. Webster described his booklet in *The American Minerva,* of which he was editor, as follows: "As Essay on Slavery: designed to exhibit in a new point of view, its effects on morals, industry, and the peace of society. Some facts and calculations are offered to prove the labor of freemen to be much more productive than that of slaves; that countries are rich, powerful and happy in proportion as the laboring people enjoy the fruits of their own Labor; and hence the necessary conclusion, that slavery is impolitic as well as unjust."

Webster rejects the idea of the innate inferiority of the Negro, attributing any inferior characteristics to the "depressed condition" of slavery, and offers one of the earliest American evaluations of colonization as an alternative to slavery. The selection which follows consists of pp. 6, 7, 33–37. All notes but one are in the original. A few of Webster's notes, of little interest to the modern reader, have been omitted.

## Effects of Slavery

It is evidently the will of heaven that men should be prompted to action by a regard to their own benefit and happiness. Whenever by the positive institutions of society, or by external force, men are stripped of the power of exerting themselves for their own benefit, the mind, having lost its spring or stimulus, either ceases to act, and men become mere machines, moving only when impelled by some extraneous power; or if the mind acts at all, it is at the impulse of violent passions, struggling to throw off an unnatural restraint, and to revenge the injury. Hence it is, that slaves, with few exceptions, may be divided into two classes, the *indolent* and the *villanous*.

In America the laziness of slaves has become proverbial: indeed the blacks are so remarkable for their inaction, their want of foresight and their disinclination to improvement, as to create very great doubts in the minds of some men of a philosophical cast, whether they are not a distinct and inferior race of beings.[1] But on examining this subject, and comparing the blacks of this country, with the slaves of other countries, who are confessedly of the same race with the most improved European nation, it will probably be found that, making the usual allowances for the effects of their native climate, all the peculiar features in the character of the African race in America, may justly be ascribed to their depressed condition.

The indolence of the slaves in the southern states, must indeed approach almost to stupidity. It is said by gentlemen, well informed on this subject, that three blacks will not perform more labor than one free white in the northern states.[2] And it is well known that on every plantation, a negro driver is required, with his whip and his cane, to compel the reluctant slave to perform his daily task. But are American slaves only distinguished for their aversion to labor? History teaches us a very different doctrine. Among the ancient Germans, who, by their vigor and bravery, conquered half the world, slavery had the same debasing stupifying influence: and it is remarkable that the word *lazzi*, which among our Saxon ancestors, was the denomination of the lowest order of bondmen or servants, is the origin of our English word *lazy*, a word expressive of that indolence and aversion to labor, which remarkably characterize the negroes in America. If slavery had this effect upon our own ancestors, the warlike heroes of the *north*, surely modern philosophers need not resort to an original difference of race, for the cause of that dullness and want of mental vigor, remarkable in the enslaved natives of the *torrid zone* and their degenerate descendants.

But if we turn our eyes upon the present nations of Europe, we shall find multiplied proofs of this important truth, that slavery necessarily enervates the vigor of the human mind, in all climates and among all nations. . . .

That freedom is the sacred right of every man whatever be his color, who has not forfeited it by some violation of municipal law, is a truth established by God himself in the very creation of human beings. No time, no circumstances, no human power or policy can change the nature of this truth, nor repeal the fundamental laws of society by which every man's right to liberty is guaranteed. The first act therefore of enslaving men is always a violation of those great primary laws of society, by which alone the master himself holds every particle of his own freedom.

But are there not cases when it is necessary to make a distinction between *abstract right and political expedience?* Is it not true that *political expedience,* properly understood, is the foundation of all *public right and justice?* The African slave trade originated when political and social rights were not generally understood, and when the few philosophers who understood and attempted to defend them could make a very feeble resistance to the suggestions of private avarice and the tyrannical policy of nations.[3] Under such circumstances, the business was begun and continued, till about 40 years ago when the society of Quakers, under the auspices of the benevolent Anthony Benezet, remonstrated against the shameful traffic. From that period powerful efforts have been made by numerous societies as well as individuals, to procure the emancipation of those already reduced to slavery, and to put a stop to further importations from Africa. These efforts have been attended with great success. In some of the northern states of America, all the slaves have been set free by constitutional declarations of rights; in almost all of them provision has been made by law to introduce a gradual abolition of the existing slavery, and the further importation is strictly prohibited. At the same time we may remark that by a late act of the British Parliament, the slave trade is to cease in the year 1796; and the revolution in France has already produced very important changes in that trade and in the condition of the slaves in some of the French Islands. What will be the final result of these measures and events in the West Indies, no man can predict with any degree of assurance.

With respect to the United States of America, no great difficulties or inconveniences occur in gradually abolishing slavery in all the States north of Delaware. In the 8 States north and east of

Delaware, the number of slaves is comparatively small; being to the free inhabitants in the proportion of only *one to forty four;* but in the six southern States, where the slaves make nearly *one third* of the inhabitants, the liberation of them is a matter of very serious consequence.[4]

To give freedom at once to almost 700,000 slaves, would reduce perhaps 20,000 white families to beggary. It would impoverish the country south of Pennsylvania; all cultivation would probably cease for a time; a famine would ensue; and there would be extreme danger of insurrections which might deluge the country in blood and perhaps depopulate it. Such calamities would be deprecated by every benevolent man and good citizen; and that zeal which some persons discover to effect a *total sudden abolition* of slavery in the United States, appears to be very intemperate. Indeed it is a zeal which counteracts its own purposes; for a sudden emancipation of such a number of slaves, instead of bettering their condition would render it worse, and inevitably expose them to perish with cold and famine. Whatever have been the means and however unjustifiable the policy by which slavery has been introduced and encouraged, the evil has taken such deep root, and is so widely spread in the southern States, that an attempt to eradicate it at a single blow would expose the whole political body to dissolution. In these ideas I shall probably be seconded by a great proportion of thinking men throughout the United States.

It has been suggested that the country may gradually be delivered from its black inhabitants by transporting a certain number of them to Africa every year, furnished with the necessary means of subsistence. A settlement of this kind has been already begun by a colony from Great-Britain, under the superintendance of Mr. Clarkson.[5] Indeed if colonial establishments of this kind could be effected, without great injury to the United States, humanity and philosophy would exult at the prospect of seeing the arts of civilized nations introduced into the heart of Africa. But the practicability of this plan of colonization seems to be yet problematical. It seems not yet decided by the experiments made, whether such colonies would not dwindle away by disease, and be perpetually exposed to the hostility of the surrounding natives. Indeed, it may be an important question, whether even well civilized blacks placed in the torrid zone, where little labor is requisite to procure their necessary food and clothing, would not neglect all arts and labor, beyond what are necessary to supply immediate wants, and gradually revert back to a savage state. How far a commercial intercourse with such colonies, by exciting a taste for luxuries and the love of wealth and splendor, would tend to preserve their habits of industry and prompt them to encourage arts and manufactures, we have perhaps no certain data from which we can draw even a probable conclusion.

But other objections oppose themselves to the project of African colonization. Who is to pay the expense? The master will think the loss of his slaves a sacrifice on his part sufficiently great, without furnishing them with food, utensils, and shipping for their transportation; and the slaves are not able to furnish themselves with these articles. The funds therefore must be raised by private subscriptions, or supplied by government; and these resources cannot be relied on in the present state of America. Besides it is not certain that the slaves themselves would be willing to risk such a change of situation; as most of them are born in this country and are total strangers to Africa and its inhabitants. In this case, to compel them to quit the country, and encounter the dangers of the sea, an insalubrious climate and the hostile tribes of Africa; together with the risk of starving, would be a flagrant act of injustice, inferior only to the first act of enslaving their ancestors.

The objection that the unhealthiness of the climate renders it impossible for whites to cultivate rice and indigo plantations, and therefore it is necessary to perform this business by blacks, seems to be of little weight; or at least, it cannot be of permanent duration. It is commonly supposed that the insalubrity of the air in the southern states, arises in great measure, from the stagnant waters which cover the rice and indigo plantations. These waters indeed increase the evil; but the principal cause is a much more extensive one; the large marshes and vast tracts of uncleared land in the flat country. Marshes and stagnant waters, in which vegetable substances putrify and dissolve, produce pestilential exhalations; and when a country is mostly covered with forests, the air itself becomes stagnant and does not carry off the noxious effluvia generated in low grounds. It is with the air as with water; its purity depends on its motion. To render any flat country healthy, it must be cleared of its forests, and laid open on all sides to the action of the wind. It is not sufficient to open here and there a plantation, and leave four fifths of the earth covered with wood. Besides the advantage of giving motion to the air on an extended plain, the clearing and cultivation of the earth lays it open to the sun, whose heat warms and dries the surface, and by removing the moisture, prevents the generation of noxious exhalations. Thus whenever most of the land in the southern states shall be cleared, the principal cause of epidemic diseases will be destroyed; and the free circulation of air near the surface of the earth will render the putrid exhalations from the plantations and marsh ground which cannot be drained, much less fatal. The New-England States, sixty years ago, were infested with the same annual fevers, which now prove so troublesome to the southern states; but by the clearing and cultivation of the earth, those diseases no longer prevail. The rice fields in Italy and Spain are all cultivated by white people, and tho they render the air about them less salubrious than it is in other parts of the country, yet it is not so fatal to the health of the people as to discourage the culture of that useful grain.

There is therefore no question that a general and high state of cultivation will, to a great degree, correct the insalubrity of the low flat country in the southern States, so as to render it cultivable with white laborers; except perhaps in the vicinity of such saltmarshes as cannot be drained. But the obstacles that present themselves to the project of *colonization,* and to that of a *general sudden abolition* of slavery, appear to be equally insurmountable. The blacks in the southern States must, it is presumed, continue there, for a great number of years, perhaps forever; government at least will not undertake the herculean task of exporting them to a foreign country, and repeopling five or six States with white inhabitants.[6]

What then can be done? What method can be devised for meliorating the condition of the blacks, without essentially injuring the slave, the master and the public. This is the great desideratum. There appears to me only one plan or expedient for effecting this desirable object, which, in its operation, will combine the three several interests which are to be consulted; this is, to raise the slaves, by gradual means, to the condition of free tenants.

## NOTES [FROM THE ORIGINAL TEXT]

1. See Hume's *Essays* vol. 1. p. 550. Note M. Jefferson's notes on Virginia, p. 237.
2. Mss. Letter from the Hon. Dr. Ramsay, Charleston, South Carolina.
3. I have heard elderly people remark, that in the early part of their lives it never once occurred to them that it was unjust and iniquitous to enslave Africans. It is within a few years only that the question has been generally discussed.
4. Of 40,384 Slaves in the States north of Delaware, 32,777 are in New-York and New-Jersey: the slaves in Pennsylvania Vermont and the four New-England States amounting only to 7607. . . .
5. Thomas Clarkson (1760–1846), English Abolitionist, devoted his life to the abolition of the slave-trade as well as of slavery in the British colonies [L.R.].
6. The project of exporting all the blacks in the United States, would, if practicable, be attended with many desireable effects. The separation of the whites from all mixture of colour, would remove the causes of much jealousy and dissention, which will otherwise prevail among the whites and blacks. But should colonization ever be attempted, the exportation of the slaves from the southern States must be slow and gradual, to prevent the impoverishment of the country. The sudden expulsion of 700,000 morescoes from Spain, in the riegn of Philip 3, gave a blow to the agriculture and manufactures of that kingdom which the efforts of almost two centuries have scarcely repaired. . . . Many of the wealthiest people in in Spain were reduced to poverty and distress!—Perhaps a more eligible scheme would be to assign the blacks a portion of land in the United States, and remove them all thither by slow degrees, furnishing them with means of cultivation.

## WARNER MIFFLIN

### On Slavery and Crime

The Quaker reformer Warner Mifflin (1745–1798) is perhaps best known for his efforts against slavery. After inheriting a number of slaves in 1774–75, he freed them all. Thereafter, he worked tirelessly to persuade Quakers to liberate their slaves, and submitted petitions against slavery and the slave trade to various state legislative bodies as well as to Congress. In 1794, he published an anti-slavery tract entitled *A Serious Expostulation With the Members of the House of Representatives of the United States,* and in 1796 he defended his efforts in a pamphlet printed in Philadelphia, entitled *The Defense of Warner Mifflin against Aspersions Cast on Him on Account of His Endeavors to Promote Righteousness, Mercy and Peace, among Mankind.* The following selection is from pp. 21–23 of the latter work in which the author denies any inherent difference in character between blacks and whites.

. . . It is urged as a very great objection to the emancipation of blacks, their disposition to pilfering, but is not the worst of Robbery in depriving them of that most valuable Property, Liberty, and keeping them under the oppression of Slavery, the very cause of this fault? being pinched at times for almost every necessary of life, they naturally put forth a hand to partake of what their labour gives them some claim to in equity from their possessors, where due support is withheld; and these practices becoming habitual, in their impoverished condition, they discriminate not sufficiently between the property of those they labour for and others; but when opportunity presents frequently supply their wants from all alike, except where a principle of religious rectitude restrains from all such acts: I attempt not to palliate the crime. I have endeavoured what lies in my power to reprobate such proceedings, labouring to inculcate the Christian doctrine of returning good for evil, whereby they may know an overcoming evil with good; and to point out the necessity of departing from these practices, being objections speciously alledged against their general liberation: But as Slavery decreases and is exploded, we may reasonably hope its concomitant habits will also decrease, and a greater nobility of Soul take place. I believe the Almighty hath arisen to Judgment in this business, and that his voice will be found to exceed the sound of many Waters, or all the clamours of the People; overpowering all opposition whatsoever.

If we proved more faithful in the discharge of our duty towards God and this People, I believe they would act differently towards us—But where does Negro crimes exceed the Crimes of White Men? when we view them, selling tender Babes from a fond Mother, a beloved Wife from an affectionate Husband, or an aged Father from his offspring with whom he hath lived from their early years; and although a Slave, capable of the ties of affection and enjoying consolation in their Society; and now, as to this life, forever parted—Ah! what language can paint in its genuine Colours this abominable practice? how rejoicing would it be to me, if with divine allowance, I might be placed in an allotment exempt from that continued grief of soul, which is almost daily renewed, from seeing and hearing of those acts of inhumanity committed by my countrymen! could I have believed myself authorized by the approbation, of Heaven, I should long 'ere this time have sought an asylum in some other Quarter—but I desire to be found in my proper allotment the little time I may be continued here—faithfully discharging my duty towards my Creator and my Country.

# CHAPTER 7

# The Early National Period

"Pro-slavery theory throughout the period 1790–1820," according to William Sumner Jenkins in *Pro-Slavery Thought in the Old South*,[1] "may be characterized generally as being in a state of quiescence. During these three decades the prevailing opinion throughout the South was in support of slavery, but its defense normally remained dormant, only occasionally being aroused from a passive condition to become articulate." This was in contrast to succeeding decades, when pro-slavery statements increased in number and became "aggressive and even belligerent."[2]

During the post-Revolutionary period, two diverse, almost contradictory trends were apparent in both the North and the South. On the one hand, the libertarian ideals of the Revolution continued to have an impact in the form of continuing efforts to emancipate Negro slaves. These resulted in the elimination of slavery in a number of northern states, including Connecticut, New York, Rhode Island and Pennsylvania. Indeed, as Guion Johnson notes in *A History of Racial Ideologies in the United States with Reference to the Negro*,[3] "It is possible that the general attitude toward the Negro for a generation after the Revolution was more kindly than at any other time in the history of the country." Even in the South, laws forbidding the manumission of slaves were "temporarily relaxed" and many slave-owners liberated their slaves. The result, Johnson continues, was that "the free Negro population of North Carolina, for example, increased 42 per cent between 1790 and 1800 and 46 per cent in the following decade."

On the other hand, a trend to conservatism which began before the adoption of the Constitution and continued into the early decades of the nineteenth century, also had its impact on race relations. This trend was a reaction against "the equalitarian ideologies of the Revolution"[4] and "the theory of the natural and inalienable rights of man." It resulted in constitutional safeguards for slavery and for the return of fugitive slaves. What may be regarded as parallel to this trend or an integral part of it was a seeming increase in prejudice against the free Negro, in both the North and the South, a tendency to place severe restrictions upon his movements and to limit his rights as a citizen.[5]

Ideologically, both prejudice and discriminatory laws assumed that the free Negro was "a social and political menace." Even opposition to the slave trade and slavery was frequently based upon "a fear of acquiring a Negro population out of proportion to the ability of the whites to police and to acculturate."[6] The attitude toward the Negro as an inferior being as well as a menace, which had existed since the earliest days of slavery and was so useful in defending it, continued to play an important role—in the North to justify repression of the free Negro, in the South to preserve slavery and repress the free Negro.

Of greatest import for the course of pro- and anti-slavery feeling, hence of racial thought in the United States, were the invention of the cotton gin and technological developments in the cotton textile industry in Europe as well as America. These resulted in a vastly increased demand for cotton, a commensurate increase in cotton production and a heightened demand for slave labor on Southern cotton plantations. Between 1790 and 1808, over 100,000 slaves were brought into this country. Even after the outlawing of the foreign slave trade in 1808, between 250,000 and 300,000 slaves were smuggled into the United States. Thus the total number of slaves grew from 697,624 in 1790 to a million and a half in 1820 and approximately two million in 1830.

Concurrently with the increase in slavery in the South and the end of slavery in the North there occurred a decline in organized anti-slavery activity in both sections. Abolition societies in the North declined during the 1790's and the early decades of the nineteenth century.[7] Southern anti-slavery societies "had also fallen away by 1803," as a result of intensified public hostility to anti-slavery efforts. Thus, "a few years after the insurrection of Gabriel, in 1800, the Alexandria Society is reported dissolved, and the Maryland and Virginia societies, which were still apparently flourishing in 1797, are not even heard from."[8]

The result was that, during the early decades of the century, slavery became deeply entrenched and accepted as an established institution in American society, the Negro came increasingly to be regarded as a natural slave or as an inferior being, and the voices of those who could challenge the dominant ideology, either from the standpoint of natural rights or the equal humanity of the Negro, were isolated and weakened, if not muted. Yet, while slavery gained increasing acceptance, one finds a paucity of considered and well-thought-out defenses of the institution on the basis of race.[9] Noteworthy writings of this nature did not appear until the institution was attacked by the new-born anti-slavery movement under the leadership of Garrison in the 1830's.

## NOTES

1. Chapel Hill, 1935, p. 48.
2. *Ibid.*
3. MS in the New York Public Library, 1943, p. 61.
4. *Ibid.*, p. 90.
5. For examples see D. F. Tingley, "The Rise of Racialistic Thinking in the Nineteenth Century" (Master's Thesis, University of Illinois, 1952), pp. 34–35.
6. Johnson, *A History of Racial Ideologies,* pp. 39–40.
7. Mary S. Locke notes that after 1798, the Abolition societies of Connecticut and Rhode Island, which had been represented up to 1796, failed to send delegates to the annual meetings of the American Convention of anti-slavery societies. *Anti-Slavery in America*, p. 109.
8. *Ibid.*, pp. 109–111.
9. Southern statements in Congress during the debate over the admission of Missouri in 1819 and 1820 do contain comments on the nature of the Negro, but these are usually not elaborated.

# THOMAS BRANAGAN

## ON THE NEGRO AND COLONIZATION

Born in Dublin, Ireland, in 1774, Thomas Branagan was at various times a sailor, plantation overseer and author. Although self-educated and without even an elementary knowledge of English grammar, he wrote two epic poems, *Avenia* and *The Penitential Tyrant,* and political treatises.

Branagan was convinced of the iniquity of slavery but believed the Negro to be a menace to the white man. He proposed to create a Negro state in the West, in which black men would be free and independent citizens, and to which all blacks could migrate. The following selection is from pp. 35–39, 41–45 of one of his books published in Philadelphia, 1805, with the following title: *Serious Remonstrances, Addressed to the Citizens of the Northern States, and their Representatives: Being an Appeal to Their Natural Feelings & Common Sense: Consisting of Speculations and Animadversions, on the Recent Revival of the Slave Trade, in the American Republic: With an Investigation Relative to the Consequent Evils Resulting to the Citizens of the Northern States From that Event, Interspersed with a Simplified Plan for Colonizing the Free Negroes of the Northern, in Conjunction with Those Who Have, or May Emigrate From the Southern States, in a Distant Part of the National Territory: Considered as the Only Possible Means of Avoiding the Deliterious evils attendant on Slavery in a Republic.* The errors in grammar and spelling are to be found in the original.

## *A Simplified Plan for Colonizing the Free Negroes . . . in a Distant Part of the National Territory*

. . . Many plans have been suggested by candid persons for the purpose of amolerating the situation of slaves, some have proposed an instantaneous emancipation of 800,000 slaves: others have proposed a gradual emancipation and to confer on the liberated negroes all the rights of citizens political, and social.

Though I revere the persons who have made these propositions, I must affirm that they utterly tend to frustrate the objects they mean to accellerate; they are encumbered with inseperable difficulties, and in some respects involve greater mischief than the original disorder designed to be cured. Without farther procrastination, I will develope my plan, which I will prove or endeavour to prove, will answer the end proposed better than any plan that has yet been adopted, which is briefly; to appropriate a proportionable part of the territory which we purchased from France for 15,000,000 dollars, as a colony, or seperate state, a particular quantum of that land to be given to each free coloured person who would emigrate gratis; funds to be established in the several states for the accommodation of the negroes, who would think proper[1] to emigrate to enable them to clear and cultivate the land, for their own use, and as their own property for ever; a governor, judges, and magistrates, to be appointed (as in New-Orleans) by the President of the United States: of the most intelligent and virtuous of the African race, so that such white persons as wish to emigrate and associate with the blacks, may likewise be under their control and governed by them. Thus the most fertile land, from a wilderness would be metamorphosed to a garden, and thousands of free negroes who are at present starving with hungar, and destitute of employ, would be put in a capacity to enrich themselves, and provide for their posterity: and the benevolent slave holders in the South, who wish to liberate their slaves, but forego their generous intentions, by this means would have an opportunity to redeem them from wretchedness, and crown them with peace, happiness, and plenty. That this plan might be very easily realized, may be demonstrated from the case of tens of thousands of Europeans, who have cleared and cultivated the Western forests, and changed the baren wilderness to flourishing states and fruitful gardens; but as facts are more convincing than the most systematical reasoning, I will contract the most reasonable plan that has yet been exhibited for the accommodation of slaves, and the one I here suggest, and that the most illiterate may see the difference, I will delineate my hypothesis in the most simple and comprehensive manner.

First, I would depict the only plan that has yet been devised, to deliver our country from the destructive evils in question, which has been even partially attended with success; and exhibit the paramount injuries attending this plan, both to the citizens of the North, and the negroes that either elope from the South, or that receive their monumission from their original proprietors. The plan I allude to is this; that the slaves should be emansipated in the South in a gradual manner, while ways and means should be provided in the North for their intellectual and moral instruction; and when capacitated, to be received as citizens of the United States, and to enjoy privileges accordingly, and be on the same state of political and social equality with the whites. This is the best method that has yet been adopted, which I will prove from experience, to be big with very unpleasant effects, and exceedingly injurious to the citizens of the North.

In the first place, it is impossible in the nature of things, for the blacks in the North ever to be reconciled to the whites; while hundreds of thousands of their countrymen are groaning, bleeding, and dying, beneath the frowns of despotism, in the South. To suppose they can be reconciled while this is the case, is the first-born of absurdities. . . .

For the sake of illustration we will suppose that a general rebellion broke out among the blacks from New Hampshire to Georgia, which I have not the least doubt will be the case sooner or later; would not the blacks in the North, be worse than the worst of tories, where last war, if they did not assist with every possible means in their power their Southern brethren, to regain their liberty, and with it all the privileges social and political peculiar to freemen? Without any manner of doubt. Are not slave-holders, and their slaves at open and perpetual war, a war that is daily carried on in the most sanguinary manner, and with unremitted efforts. In order then to ascertain what is the duty of Africans to their oppressors, we must ask ourselves, what would we conceive our duty to be, to a gang of robbers, who came by night to rob, murder, and destroy us, and our families? The answer is plain, if we had the ability and opportunity, we would destroy our enemies, preserve our families and liberties, or die in the attempt. If we consider the conditions of 8 or 900,000 blacks and colored persons, in the most abject and humiliating bondage in this country, our hypothesis will appear more sonorous. They are bound to obey the unjust laws that rob them of their all, and subjects them unconditionally to the caprice and cruelty of their tyrants. They are forced to submit to laws that bereave them of liberty, life and property. These laws, and the legislatures or government that framed them, are their mortal, their most implacable enemies: then how can such injured persons, owe any allegiance to such governments, whose laws they suffer the penalty of, for the least misdemeanors; yet without receiving the least benefit from them. If they derive any, it is only the partial protection of their life and limbs; and this only tends to perpetuate their unutterable misery.

I ask any man of common sense, must not such persons, and their progeny, be irresistibly stimulated to endeavour to regain their liberty, and punish their murderers? Must not the most superficial recollection of their wrongs, enhance a propensity for revenge in the free blacks, now in the North? Can they forget the injuries their ancestors met with from Americans, and when they remember that they were robbed, enslaved, and murdered; can they help feeling an involuntary disgust to their tyrants, their children, their color and their country? It is impossible! Let us bring the matter home to ourselves; if a certain family used my father and his family (myself excepted) as the christians do the exiled Africans, could I forget it? I could sooner forget my a, b, c, or forget I had a head upon my shoulders. If therefore my definition is correct, and I do not see how it can be incorrect, the sons of Africa in America, are the inveterate enemies of Americans, and are at perpetual war with them. With respect to the former the war is properly defensive, with the latter it is offensive; and nothing can put an end to this sanguinary warfare, but for the one party to forego the rights they bereaved the others of, and with the ill-gotten booty, exonerate the most illegal policy, destructive measures, and shocking guilt. Thus if the virtue of the citizens of the South, was paramount to their avarice, it would be more than madness for them to emancipate their slaves and let them remain with them as free men and citizens. It would be exactly as if a man who greatly injured another person, unjustly, and consequently made him his enemy has the injured person bound and in his power, he is in part out of danger; but if he liberates him, and puts a sword in his hand, there is nothing more certain, than that he will be revenged of his adversary. A man must shut his eyes against the light, and basely insult his understanding, not to see the deleterious policy[2] of keeping a numerous and at the same time a growing body of people amongst us knowing the vitals of the body politic, for the blacks in the South propagate very slowly owing to their hard usage, those in the North propagate rapidly, consequently in the course of 10 or 20 years we may expect the number of blacks in the North will be augmented to several hundred Thousands.

## NOTES [FROM THE ORIGINAL TEXT]

1. This observation is made on the supposition, that it would be incompatible with the laws of the land to force them to emigrate; but if this is not the case, I think, if comfortable provision was made for them elsewhere; if they refused to go with their families where the government thought proper to point out, they should be sent perforce. This would not be enfringing the laws of hospitality, or philanthropy, for every reasonable person must allow that it is better for the blacks themselves to be accomodated domestically, and settled politically independent by themselves, than associate with the whites with whom they never can enjoy reciprocal rights, and political privileges. Would it not be just and generous, as well as hospitable, to force a foolish or stubborn person from a place where he was surrounded with poverty, to a place where he would be crowned with plenty: from a place where he was politically a slave, where he would be politically free: certainly it would.

2. It is St. George Tucker's opinion, that by propagation alone, in 30 years the blacks will be double in number to what they are at present; and so on in following years, if (as it is in the Northern states) there is no cruelty or hardship exercised over them. If this supposition is correct, (of which there can be no doubt) what multitudes of natural enemies must our children, and grand children have to combat with. Even in Philadelphia, their number must be augmented to 50,000 at least in 60 years.

# HENRI GREGOIRE AND D. B. WARDEN

## CIVILIZATION, INTELLECT AND SLAVERY

Henri Gregoire (1750–1831), the great French revolutionist, humanitarian and constitutional bishop of Blois, is one of the towering figures in the history of racial thought. Though a Frenchman, he is included here because his work on the Negro was translated by an American and published in the United States in 1810, because of its initial impact on American thought and its comments on Jefferson, and because in recent years the book has been overlooked in this country. David Baillie Warden (1778–1845), the translator, then Secretary to the American Legation at Paris, later published a 3-volume study, *A Statistical, Political, and Historical Account of the United States of North America; from the Period of their First Colonization to the Present Day* (Edinburgh, 1819).

The selections from Gregoire's work, *An Enquiry concerning the Intellectual and Moral Faculties, and Literature of Negroes; Followed with an Account of the Life and Works of Fifteen Negroes and Mulattoes, Distinguished in Science, Literature and the Arts* (Brooklyn, 1810), include Warden's preface, extracts from Chapter II, and most of the "Conclusion." All notes are from the original, unless initialed (L. R.).

## Concerning the Intellectual and Moral Faculties, and Literature of Negroes

### Translator's Preface

I recollect to have heard the celebrated professor Millar, of the university of Glasgow, observe, in his course of civil law, "that the mind revolts at the idea of a serious discussion on the subject of slavery. Every individual, whatever be his country or complexion, is entitled to freedom. The happiness of the poor man is of as much importance as that of the rich. No man has a right to reduce another to the condition of the brute. No individual can sell his liberty. The bargain is unequal, and ought to be broken. Negro slavery is contrary to the sentiments of humanity and the principles of justice."

Notwithstanding this opinion, embraced by the just and the humane of all countries, the slave trade has been a subject of discussion for more than twenty years in the British parliament; and so distinguished for talents and sophistry, have been some of its abettors, that a refutation of their false reasonings became highly useful, and even necessary. Self-interest, or an ardent desire to amass riches, has such a powerful influence over the mind, that the English and French colonists believed, or affected to believe, that the black color of the negro was a sufficient excuse, not only for making him a slave, but for treating him even worse than the brute.

In 1796, one hundred thousand Africans, most of them kidnapped, were dragged from their habitations, and transported as slaves, to cultivate the soil of British isles. The Englishman calculates the profits of their sale, or of their labour, without reflecting even for a moment, that these unfortunates have lost their freedom, their relatives, their friends and their country. All the comforts whites can bestow, can never recompence the loss of liberty.

This subject is so ably discussed by our author, that his work must powerfully contribute to hasten in all countries, the abolition of this unjust and inhuman traffic. The plan recently adopted by the government of the United States, and the late decision of the British parliament give room to hope, that at no very distant period, absolute slavery will exist no more.

The learned senator has proven by facts, that blacks not only possess talents, but also those nobler virtues which elevate man in the scale of being. The planter, by torture and hard labour, endeavouring to render the negro as tame and submissive as the brute, creates and fosters in him that revengeful disposition, which has been considered as interwoven in his frame, and peculiar to his species. Why is the slave indolent and vindictive? he has no spur to industry; the product of his labour is not his own. He is almost naked, and his aliment is scanty and unwholsome. In the British islands, three herrings per week, and a small portion of yams constitute his allotted food. By industry and good behaviour united, he cannot disarm the master of his arbitrary power. For him there is no compassion except that of his fellow slave. He is treated as a malefactor, and under the habitual influence of malevolent passions, he naturally pants for revenge. He can hardly say that virtue is his interest. He finds that honour procures him no benefit; industry no reward. At last dejected and sad, after seven or eight years of hard labour and suffering, he sinks under the meanness of his condition, and expires with the hope that his spirit will return to his much loved country.

I beg leave to inform the reader that this translation was made from the manuscript of the author; and with such haste, that an apology for its imperfections is necessary. The only merit I dare to claim, if merit it can be called, is that of not having mistaken the sense of the author.

As this production is the result of a long and deep investigation of the subject, and composed by a man of great erudition and rare virtues, well known in the religious, political and learned societies of different countries, it will doubtless be read with a high degree of interest. Another recommendation, is, that no similar work exists.

May the day soon arrive when the defenders of justice in every country, shall have a right like the eloquent Curran to exclaim, "I speak in the spirit of our laws, which makes liberty commensurate with, and inseparable from our soil; which proclaims even to the stranger and the sojourner, the moment he sets his foot upon our native earth, that the ground on which he treads is holy, and consecrated by the genius of *universal emancipation*. No matter in what language his doom may have been pronounced; no matter what complexion incompatible with freedom, an Indian or an African sun may have burnt upon him; no matter in what disastrous battle his liberty may have been cloven down; no matter with what solemnities he may have been devoted on the altar of slavery: the first moment he touches our sacred soil, the altar and the god sink together in the dust; his soul walks abroad in her own majesty; his body swells beyond the measure of his chains, that burst from around him, and he stands redeemed, regenerated and disenthralled, by the irresistible genius of *universal emancipation*."[1]

## Chapter II.

. . . The opinion of the inferiority of negroes is not new. The pretended superiority of the whites is defended by interested judges of the same colour, whose competency might be questioned, before their decision is attacked. This reminds us of the fable of the lion, who on seeing a picture representing an animal of his species struck to the ground by a man, simply observed, that lions have no painters.

Hume, who in his essay on national character, admits that there are four or five races, affirms that the white man only is improved; that no black has distinguished himself by his actions or by his knowledge,—his translator Estwick,[2] and Chatelux have repeated the same assertion.

Barre-Saint-Venant thinks that if nature has given to negroes some combinations of ideas, which raise them above other animals, she has denied them deep reflection, genius and reason.[3]

We regret to find the same prejudice in a man, whose name is not pronounced amongst us, but with the most profound esteem or merited respect—we mean Jefferson in his "Notes on Virginia."[4] To support his opinion it was not enough to undervalue the talents of two negro writers: it was necessary to establish by argument and by a multitude of facts, that if the situation and circumstances of blacks and whites be the same, the former can never rival the latter.

With regard to the difficulty arising from the circumstance of Epictetus, Terence and Phadro, being slaves (he might have added the names of Locman, Esop, Servius Tullius, &c.) he answers, by a *petitio principii*, saying, that they were whites.

Jefferson attacked by Beattie, has been since opposed by Imlay, his countryman, with considerable warmth, especially concerning Phillis Wheatley. Of her works Imlay transcribes affecting passages, but he also is deceived, in saying to Jefferson, that to cite Terence is awkward, seeing that he was not only an African but a Numidian, and a Negro.[5] It appears that Terence was a Carthaginian. Numidia corresponds to what is now named Mauritania, whose inhabitants, of Arabian descent, having invaded Spain, were the most enlightened people of the middle age.

Besides, Jefferson furnishes arms against himself in his answer to Raynal, who reproaches America for not having produced one celebrated man. When we shall have existed, says this learned American, as a nation, as long as the Greeks before they had a Homer, the Romans a Virgil, or the French a Racine, there will be room for astonishment. We may in like manner say, that when the negroes shall have existed in a state of civilization as long as the inhabitants of the United States, without having introduced such men as Franklin, Washington, Warren, Jefferson, Rittenhouse, Rush, Barlow, Rumford, West, Putnam, Mitchell, Hancock, Alston, Vanderlyn, Copely, Miller, Trumbull, Smith, Barton, Fulton, Edwards, and Ramsay, there will be reason for believing that among them there is a total absence of genius.

Alas! how did Genty write in his work, on the *influence of the discovery of America*. "How can the genius of invention spring up from the bosom of disgrace and misery—where there is no recompence in view—no hope of relief."[6]

In most parts of the regions of Africa, civilization and the arts are yet in their infancy. If it is, that the inhabitants are negroes, explain to us the cause, why whites, or copper coloured men of other countries have remained savage, and even man eaters? Why had not the wandering tribes of hunters of North America, before the arrival of Europeans, attained the rank of Shepherds? Nevertheless their capacity for improvement is not contested; it is readily acknowledged by those who traffic with them. We may consider it as a truth well ascertained that cupidity will always find pretexts to justify their slavery. . . .

Homer tells us, that when Jupiter condemns a man to slavery, he takes from him half his mind. Liberty conducts to every thing that is sublime in genius and virtue, whilst slavery extinguishes all. What sentiments of dignity or of respect, can those mortals have for themselves, who are considered as cattle, and who are often staked, by their masters, at cards or billiards, against some barrels of rice or other merchandize. What can individuals perform when degraded below the condition of brutes, overwrought, covered with rags, famished by hunger, and for the slightest fault torn by the bloody whip of an overseer? . . .

## Conclusion

Of all countries where science is cultivated, I doubt whether there be one so much a stranger to foreign literature as France. We need not therefore be surprised that no mention is made of negro authors, in our historical dictionaries, which are little else than financiering speculations. They contain a pompous list of ephemeral romances, and theatrical pieces long forgotten. . . . We do not find even the name of Suhm, the Puffendorf of the last century, nor that of many national writers who merit distinction, such as Persini, Blarn, Jehan de Brie, John de Lois, and the good Quaker Benizet, born at St. Quintin, the friend of all men, the defender of the oppressed, who, during his whole life, combatted slavery by reason, religion and example. He established, at Philadelphia, a school for young negroes, who were taught by himself. During those intervals of leisure which the functions of his employment allowed, he sought for the unfortunate to give them comfort. At his funeral, which was honoured with the solemn attendance of an immense number of people, an American colonel, who had served as engineer in the war of freedom, exclaimed, "I would rather be Benizet in his coffin, than George Washington with all his celebrity." An exaggeration which does honour to his heart. In speaking of Benizet, Yvan Raiz, a Russian traveller, said, "the Academies of Europe resound with praises decreed to illustrious men, and the name of Benizet is not found on the list. For whom then do they reserve their crowns? This Frenchman, who so powerfully excited the attention of strangers, is not even known in France." His name is not mentioned by our compilers of dictionaries; but Benjamin Rush, and a number of English and Americans, have at least repaired this omission.

Men, who have consulted only their common sense, and who have not attended to discussions relative to colonies, will perhaps scarcely believe that many have classed negroes in the rank of brutes, and have questioned their moral and intellectual capacity. This doctrine, however, as absurd as it is abominable, is insinuated in different writings. It cannot be disputed that negroes, in general, to ignorance join absurd prejudices, gross vices, and especially those which belong to slaves of all species and all colors:—Frenchmen, Englishmen and Hollanders, what would you have been, if placed in the same circumstances? I maintain, that among errors the most stupid, and crimes the most hideous, there is not one for which you ought to reproach them.

In Europe, during ages, whites, under various forms, have made slaves of whites. Can we otherwise characterize the impressment of men in England, the conduct of *lady sellers* in Holland, and that of German Princes, who vend their regiments for the service of the colonies? But, if ever negroes, bursting their chains, should come, (which Heaven forbid) on the European coast, to drag whites of both sexes from their families; to chain them and conduct them to Africa, and mark them with a hot iron; if whites stolen, sold, purchased by crimes, and placed under the guidance of merciless inspectors, were immediately compelled, by the stroke of the whip, to work in a climate injurious to their health, where at the close of each day, they would have no other consolation than that of advancing another step to the tomb—no other perspective than to suffer and to die in all the anguish of despair—if devoted to misery and ignominy, they were excluded from all the privileges of society, and declared legally incapable of judicial action, their testimony would not have been admitted even against the black class:—if, like the slaves of Batavia, these white slaves in their turn, were not permitted to wear shoes and stockings—if driven from the side walks, they were compelled to mingle with the animals in the middle of the street—if a subscription were made to have them *lashed* in a mass, and their backs, to prevent gangrene, covered with pepper and with salt— if the forfeit for killing them were but a trifling sum, as at Barbadoes and Surinam—if a reward were offered for apprehending those who escape from slavery—if those who escape were hunted by a pack of hounds, trained to carnage—if, blaspheming the Divinity, the blacks pretended, that by their origin they had permission of heaven to preach passive obedience and resignation to the whites—if greedy hireling writers published, that for this reason, just reprisals may be exercised against the *rebellious* whites, and that white slaves are happy, more happy than the peasants in the bosom of Africa:—in a word, if all the arts of cunning and calumny, all the strength and fury of avarice, all the inventions of ferocity were directed against you, by a coalition of dogs, merchants, priests, kings, soldiers and colonists, what cry of horror would resound through these countries? To express it, new epithets would be sought; a crowd of writers, and particularly of poets, would exhaust their eloquent lamentations, provided that having nothing to fear, there was something to gain. Europeans, reverse this hypothesis, and see what you are!

During the three last centuries, tygers and panthers are less terrible to Africa, than you. For three centuries, Europe, which calls herself christian and civilized, tortures without pity, and without remorse, the people of Africa and America, who she calls savage and barbarian. To procure indigo, sugar and coffee, she has introduced amongst them drunkenness, desolation, and a forgetfulness of all the sentiments of nature. Africa is not even allowed to breathe when the powers of Europe are combined to tear her to pieces. Yes, I repeat it, there is not a vice, not a species of wickedness, of which Europe is not guilty towards negroes, of which she has not shewn them the example. Avenging God! suspend thy thunder, exhaust thy compassion, in giving her time and courage to repair, if possible, these horrors and atrocities.

I have taken upon myself the task of proving, that the negroes are capable of virtues and talents; this I have established by reasoning, and still more by facts: these facts do not announce sublime discoveries; these works are not chef d'oeuvres, but they furnish irrefutable arguments against the enemies of negroes. I shall not say with Helvetius, that all individuals at their birth, have the same dispositions, and that man is the product of his own education: though this assertion, false in a general sense, is true in many respects. A union of fortunate circumstances unfolded the genius of Copernicus, Galileo, Leibnitz and Newton: perhaps others might have surpassed them, if unfortunate circumstances had not prevented the development of their mind. Each country has its Baotia,[7] but we may say, in general, that virtue and vice, wisdom and foolishness, genius and stupidity, belong to all countries, nations, heads and complexions.

To form a comparison of the people of different countries, we must place them in the same situation and circumstances; and what likeness can be found between whites, enlightened by the truths of christianity, (which leads to almost all others) enriched by the discoveries and information of all ages, and stimulated by every species of encouragement, and blacks, deprived of all those advantages, and devoted to oppression and misery? If some of them had not given a proof of their talents, there would be no reason for surprize; what astonishes us is, that so many of them have displayed genius. What would they then be, if restored to the dignity of free men, they occupied the rank which nature has assigned and tyranny refused?

Revolutions, in the political world, on account of the disasters they occasion, may be compared to the great convulsions of nature. The planters have been guilty of another imposture, in asserting that the friends of the blacks wished for a sudden and general freedom: It is not so, they were in favour of progressive measures, which, without commotion, would accomplish the desired object. Such was the opinion of the author of this work, when in a publication addressed to negroes and free mulattoes, which brought upon him so much abuse, he announced (and he still announces it) that one day, on the banks of the Antilles, the sun will shine on free men only, and its beams no longer set on irons and slaves. But the French planters have rejected with fury all the decrees by which the constituent assembly proposed to introduce gradually those salutary reforms: their pride, says Genty, has lost them the *new world*, which will never flourish but under the auspices of personal liberty. The horrible traffic which man there makes of his own species, will never lead to a durable prosperity.

Happily the colonies, and the American continent, the last asylum of liberty, are advancing to a state of things, which will be common to the Antilles, and whose course all the combined powers will be unable to arrest. Negroes, reinstated in their rights, by the irresistible force of events, will owe no gratitude towards colonists, whose affections might have been won by means equally easy and useful.

Manual labour, voluntarily undertaken, the utility of which is acknowledged in Brazil and the Bahamas, and the successful introduction of the plough in Jamaica,[8] are sufficient to shew the order of overthrowing, or modifying the colonial system. This revolution will have an accelerated motion when industry and freedom, better acquainted with their mutual relations, shall call in the aid of the steam-engine and other mechanical inventions, which abridge labour and facilitate manipulations; when an energetic and powerful nation, to whom every thing announces a high destiny, stretching her arms across the Atlantic and Pacific Oceans, shall dart her vessels from the one to the other by a shorter route, whether by cutting the isthmus of Panama, or by forming a canal of communication, as has been proposed, by the river St. John, and the lake of Nigaragua, and thus change the face of the commercial world, and of empires; who knows whether America will not avenge herself for the outrages she has suffered, and whether old Europe, reduced to the rank of a subaltern power, will not become a colony of the new world?

There is nothing useful but what is just: there is no law of nature which makes one individual dependent on another: and all these laws, which reason disavows, have no force. Every person brings with him into the world his title to freedom.[9] Social conventions have circumscribed its use, but its limits ought to be the same for all the members of a community, whatever be their origin, colour or religion. If, says *Price,* you have a right to make another man a slave, he has a right to make you a slave: and if we have no right, says *Ramsay,* to sell him, no one has a right to purchase him.[10]

May European nations at last expiate their crimes towards Africans. May Africans, raising their humiliated fronts, give spring to all their faculties, and rival the whites in talents and virtues only; avenging themselves by benefits and effusions of fraternal kindness, at last enjoy liberty and happiness. Although these advantages be but the dream of an individual, it is at least consoling to carry to the tomb the conviction, that we have done every thing in our power to procure them for others.

## NOTES [FROM THE ORIGINAL TEXT]

1. Defense of Hamilton Rowan, Esquire.
2. Considerations on the Negro cause, by Estwick.
3. Modern Colonies under the torrid zone, particularly that of Saint-Domingo, by Barre-St.-Venant, 8vo. Paris, 1802. chap. 4.
4. Notes on Virginia, by T. Jefferson, 8vo. London.
5. Topographical description of the western country of North America, by G. Imlay, London, 1793, letter 9th.

6. Topographical description of the western country of North America, by G. Imlay, p. 167.

7. Boeotia, a district of central Greece which suffered from a heavy atmosphere and whose people, though they produced such great men as Pindar and Plutarch, were proverbially dull. (—L.R.)

8. Dallas, vol. 1, p. 4. Barre St. Venant also proposes to introduce the plough into the colonies.

9. Le Gente.

10. Essay on the treatment and conversion of slaves.

## JEFFERSON VIEWS THE NEGRO IN 1809

In the following letters to Henri Gregoire and Joel Barlow, we find additional material on Jefferson's opinions of Negro ability. The letter to Barlow, with its comments on Jefferson's letter to Gregoire, has been regarded as an example of Jefferson's insincerity on this question. See, for example, Woodson and Wesley, *The Negro in Our History,* p. 140. Both letters are reprinted from *The Writings of Thomas Jefferson,* edited by H. A. Washington (Washington, D.C., 1853), Vol. V, pp. 429, 475–6.

### *To M. Gregoire, Evêque et Senateur à Paris*

WASHINGTON, February 25, 1809.

SIR,—I have received the favor of your letter of August 17th, and with it the volume you were so kind as to send me on the "Literature of Negroes." Be assured that no person living wishes more sincerely than I do, to see a complete refutation of the doubts I have myself entertained and expressed on the grade of understanding allotted to them by nature, and to find that in this respect they are on a par with ourselves. My doubts were the result of personal observation on the limited sphere of my own State, where the opportunities for the development of their genius were not favorable, and those of exercising it still less so. I expressed them therefore with great hesitation; but whatever be their degree of talent it is no measure of their rights. Because Sir Isaac Newton was superior to others in understanding, he was not therefore lord of the person or property of others. On this subject they are gaining daily in the opinions of nations, and hopeful advances are making towards their reestablishment on an equal footing with the other colors of the human family. I pray you therefore to accept my thanks for the many instances you have enabled me to observe of respectable intelligence in that race of men, which cannot fail to have effect in hastening the day of their relief; and to be assured of the sentiments of high and just esteem and consideration which I tender to yourself with all sincerity.

## To Mr. Barlow

MONTICELLO, October 8, 1809.

DEAR SIR,—It is long since I ought to have acknowledged the receipt of your most excellent oration on the 4th of July. I was doubting what you could say, equal to your own reputation, on so hackneyed a subject; but you have really risen out of it with lustre, and pointed to others a field of great expansion. A day or two after I received your letter to Bishop Gregoire, a copy of his diatribe to you came to hand from France. I had not before heard of it. He must have been eagle-eyed in quest of offence, to have discovered ground for it among the rubbish massed together in the print he animadverts on. You have done right in giving him a sugary answer. But he did not deserve it. For, notwithstanding a compliment to you now and then, he constantly returns to the identification of your sentiments with the extravagances of the Revolutionary zealots. I believe him a very good man, with imagination enough to declaim eloquently, but without judgment to decide. He wrote to me also on the doubts I had expressed five or six and twenty years ago, in the Notes of Virginia, as to the grade of understanding of the negroes, and he sent me his book on the literature of the negroes. His credulity has made him gather up every story he could find of men of color, (without distinguishing whether black, or of what degree of mixture,) however slight the mention, or light the authority on which they are quoted. The whole do not amount, in point of evidence, to what we know ourselves of Banneker. We know he had spherical trigonometry enough to make almanacs, but not without the suspicion of aid from Ellicot, who was his neighbor and friend, and never missed an opportunity of puffing him. I have a long letter from Banneker, which shows him to have had a mind of very common stature indeed. As to Bishop Gregoire, I wrote him, as you have done, a very soft answer. It was impossible for doubt to have been more tenderly or hesitatingly expressed than that was in the Notes of Virginia, and nothing was or is further from my intentions, than to enlist myself as the champion of a fixed opinion, where I have only expressed a doubt. St. Domingo will, in time, throw light on the question. . . .

# AMOS STODDARD

## THE EFFECTS OF WORK AND HEAT ON WHITES
## AND BLACKS

Amos Stoddard (1762–1813), born in Woodbury, Conn., was a soldier in the Revolutionary War, a lawyer for several years in Massachusetts, and acting governor of Louisiana. In 1812, he wrote *Sketches, Historical and Descriptive, of Louisiana,* which was published in Philadelphia that year. The following selection consists of pp. 341–3.

. . . It is difficult, even for men of moderate tempers, to suppress their indignation at one of the pretexts adduced in support of slavery, that the whites are unable to labor in some climates on account of the excessive heats! If we be allowed to consult our convenience without regard to the means; if each white is at liberty to make fifty or a hundred blacks wretched and miserable to promote his interest, and to gratify his avarice; then let us abandon our moral and political creeds, and study only to render our consciences inaccessible to remorse. The God of nature never intended, that one part of the human race should be governed by the whims and caprices of the other; nor that artificial evil should become a substitute for attainable good. The pretext is futile in every point of view. Nature has fitted men for labor in the climate where they are born and educated. A citizen of Georgia is as well qualified to labor in that state as a Yankee in New-England; the effects of heat and cold are about the same on both. Add to this, it so happens, that in the warm latitudes the lands are much more prolific, and much more easily cultivated, than in colder ones; of course less labor is required to gain subsistence. The native inhabitants of Lower Louisiana experience no inconvenience from the heats; and those employed in navigating the rivers are exposed to more fatigue than is common to any other class of our citizens. Besides, in that country, and in the Mississippi territory, hundreds of families from the middle and eastern states, have planted themselves. For several years after their arrival, their characteristic industry was evident; and they experienced no dangerous effects from the climate, except a troublesome lassitude for the two or three first years. The accumulation of wealth enabled them to purchase slaves; after which, like their neighbors, they contracted habits of indulgence. The heats, therefore, furnish no material obstruction to manual labor; and the effects of them in the southern states and territories are more than counterbalanced by the exuberant nature, and the valuable productions, of their lands. Much indeed is due to the people of slave states, to whom slavery has become familiar from long habit, and, perhaps, in their view, necessary to their prosperity, if not to their existence. Their feelings, and even prejudices, are entitled to respect; and a system of emancipation cannot be contrived with too much caution.

The fact is, that the people of the eastern states experience more inconvenience from the rigors of the seasons than those of the south. In New-England the mercury sometimes rises to one hundred degrees, and as often falls twenty degrees below *zero*. The extremes of heat are greater in New-England; but they are not of so long continuance, nor is the air so humid and unelastic as in the southern parts of the union, which are doubtless more or less prejudicial to health. Still these traits are more tolerable than the opposite extreme in New-England, where the country is covered with snow, and bound in icy chains for nearly six months in the year. Both men and beasts suffer from the rigors of winter; and the necessary subsistence for them, is obtained at a prodigious expense and labor. In Lower Louisiana the whites may labor nine months in the year, without experiencing any inconvenience from the heats; and three months labor in that quarter is productive of more real value than twelve months in New-England. Add to this, cattle and swine need no other food than what the earth spontaneously yields; and every planter has it in his power to supply himself with almost any number he pleases. In whatever light, therefore, we view the subject, the greatest advantages are attached to the southern states and territories.

The pernicious system of slavery deserves reprehension from another motive. No country can become populous where it prevails; and this truth is attested by numerous examples. We need cast our eyes only on the West-India Islands, and on the southern states of the union. No part of the country possesses a more happy climate, or a better soil, than the great state of Virginia;

yet her white population is comparatively small. Kentucky is a slave state; and if her population be considerable, it must be attributed to accidental causes, which are not difficult to explain. The state of Ohio is now in its infancy: slavery is excluded from her bosom; and this very circumstance will induce a rapid population, augment her strength and resources, and soon enable her to rise superior to her neighbor.

## GEORGE BOURNE

### RELIGION AND RACE

A Presbyterian and Dutch Reformed Clergyman, George Bourne (1780–1845) was born in England and attended the Homerton Seminary in London. Migrating to the United States, he became pastor of a Presbyterian church in Virginia in 1814. He was one of the first advocates in this country of immediate emancipation of the slave. His book, *The Book and Slavery Irreconcilable, with Animadversions Upon Dr. Smith's Philosophy,* was published in Philadelphia in 1816. In 1833 he participated in the convention in Philadelphia which formed the American Anti-Slavery Society. In succeeding years, he published other books, most of which dealt with the evils of slavery. The following selection is from pp. 95–98 of *The Book and Slavery Irreconcilable.* The notes are in the original.

Revealed religion is predicated upon the natural equality, the individual responsibility, the reciprocal duties of the human family, and the paramount claims of the most high God to the services, and the obedience of all his creatures. Slavery does not merely diminish the energy, and mitigate the obligation of the sacred scriptures, but it totally nullifies all the fundamental principles of Christianity.

Paul assured the Areopagites, that *God made of one flesh, all nations of men.*[1] The dissimilarity of the rational species, upon the pretext of colour, is consequently a chimera; and if the members of the various countries of the globe are derived from a different origin, they cannot be bound by the same laws as ourselves. This aggravates the iniquity of Slave-holding to an inconceivable degree, because it pre-supposes the right to grasp every reasonable creature who bears not our own external conformation, or whose features differ: but the same principles in re-action would justify every country in enslaving its neighbours, and every individual, who could effect it, in stealing his inferior or dependent. . . .

Slavery is the legitimate offspring, and the frequent cause of a rejection of the BOOK. Christian Instructors may justly be alarmed; they cannot be *silent* upon *man-stealing*, much less excuse, defend, or engage in it, without a virtual admission that divine revelation is not our sole infallible directory.[2]

Men calumniate the coloured people, that they may claim a right to enslave them; and for justification of their culpable conduct. The accusers are both judges and executioners. . . .

Slavery extinguishes all the rights of man: from his equal rank in creation, the slave is ignominiously debased to a *brute;* and the immunities which naturally inhere to him, are all stolen. The Thief becomes a despot, and the kidnapped immortal is buried in terrestrial vassalage, without hope and without end. His life is at the disposal of a barbarian, who may render it as wretched as he will uncontrouled, or shorten its duration by every refinement of torture: of his freedom he is altogether divested: and his labour, his comforts, his children, and his all, are the *property* of the most guilty violator of the eighth commandment. What peculiarly daring effrontery do men display, when they assume the garb of religion, and deny its most obvious principles, its most luminous prescriptions, and its most tremendous denunciations. Can he be a Christian who abrogates the *BOOK?* . . .

## Notes [from the original text]

1. Acts 17. 24–26.
2. "If the plague had rewards and pensions to bestow, it would find apologists; but in defending the poor and the oppressed, as we must struggle against power, riches and frenzy, we may expect nothing but calumny, injuries and persecutions." *Frapolosarpi.* [Father Paul Sarpi, 1552–1623, Venetian priest and scientist.]

# JOHN QUINCY ADAMS

## On Negro Rights

The following selections from the diary of John Quincy Adams (1767–1848), who was at the time a Representative in Congress from Massachusetts, throw light upon his remarkable humanitarian views and his devotion to equal treatment for the Negro. In contrast are the typically slaveholder views of John C. Calhoun and the conservative opinions of Judge Henry Baldwin of Pennsylvania. These selections from the year 1820 consist of Vol. IV, pp. 530–531; Vol. V, pp. 10–12, 208–211, *Memoirs of John Quincy Adams, Comprising Portions of His Diary from 1795 to 1848,* edited by Charles Frances Adams (Philadelphia, 1875).

[February 24, 1820.] I had some conversation with Calhoun on the slave question pending in Congress. He said he did not think it would produce a dissolution of the Union, but, if it should, the South would be from necessity compelled to form an alliance, offensive and defensive, with Great Britain.

I said that would be returning to the colonial state.

He said, yes, pretty much, but it would be forced upon them. I asked him whether he thought, if by the effect of this alliance, offensive and defensive, the population of the North should be cut off from its natural outlet upon the ocean, it would fall back upon its rocks bound hand and foot, to starve, or whether it would not retain its powers of locomotion to move southward by land. Then, he said, they would find it necessary to make their communities all military. I pressed the conversation no further; but if the dissolution of the Union should result from the slave question, it is as obvious as anything that can be foreseen of futurity, that it must shortly afterwards be followed by the universal emancipation of the slaves. A more remote but perhaps not less certain consequence would be the extirpation of the African race on this continent, by the gradually bleaching process of intermixture, where the white portion is already so predominant, and by the destructive progress of emancipation, which, like all great religious and political reformations, is terrible in its means, though happy and glorious in its end. Slavery is the great and foul stain upon the North American Union, and it is a contemplation worthy of the most exalted soul whether its total abolition is or is not practicable: if practicable, by what means it may be effected, and if a choice of means be within the scope of the object, what means would accomplish it at the smallest cost of human sufferance. A dissolution, at least temporary, of the Union, as now constituted, would be certainly necessary, and the dissolution must be upon a point involving the question of slavery, and no other. The Union might then be reorganized on the fundamental principle of emancipation. This object is vast in its compass, awful in its prospects, sublime and beautiful in its issue. A life devoted to it would be nobly spent or sacrificed. This conversation with Calhoun led me into a momentous train of reflection. It also engaged me so much that I detained him at his office, insensibly to myself, till near five o'clock, an hour at least later than his dining-time.

March 3, 1820 . . . I walked home with Calhoun, who said that the principles which I had avowed were just and noble; but that in the Southern country, whenever they were mentioned, they were always understood as applying only to white men. Domestic labor was confined to the blacks, and such was the prejudice, that if he, who was the most popular man in his district, were to keep a white servant in his house, his character and reputation would be irretrievably ruined.

I said that this confounding of the ideas of servitude and labor was one of the bad effects of slavery; but he thought it attended with many excellent consequences. It did not apply to all kinds of labor—not, for example, to farming. He himself had often held the plough; so had his father. Manufacturing and mechanical labor was not degrading. It was only manual labor—the proper work of slaves. No white person could descend to that. And it was the best guarantee to equality among the whites. It produced an unvarying level among them. It not only did not excite, but did not even admit of inequalities, by which one white man could domineer over another.

I told Calhoun I could not see things in the same light. It is, in truth, all perverted sentiment—mistaking labor for slavery, and dominion for freedom. The discussion of this Missouri question has betrayed the secret of their souls. In the abstract they admit that slavery is an evil, they disclaim all participation in the introduction of it, and cast it all upon the shoulders of our old Grandam Britain. But when probed to the quick upon it, they show at the bottom of their souls pride and vainglory in their condition of masterdom. They fancy themselves more generous and noble-hearted than the plain freemen who labor for subsistence. They look down upon the simplicity of a Yankee's manners, because he has no habits of overbearing like theirs and cannot treat negroes like dogs. It is among the evils of slavery that it taints the very sources of moral principle. It establishes false estimates of virtue and vice; for what can be more false and heartless than this doctrine which makes the first and holiest rights of humanity to depend upon the color of the skin? It perverts human reason, and reduces man endowed with logical powers to maintain that slavery is sanctioned by the Christian religion, that slaves are happy and contented in their condition, that between master and slave there are ties of mutual attachment and affection, that the virtues of the master are refined and exalted by the degradation of the slave; while at the same time they vent execrations upon the slave-trade, curse Britain for having given them slaves, burn at the stake negroes convicted of crimes for the terror of the example, and writhe in agonies of fear at the very mention of human rights as applicable to men of color. The impression produced upon my mind by the progress of this discussion is, that the bargain between freedom and slavery contained in the Constitution of the United States is morally and politically vicious, inconsistent with the principles upon which alone our Revolution can be justified; cruel and oppressive, by riveting the chains of slavery, by pledging the faith of freedom to maintain and perpetuate the tyranny of the master; and grossly unequal and impolitic, by admitting that slaves are at once enemies to be kept in subjection, property to be secured or restored to their owners, and persons not to be represented themselves, but for whom their masters are privileged with nearly a double share of representation. The consequence has been that this slave representation has governed the Union. Benjamin portioned above his brethren has ravined as a wolf. In the morning he has devoured the prey, and at night he has divided the spoil. It would be no difficult matter to prove, by reviewing the history of the Union under this Constitution, that almost everything which has contributed to the honor and welfare of the nation has been accomplished in despite of them or forced upon them, and that everything unpropitious and dishonorable, including the blunders and follies of their adversaries, may be traced to them. I have favored this Missouri compromise, believing it to be all that could be effected under the present Constitution, and from extreme unwillingness to put the Union at hazard. But perhaps it would have been a wiser as well as a bolder course to have persisted in the restriction upon Missouri, till it should have terminated in a convention of the States to revise and amend the Constitution. This would have produced a new Union of thirteen or fourteen States unpolluted with slavery, with a great and glorious object to effect, namely, that of rallying to their standard the other States by the universal emancipation of their slaves. If the Union must be dissolved, slavery is precisely the question upon which it ought to break. For the present, however, this contest is laid asleep.

[November 29, 1820.] I returned Mr. Baldwin's[1] visit, and had a long conversation with him on the subject of the Missouri question of the present session, which he agreed was a totally different question from that of the last. He said, however, that those who now objected to the admission of Missouri, on the ground of the exceptionable article in her Constitution, connected the restriction question of the last session with it, and wished to reopen the whole controversy.

I told him I believed there would be a very small portion of the House for that, and I thought it would be quite unjustifiable; but the article in the Missouri Constitution was directly repugnant to the rights reserved to every citizen of the Union in the Constitution of the United States. Its purport went to disfranchise all the people of color who were citizens of the free States. The Legislatures of those States were bound in duty to protect the rights of their own citizens; and if Congress, by the admission of Missouri with that clause in her Constitution, should sanction this outrage upon those rights, the States, a portion of whose citizens should be thus cast out from the pale of the Union, would be bound to vindicate them by retaliation. And if I were a member of the Legislature of one of those States, I would move for a declaratory act, that so long as the article in the Constitution of Missouri depriving the colored citizens of the State, say of Massachusetts, of their rights as citizens of the United States within the State of Missouri, should subsist, so long the white citizens of the State of Missouri should be held as aliens within the Commonwealth of Massachusetts, not entitled to claim or enjoy within the same any right or privilege of a citizen of the United States. And I would go further, and declare that Congress having, by their sanction of the Missouri Constitution, by admitting that State into the Union without excepting against that article which disfranchised a portion of the citizens of Massachusetts, had violated the Constitution of the United States; wherefore, until that portion of the citizens of Massachusetts whose rights are violated by the article in the Missouri Constitution should be redintegrated in the full enjoyment and possession of those rights, no clause or article of the Constitution of the United States should, within the Commonwealth of Massachusetts, be so construed as to authorize any person whomsoever to claim the property or possession of a human being as a slave. And I would prohibit by law the delivery of any fugitive slave upon the claim of his master. All which I would do, not to violate, but to redeem from violation, the Constitution of the United States. It was indeed to be expected that such laws would again be met by retaliatory laws of Missouri and the other slave-holding States, and the consequence would be the dissolution "de facto" of the Union, but that dissolution would have commenced by the article in the Missouri Constitution. That article was in itself a dissolution of the Union. If acquiesced in, it would change the terms of the federal compact—change its terms by robbing thousands of citizens of their rights. And what citizens? The poor, the unfortunate, the helpless. Already cursed by the mere color of their skin, already doomed by their complexion to drudge in the lowest offices of society, excluded by their color from all the refined enjoyments of life accessible to others, excluded from the benefits of a liberal education, from the bed, from the table, and from all the social comforts of domestic life, this barbarous article deprives them of the little remnant of right yet left them—their rights as citizens and as men. Weak and defenceless as they are, so much the more sacred is the obligation of the Legislature of the States to which they belong to defend their lawful rights; and I would defend them should the dissolution of the Union be the consequence. For it would not be the defence, it would be the violation of their rights, to which all the consequences would be imputable; and if the dissolution of the Union must come, let it come from no other cause but this. If slavery be the destined sword in the hand of the destroying angel which is to sever the ties of this Union, the same sword will cut in sunder the bonds of slavery itself. A dissolution of the Union for the cause of slavery would be followed by a servile war in the slave-holding States, combined with a war between the two severed portions of the Union. It seems to me that its result must be the extirpation of slavery from this whole continent; and, calamitous and desolating as this course of events in its progress must be, so glorious would be its final issue, that, as God shall judge me, I dare not say that it is not to be desired.

Baldwin said that he entertained different opinions from mine of this class of our population; that he thought them far more mischievous than useful; that of all the petty crimes committed in the part of the country where he resided, nine-tenths were by free people of color; that he believed it to be the same throughout the country, though there might be an exception in the Eastern States; that all the States made laws for the exclusion of paupers and vagabonds, and persons whose residence within the State would become a nuisance; but that, for his part, he was willing to admit Missouri in any form in which it had been proposed, with the condition or without it.

## NOTE

1. Judge Henry Baldwin of Pennsylvania; at the time, a Representative in Congress; appointed an Associate Justice of the Supreme Court by President Jackson in 1830.

## DANIEL RAYMOND

### RACE, SLAVERY AND FERTILITY

Born in New Haven, Connecticut, Daniel Raymond (1786–1849) was admitted to the bar in Baltimore in 1814 and lived in Cincinnati after 1840. Though a lawyer, he was best known for his original writings on political economy. His most widely read works are *Thoughts on Political Economy*, which first appeared in 1820, with later editions; *Elements of Constitutional Law*, published in 1840; and *The Missouri Question*, a large pamphlet printed in Baltimore in 1819. In the latter, he set forth a plan for the elimination of slavery which he based upon statistics showing the differential fertility rates of free and enslaved Negroes and a comparison of these with the fertility rates of whites. His pamphlet is also noteworthy as one of the earliest and most devastating critiques of Negro colonization. The selections which follow are from pp. 3–9, 18–23, 25–26, 27–29, of *The Missouri Question*.

## The Missouri Question

There is no subject so interesting and important to the real lovers of their country, as that of slavery, because there is none which involves the happiness, prosperity and glory of our country in so great a degree—none attended with so many difficulties in remedying. It is admitted by all parties, slave-holders or not, that slavery is the greatest curse our country is afflicted with—it is a foul stain upon our national escutcheon—A canker which is corroding the moral and political vitals of our country. There is but one voice on this subject, and that is the voice of condemnation, as an enormous, and an alarming evil.

But although there is such an union of sentiment, as to the existence and nature of the evil, there is a vast diversity of opinion as to the remedy to be applied, for its correction or its cure.

The true policy of every wise legislator is to consider his country immortal, and to legislate for it as if it were to exist forever; but unfortunately, most legislators act as though they thought their country as short lived as themselves, and instead of adopting a policy, which is to look prospectively to future generations and centuries; they adopt a policy which looks only to themselves and to the present race. Unless the fruits of a policy are to be gathered by themselves, they think it unworthy of their attention. This is eminently the case in the Southern States, in regard to their policy towards their slaves. They reprobate slavery as the eldest and greatest curse, and *at the same time* adopt measures *calculated* to increase and perpetuate it to the latest generations. They affect to despise the traitor, but they *love* the treason. This may appear to be a bold charge, but I trust, I shall be able to make it good; which, if I do not, I shall be very ready to retract.

A writer in the Federal Gazette of the 23d Nov. under the signature of Phocion, says, "since the establishment of our independence, every state has engaged in the humane work of freeing our country from this curse, or where this could not be done with safety to the state or advantage to the slaves, in ameliorating their condition." This writer speaks the general sentiment of the southern public on this subject; but I trust I shall show before I conclude, that the southern states, Maryland excepted, not only have not done any thing towards freeing our country from this curse; but that they have on the contrary done and are doing all in their power, both to magnify the *curse* beyond all calculation, and to perpetuate it to the latest ages. That under the policy they are now pursuing, the evil will continue to increase in a geometrical ratio, and that there can be no hope of its ever being ameliorated—nay farther, that *the policy* they are now pursuing, and *the policy* they wish the United States to adopt, will not only magnify and perpetuate the evil in the present slave holding states, but will extend it in all its horrors over a vast and boundless tract of country. I allude to the policy of permitting the new states west of the Mississippi, to become slave holding states. And here I will observe, that if the admission of slaves into the western world, would diminish the evil in the old slave states, I would say, *let them be admitted.* But I believe, I shall be able to prove upon the soundest principles of political economy, that the admission of slaves into those western states, so far from diminishing the evil in the old states, will have directly the contrary effect—that it will be the very means of preventing the southern states from ever ridding themselves of that *curse*. I shall also endeavour to free myself from the charge which Phocion brings against the eastern writers and eastern presses, of "upbraiding their neighbours, when they can suggest no remedy for the evil for which they upbraid them."

The idea, however, that this curse is to be increased and perpetuated through all succeeding generations, is very appalling, and our southern politicians either refrain from looking at so forbidding a picture, or they cast about for some remedy, which they flatter themselves, may mitigate its horrors. I shall attempt to show that they have not yet devised any plan that can in the smallest perceptible degree, effect their purpose, and that their policy is in fact increasing and perpetuating the evil upon their posterity. Slavery is a poisonous plant of vigorous and rapid growth—plant but a scion in any soil, and it will soon spread forth its pestiferous branches, overshadowing, choaking and finally destroying every thing within the sphere of its influence.

The scheme most relied on at present for eradicating the curse of slavery from our soil, is the Colonization Society, and if we will listen without examination of the premises, to the fair and flattering promises and anticipations of some of its zealous, philanthropic and highly praiseworthy members, we shall be led to believe, that it will one day accomplish the object of its founders. But let us take heed that we do not deceive ourselves, and in so doing, be induced to rely upon a fallacious hope; to the neglect of more efficient means. Let it not be supposed that I am unfriendly to the Colonization Society. Such is not the fact—I am a member of that Society—I applaud the motives of its founders —and I believe it may be the means of doing much good, and so believing, I am ready to lend them all the assistance in my power.

But I say it is wholly and totally inadequate to the accomplishment of its professed object; and must and would in the nature of things be so; if it should receive the united support of the whole nation. It is not possible in the nature of things, to colonize the whole, or any considerable portion of the black population of this country; and of course no sensible impression can be made upon the evil of slavery. I am ready to grant, and I have no doubt the fact is so, that a flourishing colony may be established in Africa, but I deny that it is possible for us to send to that colony a twentieth part of the annual increase of the black population of this country. That being the fact, and as population increases in a geometrical ratio, it is utterly impossible by that means, to make any perceptible diminution of the number of blacks in our country. On the contrary, the curse of slavery will continue to increase and that in a geometrical ratio too, in spite of the utmost efforts of the Society. But suppose it were possible for the Society to send a greater number annually to this colony, than the annual increase of the blacks by procreation; a supposition necessary in order to make any diminution of the present number of our blacks, would it be possible for the colony to receive them into its bosom? Suppose the colony were now established, and in as flourishing a condition as could be expected by its most sanguine promoters? and suppose it contained 10,000 inhabitants. How many emigrants would it be able to receive in one year? Could it receive ten thousand? Surely not—that number could neither find employment nor support— they would endanger and probably overturn the government. I should suppose one or two thousand at most, would be as many as it could with safety receive. How many could one of our western territories (containing 10,000 inhabitants) receive in one year? Could it receive any indefinite number? Must not that number bear a proportion to the numbers already there, in order to find support, protection, employment, and be subject to the existing government? And can it be supposed a colony in Africa will enjoy more advantages, or be on a more favorable footing, than a colony in our own country, and of our own free, enlightened and industrious citizens. Suppose half a million of emigrants, a twentieth part of our population were to land in our country, in one year, could we find them support and employment, and would they not endanger our government?

I say then that emigrants to a colony, must bear a proportion, and that a small one, to the existing numbers in the colony, and of course that if the colony was now established under the most favorable circumstances, it would be utterly impossible for it to receive a twentieth part of the annual increase of our black population.

The present annual increase of the black population by procreation is at least 40,000; and does any man believe that it would be in the power of the whole United States, in one hundred years to establish a colony in Africa, capable of receiving 40,000 emigrants? It will be recollected also, that population increases in a geometrical ratio, and that our black population doubles at a moderate calculation at least three times in a century. Let any one then, who is apt at arithmetic, tell what will be the annual increase of our black population, a century hence, and then say whether he thinks it will be in the power of any Society, however powerful, to colonize a number equal to the then annual increase; a thing that must be done in order to keep down the black population to the number it shall then be. The idea then that the Colonization Society, can under any circumstances, have any perceptible effect in eradicating slaves from our soil, is utterly chimerical. It follows also, that we and our posterity are to be afflicted with the curse, to the latest ages, unless some other remedy is provided. And can the idea be for a moment endured, that for countless ages this poisonous plant is to infest our soil, blasting as with mildew, the beautiful tree of liberty? Can we endure the thought that millions and millions of our fellow creatures for ages to come shall be born to drag out wretched lives of slavery! Shall we leave our posterity to grapple with this monster of iniquity, and possibly if not probably be finally overcome in the struggle? Or shall we not rather if it be possible, labour to eradicate it ourselves, before it takes deeper root in our soil and before its present formidable trunk shall become tenfold more formidable? It is an axiom as true as the first problem in Euclid, that if left to itself it will every year become more inveterate and more formidable. The policy that the southern states have for twenty years pursued and are now pursuing, will as surely and rapidly increase the curse as that the human species themselves will increase and multiply.

But I am asked what remedy can we adopt for the evil? Is there any means by which we can rid ourselves of this curse, without doing violence to the poor slaves, and without violating the laws of morality and religion, and without endangering our own safety? I do humbly trust there are such means—I do verily believe, we can rid ourselves of this curse, without doing violence or injustice to any man; without offending against the laws of religion or morality, and without endangering our own safety; and these means I will take the liberty of stating. Previous, however, to doing this, I must crave the patience of the reader, while I state a few statistical facts and calculations, as premises from which my conclusions are to be drawn—I will also observe that the extirpation of slavery from our country, is, and necessarily must be a work of time. A century to an individual is a long time; but to a nation, a short one, and a policy which looks prospectively a century and no more, may be a short sighted policy for a young, a rising, and rapidly growing nation in numbers, wealth, power and glory. Our policy in regard to the black population of our country, must not be a policy of years, but of centuries.

The first proposition which I will lay down, is *That in our country, a free black population does not increase by procreation so fast by nearly 50 per cent. in twenty years, as a white population in a non slave holding state.*

2. *That a free black population does not increase so fast by procreation as a slave population.*

3. *That the white population in a slave state, does not increase so fast by at least 30 or 40 per cent. in twenty years, as the same population does in a state where there are none, or few slaves.*

4. *That a slave population increases by procreation, faster than the white population in a slave state.*

And 5. (As a corollary from the foregoing propositions) *that in proportion as you restrain the increase of a slave population, you promote the increase of the white population;* and then the question for politicians to decide, arises, to wit: Whether that policy is best which promotes the increase of a free white population, by restraining the increase of a slave population, or that which promotes the increase of a slave population, by restraining the increase of a free white population. And can there be any doubt upon this question? Does that man live and breathe the air of this free country, who would dare to say, that a legislature ought to hesitate for a moment, in adopting that policy which would promote the increase of a white population, rather than of a black slave population? If there be such a man, he is a disgrace to his species. . . .

The fact, then, incontestibly is, that the difference between the increase of a white population and a free black population in our country, is much greater than appears by the above estimate, that is, that a white population will more than double twice, while a free black population is doubling once.

It is unnecessary to account for this curious fact,—it is enough for my purpose to show that it is a fact; but there is no difficulty in accounting for it upon philosophical principles. The blacks do not stand upon an equal footing with the whites in a civil point of view.—They are more degraded—they have not the same motives for exertion and of course they are not so industrious, enterprising, and provident as the whites, and do not marry and raise so many children. It certainly is not a new discovery in the science of population, that the lowest classes of society do not raise so many children as the middle classes. . . .

From all these estimates, it is clear, that the white population in a slave state, does not increase so fast as the white population in a non slave holding state, nor is this difference a small one. It is at a moderate calculation a difference of from 40 to 60 per cent. in 20 years. The difference is 86 per cent. against Maryland, 74 against Virginia, 68 against North Carolina, and 35 per cent. against South Carolina. This is certainly a matter of no trifling consideration. The great end of government in our country, is to promote the increase of our species, especially the free portion of them; and any cause, whatever it be, that prevents their increase, ought to be removed. There can be no doubt that slavery is the primary cause of the white population in the southern states, not increasing so fast as in the northern. I admit there may, and doubtless are at present, other immediate causes to be found in the manners, customs and habits of the people; but this difference in the manners, customs and habits of the people, is traceable to slavery as the primary cause. If the southern people are less industrious, less enterprising, less provident, it is because they are and have been cursed with slavery. It is an old maxim, that idleness is the parent of vice and dissipation, but there is nothing which so much conduces to idleness in a white popula-

tion as slavery.—May it not then be said that slavery is a poisonous plant which takes deep root in any soil, and shoots forth its
vigorous branches in all directions, blasting, withering, and
ultimately destroying every goodly plant. Is it not in fact that
*bohun upas* which has been supposed to exist only in the
imagination of fanciful travellers?

The reasons why the white population does not increase so fast
in a slave state, as in a state where there are no slaves, are neither
doubtful nor mysterious. They are apparent to the most superficial observer.

It is a self-evident axiom, that population or the increase of
population must be limited to the means of subsistence. The
human species cannot increase where there is nothing to subsist
on. It is an established fact, that the human species, where the
means of subsistence are abundant, are capable of doubling their
numbers every fifteen years at least, some say less. We have seen
already that they doubled in a portion of our country, by natural
increase, in about twenty years. If they are capable of doubling
in twenty years, or in any given time, then they increase in a
geometrical ratio. In other words, if one million will increase to
two millions in twenty years, then upon the same principle that
two will, provided the means of subsistence are equally abundant,
increase to four in forty years, that four to eight in eighty years,
that eight to sixteen millions in a century, and so on to thirty-
two millions in twenty years more. It is however manifest that
the earth cannot be made to produce an equal increase of the
means of subsistence. Hence it follows that the increase of the
human species is by the laws of God (for the laws of nature are
God's laws,) restrained or limited to the power of the earth to
yield them subsistence. If all the product of the earth be consumed by slaves, a white population cannot subsist; and whatever portion of the product of the earth be consumed by slaves,
in the same proportion will the means of subsistence be taken
from a white population, and in the same proportion will the
increase of the white population be limited or restrained. In
other words, every slave in the world, especially in our country
occupies the place of a free man. Nay he does much more than
this, for I will show hereafter that no country can in the nature

of things contain or support so many human beings where slavery exists, as it would do if there was no slavery.

In all countries the great mass of the population is poor and obliged to depend upon manual labour for the subsistence of themselves and families. This is as much the case in the slave states, as in those where there are no slaves. A large portion of the white population in the southern states, are neither slave owners nor land owners, and are as much dependant on the labor of their lands for subsistence as the eastern people. But where slavery abounds they have no market for their labour—they cannot obtain employment. How then are they to raise families? Besides, it is in slave states a disgrace for white people to labour—the labourer is reduced to the level of slaves. No man will therefore labour, who can avoid it. Hence the middling classes of society, what are properly called the yeomanry of the country, and by the way the most valuable part of every community, not having property enough to raise families without their own manual labour, prefer living single, (and as they call it respectably) to marrying and raising families, which they would be obliged to disgrace by manual labour. That this is universally the case I do not pretend; that it is very generally so cannot be denied.

I have said that no country can support as many human beings where slavery exists, as it would do if there was no slavery. We have already seen that population is always restrained and kept down to the means of subsistence. The means of subsistence depends upon the industry of man—the earth yielding more or less abundantly, in proportion to the labour bestowed upon it. It is ordained of God that it shall be so. There certainly needs no argument to prove that slaves are less industrious, and less faithful in their labours, than a free white population who labour for their own benefit, and reap that which they sow, universal experience proves that this is the case. It follows then that slaves will never produce the means of subsistence so abundantly as free whites, and of course so many of them cannot subsist in the same country.

The most important proposition still remains to be examined, which is, *that a slave population increases faster than the white population in a slave state.* A most momentous and alarming proposition this! one which portends more mischief, misery, insurrection, bloodshed and desolation to our country and our race, than any the imagination can conceive, provided the present policy of the southern states in regard to their slaves is still pursued. Who can tell what is to be the issue of this, and where it is to end? If the slave population increase faster than the white, it will ere long be the most numerous, and not only the most numerous, but vastly the most numerous. And shall ten men be in subjection to one, or will a thousand quietly remain in bondage to an hundred? Such things cannot be—it was not intended by Him who made the black man as well as the white, that such things should be. We may put far off the evil day, but it will surely come upon us or our posterity.—The day of desolation and wrath is sure to overtake us, unless we avert it by a timely reformation of our policy. But before we frighten ourselves with this picture, let us see whether it be a true representation. . . .

That the slave population does increase faster than the white in the slave states is an undoubted fact, nor is there any difficulty in accounting for it. A population increases always faster or slower in proportion to the means of subsistence. If the means of subsistence are sufficiently abundant, it will double in fifteen, twenty, fifty or an hundred years in proportion to that abundance. In many of the countries of Europe, the population does not double in less than a century, and in some others the increase is still slower. This certainly is not owing to any deficiency in the power of procreation, nor to wars or pestilence, but to a want of the means of subsistence. If the population of Great Britain were to increase as fast as the population of some of our states, the island could not contain them a century hence if they stood side by side.

The reason then why a slave population increases faster than the white in a slave state, is because their means of subsistence are more abundant. The slaves usually belong to men of wealth, who have the means of supplying them with food, and whose interest it is that the slaves should multiply as fast as possible, at least it is their interest so long as there is a demand for slaves, and the increase of the slaves will always be proportionate to the demand. The greater and more extensive the market, therefore the faster they will increase. They are raised as an article of traffic, the same as cattle and horses, and the market regulates the increase of the one in the same manner that it does the other. If the market would justify it, we should see master promoting the increase of their slaves, treating their breeding slaves with the same care, and nursing their offspring with the same attention and tenderness, that they now bestow upon their breeding mares and their foals. When this comes to be the case we shall find that the slave population will double at least every fifteen or twenty years, and there is nothing wanting to make this the case but an extensive demand and a high market. . . .

The question is not, as a superficial observer might at first view suppose, whether the increase of the human species ought to be restrained in an absolute sense, but whether the increase of one portion of them, ought to be restrained, in order to promote the increase of another. In other words, whether the best policy is to raise a million of free white men, or a million of slaves, or rather, whether the best policy is to raise a million of free men, or half a million of slaves, for we have already seen, that the earth will not support so many slaves as free men. Both we cannot raise, for the earth cannot support both. The earth cannot support an unlimited number.—There must be a restraint placed directly or indirectly somewhere. On whom shall it be placed? that is the question. And does this question admit of a doubt? In a political, a moral, an intellectual, and a religious point of view, is not a white population better than a black one?

But this is not the only light in which this question ought to be viewed. If the present policy of increasing, extending, and perpetuating slavery, is persisted in, what are to be, sooner or later, the consequences to posterity, to our country, to the glory of our young and rising empire? These consequences are portentous and terrifying. It is ordained of God, (however sceptical some may be on this subject,) that the iniquities of men shall punish themselves; and if some measures are not taken to remedy the iniquity of slavery,—if it be permitted to descend to posterity with accumulated force, there will, as surely, sooner or later, be a day of retribution and wrath, as there is a God in Heaven. This may not happen in one century, or perhaps in two, but happen it will. And what is a century in the probable period allotted to a nation's existence? Am I asked how I propose to remedy this enormous evil, and avert these threatening calamities? By adopting directly the opposite policy from that at present pursued by all the slave states, Maryland excepted.—By passing laws authorising masters to manumit their slaves, and by promoting their manumission as fast as possible. In Maryland, masters have been permitted to manumit their slaves since 1796, and at this day, nearly one third of the black population of the state, are free, and in less than fifty years, the slaves will be a very small portion of the black population, and the whole, will bear a much smaller proportion to the white population than it now does.— The white population will increase in a greater, and the black, in a smaller ratio, until this eldest curse shall be eradicated. For we have already seen that a white population will increase faster than a black one. In all the other slave states, the manumission of slaves, is, I believe, prohibited by law,—at any rate, such is the case in most of them. In Virginia, there is a manumission law, qualified with a proviso, that the manumitted leave the state, which, in effect, amounts to an absolute prohibition, as to all practical effects. It has already, I think, been satisfactorily shown, that this policy is calculated not only to perpetuate the evil to all eternity, but to increase its magnitude in each succeeding generation. . . .

But we are told, by those who oppose the manumission of slaves, that when manumitted they become a nuisance to society, and that their condition is worse, when free, than when slaves. And suppose we admit this: does it at all affect the great points of the case? If free negroes are a nuisance to society, are not slaves, and the consequences of slavery, an infinitely greater nuisance? What are the mischiefs of a parcel of idle, vagabond, pilfering blacks, admitting them all to be such, in comparison to the incalculable mischiefs of slavery? The mischiefs of one, are only for a generation or two at most, for the idle, vagabond blacks do not raise families, or comparatively none.—If they are industrious, provident, and raise families, then they are good citizens, and teach their children to become such. The mischiefs of the other are interminable. In short, the character of manumitted slaves, materially changes in the course of one or two generations. The industrious thrive and increase,—their off-spring, accustomed to liberty, acquire the habits of the whites, and make equally as good citizens, that is, the laboring class.— Such is the fact in Maryland,—experience proves, that such will be the fact every where. The worthless come to nought.

And as to the slaves being in a worse condition after manumission than before, it is all idle cant, prompted by the self-interest of those who are unwilling to emancipate their slaves, because of that self-interest. What would you say of a father, who should keep an idle, dissolute son in perpetual bondage, because if permitted to have his liberty, he would prejudice himself? You would say he was a brutal tyrant, because he undertook to exercise authority where he had no right. The son is a free agent as well as the father, and has the same right to exercise his volition, and to judge of his own conduct, being himself solely accountable for his actions. The same reasoning applies with still stronger force in the case of slaves, especially when we consider the pernicious consequences of the opposite doctrine. It has been a favorite dogma with some politicians, as well as with a certain denomination of Christians, that we are justified in doing evil, that good may come, and such, in effect, is the doctrine of those who hold that we ought not to manumit our slaves, lest an injury should be done them instead of a benefit. This abominable doctrine, however, is, thank God, very nearly exploded from modern political, as well as modern religious creeds. There is no safer rule, in all the relations of life, than to do our own duty, and leave the result to God.—This is the rule I would have adopted in regard to our slaves.

But I may, perhaps, be asked, whether I would have the slaves forcibly manumitted by law? By no means. Let masters be permitted to manumit their slaves, or not, as seemeth to them good.—This is all that is required. Such a law would promote their manumission fast enough for the present. It would also cause the manumission to be gradual, so that no great and sudden change would be produced in Society. This would open a vein which would let out the polluted blood of slavery from the body politic, silently, constantly, and gradually, without endangering its health. The manumitted slaves would gradually acquire the habits of free men, and become good citizens, or dwindle to nothing. After a large portion of this poisonous blood had thus escaped, its final extinction might be forced by a law such as has been passed by most of the eastern states, limiting a period, after which, all that were born should be free at a certain age. This is not merely a plausible theory, but it is founded on fact and experience. . . .

# JAMES MADISON

## ON BLACKS, SLAVERY AND EMANCIPATION

The fourth President of the United States, Madison retired from the presidency in 1817 and lived the remainder of his life on his estate, at Montpellier (now Montpelier), Virginia. The following letter was written in response to one from Robert J. Evans, who had suggested that the time had arrived for adopting a plan of slavery emancipation. Evans wrote newspaper articles under the name of Benjamin Rush. He was not, of course, the real Benjamin Rush, who had died in 1813.

## To Robert J. Evans

MONTPELLIER, June 15, 1819

SIR,—I have rec[eive]d your letter of the 3ᵈ instant, requesting such hints as may have occurred to me on the subject of an eventual extinguishment of slavery in the U.S.

Not doubting the purity of your views, and relying on the discretion by which they will be regulated, I cannot refuse such a compliance as will at least manifest my respect for the object of your undertaking.

A general emancipation of slaves ought to be 1. gradual. 2. equitable & satisfactory to the individuals immediately concerned. 3. consistent with the existing & durable prejudices of the nation.

That it ought, like remedies for other deep-rooted and widespread evils, to be gradual, is so obvious that there seems to be no difference of opinion on that point.

To be equitable & satisfactory, the consent of both the Master & the slave should be obtained. That of the Master will require a provision in the plan for compensating a loss of what he held as property guarantied by the laws, and recognised by the Constitution. That of the slave, requires that his condition in a state of freedom, be preferable in his own estimation, to his actual one in a state of bondage.

To be consistent with existing and probably unalterable prejudices in the U.S. the freed blacks ought to be permanently removed beyond the region occupied by, or allotted to a White population. The objections to a thorough incorporation of the two people are, with most of the Whites, insuperable; and are admitted by all of them to be very powerful. If the blacks, strongly marked as they are by Physical & lasting peculiarities, be retained amid the Whites, under the degrading privation of equal rights political or social, they must be always dissatisfied with their condition as a change only from one to another species of oppression; always secretly confederated ag[ain]st the ruling & privileged class; and always uncontroulled by some of the most cogent motives to moral and respectable conduct. The character of the free blacks, even where their legal condition is least affected by their colour, seems to put these truths beyond question. It is material also that the removal of the blacks be to a distance precluding the jealousies & hostilities to be apprehended from a neighboring people, stimulated by the contempt known to be entertained for their peculiar features; to say nothing of their vindictive recollections, or the predatory propensies which their State of Society might foster. Nor is it fair, in estimating the danger of Collisions with the Whites, to charge it wholly on the side of the Blacks. There would be reciprocal antipathies doubling the danger.

The colonizing plan on foot, has as far as it extends, a due regard to these requisites; with the additional object of bestowing new blessings civil & religious on the quarter of the Globe most in need of them. The Society proposes to transport to the African Coast all free & freed blacks who may be willing to remove thither; to provide by fair means, &, it is understood with a prospect of success, a suitable territory for their reception; and to initiate them into such an establishment as may gradually and indefinitely expand itself.

The experiment, under this view of it, merits encouragement from all who regard slavery as an evil, who wish to see it diminished and abolished by peaceable & just means; and who have themselves no better mode to propose. Those who have most doubted the success of the experiment must at least have wished to find themselves in an error.

But the views of the Society are limited to the case of blacks already free, or who may be *gratuitously* emancipated. To provide a commensurate remedy for the evil, the plan must be extended to the great Mass of blacks, and must embrace a fund sufficient to induce the Master as well as the slave to concur in it. Without the concurrence of the Master, the benefit will be very limited as it relates to the Negroes; and essentially defective, as it relates to the U[nited] States; and the concurrence of Masters, must, for the most part, be obtained by purchase.

Can it be hoped that voluntary contributions, however adequate to an auspicious commencement, will supply the sums necessary to such an enlargement of the remedy? May not another question be asked? Would it be reasonable to throw so great a burden on the individuals distinguished by their philanthropy and patriotism?

The object to be obtained, as an object of humanity, appeals alike to all; as a National object, it claims the interposition of the nation. It is the nation which is to reap the benefit. The nation therefore ought to bear the burden.

Must then the enormous sums required to pay for, to transport, and to establish in a foreign land all the slaves in the U.S. as their Masters may be will[in]g to part with them, be taxed on the good people of the U.S. or be obtained by loans swelling the public debt to a size pregnant with evils next in degree to those of slavery itself?

Happily it is not necessary to answer this question by remarking that if slavery as a national evil is to be abolished, and it be just that it be done at the national expence, the amount of the expence is not a paramount consideration. It is the peculiar fortune, or, rather a providential blessing of the U.S. to possess a resource commensurate to this great object, without taxes on the people, or even an increase of the public debt.

I allude to the vacant territory the extent of which is so vast, and the vendible value of which is so well ascertained.

Supposing the number of slaves to be 1,500,000, and their price to average 400 d[olla]rs, the cost of the whole would be 600 millions of doll[ar]s. These estimates are probably beyond the fact; and from the no. of slaves should be deducted 1. those whom their Masters would not part with. 2. those who may be gratuitously set free by their Masters. 3. those acquiring freedom under emancipating regulations of the States. 4. those preferring slavery where they are, to freedom in an African settlement. On the other hand, it is to be noted that the expence of removal & settlement is not included in the estimated sum; and that an increase of the slaves will be going on during the period required for the execution of the plan.

On the whole the aggregate sum needed may be stated at about 600 Mil[lion]s of dollars.

This will require 200 mil[lion]s of Acres at 3 dol[lar]s per Acre; or 300 mil[lion]s at 2 doll[a]rs per Acre a quantity which tho' great in itself, is perhaps not a third part of the disposable territory belonging to the U.S. And to what object so good so great & so glorious, could that peculiar fund of wealth be appropriated? Whilst the sale of territory would, on one hand be planting one desert with a free & civilized people, it would on the other, be giving freedom to another people, and filling with them another desert. And if in any instances, wrong has been done by our forefathers to people of one colour, by dispossessing them of their soil, what better atonement is now in our power than that of making what is rightfully acquired a source of justice & of blessings to a people of another colour?

As the revolution to be produced in the condition of the negroes must be gradual, it will suffice if the sale of territory keep pace with its progress. For a time at least the proceeds w[oul]d be in advance. In this case it might be best, after deducting the expence incident to the surveys & sales, to place the surplus in a situation where its increase might correspond with the natural increase of the unpurchased slaves. Should the proceeds at any time fall short of the calls for their application, anticipations might be made by temporary loans to be discharged as the land should find a Market.

But it is probable that for a considerable period, the sales would exceed the calls. Masters would not be willing to strip their plantations & farms of their laborers too rapidly. The slaves themselves, connected as they generally are by tender ties with others under other Masters, would be kept from the list of emigrants by the want of the multiplied consents to be obtained. It is probable indeed that for a long time a certain portion of the proceeds might safely continue applicable to the discharge of the debts or to other purposes of the Nation. Or it might be most convenient, in the outset, to appropriate a certain proportion only of the income from sales, to the object in view, leaving the residue otherwise applicable.

Should any plan similar to that I have sketched, be deemed eligible in itself no particular difficulty is foreseen from that portion of the nation which with a common interest in the vacant territory has no interest in slave property. They are too just to wish that a partial sacrifice sh[oul]d be made for the general good; and too well aware that whatever may be the intrinsic character of that description of property, it is one known to the constitution, and, as such could not be constitutionally taken away without just compensation. That part of the Nation has indeed shewn a meritorious alacrity in promoting, by pecuniary contributions, the limited scheme for colonizing the Blacks, & freeing the nation from the unfortunate stain on it, which justifies the belief that any enlargement of the scheme, if founded on just principles would find among them its earliest & warmest patrons. It ought to have great weight that the vacant lands in question have, for the most part been derived from grants of the States holding the slaves to be redeemed & removed by the sale of them.

It is evident however that in effectuating a general emancipation of slaves, in the mode which has been hinted, difficulties of other sorts would be encountered. The provision for ascertaining the joint consent of the masters & slaves; for guarding ag[ain]st unreasonable valuations of the latter; and for the discrimination of those not proper to be conveyed to a foreign residence, or who ought to remain a charge on Masters in whose service they had been disabled or worn out and for the annual transportation of such numbers, would Require the mature deliberations of the National Councils. The measure implies also the practicability of procuring in Africa, an enlargement of the district or districts, for receiving the exiles, sufficient for so great an augmentation of their numbers.

Perhaps the Legislative provision best adapted to the case would be an incorporation of the Colonizing Society or the establishment of a similar one, with proper powers, under the appointment & superintendence of the National Executive.

In estimating the difficulties however incident to any plan of general emancipation, they ought to be brought into comparison with those inseparable from other plans, and be yielded to or not according to the result of the comparison.

One difficulty presents itself which will probably attend every plan which is to go into effect under the Legislative provisions of the National Gov[ernmen]t. But whatever may be the defect of existing powers of Congress, the Constitution has pointed out the way in which it can be supplied. And it can hardly be doubted that the requisite powers might readily be procured for attaining the great object in question, in any mode whatever approved by the Nation.

If these thoughts can be of any aid in your search of a remedy for the great evil under which the nation labors, you are very welcome to them. You will allow me however to add that it will be most agreeable to me, not to be publickly referred to in any use you may make of them.

## ELIHU EMBREE

### CHARITY AND RACE

Born in Pennsylvania, Elihu Embree (1782–1820) moved to Tennessee with his parents in 1790 and lived in that state the remainder of his life. He joined the newly formed Manumission Society of Tennessee in 1815, soon after he had joined the Society of Friends and had freed his own slaves. In March 1819, in Jonesboro, he began to publish a weekly newspaper, the *Manumission Intelligencer*. Renamed *The Emancipator* and converted into a monthly in April 1820, it became "the first periodical in the United States devoted exclusively to the abolition of slavery."[1] However, it went out of existence with Embree's death on December 4, 1820.

Students of American history are indebted to B. H. Murphy, of Nashville, Tennessee, who published the complete run of *The Emancipator* in 1932, in a volume entitled *The Emancipator,* together with a short biography of Embree by Dr. Robert H. White, of Nashville, and the addition of two previously unpublished anti-slavery memorials bearing the signature of Elihu Embree. The following selection is an editorial by Embree which appeared in *The Emancipator* on April 30, 1820.

### Savannah

It appears that the people of Savannah have returned the donation of the citizens of New-York of 10 or 12 thousand dollars, because they expressed a wish that the donation be applied exclusively to the relief of such sufferers by the late fire as had to labor for a livelihood, without respect to COLOUR.—This last word, *colour,* seems to have insulted their haughty spirits, to find that the donors had once thought of and felt a disposition to relieve the distresses of the unfortunate black people as well as the white. Some most insolent reproachful language is used by the mayor of Savannah to the mayor and aldermen of New York, without any other apparent provocation than the above expressed wish respecting the appropriation of their said donation. Such are some of the effects of slavery on the minds of slaveholders. Pride, haughtiness, ingratitude and tyranny, are some of the general effects produced by suffering men to assume an undue controul over others.

When I heard the letter of the mayor of Savannah to the mayor of Jonesborough read, it called up feelings in me which I am always happy to cherish, a disposition to alleviate the condition of the distressed, and accordingly out of my little I subscribed $100, payable in *Bacon* at 10 *cts* per pound, which I have paid over to the person appointed in this place to receive it; but had I seen the above statement before delivery I have no hesitation in believing I should have retained it, until I could have found some person or persons more deserving, and more in need than I now believe the people of Savannah are. They certainly are not reduced to that extremity that the mayor's letter described, or it would doubtless have humbled these haughty people at least so much as to have been willing to allow their sable brethren who were their fellow sufferers, to share in the relief offered them.—Nay, they would have been willing to have taken the money on loan, or in almost any way, rather than to have done without it, as present relief seems to be asked for in the most pathetic language. I always thought (until these haughty slave holders told me otherwise) that a *donor* has the right of directing his donation as he pleases, and I still think that where justice is not entirely turned out of doors, it continues to be a donors previlege. I pitied their circumstances when I first heard of their late calamity; I now am truly ashamed that they are human beings, as this act of theirs disgraces human nature. But when I reflect that these monsters in human shape are citizens of America, the land of boasted LIBERTY, and that these very men have the audacity to take that sacred word in their po[l]luted lips, I am struck with astonishment, amaze and wonder at the mercy of the supreme being, that instead of burning the town of Savannah, he has not destroyed its proud inhabitants with fire unquenchable!!!

## NOTE

1. Clement Eaton, *The Freedom-of-Thought Struggle in the Old South* (New York, Evanston and London, 1964), p. 166.

## FRANCES WRIGHT

### RACE RELATIONS IN THE UNITED STATES

Reformer and Freethinker Frances Wright (1795–1852) published her book, *Views of Society and Manners in America,* in London in 1821. It was based upon material gathered in her travels in the United States in 1818, 1819 and 1820. Her views concerning the condition of the Negro in the North are an excellent example of the myopia often induced by ideological sympathies. Viewing this country during those years as the most democratic and enlightened country in the world, which, in general, it was, she was unable to see the deep racial flaws which marred its political and economic structure. The following selection is from pp. 70–78. The notes are in the original. The reader may wish to consult the edition edited by Paul R. Baker, with an excellent introduction, published by Harvard University Press in 1963.

### *Condition of the Negro*

. . . I have not as yet replied to your enquiry, and that of your friend, concerning the appearance of the black population in those districts of these northern republics which we have hitherto visited. I hope you did not suspect me of having thrown your questions aside; I have been slow to answer, only because I was unwilling to pronounce hastily.

It has appeared to me, so far as my observations and enquiries may authorize an opinion, that, in no one particular, has the American character been more unfairly represented, than as regards the treatment and condition of the negro. The feelings of a European, when he lands in one of these northern cities, are, I have observed, of a mixed and somewhat contradictory nature. When he sees a crowd of black faces assembled at the corner of a street, or descries the sable cheeks and clumsy features of a negro girl under a pink silk bonnet, the sight offends him from its ugliness, and an immediate distaste at the country, defaced by a mixture of so novel and unseemly a population, takes possession of his mind. It is from foreigners, themselves professing an un-willingness, or even an absolute disgust at being served by black hands, that I have heard complaints of the prejudice entertained towards them on the part of Americans.[1] So little of this preju-dice have I observed among this people, that recollecting how very lately it was that the black citizens were their slaves, I was for some time absolutely at a loss to understand how there was not more. I believe, however, that the very cause which I had expected to operate in an opposite manner, explains the gentle-ness of their feelings towards these their freed bondsmen. So much has been said and written in favor of the unhappy African, he had been so long held up to their view as the object of com-passion, the slave-trade had been for so many years carried on in absolute defiance of the laws of their colonial assemblies, that the majority may be supposed to have been gradually disposed to befriend them in the spirit of political opposition, as well as from the gentler dictates of human pity. There is yet another cause which, in the northern republics, interests the public feeling in behalf of the African;—it is his condition in the old republics of the south. The compassion felt in England for the degradation of the black population in her islands, cannot necessarily equal that which is here felt for those who are kept in bondage within the bosom of their own America. The strict bond of union which unites the interests of the numerous states, seems as it were to approximate the most distant inhabitants of this vast empire to each other. The blot which defaces a portion of the Union is felt as reflecting disgrace upon the whole. The shame and the sorrow which the consideration of the southern slavery keeps alive throughout the great northern and free western states, in quick-ening their desire to hurry forward the day of its termination, awaken often a bitterness of feeling, perhaps unjust and unwise, towards the unfortunate masters of more unfortunate slaves. Much do the southern planters merit of their country for their energetic patriotism in the hour of danger. Well have they often fought the battle in the senate and the field, when transatlantic power has threatened the rights and lives of America's citizens! If they are yet cursed with an institution, at once a misfortune and a disgrace, from which their more fortunate brethren are re-lieved, let these trace it less to superior humanity or justice, than to those happier circumstances which encouraged them at first to resist the evil, and enabled them afterwards to correct it. The counsel, and perhaps ultimately the assistance, of the great and numerous northern and western states, may in time be useful in relieving their sister states from this crime and calamity;—if the former be given with temper, and the latter yielded with unpretending generosity.

I apprehend that the friend of humanity may consider with much satisfaction the condition of the negro in the great northern portion of this union. Everywhere are schools open for his instruction. In small towns, he will find him taught by the same master, and attending the same church with the white population. Would it not be more wise to rejoice in this visible decay of prejudice, than to dwell on what remains, and which still ranges the black and white children on different forms in the schoolroom, or the place of worship? In cities, the Africans have churches as well as preachers of their own, a fact from which we can only draw a satisfactory proof of their rapid advance in situation and knowledge. A European has learned, perhaps before he lands on these shores, that black and white servants sit down to meat at different tables; and should he find the fact substantiated in the first hotel in which he takes up his lodging, he marks it in his memorandum-book with a note of admiration, and follows it up with some reflection upon the liberal opinions that prevail under a democracy. Did he reflect upon the history of this country, and the history of the African in every country, and did he consult his own feelings, which, I believe, seldom acknowledge—I do not say an *equality*, but a *similarity* of race between the negro and himself, he would perhaps find little in the circumstance to argue the existence of any peculiar illiberality in the sentiments of this people. That wise institutions will do much towards improving both the physical condition and moral feelings of men, I am ready to admit, but I do not believe that they can perfect either. It seems to me, however, that such an expectation must have been formed by those who are surprised to find in this community an unwillingness to associate with the negro as with an equal. Nature has stamped a mark upon the unhappy African which, though the more cultivated and liberal will account an accidental distinction, the vulgar will regard as a symbol of inferiority. Had not the European of a less humane age degraded the African below the human standard, and laid the benumbing hand of oppression on his intellect, it is doubtful whether the least enlightened of us should ever have seen any thing in a sable skin but a whim of nature, or attributed the ignorance and slavishness of the African tribes on their own soil to any other causes than those which variously operate on the human race in all the differing climates and countries of the globe. As it is, an invidious comparison has often been drawn between the black man and the white, which, considering the actual condition of the former, is perhaps neither wise nor humane. In these northern republics, where alone such a comparison could be instituted with any seeming plausibility, a thousand hidden causes conspire to retain the African in a lower scale of being than that of the American. The latter looks around him upon a world of his creation, upon a race of men, his brethren and equals, who, like him, acknowledge no superior but the one great Being who blessed the exertions of their heroic ancestors, and to whom their hearts rise in grateful adoration for the blessings showered on their country. What great and invigorating thoughts are here which are unknown to the sons of slaves! It was but yesterday, that they were "hewers of wood and drawers of water" in the land which yields them their subsistence; for the very rights with which they are now endowed, (and of which their minds can, as yet, scarcely feel the value or understand the meaning,) for these very rights, for all they know, and all that they enjoy, they are indebted to the repenting justice of *masters*. This repentance, however complete, cannot obliterate in a moment the wrongs of years; cannot transform an abject slave into a virtuous citizen; cannot banish from his mind that he lately trembled at the frown of those who are now his equals, nor banish from the minds of these, that it was only by the law of their own lips that he ceased to be the tool of their will. It requires no deep insight into the secrets of human nature to read the consequences of this state of things. There must inevitably exist a barrier between the American and the negro, similar to that which separates the higher from the poorer and less polished classes of society in Europe. The black and the white man are a distinct race; and the distinction is, as yet, no less marked in the internal than the external man. How far a nearer approach in thought, feeling, and moral character, in future generations, may tend to remove the barrier, it is not easy to judge. I must observe that, considering the inferior grade in society that the African as yet holds; and considering also the fraction that he constitutes in the sum of the population, it speaks honourably for the morals of the American community, that the two races continue so distinctly marked.

Notwithstanding the inferior estimation in which the blacks are held, not so much on account of complexion and feature, as from the greater laxity of their morals, they may be more properly said to constitute a distinct than a degraded race. They are equally under the protection of mild and impartial laws; possess, in general, the same political rights with the mass of the community; are more peculiarly the objects of humane consideration with the benevolent and the religious; and are enabled, from the very condition of the country, to procure a subsistence, in spite of their indolence and thoughtless forgetfulness of the morrow. Though neither a frugal, nor, compared with the American population, a moral people, they are singularly cheerful and good-humoured, and are bound in close ties of social intercourse with each other. They are every where immoderately fond of dancing, and, when assembled for that purpose in the room of a country tavern, or in the hall or kitchen of some one of their employers, exhibit a show of finery which might amaze Harlequin himself. It is always thus that man, emerging from the savage or the slavish state, seizes on the indulgencies and the tinsel of luxury, before he discovers the value of those higher enjoyments, derived from the acquirement of knowledge and the cultivation of refined and elevated sentiment. In spite of the many disadvantages under which the African has hitherto laboured, instances are not wanting where he has risen to considerable wealth and respectability, particularly, I believe, in the New England states. Nothing indeed is here necessary but his own exertions to raise him in the scale of being. His political rights must in time awaken in him political ambition, in which he has yet been usually found deficient. In some of the states, the blacks now frequently exercise their right of suffrage; and it is a curious fact, that in Massachusetts some black votes were given so long back as the election for the general Convention, appointed to digest the plan of the Federal Government. In some of the northern states, the right of suffrage is still withheld from the negro; and with seeming reason, for he is evidently, as yet, but ill fitted to exercise it.[2]

I have wandered into more general observations than I had intended at the commencement of this letter, but, as they rose naturally out of a subject upon which you have expressed some curiosity, I hope they will not appear altogether misplaced.

## NOTES [FROM THE ORIGINAL TEXT]

1. It was with surprise, that I heard this illiberal disgust expressed, by word and gesture, with peculiar vehemence, by foreign *women,* and these often *ladies.*

2. Where the negro holds the right of suffrage, I do not believe the *law* excludes him from any public office of the state; the qualifications demanded are, of course, such as he is not likely to be found possessed of. This and custom operate sufficiently to ensure his exclusion.

## SAMUEL WORCESTER AND OTHERS

### On the Racial Theory of Slavery

The following essay is reprinted from a volume entitled *Essays on Slavery; Re-Published from the Boston Recorder & Telegraph, for 1825,* by Vigornius, and Others, printed in Amherst, Massachusetts, in 1826. "Vigornius" was the pen name of Samuel M. Worcester (1801–1866), a member of the Amherst College faculty from 1823 to 1834 and, thereafter, pastor of the Tabernacle Church in Salem, Mass. The essay reprinted here, by "Hieronymus," was apparently written by a liberal Southerner who presents the dominant Southern racial rationale for slavery, although he does not agree with it.

### Slavery. No. VII

Nov. 11, 1825.

MESSRS. EDITORS,—My last closed with a summary exhibition of the unscriptural character of slavery, as it is found to exist in the West Indies and in the United States; and I laboured to point out various specific and essential characteristics of dissimilarity between the system as it exists in our country, and as it existed by command or by permission, in the church and among the people of God.

Having disposed of that branch of the subject, very little, it would seem need be said in proof of the entire contrariety, the diametrical opposition between slavery and the principles upon which the American government professes to be founded, as recognized in the Declaration of Independence. That instrument expressly enumerates *liberty,* as among other cons[t]ituents, one of the unalienable rights of *all mankind.* At first sight it appears utterly inexplicable, that the natural rights of the American negro should not have come within the purview of those, who, with so much ability, good sense, and feeling, drew up that interesting document; and that it should have been still farther totally overlooked by the statesmen of the country in Congress assembled. But it appears practicable to account for the omission *at that time,* by considering how much the delegates from the different colonies had to accomplish—how they were surrounded with difficulties, beset with dangers, and struggling for national existence. They had enough on their hands to lay all the energies of body, mind, and heart, under contribution; and the adjustment of the rights of the American slave was, under the circumstances then existing, too delicate, and difficult, and intricate a business, to be despatched with facility or with speed. These considerations seem rationally to account for the oversight of the slave question, at the time *the rights of man* were undergoing argument and adjustment. We could not then be expected to do, as the South American Republics have recently done,—emancipate the slaves,—and thus act consistently. They had got through their struggle; and their fears were over. We were at the commencement of ours, and knew not then how it would terminate.

But after North American Independence was not only declared but established, and the tumult of war was visible, and the clangor of arms was audible no more;—when peace spread her wings over the land, and prosperity was following in her train;—when one interesting event after another was transpiring to give solidity to the Republic; and to shed an increase of glory around her;—how, *how* came it to pass, that *even then* the groans of Africa continued, as much as ever before, unheard; and no solitary tongue lifted an appeal in her behalf. Perhaps in part, we may charitably account for this strange and singular omission, from the *comparitive* darkness of the age; for much additional light has been since shed upon the rights of man. Perhaps too the national Legislature took it for granted (and as since has appeared, much too readily) that the different states could easily discover, and would readily take speedy preparatory steps to perform an obvious duty,—to save our consistency in particular, as well as our character in general.

Or shall we resort to some other hypothesis to account for this anomaly? This question seems to have considerably perplexed Vigornius; (see No. IV,) and he says, after quoting the "self-evident truths" to which we have just referred in the Declaration of Independence, "Either the slave was forgotten—or he was not recognized as a human being—or he is an exception to the universal rule—or lastly his right is abrogated or superseded by the paramount right of his master," &c. Vigornius has not told us, which of these four modes of accounting for the singular fact, he is inclined to adopt. As a dweller at the South from my cradle, and from my acquaintance with the state of things there for a score of years and upwards, I am strongly tempted to make choice of the 2d hypothesis to account for this remarkably insulated fact. I cannot think, that the memory of our statesmen was so treacherous, that they "forgot the slave" nor that they regarded him as "an exception to the universal rule," as in that case, I think, they would, in the instrument itself, have *at least alluded to* the exception—nor can I admit, that they regarded the rights of the slave as set aside or "superseded or abrogated by any prior or paramount right of his master." Those who were willing to tug through an eight years' war, rather than be taxed three pence a pound on tea, would never have overlooked the hundred fold more aggravated suffering, and degrading debasement of the sons of Africa in our midst. I am morally compelled then to take up with the *second* hypothesis—the slave "was not recognized as a human being."—The whole history of slavery at the South, as far and as long as I have been acquainted with it (until within a few years, say between 12 and 20, during which there has been a manifest and growing alteration in the conceptions of the whites and in the treatment of the blacks) rivets the conviction, that the slave was not regarded, *strictly speaking*, as a human being; but a sort of mid-link between brute and man—partly belonging to each and wholly to neither. For if the slave was murdered, a *paltry fine* was all the penalty; and that because the murdered individual was *nothing but a negro.* But if the slave was *stolen*, and *property* thus to the amount of several hundred dollars *lost*, then the gallows and the halter appeared in view, as the remuneration of the thief. Nay, I have known, during the period of my life, more, many more than one or two or three cases, in which a dog or a horse was a dearer object to his master, than his slave, and he would be more angry, and more vengeful at an injury done to the former than the latter. Was I not right, Messrs. Editors, in looking at such a fact as this, to infer that a negro cannot be a human being? Again, another fact—a fact I have already alluded to, and one which still exists—confirms my convictions. It is this—the declaration of a hundred negro witnesses, (even though their uniformly good character could be testified by their masters,) to any fact, in which the disadvantage of a white man *of no character* was concerned, availed, and I believe *now* avails, nothing. Was I not right, in believing that the negro was hardly recognized as a human being? And other facts I might mention of a similar complexion, but I would not be needlessly tedious.

But it is time I should say something to redeem the pledge given at the close of my first number, and this seems a suitable place to introduce something of this kind. In that part of my discussion, I ventured to say, in opposition to the writer in the Christian Spectator, on whose pieces I had commenced some re-marks, that there was an approximation at least, to acknowledge-ment of the negro's rights, in the slave-holding states. In some of the slave-holding states, negro-killing has recently been construed as murder: this looks like giving the slave a right to *"life,"* though that of "liberty and the pursuit of happiness" be still denied him. I have not indeed yet heard of a case under this recent law, in which the penalty of murder has actually overtaken any slave-killer, and I apprehend it would be exceedingly difficult actually to carry into execution this new statute: and especially, if the breach of it was committed by a man of importance and influence in society. I trust however our Northern brethren will not be reluctant, as they in too many instances are, to give us credit for passing such a law. We have rigid laws too against duelling: but while our very legislators are duellists and slave-holders, I hardly dare anticipate the execution of a duellist, a murderer of one description,—or of a negro-killer, a murderer of another kind.

And now what shall we do or say? That slavery, I mean such as it now exists in the United States, is against the Bible, against common sense, against the natural rights of man, against the first principles, the very stamina of our free republic, and against our interests too, (a point indeed, which I have not and shall not discuss, but which has been abundantly demonstrated by abler pens,) if I mistake not is sufficiently obvious. We have within these United States a million and a half, rather near two millions of men, who, if they are not, yet "of right, ought to be free and independent;" whom, according to our Declaration of Independence, "their Creator has endowed with certain unalienable rights." But while it is just, would it be safe, or wise, or benevolent, either to them, or to their owners, to invest them *immediately* with those rights? And if it would not, does not this very important circumstance peremptorily forbid the discharge of this obligation *at present. "Salus populi suprema lex."* Among writers on this subject, I know not that I have met with one, who has advocated immediate emancipation for a moment, professing at the same time his belief, that the above impediments do exist. But I observe a difference of opinion as to the point whether there would be that interference with safety and with happiness to either party,—some maintaining the affirmative, others the negative,—and I hope both are equally philanthropic in their intentions, though widely differing in their conceptions. The practicability of gradual emancipation no one pretends to doubt; and all throughout the United States, except the selfish and the sordid, the covetous and the tyrannical, I presume, desire it.

Having been occupied in this discussion so much longer than I intended when I began it, I must forego, or at least postpone the examination of this question, as I have still much more to add on other topics, connected with this subject. All I would now say is, that Providence seems to have opened the door for *beginning* to do something, *without further delay.* The Colonization Society, slow at first in its operations, and looked upon with the scowling eye of suspicion, alike at the North and at the South, has been doing its work surely—triumphing over one difficulty, disappointment, and opposition after another, till it can now stamp the seal "probatum est," on its fair and successful experiment.

*There is* a Colony of free, enlightened, civilized, christianized blacks in Africa, an American Colony—*there are* in it at least two Christian denominations—*there are* churches and *there are* schools—*there is* protection—*there are* fortifications and munitions of war, if conflict be still necessary—a handful of these colonists *have vanquished* a host of natives, who on one occasion rose up against them, and threatened to destroy them. They have selected a healthy and fertile spot—400 colonists are there already—100 more are just ready to embark, if not actually now on their way. This scheme, derided by some, for its visionary character, opposed by others, on one ground by one, for another reason by another, is now (to use Mr. Jefferson's language,) "in the full tide of successful experiment." The immediate and ostensible object of this Society, and that which was avowed as its exclusive object, at the commencement of its operations, and of its calls on Christian charity, was, the transfer, with their own consent, of as many of the free blacks in our country (the whole of whom I believe amount to nearly half a million) as provision could be made for. The condition of the free blacks in the Northern and still more in the Middle states, is much less respectable and much more wretched, than that of the same class of persons at the South; nay, than that of very many slaves themselves, who have the happiness to be blessed with good owners. After all that our Northern brethren say of the hardships of Southern slavery, the distance, and hauteur, and tyranny of masters, they have very little cause to "glory over us." The complexion of a black freeman at the North keeps him at nearly the same distance from the white freeman,—as to social intercourse with them,—as to rights of electing or being elected to office, as to prospect of rising to eminence and distinction,—as to a multitude of other things,—as the complexion and condition both of a colored slave at the South does. The Northern free black is not unfrequently more degraded mentally, morally, and physically, than the Southern Slave. So say Courts of Justice and jails.

In one of the numbers (I think) of the Christian Spectator, a Captain Otis is said to state, that the colonists (at Liberia) from the country are preferable to those from the cities, and those *from the South* to those from the North, as being more easily satisfied, more tractable and less averse to labor. Free blacks at the North are as troublesome in some respects, as slaves at the South are in others. The Colonization Society proposes to throw off this burden by degrees, thus relieving the North of a cumbrous and expensive population, and hoping to improve at the same time the character and condition, and increase the usefulness of this population by transplantation. This great and good institution, has had much to encounter, on opposite grounds, from the different latitudes of the United States. With what propriety in each case, I propose to inquire in my next.

HIERONYMUS.

# Part Three

# THE EVE OF CONFLICT, 1830-1860

The rise of Garrisonian Abolition, with its uncompromising insistence upon immediate emancipation and equality for Negroes everywhere in the United States, represented a powerful new force on the American scene. The publication of the *Liberator* in 1831, followed by the organization of the New England Anti-Slavery Society in 1832 and the American Anti-Slavery Society in 1833, constituted the beginning of a challenge to slavery which ultimately resulted in its overthrow. Acting as a catalyst, the Abolition movement spurred the publication of editorials, articles and books by anti-slavery thinkers on slavery and the Negro. These emphasized the humanity of the Negro, the evils of slavery and the inherent equality of both races.

The seriousness of the challenge, even in its earliest stages, was soon recognized in the South by politicians and ideologists alike, who responded with laws and propaganda designed to defend and support the institution. Their cause was strengthened by the continued growth of the institution itself. Thus, the output of cotton, which had been only a few thousand pounds in 1790, grew to "four million bales of four hundred pounds weight in 1859."[1] The slave population grew from 2,009,043 in 1830 to 3,953,760 in 1860.[2]

Although a variety of arguments were summoned in defense of slavery—Biblical, political, constitutional, economic and biological-racial—it was the last which proved to be the foundation of the others. Ultimately, every important argument sought to prove that, as distinguished from the white man, the Negro was constitutionally and racially suited for slavery; he was fulfilling his inherent destiny as a person and as a member of the black race, by serving as a slave; and his supreme happiness lay in his condition.[3]

The interest in race resulting from slavery coincided with and stimulated the scientific study of races. The question of the derivation of races, of the Biblical view of the single origin of mankind versus that of the multiple origins of races in different parts of the world, the question whether blacks and whites were members of separate species or were simply varieties of one species, the problem of racial characteristics, the nature of racial differences and the source of such differences, became vital issues for scholars, North and South. The result was a vast increase in the literature on race, yet a lag in scientific investigation and development of the subject itself. Indeed, as one examines the writings of those who were regarded as scientists, both in the North and the South, one finds far more apologetics and rationalizations for Negro slavery and the dogma of Negro inferiority than a dispassionate pursuit of objective truth. This situation probably stemmed from the fact that scholars in the South took slavery for granted while those in the North tended to accept without question the segregation and inferior social status of the Negro in that area. As a result, one finds far more of true scientific value and a closer approximation to modern racial thought in the writings of the anti-slavery men and women, who questioned the status quo and its associated dogma of Negro inferiority, than among the reputed scientists and academic scholars.

## NOTES

1. Ulrich B. Phillips, "Slavery," *Encyclopedia of the Social Sciences*, XIV, 87.
2. Cited in E. Franklin Frazier, *The Negro in the United States*, rev. ed. (New York, 1957) , p. 39.
3. Kenneth M. Stampp, *The Peculiar Institution: Slavery in the Ante-Bellum South* (New York, 1956) , p. 8.

# CHAPTER 8

---

# The Anti-Slavery Movement

## WILLIAM LLOYD GARRISON

### On Interracial Marriage and Colonization

The first of the following two selections by William Lloyd Garrison (1805–1879) appeared in *The Liberator* on May 7, 1831, in the midst of a campaign initiated by Garrison to eliminate a Massachusetts law forbidding marriages between whites, Negroes and Indians. The law had existed on the statute books since 1705 and was finally removed in 1843.[1] The second selection is from a pamphlet by Garrison published in Boston in 1832 (pp. 120–1, 141–147), entitled "Thoughts on African Colonization: or an Impartial Exhibition of the Doctrines, Principles and Purposes of the American Colonization Society. Together with the Resolutions, Addresses and Remonstrances of the Free People of Color." Garrison's footnotes have been omitted.

Garrison was the founder of the pre-Civil War militant Abolitionist movement. On January 1, 1831, he began publication of his weekly newspaper, *The Liberator,* in which he raised the slogan of immediate, unconditional and universal emancipation of the slave in the United States. Largely through his efforts the New England Anti-Slavery Society was formed in January 1832, and he was a major force in the organization of the American Anti-Slavery Society in December 1833. This striving on behalf of the Negro included opposition to segregation and discrimination in the North as well as to slavery in the South. For a collection of the writings of Garrison and other Abolitionists, see *The Abolitionists: A Collection of Their Writings,* edited by Louis Ruchames (New York, 1963).

## The Marriage Law

The pursuit of happiness is among the inalienable rights of man: it is inseparable from his existence, and no legislative body has a right to deprive him of it, any more than to abridge his liberty or to destroy his life without any specification of crime. The institution of marriage, by the Creator, was wisely designed to promote this happiness, by uniting those, whose affections mingle together, in a lasting bond of union. If He has 'made of one blood all nations of men for to dwell on all the face of the earth,' then they are one species, and stand on a perfect equality: their intermarriage is neither unnatural nor repugnant to nature, but obviously proper and salutary; it being designed to unite people of different tribes and nations, and to break down those petty distinctions which are the effect of climate or locality of situation, and which lead to oppression, war and division among mankind.

A union of the sexes is a matter of choice, as well of duty. To limit this choice to a particular family, neighborhood or people, is to impoverish and circumscribe human happiness, and to create an odious aristocracy. Its occasional perversion is inseparable from its exercise, because all are not equally cautious, wise or virtuous; but this cannot destroy the right. The abuse of wealth cannot authorise a legislative or judicial body to deny men the privilege of accumulating riches. The prostitution of official power furnishes no reason why a nation should be without rulers. The corruption of religion does not exonerate men from moral obligation, nor justify them in resorting to atheism. So in marriage: there will be profligate aberrations of choice, but the common sense of mankind and the usages of society will regulate this indispensable union.

These propositions we conceive to be reasonable, plain, undeniable, self-evident. There is, therefore, nothing unnatural in the amalgamation of our species. As civilization, and knowledge, and republican feelings, and christianity prevail in the world, the wider will matrimonial connexions extend; and finally people of every tribe and kindred and tongue will freely intermarry. By the blissful operation of this divine institution, the earth is evidently to become one neighborhood or family. Herein is seen the excellency of Divine Wisdom; here is the cord which is to bind the universe; here is an influence, which, regulated by the principles of the gospel, is to subdue the most stubborn prejudices and to harmonise the most discordant qualities; here is an association, which, formed by the strongest interests and united by the dearest ties, is to elevate, improve and liberalize our nature.

An unnatural alliance is not that which joins in wedlock an African descendant with an American, or an Indian with a European, who are equal in moral worth; but that which unites virtue with vice, knowledge with ignorance, sobriety with drunkenness, and piety with profligacy. The standard of matrimony is erected by affection and purity, and does not depend upon the height, or bulk, or color, or wealth, or poverty, of individuals. Water will seek its level; nature will have free course; and heart will answer to heart. To attempt to force or obstruct the flow of the affections, is ridiculous and cruel. If men and women begin to proscribe and ridicule each other for the choice of their partners, there will be a marvellous disruption and an almost universal hissing; for each perchance wonders at the taste of the other, and is ready at any moment to scandalise.

With these preliminary observations, we again republish the following tyrannical, absurd, unnatural, *unconstitutional* section of an article which was passed by our Legislature in 1786, and which, to the discredit of the age and the burning shame of the Commonwealth, is still in force:

'SEC. 7. *And be it further enacted,* That no person by this Act authorised to marry, shall join in marriage any white person with any Negro, Indian, or Mulatto, on penalty of the sum of *Fifty Pounds,* two third parts thereof to the use of the county wherein such shall be committed, and the residue to the prosecutor, to be recovered by the Treasurer of the same county, in manner as aforesaid; and all such marriages shall be absolutely null and void.'

Our readers are aware, that, at the last session of the General

Court, on motion of Mr Bigelow of this city, this scandalous section was obliterated by a vote of the House, but subsequently retained in consequence of a rejection of the New Marriage Bill altogether. For this manly and common sense effort, Mr Bigelow has been assailed from different quarters in the most scurrilous and savage manner, by editors whose brutality is exceeded only by their folly—pompous blockheads, callous to shame, and glorying in their littleness—delicate corinthians, who deserve to be literally tied to the blackest creatures in the land until their silly pride be subdued. We have already noticed the vulgar assaults on Mr B. by the editors of the Pennsylvania Inquirer and Philadelphia Gazette; and we have rods in pickle for the backs of the editor of the Boston Press and a correspondent of the Commercial Gazette of this city, which we shall apply next week.

## Thoughts on African Colonization

. . . If I must become a colonizationist, I insist upon being consistent: there must be no disagreement between my creed and practice. I must be able to give a reason why all our tall citizens should not conspire to remove their more diminutive brethren, and all the corpulent to remove the lean and lank, and all the strong to remove the weak, and all the educated to remove the ignorant, and all the rich to remove the poor, as readily as for the removal of those whose skin is 'not colored like my own;' for Nature has sinned as culpably in diversifying the size as the complexion of her progeny, and Fortune in the distribution of her gifts has been equally fickle. I cannot perceive that I am more excusable in desiring the banishment of my neighbor because his skin is darker than mine, than I should be in desiring his banishment because he is a smaller or feebler man than myself. Surely it would be sinful for a black man to repine and murmer, and impeach the wisdom and goodness of God, because he was made with a sable complexion; and dare I be guilty of such an impeachment, by persecuting him on account of his color? I dare not: I would as soon deny the existence of my Creator, as quarrel with the workmanship of his hands. I rejoice that he has made one star to differ from another star in glory; that he has not given to the sun the softness and tranquillity of the moon, nor to the

moon the intensity and magnificence of the sun; that he presents
to the eye every conceivable shape, and aspect, and color, in the
gorgeous and multifarious productions of Nature; and I do not
rejoice less, but admire and exalt him more, that, notwithstanding he has made of one blood the whole family of man, he has
made the whole family of man to differ in personal appearance,
habits and pursuits.

I protest against sending any to Africa, in whose blood there is
any mixture of our own; for, I repeat it, white blood in Africa
would be as repugnant to Nature, as black blood is in this
country. Now, most unfortunately for colonizationists, the spirit
of amalgamation has been so active for a long series of years,—
especially in the slave States,—that there are comparatively few,
besides those who are annually smuggled into the south from
Africa, whose blood is not tainted with a foreign ingredient.
Here, then, is a difficulty! What shall be done? All black blood
*must* be sent to Africa; but how to collect it is the question.
What shall be done! Why, we must resort to *phlebotomy!* . . .

Of this I am sure: no man, who is truly willing to admit the
people of color to an equality with himself, can see any insuperable difficulty in effecting their elevation. When, therefore, I
hear an individual—especially a professor of christianity—strenuously contending that there can be no fellowship with them, I
cannot help suspecting the sincerity of his own republicanism or
piety, or thinking that the beam is in his own eye. My bible
assures me that the day is coming when even the 'wolf shall dwell
with the lamb, and the leopard shall lie down with the kid, and
the wolf and the young lion and the fatling together;' and, if this
be possible, I see no cause why those of the same species—God's
rational creatures—fellow countrymen, in truth, cannot dwell in
harmony together.

How abominably hypocritical, how consummately despicable,
how incorrigibly tyrannical must this whole nation appear in the
eyes of the people of Europe!—professing to be the *friends* of the
free blacks, actuated by the purest motives of benevolence toward
them, desirous to make atonement for past wrongs, challenging
the admiration of the world for their patriotism, philanthropy
and piety—and yet (hear, O heaven! and be astonished, O
earth!) shamelessly proclaiming, with a voice louder than thun-

der, and an aspect malignant as sin, that while their colored
countrymen remain among them, they must be trampled beneath
their feet, treated as inferior beings, deprived of all the invaluable privileges of freemen, separated by the brand of indelible ignominy, and debased to a level with the beasts that
perish! Yea, that they may as soon change their complexion as
rise from their degradation! that no device of philanthropy can
benefit them here! that they constitute a class out of which *no
individual can be elevated,* and below which, *none can be
depressed!* that no talents however great, no piety however pure
and devoted, no patriotism however ardent, no industry however
great, no wealth however abundant, can raise them to a footing
of equality with the whites! that 'let them toil from youth to old
age in the honorable pursuit of wisdom—let them store their
minds with the most valuable researches of science and literature—and let them add to a highly gifted and cultivated intellect, a piety pure, undefiled, and unspotted from the world, *it is
all nothing*—they would not be received into the *very lowest
walks of society*—admiration of such uncommon beings would
mingle with *disgust!*' Yea, that 'there is a broad and impassible
line of demarcation between every man who has *one drop* of
African blood in his veins and every other class in the community'! Yea, that 'the habits, the feelings, all the prejudices of
society—prejudices which neither *refinement,* nor *argument,*
nor *education,* nor RELIGION itself can subdue—mark the people
of color, whether bond or free, as the subjects of a degradation
*inevitable* and *incurable*'! Yea, that '*Christianity* cannot do for
them here, what it will do for them in Africa'! Yea, that 'this is
not the fault of the colored man, NOR OF THE WHITE MAN, nor of
Christianity; but AN ORDINATION OF PROVIDENCE, *and no more to
be changed than the* LAWS OF NATURE'!!!

Again I ask, are we pagans, are we savages, are we devils?
Search the records of heathenism, and sentiments more hostile to
the spirit of the gospel, or of a more black and blasphemous
complexion than these, cannot be found. I believe that they are
libels upon the character of my countrymen, which time will
wipe off. I call upon the spirits of the just made perfect in
heaven, upon all who have experienced the love of God in their
souls here below, upon the christian converts in India and the

islands of the sea, to sustain me in the assertion that there *is* power enough in the religion of Jesus Christ to melt down the most stubborn prejudices, to overthrow the highest walls of partition, to break the strongest caste, to improve and elevate the most degraded, to unite in fellowship the most hostile, and to equalize and bless all its recipients. Make me *sure* that there is not, and I will give it up, now and for ever. 'In Christ Jesus, all are one: there is neither Jew nor Greek, there is neither bond nor free, there is neither male nor female.'

These sentiments were not uttered by infidels, nor by worthless wretches, but in many instances by professors of religion and *ministers of the gospel!* and in almost every instance by reputedly the most enlightened, patriotic and benevolent men in the land! Tell it not abroad! publish it not in the streets of Calcutta! Even the eminent President of Union College, (Rev. Dr. Nott,) could so far depart, unguardedly I hope, from christian love and integrity, as to utter this language in an address in behalf of the Colonization Society:—'With us they [the free people of color] have been degraded by slavery, and *still further degraded by the mockery of nominal freedom.*' Were this true, it would imply that we of the free States are more barbarous and neglectful than even the traffickers in souls and men-stealers at the south. We have not, it is certain, treated our colored brethren as the law of kindness and the ties of brotherhood demand; but have we outdone slaveholders in cruelty? Were it true, to forge new fetters for the limbs of these degraded beings would be an act of benevolence. But their condition is as much superior to that of the slaves, as happiness is to misery. The second portion of this work, containing their proceedings in a collective capacity, shows whether they have made any progress in intelligence, in virtue, in piety, and in happiness, since their liberation. Again he says: '*We have endeavored,* but endeavored in vain, *to restore them either to self-respect, or to the respect of others.*' It is painful to contradict so worthy an individual; but nothing is more certain than that this statement is altogether erroneous. We have derided, we have shunned, we have neglected them, in every possible manner. They have had to rise not only under the mountainous weight of their own ignorance and vice, but with the additional and constant pressure of our contempt and injustice.

In despite of us, they have done well. Again: *'It is not our fault
that we have failed; it is not theirs.'* We *are* wholly and exclusively in fault. What have we done to raise them up from the
earth? What have we *not* done to keep them down? Once more:
'It has resulted from a cause over which neither they, nor we, can
ever have control.' In other words, they have been made with
skins 'not colored like our own,' and *therefore* we cannot recog-
nise them as fellow-countrymen, or treat them like rational
beings! One sixth of our whole population *must,* FOR EVER, in
this land, remain a wretched, ignorant and degraded race,—and
yet nobody be culpable—*none but the Creator* who has made us
*incapable* of doing unto others as we would have them do unto
us! Horrible—horrible! If this be not an impeachment of Infinite
Goodness,—I do not say intentionally but *really,*—I cannot
define it. . . .

Nature, we are positively assured, has raised up impassable
barriers between the races. I understand by this expression, that
the blacks are of a different species from ourselves, so that all
attempts to generate offspring between us and them must prove
as abortive, as between a man and a beast. It is a law of Nature
that the lion shall not beget the lamb, or the leopard the bear.
Now the planters at the south have clearly demonstrated, that an
amalgamation with their slaves is not only possible, but a matter
of course, and eminently productive. It neither ends in abortion
nor produces monsters. In truth, it is often so difficult in the slave
States to distinguish between the fruits of this intercourse and
the children of white parents, that witnesses are summoned at
court to solve the problem! Talk of the barriers of Nature, when
the land swarms with living refutations of the statement! Happy
indeed would it be for many a female slave, if such a barrier
could exist during the period of her servitude to protect her from
the lust of her master!

In France, England, Spain, and other countries, persons of
color maintain as high a rank and are treated as honorably as
any other class of the inhabitants, in despite of the 'impassable
barriers of Nature.' Yet it is proclaimed to the world by the
Colonization Society, that the American people can never be as
republican in their feelings and practices as Frenchmen, Spaniards, or Englishmen! Nay, that *religion* itself cannot subdue

their malignant prejudices, or induce them to treat their dark skinned brethren in accordance with their professions of republicanism! My countrymen! is it so? Are you willing thus to be held up as tyrants and hypocrites for ever? as less magnanimous and just than the populace of Europe? No—no! I cannot give you up as incorrigibly wicked, nor my country as sealed over to destruction. My confidence remains, like the oak—like the Alps —unshaken, stormproof. I am not discouraged—I am not distrustful. I still place an unwavering reliance upon the omnipotence of truth. I still believe that the demands of justice will be satisfied; that the voice of bleeding humanity will melt the most obdurate hearts; and that the land will be redeemed and regenerated by an enlightened and energetic public opinion. As long as there remains among us a single copy of the Declaration of Independence, or of the New Testament, I will not despair of the social and political elevation of my sable countrymen. Already a rallying-cry is heard from the East and the West, from the North and the South; towns and cities and states are in commotion; volunteers are trooping to the field; the spirit of freedom and the fiend of oppression are in mortal conflict, and all neutrality is at an end. Already the line of division is drawn: on one side are the friends of truth and liberty, with their banner floating high in the air, on which are inscribed in letters of light, 'IMMEDIATE ABOLITION'—'NO COMPROMISE WITH OPPRESSORS'—'EQUAL RIGHTS' —'NO EXPATRIATION'—'DUTY, AND NOT CONSEQUENCES'—'LET JUSTICE BE DONE, THOUGH THE HEAVENS SHOULD FALL!'—On the opposite side stand the supporters and apologists of slavery in mighty array, with a black flag on which are seen in bloody characters, 'AFRICAN COLONIZATION'—'GRADUAL ABOLITION'— 'RIGHTS OF PROPERTY'—'POLITICAL EXPEDIENCY'—'NO EQUALITY'— 'NO REPENTANCE'—'EXPULSION OF THE BLACKS'—'PROTECTION TO TYRANTS!'—Who can doubt the issue of this controversy, or which side has the approbation of the Lord of Hosts? . . .

## NOTE

1. See Louis Ruchames, "Race, Marriage, and Abolition in Massachusetts," *The Journal of Negro History*, XL (July 1955), 250–273.

# LYDIA MARIA CHILD

## ON NEGRO INTELLECT

Lydia Maria Child (1802–1880) was a popular Massachusetts novelist when she wrote *An Appeal in Favor of that
Class of Americans Called Africans,* published in July 1833,
in Boston, by Allen and Ticknor. The volume helped create
anti-slavery sentiment, especially in Massachusetts, and influenced William Ellery Channing to speak out against
slavery. Thereafter, she wrote many other works of an anti-
slavery nature, and was closely identified with the anti-
slavery movement. In 1828, she married a Whig reformer,
lawyer and editor, David Lee Child (1794–1874). Both were
deeply influenced by *The Liberator* and their personal
association with Garrison. Mr. Child was one of the founders
of the New England Anti-Slavery Society in 1832 and contributed many essays to anti-slavery publications. The following selection is from pp. 155–187 of Mrs. Child's *Appeal.*
It reveals the vast research which she and other Abolitionist
writers carried on to ascertain the true racial character of the
Negro.

## Intellect of Negroes

"We must not allow negroes to be *men,* lest we ourselves should be
suspected of not being *Christians.*"   MONTESQUIEU.

In order to decide what is our duty concerning the Africans
and their descendants, we must first clearly make up our minds
whether they are, or are not, human beings—whether they have,
or have not, the same capacities for improvement as other men.

The intellectual inferiority of the negroes is a common, though
most absurd apology, for personal prejudice, and the oppressive
inequality of the laws; for this reason, I shall take some pains to
prove that the present degraded condition of that unfortunate
race is produced by artificial causes, not by the laws of nature.

In the first place, naturalists are universally agreed concerning
"the identity of the *human* type;" by which they mean that all

living creatures, that can, by any process, be enabled to perceive moral and intellectual truths, are characterized *by similar peculiarities of organization.* They may differ from each other widely, but they still belong to the same class. An eagle and a wren are very unlike each other; but no one would hesitate to pronounce that they were both birds: so it is with the almost endless varieties of the monkey tribe. We all know that beasts, however sagacious, are incapable of abstract thought, or moral perception. The most wonderful elephant in the world could not command an army, or govern a state. An ourang-outang may eat, and drink, and dress, and move like a man; but he could never write an ode, or learn to relinquish his own good for the good of his species. The *human* conformation, however it may be altered by the operation of physical or moral causes, differs from that of all other beings, and on this ground, the negro's claim to be ranked as a *man,* is universally allowed by the learned.

The condition of this people in ancient times is very far from indicating intellectual or moral inferiority.—Ethiopia held a conspicuous place among the nations.—Her princes were wealthy and powerful, and her people distinguished for integrity and wisdom. Even the proud Grecians evinced respect for Ethiopia, almost amounting to reverence, and derived thence the sublimest portions of their mythology. The popular belief that all the gods made an annual visit to the Ethiopians, shows the high estimation in which they were held; for we are not told that such an honor was bestowed on any other nation. . . .

In Africa was the early reign of Saturn, under the appellation of Ouranus, or Heaven; there the impious Titans warred with the sky; there Jupiter was born and nursed; there was the celebrated shrine of Ammon, dedicated to Theban Jove, which the Greeks reverenced more highly than the Delphic Oracle; there was the birth-place and oracle of Minerva; and there, Atlas supported both the heavens and the earth upon his shoulders.

It will be said that fables prove nothing.—But there is probably much deeper meaning in these fables than we now understand; there was surely some reason for giving them such a "local habitation." Why did the ancients represent Minerva as born in Africa,—and why are we told that Atlas there sustained the heavens and the earth, unless they meant to imply that Africa was the centre, from which religious and scientific light had been diffused? . . .

It is well known that Egypt was the great school of knowledge in the ancient world. It was the birth-place of Astronomy; and we still mark the constellations as they were arranged by Egyptian shepherds. The wisest of the Grecian philosophers, among whom were Solon, Pythagoras and Plato, went there for instruction, as our young men now go to England and Germany. The Eleusinian mysteries were introduced from Egypt; and the important secret which they taught, is supposed to have been the existence of one, invisible God. A large portion of Grecian mythology was thence derived; but in passing from one country to the other, the form of these poetical fables was often preserved, while the original meaning was lost.

Herodotus, the earliest of the Greek historians, informs us that the Egyptians were negroes. This fact has been much doubted, and often contradicted. But Herodotus certainly had the best means of knowing the truth on this subject; for he travelled in Egypt, and obtained his knowledge of the country by personal observation. He declares that the Colchians must be a colony of Egyptians, because, "like them, they have a black skin and frizzled hair."

The statues of the Sphinx have the usual characteristics of the negro race. This opinion is confirmed by Blumenbach, the celebrated German naturalist, and by Volney, who carefully examined the architecture of Egypt. . . .

All travellers in Africa agree, that the inhabitants, particularly of the interior, have a good deal of mechanical skill. They tan and dye leather, sometimes thinning it in such a manner that it is as flexible as paper. In Houssa, leather is dressed in the same soft, rich style as in Morocco; they manufacture cordage, handsome cloths, and fine tissue. Though ignorant of the turning machine, they make good pottery ware, and some of their jars are really tasteful. They prepare indigo, and extract ore from minerals. They make agricultural tools, and work skilfully in gold, silver and steel. Dickson, who knew jewellers and watch-makers among them, speaks of a very ingenious wooden clock made by a negro. Hornemann says the inhabitants of Haissa give their cutting instruments a keener edge than European artists, and their files are superior to those of France or England. Golberry assures us that some of the African stuffs are extremely fine and beautiful. . . .

In addition to the arguments drawn from the ancient conditions of Africa, and the present character of people in the interior of that country, there are numerous individual examples of spirit, courage, talent, and magnanimity.

History furnishes very few instances of bravery, intelligence, and perseverance, equal to the famous Zhinga, the negro queen of Angola, born in 1582. Like other despotic princes, her character is stained with numerous acts of ferocity and crime; but her great abilities cannot be for a moment doubted. . . .

*Job Ben Solomon,* was the son of the Mohammedan king of Bunda, on the Gambia. He was taken in 1730, and sold in Maryland. By a train of singular adventures he was conveyed to England, where his intelligence and dignified manners gained him many friends; among whom was Sir Hans Sloane, for whom he translated several Arabic manuscripts. After being received with distinction at the Court of St James, the African Company became interested in his fate, and carried him back to Bunda, in the year 1734. His uncle embracing him, said, "During sixty years, you are the first slave I have ever seen return from the American isles." At his father's death, Solomon became king, and was much beloved in his states. . . .

*Antonio Perura Rebouças,* who is at the present time Deputy from Bahia, in the Cortes of Brazil, is a distinguished lawyer, and a good man. He is learned in political economy, and has written ably upon the currency of Brazil. . . .

*Henry Diaz,* who is extolled in all the histories of Brazil, was a negro and slave. He became Colonel of a regiment of foot-soldiers, of his own color; and such was his reputation for sagacity and valor, that it was considered a distinction to be under his command. In the contest between the Portuguese and Hollanders, in 1637, Henry Diaz fought bravely against the latter. He compelled them to capitulate at Arecise, and to surrender Fernanbon. . . .

*Antony William Amo,* born in Guinea, was brought to Europe when very young. The Princess of Brunswick, Wolfenbuttle, defrayed the expenses of his education. He pursued his studies at

Halle and at Wittemberg, and so distinguished himself by his character and abilities, that the Rector and Council of Wittemberg thought proper to give public testimony of their respect in a letter of congratulation. In this letter they remark that Terence also was an African—that many martyrs, doctors, and fathers of the church were born in the same country, where learning once flourished, and which by losing the christian faith, again fell back into barbarism. Amo delivered private lectures on philosophy, which are highly praised in the same letter. He became a doctor.

*Lislet Geoffrroy*, a mulatto, was an officer of Artillery and guardian of the Depot of Maps and Plans of the Isle of France. He was a correspondent of the French Academy of Sciences, to whom he regularly transmitted meteorological observations, and sometimes hydrographical journals. His map of the Isles of France and Reunion is considered the best map of those islands that has appeared. In the archives of the Institute of Paris is an account of Lislet's voyage to the Bay of St Luce. He points out the exchangeable commodities and other resources which it presents; and urges the importance of encouraging industry by the hope of advantageous commerce, instead of exciting the natives to war in order to obtain slaves. Lislet established a scientific society at the Isle of France, to which some white men refused to belong, because its founder had a skin more deeply colored than their own.

*James Derham*, originally a slave at Philadelphia, was sold to a physician, who employed him in compounding drugs; he was afterward sold to a surgeon, and finally to Doctor Robert Dove, of New Orleans. In 1788, at the age of twenty one, he became the most distinguished physician in that city, and was able to talk with French, Spanish, and English in their own languages. Doctor Rush says, "I conversed with him on medicine, and found him very learned. I thought I could give him information concerning the treatment of diseases; but I learned from him more than he could expect from me."

*Thomas Fuller*, an African residing in Virginia, did not know how to read or write, but had great facility in arithmetical calculations. He was once asked how many seconds has an individual lived when he is seventy years, seven months, and seven days old? In a minute and a half he answered the question. One of the company took a pen, and after a long calculation, said Fuller had made the sum too large. "No," replied the negro, "the error is on your side. You did not calculate the leap-years." These facts are mentioned in a letter from Doctor Rush, published in the fifth volume of the American Museum.

In 1788, *Othello*, a negro, published at Baltimore an Essay against Slavery. Addressing white men, he says, "Is not your conduct, compared with your principles, a sacrilegious irony? When you dare to talk of civilization and the gospel, you pronounce your own anathema. In you the superiority of power produces nothing but a superiority of brutality and barbarism. Your fine political systems are sullied by the outrages committed against human nature and the divine majesty."

*Olandad Equiano*, better known by the name of Gustavus Vasa, was stolen in Africa, at twelve years old, together with his sister. They were torn from each other; and the brother, after a horrible passage in a slave ship, was sold at Barbadoes. Being purchased by a lieutenant, he accompanied his new master to England, Guernsey, and the siege of Louisbourg. He afterwards experienced great changes of fortune, and made voyages to various parts of Europe and America. In all his wanderings, he cherished an earnest desire for freedom. He hoped to obtain his liberty by faithfulness and zeal in his master's service; but finding avarice stronger than benevolence, he began trade with a capital of three pence, and by rigid economy was at last able to purchase—*his own body and soul;* this, however, was not effected, until he had endured much oppression and insult. He was several times shipwrecked, and finally, after thirty years of vicissitude and suffering, he settled in London and published his Memoirs. The book is said to be written with all the simplicity, and something of the roughness, of uneducated nature. He gives a *naive* description of his terror at an earthquake, his surprise when he first saw snow, a picture, a watch, and a quadrant.

He always had an earnest desire to understand navigation, as a probable means of one day escaping from slavery. Having persuaded a sea-captain to give him lessons, he applied himself with great diligence, though obliged to contend with many obstacles, and subject to frequent interruptions. Doctor Irving, with whom he once lived as a servant, taught him to render salt water fresh by distillation. Some time after, when engaged in a northern expedition, he made good use of this knowledge, and furnished the crew with water they could drink.

His sympathies were, very naturally, given to the weak and the despised, wherever he found them. He deplores the fate of modern Greeks, nearly as much degraded by the Turks as the negroes are by their white brethren. In 1789, Vasa presented a petition to the British parliament, for the suppression of the slave trade. His son, named Sancho, was assistant librarian to Sir Joseph Banks, and Secretary to the Committee for Vaccination.

Another negro, named *Ignatius Sancho,* was born on board a Guinea ship, where his parents were both captives, destined for the South American slave market.—Change of climate killed his mother, and his father committed suicide. At two years old the orphan was carried to England, and presented to some ladies residing at Greenwich. Something in his character reminded them of Don Quixote's squire, and they added Sancho to his original name of Ignatius. The Duke of Montague saw him frequently and thought he had a mind worthy of cultivation. He often sent him books, and advised the ladies to give him a chance for education; but they had less liberal views, and often threatened to send the poor boy again into slavery. After the death of his friends, he went into the service of the Duchess of Montague, who at her death left him an annuity of thirty pounds; beside which he had saved seventy pounds out of his earnings.

Something of dissipation mixed with his love of reading, and sullied the better part of his character.—He spent his last shilling at Drury Lane, to see Garrick, who was extremely friendly to him. At one time he thought of performing African characters on the stage, but was prevented by a bad articulation.

He afterward became very regular in his habits, and married a worthy West Indian girl. After his death, two volumes of his letters were printed, of which a second edition was soon published, with a portrait of the author, designed by Gainsborough, and engraved by Bartolozzi.

Sterne formed an acquaintance with Ignatius Sancho; and in the third volume of his letters, there is an epistle addressed to this African, in which he tells him that varieties in nature do not sunder the bands of brotherhood; and expresses his indignation that certain men wish to class their equals among the brutes, in order to treat them as such with impunity. Jefferson criticises Sancho with some severity, for yielding too much to an eccentric imagination; but he acknowledges that he has an easy style, and a happy choice of expressions.

The letters of Sancho are thought to bear some resemblance to those of Sterne, both in their beauties and defects.

*Francis Williams,* a negro, was born in Jamaica.—The Duke of Montaigne, governor of the island, thinking him an unusually bright boy, sent him to England to school. He afterward entered the University of Cambridge, and became quite a proficient in mathematics.—During his stay in Europe, he published a song which became quite popular, beginning "Welcome, welcome, brother debtor." After his return to Jamaica, the Duke tried to obtain a place for him in the council of the government, but did not succeed. He then became a teacher of Latin and mathematics. He wrote a good deal of Latin verse, a species of composition of which he was very fond. This negro is described as having been pedantic and haughty; indulging a profound contempt for men of his own color. Where learning is a rare attainment among any people, or any class of people, this effect is very apt to be produced.

*Phillis Wheatly,* stolen from Africa when seven or eight years old, was sold to a wealthy merchant in Boston, in 1761. Being an intelligent and winning child, she gained upon the affections of her master's family, and they allowed her uncommon advantages. When she was nineteen years old, a little volume of her poems was published, and passed through several editions, both in England and the United States. Lest the authenticity of the poems should be doubted, her master, the governor, the lieutenant governor, and fifteen other respectable persons, acquainted with her character and circumstances, testified that they were really her own productions. Jefferson denies that these poems have any merit; but I think he would have judged differently, had he been perfectly unprejudiced. It would indeed be absurd to put Phillis Wheatly in competition with Mrs

Hemans, Mary Hewitt, Mrs Sigourney, Miss Gould, and other modern writers; but her productions certainly appear very respectable in comparison with most of the poetry of that day.

Phillis Wheatly received her freedom in 1775; and two years after married a colored man, who, like herself was considered a prodigy. He was at first a grocer; but afterward became a lawyer, well known by the name of Doctor Peter. He was in the habit of pleading causes for his brethren before the tribunals of justice, and gained both reputation and fortune by his practice. Phillis had been flattered and indulged from her earliest childhood; and, like many literary women in old times, she acquired something of contempt for domestic occupations. This is said to have produced unhappiness between her and her husband. She died in 1780.

Mr Wilberforce, (on whom may the blessing of God rest forever!) aided by several benevolent individuals, established a seminary for colored people at Clapham, a few leagues from London. The first scholars were twenty one young negroes, sent by the Governor of Sierra Leone. The Abbé Grégoire says, "I visited this establishment in 1802, to examine the progress of the scholars; and I found there existed no difference between them and European children, except that of color. The same observation has been made, first at Paris, in the ancient college of La Marche, where Coesnon, professor of the University, taught a number of colored boys.—Many members of the National Institute, who have carefully examined this college, and watched the progress of the scholars in their particular classes, and public exercises, will testify to the truth of my assertion." . . .

Among Bonaparte's officers there was a mulatto General of Division, named Alexander Dumas. In the army of the Alps, with charged bayonet, he ascended St Bernard, defended by a number of redoubts, took possession of the enemy's cannon, and turned their own ammunition against them. He likewise signalized himself in the expedition to Egypt. His troop, composed of blacks and mulattoes, were everywhere formidable. Near Lisle, Alexander Dumas, with only four men, attacked a post of fifty Austrians, killed six, and made sixteen prisoners. Napoleon called him the Horatius Cocles of the Tyrols.

On his return from Egypt, Dumas unluckily fell into the hands of the Neapolitan government, and was two years kept in irons. He died in 1807. . . .

*Toussaint L'Ouverture,* the celebrated black chieftain, was born a slave, in the year 1745, upon the plantation of Count de Noé. His amiable deportment as a slave, the patience, mildness, and benevolence of his disposition, and the purity of his conduct amid the general laxity of morals which prevailed in the island, gained for him many of those advantages which afterwards gave him such absolute ascendency over his insurgent brethren. His good qualities attracted the attention of M. Bayou de Libertas, the agent on the estate, who taught him reading, writing, and arithmetic,—elements of knowledge, which hardly one in ten thousand of his fellow slaves possessed. M. Bayou made him his postillion, which gave him advantages much above those of the field slaves. When the general rising of the blacks took place, in 1791, much solicitation was used to induce Toussaint to join them; but he declined, until he had procured an opportunity for the escape of M. Bayou and his family to Baltimore, shipping a considerable quantity of sugar for the supply of their immediate wants. In his subsequent prosperity, he availed himself of every occasion to give them new marks of his gratitude. Having thus provided security for his benefactor, he joined a corps of blacks, under the orders of General Biassou; but was soon raised to the principal command, Biassou being degraded on account of his cruelty and ferocity. Indeed, Toussaint was every way so much superior to the other negroes, by reason of his general intelligence and education, his prudence, activity and address, not less than his bravery, that he immediately attained a complete ascendency over all the black chieftains. In 1797, Toussaint received from the French government a commission of General-in-Chief of the armies of St Domingo, and as such signed the convention with General Maitland for the evacuation of the island by the British. From 1798 until 1801, the island continued tranquil under the government of Toussaint, who adopted and enforced the most judicious measures for healing the wounds of his country, and restoring its commercial and agricultural prosperity. His efforts would have been attended with much success, but for the ill-judged expedition, which Bonaparte sent against the island, under the command of Le Clerc. This expedition, fruitless as it was in respect of its general object, proved fatal to the negro chieftain.

Toussaint was noted for private virtues; among the rest, warm affection for his family. Le Clerc brought out from France Toussaint's two sons, with their preceptor, whose orders were to carry his pupils to their father, and make use of them to work on his tenderness, and induce him to abandon his countrymen. If he yielded, he was to be made second in command to Le Clerc; if he refused, his children were to be reserved as hostages of his fidelity to the French. Notwithstanding the greatness of the sacrifice demanded of him, Toussaint remained faithful to his brethren. We pass over the details of the war, which at length, ended in a treaty of peace concluded by Toussaint, Dessalines and Christophe, against their better judgment, but in consequence of the effect of Le Clerc's professions upon their simple followers, who were induced to lay down their arms. Toussaint retired to his plantation, relying upon the solemn assurances of Le Clerc, that his person and property should be held sacred. Notwithstanding these assurances, he was treacherously seized in the night, hurried on board a ship of war, and conveyed to Brest. He was conducted first to close prison in Chateaux de Joux, and from thence to Besançon, where he was plunged into a cold, wet, subterranean prison, which soon proved fatal to a constitution used only to the warm skies and free air of the West Indies. He languished through the winter of 1802–1803; and his death, which happened in April, 1803, raised a cry of indignation against the government, which had chosen this dastardly method of destroying one of the best and bravest of the negro race. . . .

The enemies of true freedom were very ready to predict that the government of Hayti could not continue for any length of time; but it has now lasted nearly thirty years, constantly increasing in respectability and wealth. The affairs of Greece have been managed with much less ability and discretion, though all the cabinets of Europe have given assistance and advice. St Domingo achieved her independence alone and unaided—nay, in the very teeth of prejudice and scorn. The Greeks had loans from England, and contributions from America, and sympathy from half the world; the decisive battle of Navarino was gained by the combined fleets of England, France and Russia. Is it asked why

Hayti has not produced any examples of splendid genius? In reply let me inquire, how long did the Europeans ridicule *us* for our poverty in literature? When Raynal reproached the United States with not having produced one celebrated man, Jefferson requested him to wait until we had existed "as long as the Greeks before they had a Homer, the Romans a Virgil, and the French a Racine." Half a century elapsed before our republic produced Irving, Cooper, Sedgwick, Halleck, and Bryant. We must not forget that the cruel prejudice, under which colored people labor, makes it extremely difficult for them to gain admission to the best colleges and schools; they are obliged to contend with obstacles, which white men never encounter.

It might seem wonderful that the descendants of wise Ethiopia, and learned Egypt, are now in such a state of degradation, if history did not furnish a remarkable parallel in the condition of the modern Greeks. The land of Homer, Pericles, and Plato, is now inhabited by ignorant, brutal pirates. Freedom made the Grecians great and glorious—tyranny has made them stupid and miserable. Yet their yoke has been light, compared with African bondage. In both cases the wrongs of the oppressed have been converted into an argument against them. We first debase the nature of man by making him a slave, and then very coolly tell him that he must always remain a slave because he does not know how to use freedom. We first crush people to the earth, and then claim the right of trampling on them forever, because they are prostrate. Truly, human selfishness never invented a rule, which worked so charmingly both ways!

No one thinks of doubting the intellect of Indians; yet civilization has certainly advanced much farther in the interior of Africa, than it did among the North American tribes. The Indians have strong untutored eloquence,—so have the Africans. And where will you find an Indian chieftain, whose pride, intellect, and valor, are more than a match for Zhinga's? Both of these classes have been most shamefully wronged; but public prejudice, which bows the negro to the earth, has borne with a far less crushing power upon the energies of the red man; yet they have not produced a Shakspeare or a Newton. But I shall be asked how it is that the nations of Africa, having proceeded so far in the arts of civilization, have made a full stop, and remained century after century without any obvious improvement? I will answer this by another question: How long did the ancient Helvetians, Gauls, and Saxons remain in such a state of barbarism, that what they considered splendor and refinement, would be called poverty and rudeness, by their German, French, and English descendants?—What was it that changed the intellectual and moral character of these people, after ages of ignorance and ferocity? It was the *art of printing*. But, alas, with the introduction of printing, modern slavery was introduced! While commerce has carried books and maps to other portions of the globe, she has sent kidnappers, with guns and cutlasses into Africa. We have not preached the Gospel of peace to her princes; we have incited them to make war upon each other, to fill our markets with slaves. While knowledge, like a mighty pillar of fire, has guided the European nations still onward, and onward, a dark cloud has settled more and more gloomily over benighted Africa. The lessons of time, the experience of ages, from which we have learned so much, are entirely lost to this vast continent.

I have heard it asserted that the Indians were evidently superior to the negroes, because it was impossible to enslave *them*. Our slave laws prove that there are some exceptions to this remark; and it must be remembered that the Indians have been fairly met in battle, contending with but one nation at a time; while the whole world have combined against the Africans— sending emissaries to lurk for them in secret places, or steal them at midnight from their homes. The Indian will seek freedom in the arms of death—and so will the negro. By thousands and thousands, these poor people have died for freedom. They have stabbed themselves for freedom—jumped into the waves for freedom—starved for freedom—fought like very tigers for freedom! But they have been hung, and burned, and shot—and their tyrants have been their historians! When the Africans have writers of their own, we shall hear their efforts for liberty called by the true title of heroism in a glorious cause. We are told in the fable that a lion, looking at the picture of one of his own species, conquered and trampled on by man, calmly said, "We lions have no painters."

I shall be told that in the preceding examples I have shown only the bright side of the picture. I readily grant it; but I have deemed it important to show that the picture *has* a bright side. I am well aware that most of the negro authors are remarkable, principally because they are negroes. With considerable talent, they generally evince bad taste. I do not pretend that they are Scotts or Miltons; but I wish to prove that they are *men,* capable of producing their proportion of Scotts and Miltons, if they could be allowed to live in a state of physical and intellectual freedom. But where, at the present time, *can* they live in perfect freedom, cheered by the hopes and excited by the rewards, which stimulate white men to exertion? Every avenue to distinction is closed to them. Even where the body is suffered to be free, a hateful prejudice keeps the soul in fetters. I think every candid mind must admit that it is more wonderful they have done so much, than that they have done no more.

As a class, I am aware that the negroes, with many honorable exceptions, are ignorant, and show little disposition to be otherwise; but this ceases to be the case just in proportion as they are free. The fault is in their unnatural situation, not in themselves. Tyranny always dwarfs the intellect. Homer tells us, that when Jupiter condemns a man to slavery, he takes from him half his mind. A family of children treated with habitual violence or contempt, become stupid and sluggish, and are called fools by the very parents or guardians who have crushed their mental energies. It was remarked by M. Dupuis, the British Consul at Mogadore, that the generality of Europeans, after a long captivity and severe treatment among the Arabs, seemed at first exceedingly dull and insensible. "If they had been any considerable time in slavery," says he, "they appeared lost to reason and feeling; their spirits broken; and their faculties sunk in a species of stupor, which I am unable adequately to describe. They appeared degraded even below the negro slave. The succession of hardships, without any protecting law to which they can appeal for alleviation, or redress, seems to destroy every spring of exertion, or hope in their minds. They appear indifferent to everything around them; abject, servile, and brutish." . . .

Then let the slave-holder no longer apologize for himself by urging the stupidity and sensuality of negroes. It is upon the *system,* which thus transforms men into beasts, that the reproach rests in all its strength and bitterness. And even if the negroes were, beyond all doubt, our inferiors in intellect, this would form no excuse for oppression, or contempt. The use of law and public opinion is to protect the weak against the strong; and the government which perverts these blessings into means of tyranny, resembles the priest who administered poison with the Holy Sacrament.

Is there an American willing that the intellectual and the learned should bear despotic sway over the simple and the ignorant? If there be such an one, *he* may consistently vindicate our treatment of the Africans.

## THEODORE WELD

### RACIAL PROBLEMS OF THE ANTI-SLAVERY MOVEMENT

Leader of the famous student anti-slavery revolt which erupted early in 1834 at Lane Seminary in Ohio, Theodore Dwight Weld (1803–1895) resigned from the seminary in October 1834 and immediately enlisted as an agent of the American Anti-Slavery Society. It was in 1836 that Weld, as an agent of the society, wrote the following letter to Lewis Tappan, prominent philanthropist-reformer and a member of its executive committee. Lewis Tappan's brother, Arthur, was the organization's first president. Later in 1836, Weld helped to organize and train a group of seventy anti-slavery agents who were employed by the society to further its message and organization. A brilliant lecturer and writer, Weld produced one of the most important works in anti-slavery literature, *American Slavery As It Is: Testimony of a Thousand Witnesses,* published by the society in New York in 1839. The letter reprinted here is from *Letters of Theodore Dwight Weld, Angelina Grimké Weld and Sarah Grimké, 1822–1844,* edited by Gilbert H. Barnes and Dwight L. Dumond, published under the direction of the American Historical Association by D. Appleton-Century Company (New York, 1934), Vol. I, pp. 270–74. The notes are by Dumond and Barnes. The letter is reprinted with the permission of Dwight L. Dumond, the American Historical Association, and the Clements Library at the University of Michigan, which owns the original.

### *Weld to Lewis Tappan*[1]

[ROCHESTER, N.Y., March 9, 1836]

MY DEAR BROTHER TAPPAN

I *must* answer one point in your last letter just received, and also in the letter received by brother Stanton. It is *this*—my views explicitly about our intercourse with the people of Color. Really, after so long a time I must forsooth solemnly avow my principles on this subject!! Has it come to this!! Two years ago nearly, I was threatened with expulsion from Lane Seminary, mainly because I advocated the doctrine that "persons are to be treated according to their intrinsic worth *irrespective of Color, shape, condition* or what not"—and further and mostly because I acted out this principle from day to day in my intercourse with the Colored people. But to the point. I have *always* taken this ground and acted upon it: Take *more pains* to treat with attention, courtesy, and cordiality a colored person than a white, from the *fact* that he *is* colored. But you say in your letter: "you did not act on this principle when you excluded 3 or 4 colored men from your Convention in Ohio." Answer 1st. Only *one* colored brother came to the Convention. He did *not* sit with us. The facts are these. For many weeks before our State Convention I was writing into all parts of the state urging to the Convention. I wrote to a number of Colored gentlemen urging their attendance, and assigning as a reason that it was very important to the cause for the convention to testify in its corporate capacity that God had made all men of one blood. After this I went to Zanesville and Putnam in order to prepare the way for the Convention. Zanesville was locked up. Could get no place to lecture, not a shanty even. Putnam on the opposite side of the river a little better. Could get one public room. Lectured. Mob came, broke the windows [and] doors, tore off the gate, attacked me when I came out with stones and clubs, etc. This continued until the trustees of the room shut it up. Then adjourned to private room. In short, every ki[n]d of outrage was committed upon the Abolitionists and Colored people. Large numbers of poor Colored were turned out of employ, men were prosecuted under the vandal laws of Ohio for employing them, and the four hundred Colored people in Zanesville and Putnam were greatly oppressed in continued apprehension and panic. Of their own accord they called a meeting, [and] privately and after much consultation resolved to stay away from the lectures entirely, and assigned these two common sense reasons: 1. If *they* attended, it would keep away that very class of persons which they wished to go—the *prejudiced* ones. 2. If they attended, it would expose them not only to insult and outrage while there, but it would be seized as ground for the pretence of mobbing them, tearing down their houses, etc. They appointed a Committee to meet me privately, tell me what they had resolved on and the reasons, and to say to me: "Persevere. We will stay at home and pray". I told them "You have done just right". One Colored person attended one of the lectures and was knocked down on the bridge going home. When the Colored people were told that Colored persons were expected to be at the Convention, they flocked around me in agony and terror. They begged that they might be prevented from going, or if any came they might be prevailed upon not to go into the Convention. Only one came. In our *private* preparatory meeting two hours before the Convention the matter came up. There was not one member of the Convention who didnt rejoice in the privilege of sitting in Convention, at table, anywhere with this Colored brother. But we were all perfectly unanimous. Birney, all the Lane Seminary students, John Rankin, brothers,[2] the Dickeys,[3] and all Quakers, the Colored brother and all, that for him to sit in the Convention would peril his limbs at least if not his life, and would without doubt bring down on our poor panic struck brethren, the Colored people in Z. and P., the vengeance of the mob. This the people of Color without exception verily believed and besought that he would not sit in Convention. The Convention to a man were willing to peril themselves and if need be go to prison and to death, but they were not willing to call down fire upon their Colored friends. When the Colored brethren [i.e., brother] saw the state of the case, he said at once nothing would induce me to go into the Convention, and even if I wished to do it the Convention ought to advise me against it, and if they did not they would be wanting in love to the Colored people. These are the *facts*. We acted on the law of Love. The statement of the case is its *argument*. I shall not *argue* the point. I believe you have common sense. Well, but you will ask, Did we do wrong to insist upon the Colored Choir mingling with the white choir at the Anniversary of 1835? Answer, that will depend on various things of which I know nothing. *One* of them is *this:* will the effects of that public development be a *blessing* or a *curse* to the Colored people? At our Convention a specific case. It was a plain case to us all—we all knew the *facts*—and that "circumstances alter cases". As to the New York matter, those who were on the ground have all the *facts* before them and are best qualified to decide. I cannot say decidedly until I have all the facts. My views on this whole subject are expressed in our Expose of the Lane Sem. If I mistake not, I this moment recollect that a long paragraph was stricken out by vote of the majority of the brethren which they thought was so strong *amalgamationally* that the Anti Slavery community would kick. I wish I could see you and talk over this subject ten minutes, and some half a dozen other points. From all I can find out from your letters, I have made up my mind that in *carrying out principles* you dont always take into consideration the *modifications* produced in those principles by the *bearings* of *other* principles. You think so rapidly and act so promptly that you are greatly tempted *not to stop,* and trace the influence and relations of *collateral* principles to the main one. The course of a river you know may be turned clear round the compass by the action of insignificant tributaries on its current. As to my feelings toward the Colored people, suffice it to say [that] while I was at Lane Seminary my intercourse was with the Colored people of Cincinnati I think I may say *exclusively.* If I ate in the City it was at *their* tables. If I slept in the City it was at their homes. If I attended parties, it was *theirs—weddings—theirs —Funerals—theirs—Religious meetings—theirs*—Sabbath schools —Bible classes—theirs. During the 18 months that I spent at Lane Seminary I *did not attend Dr. Beechers Church once.* Nor did I ever attend any other of the Presbyterian Churches in the City except brother Mahans, and did not attend there more than half a dozen times during the whole time. The white methodist I attended once only. The rest of the time, when not called out to labor in the country, I was with the Colored people in their meetings by day and by night. If any one wishes to know what my *principles* and *practice* have been and are as to Intercourse with the Colored people, I say let him ask the three thousand colored people in Cincinnati and if he ask it soberly they will laugh in his face. But, says brother Tappan, would you have walked arm in arm with a Colored lady at mid-day down main street in Cincinnati? Answer *No.* Why?! *Not* because I had any prejudice against colored people: I never had any. When seven years old I begged the privilege of sitting on the "nigger seat" at school with a little colored boy, who was hissed and trodden by scholars and teacher. 2. *Not* Because I am afraid to go against public sentiment; that I have shown in something besides words. But 1st. *Because* to do it would bring down a storm of venge[a]nce upon the defenceless people of Color, throw them out of employ, drive them out homeless, and surrender them up victims to popular fury. 2. Because it would be in its inevitable effect upon all classes and parties an ostentatious display of superiority to prejudice and *a blustering bravado defiance,* which would produce an entire misconstruction of motives, and turn public attention violently from the main point to a collateral one, which is true as really involves the *principle* of the *main* point, but which will be far more rapidly advanced as an *appendage* of the main point, than by making *it* the main point, and that the appendage. Crowd ahead the *hub* and you crowd ahead the spokes and [mutilated]. As to the treatment of colored people in *specific cases,* such as that at the Ohio Convention, I say give me the colored people for counsellors. They have vastly more common sense in such matters than any of the rest of us. I have talked these matters all over a hundred times with Colored men and women, and never found one who did not agree with me in toto on this point.

One word further, If just such a project had been on foot in Cincinnati when I lived there as you have now in New York, I should have insisted upon it that colored men should be elected members of Boards of Trustees, seniors, etc., if any could be fo[u]nd at all fit for the offices—yea more, if no *absolutely unfit* for them. While I was there I was all the time on Committees, in boards of Trustees, etc., with them. Finally the principle in short is this: To make a distinction between a white man and a black on acco[u]nt of their color in organization is the very *principle of slavery.* Treatment according to worth irrespective of color is the doctrine. We may never ill treat them, never manifest the least unkindness; that would be sin. But there are times when we *may refrain* from making *public visible demonstrations* of feelings about differences of color in practical exhibitions, when such demonstrations would bring down persecutions on them.

When one of the mob at Utica asked C. Stuart where Lewis Tappan was, "I shant tell you" said Stuart.[4] Now Stuart on the same principle would not *act* in such a way the mobite would find out L. T. any more than *speak.* He would refrain from those *visible* demonstrations of affection which his heart is full of because they would [be] singling out the victim. And if he would not point out the victim to the man thirsting for his blood, he surely would not just *inflame* the thirst, and then point out the victim. Well, here I am all over the sheet—cant say any more. I want to write you about half a dozen things of much moment in a few days. I am waiting here a few days for two protracted meetings now in Progress to close before beginning to lecture. Meanwhile, every moment is occupied in answering letters an[d] tying up the loose strings of m[an]y little matters. In haste, ever your brother in bond with the bound

WELD

## NOTES

1. Addressed: New York City. [This and following notes are by editors Dumond and Barnes]
2. The Lane rebels.
3. William Dickey (1774–1858) and his brother, James H. Dickey, were leading ministers in the Chillicothe Presbytery. Born in South Carolina, and reared in Kentucky, they had begun their ministry in that State, and in 1817 had moved to Ohio. William Dickey was pastor of the Presbyterian Church in Bloomington, Ohio, for forty years, and James Dickey preached in Ross County. Together with John Rankin, Dyer Burgess, Samuel Crothers, Van Dyke, and the Gillilands, all of them former Kentuckians, they made the Chillicothe Presbytery almost solidly anti-slavery in sentiment.
4. This incident occurred at the organization meeting of the New York State Anti-Slavery Society in 1835.

## CATHERINE E. BEECHER
## AND ANGELINA GRIMKÉ

### A Critique and Defense of Abolitionist Strategy

Catherine Beecher (1800–1878), the eldest of Rev. Lyman Beecher's nine children and sister of Henry Ward Beecher, was an early advocate of higher education for women. Conservative in her political views, she opposed feminine suffrage, as well as Abolitionist efforts to achieve Negro equality and their interference with Southern slavery. In the following selection from pp. 26–32 of her volume, *An Essay on Slavery and Abolitionism, with Reference to the Duty of American Females* (Philadelphia, 1837), she criticizes the methods used by the Abolitionists of her day in seeking to eliminate anti-Negro discrimination. The book was addressed to Angelina Grimké. Miss Grimké, daughter of a prominent South Carolina slaveholding family, who left the South with her sister Sarah and became an outstanding anti-slavery leader, replied in a volume entitled *Letters to Catherine E. Beecher, in Reply to an Essay on Slavery and Abolitionism, Addressed to A. E. Grimké* (Boston, 1838). The selection following Miss Beecher's statement is from pp. 42–50 of Angelina Grimké's book.

### Catherine Beecher on Prejudice and Abolition

. . . The next measure of Abolitionism was an attempt to remove the prejudices of the whites against the blacks, on account of natural peculiarities. Now, prejudice is an *unreasonable* and *groundless* dislike of persons or things. Of course, as it is unreasonable, it is the most difficult of all things to conquer, and the worst and most irritating method that could be attempted would be, to attack a man as guilty of sin, as unreasonable, as ungenerous, or as proud, for allowing a certain prejudice.

This is the sure way to produce anger, self-justification, and an increase of the strength of prejudice, against that which has caused him this rebuke and irritation.

The best way to make a person like a thing which is disagree-

able, is to try in some way to make it agreeable; and if a certain
class of persons is the subject of unreasonable prejudice, the
peaceful and christian way of removing it would be to endeavour
to render the unfortunate persons who compose this class, so
useful, so humble and unassuming, so kind in their feelings, and
so full of love and good works, that prejudice would be supplanted by complacency in their goodness, and pity and sympathy for their disabilities. If the friends of the blacks had
quietly set themselves to work to increase their intelligence, their
usefulness, their respectability, their meekness, gentleness, and
benevolence, and then had appealed to the pity, generosity, and
christian feelings of their fellow citizens, a very different result
would have appeared. Instead of this, reproaches, rebukes, and
sneers, were employed to convince the whites that their prejudices were sinful, and without any just cause. They were accused
of pride, of selfish indifference, of unchristian neglect. This
tended to irritate the whites, and to increase their prejudice
against the blacks, who thus were made the causes of rebuke and
exasperation. Then, on the other hand, the blacks extensively
received the Liberator, and learned to imbibe the spirit of its
conductor.

They were taught to feel that they were injured and abused,
the objects of a guilty and unreasonable prejudice—that they occupied a lower place in society than was right—that they ought to
be treated as if they were whites; and in repeated instances,
attempts were made by their friends to mingle them with whites,
so as to break down the existing distinctions of society. Now. the
question is not, whether these things, that were urged by Abolitionists, were true. The thing maintained is, that the method
taken by them to remove this prejudice was neither peaceful nor
christian in its tendency, but, on the contrary, was calculated to
increase the evil, and to generate anger, pride, and recrimina-
tion, on one side, and envy, discontent, and revengeful feelings
on the other.

These are some of the general measures which have been
exhibited in the Abolition movement. The same peculiarities
may be as distinctly seen in specific cases, where the peaceful and
quiet way of accomplishing the good was neglected, and the one
most calculated to excite wrath and strife was chosen. Take, for

example, the effort to establish a college for coloured persons. The quiet, peaceful, and christian way of doing such a thing, would have been, for those who were interested in the plan, to furnish the money necessary, and then to have selected a retired place, where there would be the least prejudice and opposition to be met, and there, in an unostentatious way, commenced the education of the youth to be thus sustained. Instead of this, at a time when the public mind was excited on the subject, it was noised abroad that a college for blacks was to be founded. Then a city was selected for its location, where was another college, so large as to demand constant effort and vigilance to preserve quiet subordination; where contests with "sailors and town boys" were barely kept at bay; a college embracing a large proportion of southern students, who were highly excited on the subject of slavery and emancipation; a college where half the shoe-blacks and waiters were coloured men. Beside the very walls of this college, it was proposed to found a college for coloured young men. Could it be otherwise than that opposition, and that for the best of reasons, would arise against such an attempt, both from the faculty of the college and the citizens of the place? Could it be reasonably expected that they would not oppose a measure so calculated to increase their own difficulties and liabilities, and at the same time so certain to place the proposed institution in the most unfavourable of all circumstances? But when the measure was opposed, instead of yielding meekly and peaceably to such reasonable objections, and soothing the feelings and apprehensions that had been excited, by putting the best construction on the matter, and seeking another place, it was claimed as an evidence of opposition to the interests of the blacks, and as a mark of the force of sinful prejudice. The worst, rather than the best, motives were ascribed to some of the most respectable, and venerated, and pious men, who opposed the measure; and a great deal was said and done that was calculated to throw the community into an angry ferment.

Take another example. If a prudent and benevolent female had selected almost any village in New England, and commenced a school for coloured females, in a quiet, appropriate, and unostentatious way, the world would never have heard of the case, except to applaud her benevolence, and the kindness of the villagers, who aided her in the effort. But instead of this, there appeared public advertisements, (which I saw at the time,) stating that a seminary for the education of young ladies of colour was to be opened in Canterbury, in the state of Connecticut, where would be taught music on the piano forte, drawing, &c., together with a course in English education. Now, there are not a dozen coloured families in New England, in such pecuniary circumstances, that if they were whites it would not be thought ridiculous to attempt to give their daughters such a course of education, and Canterbury was a place where but few of the wealthiest families ever thought of furnishing such accomplishments for their children. Several other particulars might be added that were exceedingly irritating, but this may serve as a specimen of the method in which the whole affair was conducted. It was an entire disregard of the prejudices and proprieties of society, and calculated to stimulate pride, anger, ill-will, contention, and all the bitter feelings that spring from such collisions. Then, instead of adopting measures to soothe and conciliate, rebukes, sneers and denunciations, were employed, and Canterbury and Connecticut were held up to public scorn and rebuke for doing what most other communities would probably have done, if similarly tempted and provoked.

### Angelina Grimké Replies

HAVERHILL, MASS. 7*th mo.* 23, 1837.

DEAR FRIEND:—Thou sayest, 'the *best* way to make a person like a thing which is disagreeable, is to try in some way to make it agreeable.' So, then, instead of convincing a person by sound argument and pointed rebuke that sin is *sin,* we are to *disguise* the opposite virtue in such a way as to make him like that, in preference to the sin he had so dearly loved. We are to *cheat* a sinner out of his sin, rather than to compel him, under the stings of conviction, to give it up from deep-rooted principle.

If this is the course pursued by ministers, then I wonder not at the kind of converts which are brought into the church at the present day. Thy remarks on the subject of prejudice, show but too plainly how strongly thy own mind is imbued with it, and how little thy colonization principles have done to exterminate this feeling from thy own bosom. Thou sayest, 'if a certain class of persons is the subject of unreasonable prejudice, the peaceful and christian way of removing it would be to endeavor to render the unfortunate persons who compose this class, so useful, so *humble,* so *unassuming,* &c. that prejudice would be supplanted by complacency in their goodness, and *pity* and sympathy for their disabilities.' 'If the friends of the blacks had quietly set themselves to work to increase their intelligence, their usefulness, &c. and then had appealed to the *pity* and benevolence of their fellow citizens, a very different result would have appeared.' Or, in other words, if one person is guilty of a sin against another person, I am to let the sinner go entirely unreproved, but to persuade the injured party to bear with humility and patience all the outrages that are inflicted upon him, and thus try to soothe the sinner 'into complacency with their goodness' in 'bearing all things, and enduring all things.' Well, suppose I succeed:—is that sinner won from the evil of his ways by *principle?* No! Has he the principle of love implanted in his breast? No! Instead of being in love with the virtue exhibited by the individual, because *it is virtue,* he is delighted with the personal convenience he experiences from the exercise of that virtue. He feels kindly toward the individual, *because* he is an *instrument* of his enjoyment, a mere *means* to promote his wishes. There is *no* reformation there at all. And so the colored people are to be taught to be 'very *humble*' and '*unassuming,*' '*gentle*' and '*meek,*' and then the '*pity* and generosity' of their fellow citizens are to be appealed to. Now, no one who knows anything of the influence of Abolitionists over the colored people, can deny that it has been *peaceful* and christian; had it not been so, they never would have seen those whom they had regarded as their best friends, mobbed and persecuted, without raising an arm in their defence. Look, too, at the rapid spread of thorough temperance principles among them, and their moral reform and other laudable and useful associations; look at the rising character of this people, the new life and energy which have been infused into them. Who have done it? Who have exerted by far the greatest influence on these oppressed Americans? I leave thee to answer. I will give thee one instance of this salutary influence. In a letter I received from one of my colored sisters, she incidentally makes this remark:—'Until very lately, I have lived and acted more for *myself* than for the good of others. I confess that I am *wholly indebted to the Abolition cause* for arousing me from apathy and indifference, and shedding light into a mind which has been too long wrapt in selfish darkness.' The Abolition cause has exerted a powerful and healthful influence over this class of our population, and it has been done by quietly going into the midst of them, and identifying ourselves with them.

But Abolitionists are complained of, because they, at the same time, fearlessly exposed the *sin* of the unreasonable and unholy prejudice which existed against these injured ones. Thou sayest 'that reproaches, rebukes and sneers were employed to convince the whites that their prejudices were sinful, and *without* any just cause.' *Without any just cause!* Couldst thou think so, if thou really loved thy colored sisters *as thyself*? The unmeasured abuse which the Colonization Society was heaping upon this despised people, was no *just cause* for pointed rebuke, I suppose! The manner in which they are thrust into one corner of our meeting-houses, as if the plague-spot was on their skins; the rudeness and cruelty with which they are treated in our hotels, and steamboats, rail road cars and stages, is *no just cause* of reproach to a professed christian community, I presume. Well, all that I can say is, that I believe if Isaiah or James were now alive, they would pour their reproaches and rebukes upon the heads and *hearts* of those who are thus despising the Lord's poor, and saying to those whose spirits are clothed by God in the 'vile raiment' of a *colored skin,* Stand thou there in yonder gallery, or sit thou here in 'the negro-pew.' 'Sneers,' too, are complained of. Have abolitionists ever made use of greater sarcasm and irony than did the prophet Elijah? When things are ridiculous as well as wicked, it is unreasonable to expect that every cast of mind will treat them with solemnity. And what is more ridiculous than American prejudice; to proscribe and persecute men and women, because their *complexions* are of a darker hue than our own? Why, it is an outrage upon common sense; and as my brother Thomas S. Grimke remarked only a few weeks before his death, 'posterity will laugh at our prejudices.' Where is the harm, then, if abolitionists should laugh now at the wicked absurdity?

Thou sayest, 'this tended to irritate the whites, and to increase their prejudices against the blacks.' The *truth always* irritates the proud, impenitent sinner. To charge abolitionists with this irritation, is something like the charge brought against the English government by the captain of the slaver I told thee of in my second letter, who threw all his human merchandize overboard, in order to escape detection, and then charged this horrible wholesale murder upon the government; because, said he, they had no business to make a law to hang a man if he was found engaged in the slave trade. So *we* must bear the guilt of man's angry passions, because the *truth* we preach is like a two-edged sword, cutting through the bonds of interest on the one side, and the cords of caste on the other.

As to our increasing the prejudice against color, this is just like the North telling us that we have increased the miseries of the slave. Common sense cries out against the one as well as the other. With regard to prejudice, I believe the truth of the case to be this: the rights of the colored man *never* were advocated by any body of men in their length and breadth, before the rise of the Anti-Slavery Society in this country. The propagation of these ultra principles has produced in the northern States exactly the same effect, which the promulgation of the doctrine of immediate emancipation has done in the southern States. It has *developed* the latent principles of pride and prejudice, not *produced* them. Hear John Green, a Judge of the Circuit Court of Kentucky, in reference to abolition efforts having given birth to the opposition against emancipation now existing in the South: 'I would rather say, it has been the means of *manifesting* that opposition, which *previously* existed, but *laid dormant* for want of an exciting cause.' And just so has it been with regard to prejudice at the North—when there was no effort to obtain for the colored man his *rights* as a man, as an American citizen, there was no opposition exhibited, because it 'laid dormant for want of an exciting cause.'

I know it is alleged that some individuals, who treated colored people with the greatest kindness a few years ago, have, since abolition movements, had their feeling so embittered towards them, that they have withdrawn that kindness. Now I would ask, could such people have acted from *principle?* Certainly not; or nothing that others could do or say would have driven them from the high ground they *appeared* to occupy. No, my friend, they acted precisely upon the false principle which thou hast recommended; their *pity* was excited, their *sentiments of generosity* were called into exercise, because they regarded the colored man as an *unfortunate inferior,* rather than as an *outraged* and *insulted* equal. Therefore, as soon as abolitionists demanded for the oppressed American the *very same treatment,* upon the high ground of *human rights,* why, then it was instantly withdrawn, simply because *it never had been conceded on the right ground;* and those who had previously granted it became afraid, lest, during the era of abolition excitement, persons would presume *they* were acting on the fundamental principle of abolitionism— the principle of *equal rights,* irrespective of color or condition, instead of on the mere principle of *'pity* and *generosity.'*

It is truly surprising to find a professing christian excusing the unprincipled opposition exhibited in New Haven, to the erection of a College for young men of color. Are we indeed to succumb to a corrupt public sentiment at the North, and the abominations of slavery at the South, by refraining from asserting the *right* of Americans to plant a literary institution in New Haven, or New York, or *any where* on the American soil? Are we to select 'some retired place,' where there would be the least prejudice and opposition to meet, rather than openly and fearlessly to face the American monster, who, like the horse-leach, is continually crying give, give, and whose demands are only increased by compromise and surrender? No! there is a spirit abroad in this country, which will not consent to barter principle for an *unholy* peace; a spirit which seeks to be 'pure from the blood of all men,' by a bold and christian avowal of truth; a spirit which will not hide God's eternal principles of right and wrong, but will stand erect in the storm of human passion, prejudice and interest, 'holding forth the light of truth in the midst of a crooked and perverse generation;' a spirit which will never slumber nor sleep, till man ceases to hold dominion over his fellow creatures, and the trump of universal liberty rings in every forest, and is re-echoed by every mountain and rock.

Art thou not aware, my friend, that this College was projected in the year 1831, previous to the formation of the first Anti-Slavery Society, which was organized in 1832? How, then, canst thou say that the circumstances relative to it occurred 'at a time when the public mind was excited on the subject?' I feel quite amused at the *presumption* which thou appearest to think was exhibited by the projectors of this institution, in wishing it to be located in New Haven, where was another College 'embracing a large proportion of southern students,' &c. It was a great offence, to be sure, for colored men to build a College by the walls of the white man's 'College where half the shoe-blacks and waiters were *colored men.*' But why so? The other half of the shoe-blacks and waiters were *white,* I presume; and if these *white* servants could be satisfied with *their* humble occupation *under the roof* of Yale College, why might not the colored waiters be contented also, though an institution for the education of colored Americans might *presume* to lift its head 'beside the very walls of this College?' Is it possible that any professing christian can calmly look back at these disgraceful transactions, and tell me that such opposition was manifested '*for the best reasons?*' And what is still worse, censure the projectors of a literary institution, in free, republican, enlightened America, because they did not meekly yield to '*such reasonable objections,*' and refused 'to soothe the feelings and apprehensions of those who had been excited' to opposition and clamor by the simple fact that some American born citizens wished to give their children a liberal education in a separate College, only because the white Americans despised their brethren of a darker complexion, and scorned to share with them the privileges of Yale College? It was very wrong, to be sure, for the friends of the oppressed American to consider such outrageous conduct 'as a mark of the force of sinful prejudice!' Vastly uncharitable! Great complaints are made that 'the worst motives were ascribed to some of the most respectable, and venerated, and *pious* men who opposed the measure.' Wonderful indeed, that men should be found so true to their principles, as to dare in this age of sycophancy to declare the truth to those who stand in high places, wearing the badges of office or honor, and fearlessly to rebuke the puerile and unchristian prejudice which existed against their colored brethren! 'Pious men!' Why, I would ask, how are we to judge of men's piety—by professions or products? Do men gather thorns of grapes, or thistles of figs? Certainly not. If, then, in the lives of men we do not find the fruits of christian principle, we have no right, according to our Saviour's criterion, 'by their fruits ye shall know them,' to suppose that men are really pious who can be perseveringly guilty of despising others, and denying them equal rights, because they have colored skins. 'A great deal was said and done that was calculated to throw the community into an angry ferment.' Yes, and I suppose the friends of the colored man were just as guilty as was the great Apostle, who, by the angry, and excited, and *prejudiced* Jews, was accused of being 'a pestilent fellow and a mover of sedition,' because he declared himself called to preach the everlasting gospel to the Gentiles, whom they considered as 'dogs,' and utterly unworthy of being placed on the same platform of human rights and a glorious immortality.

Thy friend,

A. E. GRIMKÉ.

# WILLIAM ELLERY CHANNING

## ON ABOLITIONISTS AND INTEGRATION

William Ellery Channing (1780–1842) was the most eminent Unitarian clergyman of the early nineteenth century,
pastor of the Federal Street Church in Boston, reformer and
peace advocate. Although he was anti-slavery, Channing
opposed Garrison's strong condemnation of slaveholders and
his call for immediate emancipation. The following selection
is from his *Remarks on the Slavery Question, in a Letter to
Jonathan Phillips, Esq.* (Boston, 1839), pp. 76–79. The Hall
of Freedom to which he refers was Pennsylvania Hall in
Philadelphia, built by the Abolitionists as a meeting place
and dedicated on May 14, 1838. Three days later, the
building was burnt down by a frenzied anti-Abolitionist
mob. Jonathan Phillips was Channing's lifelong friend.

. . . But we have not yet touched the great cause of the
conflagration of the Hall of Freedom. Something worse than
fanaticism or separation of the Union, was the impulse to this
violence. We are told, that white people and black sat together
on the benches of the Hall, and were even seen walking together
in the streets! This was the unheard of atrocity which the virtues
of the people of Philadelphia could not endure. They might have
borne the dissolution of the national tie; but this junction of
black and white was too much for human patience to sustain.
And has it indeed come to this? For such a cause, are mobs and
fires to be let loose on our persons and most costly buildings?
What! Has not an American citizen a right to sit and walk with
whom he will? Is this common privilege of humanity denied us?
Is society authorized to choose our associates? Must our neighbour's tastes as to friendship and companionship control our own?
Have the feudal times come back to us, when to break the law of
caste was a greater crime than to violate the laws of God? What
must Europe have thought, when the news crossed the ocean of
the burning of the Hall of Freedom, because white and colored
people walked together in the streets? Europe might well open its

eyes in wonder. On that continent, with all its aristocracy, the colored man mixes freely with his fellow-creatures. He passes for a man. He sometimes receives the countenance of the rich, and has even found his way into the palaces of the great. In Europe, the doctrine would be thought too absurd for refutation, that a colored man, of pure morals and piety, of cultivated intellect and refined manners, was not a fit companion for the best in the land. What must Europe have said, when brought to understand, that in a republic, founded on the principles of human rights and equality, people are placed beyond the protection of the laws, for treating an African as a man? This Philadelphia doctrine deserves no mercy. What an insult is thrown on human nature, in making it a heinous crime to sit or walk with a human being, whoever he may be!

It just occurs to me, that I have forgotten the circumstance, which filled to overflowing the cup of Abolitionist wickedness in Philadelphia. The great offence was this, that certain young women of anti-slavery faith, were seen to walk the streets with colored young men! Of the truth of this allegation, which has been denied, I am not able to judge; but allowing its correctness, I must think, that to violate the majesty of the laws, and to convulse a whole city, because a few young women thought fit to manifest in this way their benevolence towards a despised race,

> "Resembles ocean into tempest wrought,
> To waft a feather, or to drown a fly."

Offences against manners are wisely left to the scourge of public opinion, which proves itself, in such cases, a more effectual as well as more merciful discipline than burning or the gallows. If ridicule and indignation will not put down supposed misdemeanors of this class, what will force avail?—May I be here allowed to counsel my fair abolitionist friends, (if they have really fallen into the "unpardonable transgression" laid to their charge,) to respect hereafter the usages of society in regard to their communications with the other sex. If their anti-slavery zeal compels them to bear testimony against the prejudice, which excludes the colored people from the society of the whites, let them choose for their associates the women of the despised caste.

With less defiance of opinion, they will thus give equal expression to their interest in the wronged. I believe, however, that the less conspicuous their zeal in this and other public movements, the better. There are none, for whom I feel a deeper and more affectionate solicitude, than for the young of the other sex; and when I think of their inexperience, and of the strength of their sensibility, and then consider how exposed they are, on occasions of struggle and excitement, to unconscious imprudences, which may throw a shade over their characters not soon to be dispelled, and which, in their calmer hours, may visit them with secret upbraidings, or with fears of having started from the proper path, I cannot but desire, that, whilst they open their hearts to all generous sympathies, they should postpone the public manifestation of their zeal to a riper age.

The violence, which was offered the Abolitionists for their reception of the colored people to freer social intercourse, was the more aggravated, because, if they erred in the matter, their motive was a generous one, not got up for the occasion, but proved to be sincere by their whole conduct. They say, that the colored race, ground as they have been in the dust by long tyranny, and still suffering under prejudices which forbid their elevation, are entitled to peculiar regard from the disciples of him who came to raise the fallen, "to seek and save the lost." They look on this people with peculiar sympathy, because subjected to peculiar hardships. With this view, they are anxious to break down the distinction, or at least, to diminish the distance, between the black man and the white, believing that in this way only the degrading influences of the injuries of years can be overcome. Allow this to be an error; is it not a generous one? Is there nothing holy in sympathy with the wronged? Are feelings of benevolent concern, for whatever portion of our race, to be insulted, and to bring down violence on our heads, because they transgress conventional rules and forms of "good society"? That ignorant and coarse people should treat the motives of the Abolitionists with scorn, cannot surprise us; but that any, who belong to what is called the respectable and refined class, should join the fierce multitude in persecuting men of worth and humanity, admits no excuse. Does it not show, that the line of

separation between the high and low is not as broad as we sometimes imagine; that much which passes for refinement is mere
gloss; and that when the passions are stirred up by the concurrence of numbers, "the friends of order" can set laws at defiance
as boldly as the multitude?

# RALPH WALDO EMERSON

## A TRIBUTE TO THE NEGRO RACE

Though never apparently a member of either the American or the Massachusetts Anti-Slavery Society, Emerson sympathized with their aims and frequently spoke at their meetings. He also actively opposed racial segregation and discrimination. The following selection is the close of Emerson's first West India Emancipation Address, delivered in Concord on August 1, 1844, at a meeting sponsored by the Massachusetts Anti-Slavery Society, on the anniversary of the emancipation of the Negroes in the British West Indies. For additional remarks by Emerson on the question of race, see his *English Traits,* Chapter IV, "Race." A comprehensive treatment of Emerson's views on race is to be found in Philip L. Nicoloff, *Emerson on Race and History, An Examination of "English Traits"* (New York, 1961).

## *West India Emancipation*

. . . The First of August marks the entrance of a new element into modern politics, namely, the civilization of the negro. A man is added to the human family. Not the least affecting part of this history of Abolition is the annihilation of the old indecent nonsense about the nature of the negro. In the case of the ship Zong, in 1781, whose master had thrown one hundred and thirty-two slaves alive into the sea, to cheat the underwriters, the first jury gave a verdict in favor of the master and owners: they had a right to do what they had done. Lord Mansfield is reported to have said on the bench, "The matter left to the jury is,—Was it from necessity? For they had no doubt,—though it shocks one very much,—that the case of slaves was the same as if horses had been thrown overboard. It is a very shocking case." But a more enlightened and humane opinion began to prevail. Mr. Clarkson, early in his career, made a collection of African productions and manufactures, as specimens of the arts and culture of the negro; comprising cloths and loom, weapons, polished stones and woods, leather, glass, dyes, ornaments, soap, pipe-bowls and trinkets. These he showed to Mr. Pitt, who saw and handled them with extreme interest. "On sight of these," says Clarkson, "many sublime thoughts seemed to rush at once into his mind, some of which he expressed"; and hence appeared to arise a project which was always dear to him, of the civilization of Africa,—a dream which forever elevates his fame. In 1791, Mr. Wilberforce announced to the House of Commons, "We have already gained one victory: we have obtained for these poor creatures the recognition of their human nature, which for a time was most shamefully denied them." It was the sarcasm of Montesquieu, "it would not do to suppose that negroes were men, lest it should turn out that whites were not"; for the white has, for ages, done what he could to keep the negro in that hoggish state. His laws have been furies. It now appears that the negro race is, more than any other, susceptible of rapid civilization. The emancipation is observed, in the islands, to have wrought for the negro a benefit as sudden as when a thermometer is brought out of the shade into the sun. It has given him eyes and ears. If, before, he was taxed with such stupidity, or such defective vision, that he could not set a table square to the walls of an apartment, he is now the principal if not the only mechanic in the West Indies; and is, besides, an architect, a physician, a lawyer, a magistrate, an editor, and a valued and increasing political power. The recent testimonies of Sturge, of Thome and Kimball, of Gurney, of Philippo, are very explicit on this point, the capacity and the success of the colored and the black population in employment of skill, of profit and of trust; and best of all is the testimony to their moderation. They receive hints and advances from the whites that they will be gladly received as subscribers to the Exchange, as members of this or that committee of trust. They hold back, and say to each other that "social position is not to be gained by pushing."

I have said that this event interests us because it came mainly from the concession of the whites; I add, that in part it is the earning of the blacks. They won the pity and respect which they have received, by their powers and native endowments. I think this a circumstance of the highest import. Their whole future is in it. Our planet, before the age of written history, had its races of savages, like the generations of sour paste, or the animalcules that wriggle and bite in a drop of putrid water. Who cares for these or for their wars? We do not wish a world of bugs or of birds; neither afterward of Scythians, Caraibs or Feejees. The grand style of Nature, her great periods, is all we observe in them. Who cares for oppressing whites, or oppressed blacks, twenty centuries ago, more than for bad dreams? Eaters and food are in the harmony of Nature; and there too is the germ forever protected, unfolding gigantic leaf after leaf, a newer flower, a richer fruit, in every period, yet its next product is never to be guessed. It will only save what is worth saving; and it saves not by compassion, but by power. It appoints no police to guard the lion, but his teeth and claws; no fort or city for the bird, but his wings; no rescue for flies and mites, but their spawning numbers, which no ravages can overcome. It deals with men after the same manner. If they are rude and foolish, down they must go. When at last in a race, a new principle appears, an idea,—*that* conserves it; ideas only save races. If the black man is feeble and not important to the existing races, not on a parity with the best race, the black man must serve, and be exterminated. But if the black man carries in his bosom an indispensable element of a new and coming civilization; for the sake of that element, no wrong, nor strength nor circumstance can hurt him: he will survive and play his part. So now, the arrival in the world of such men as Toussaint, and the Haytian heroes, or of the leaders of their race in Barbadoes and Jamaica, outweighs in good omen all the English and American humanity. The anti-slavery of the whole world is dust in the balance before this,—is a poor squeamishness and nervousness: the might and the right are here: here is the anti-slave: here is man: and if you have man, black or white is an insignificance. The intellect,—that is miraculous! Who has it, has the talisman: his skin and bones, though they were of the color of night, are transparent, and the everlasting stars shine through, with attractive beams. But a compassion for that which is not and cannot be useful or lovely, is degrading and futile. All the songs and newspapers and money-subscriptions and vituperation of such as do not think with us, will avail nothing against a fact. I say to you, you must save yourself, black or white, man or woman; other help is none. I esteem the occasion of this jubilee to be the proud discovery that the black race can contend with the white; that, in the great anthem which we call history, a piece of many parts and vast compass, after playing a long time a very low and subdued accompaniment, they perceive the time arrived when they can strike in with effect and take a master's part in the music. The civility of the world has reached that pitch that their more moral genius is becoming indispensable, and the quality of this race is to be honored for itself. For this, they have been preserved in sandy deserts, in rice-swamps, in kitchens and shoe-shops, so long: now let them emerge, clothed and in their own form.

There remains the very elevated consideration which the subject opens, but which belongs to more abstract views than we are now taking, this namely, that the civility of no race can be perfect whilst another race is degraded. It is a doctrine alike of the oldest and of the newest philosophy, that man is one, and that you cannot injure any member, without a sympathetic injury to all the members. America is not civil, whilst Africa is barbarous.

These considerations seem to leave no choice for the action of the intellect and the conscience of the country. There have been moments in this, as well as in every piece of moral history, when there seemed room for the infusions of a skeptical philosophy; when it seemed doubtful whether brute force would not triumph in the eternal struggle. I doubt not that sometimes, a despairing negro, when jumping over the ship's sides to escape from the white devils who surrounded him, has believed there was no vindication of right; it is horrible to think of, but it seemed so. I doubt not that sometimes the negro's friend, in the face of scornful and brutal hundreds of traders and drivers, has felt his heart sink. Especially, it seems to me, some degree of despondency is pardonable, when he observes the men of conscience and of intellect, his own natural allies and champions,—those whose attention should be nailed to the grand objects of this cause, so hotly offended by whatever incidental petulances or infirmities of indiscreet defenders of the negro, as to permit themselves to be ranged with the enemies of the human race; and names which should be the alarums of liberty and the watchwords of truth, are mixed up with all the rotten rabble of selfishness and tyranny. I assure myself that this coldness and blindness will pass away. A single noble wind of sentiment will scatter them forever. I am sure that the good and wise elders, the ardent and generous youth, will not permit what is incidental and exceptional to withdraw their devotion from the essential and permanent characters of the question. There have been moments, I said, when men might be forgiven who doubted. Those moments are past. Seen in masses, it cannot be disputed, there is progress in human society. There is a blessed necessity by which the interest of men is always driving them to the right; and, again, making all crime mean and ugly. The genius of the Saxon race, friendly to liberty; the enterprise, the very muscular vigor of this nation, are inconsistent with slavery. The Intellect, with blazing eye, looking through history from the beginning onward, gazes on this blot and it disappears. The sentiment of Right, once very low and indistinct, but ever more articulate, because it is the voice of the universe, pronounces Freedom. The Power that built this fabric of things affirms it in the heart; and in the history of the First of August, has made a sign to the ages, of his will.

## CASSIUS M. CLAY

### ON SLAVERY AND RACIAL EQUALITY

Kentucky-born legislator Cassius Marcellus Clay (1810–1903) was an anti-slavery Southerner who "sacrificed a promising career in politics to advocate the gradual emancipation of the slaves."[1] It was at Yale that Clay was first attracted to the anti-slavery cause by hearing Garrison speak, although he did not become a militant opponent of slavery until 1840 and was never a Garrisonian. In 1845 he began to publish the *True American*, a newspaper devoted to the overthrow of slavery, at Lexington, Kentucky. A few months later the press was dismantled by a mob and shipped to Cincinnati, and Clay threatened with assassination, but he continued to print the paper in Cincinnati and publish it in Lexington.

Clay opposed slavery, yet he was not always consistent in his views. Although the following excerpt emphasizes Negro equality, elsewhere he expresses a belief in Negro inferiority. While he opposed the annexation of Texas, he volunteered in the Mexican War. He supported Lincoln in 1860 and was rewarded with a diplomatic post in Russia. After 1869 he again lived in Kentucky. The selection reprinted here is from his speech against the annexation of Texas—which he denounced as a scheme to extend slavery—delivered on December 30, 1843 at White Sulphur Springs, Kentucky; it is reprinted from Horace Greeley, ed., *The Writings of Cassius Marcellus Clay: Including Speeches and Addresses* (New York, 1848), pp. 93–4.

. . . They further tell us, with most reverential gravity, that "God has designed some men for slaves, and man need not attempt to reverse the decree: it is better that the blacks should be slaves, than the whites." This proposition, which I denounce as utterly false, passes away before the glance of reason, as the dew before the summer's sun.

I shall admit, merely for the sake of argument, that some men always have, and possibly will perform menial offices for the more fortunate. Let the law of nature or of God, have its undisturbed action—let the performance of those offices be voluntary on the part of servants, and that beautiful harmony by which the highest intellect is united, by successive inferior links to the lowest mind, will never be disturbed. The sensitive and highly organized, the intellectual, will gradually rise from servitude to command: the stolid, the profligate, the insensible, and coarsely organized will sink into their places: the law of God and enlightened freedom will still be preserved, and the greatest good to the greatest number be secured for ever. But when, by municipal law, and not by the law of fitness, which is the law of nature, not regarding the distinctions of morals, mind, or body, whole classes are doomed to servitude: when the intellectual, the sensitive, the foolish, the rude, the good, the bad, the refined, the degraded, are all depressed to one level, never more to rise forever; then comes evil, nothing but evil, like as from dammed up waters, or pent up steam, floods and explosions come slowly, but come at last—so nature mocks with temporary desolation, at the obstacles man would oppose to her progress, and at length, moves on once more in all the untrammeled vigor and unfading loveliness which, from eternity, was decreed. That the black is inferior to the white, I readily allow; but that vice may depress the one, and virtue, by successive generations, elevate the other, till the two races meet on one common level, I am also firmly convinced. Modern science, in the breeding and culture of other animals than man, has most fully proved this fact, which the ablest observers of man himself, all allow, that mental, and moral, and physical development transmit their several properties to the descendants—corroborating by experience, the divine decree, that the virtues and the vices of the father shall be visited on the children, to the third and fourth generation. In the capitals of Europe, blacks have attained to the highest places of social and literary eminence. That they are capable of a high degree of civilization, Hayti daily illustrates. There we have lately seen a revolution, conducted in a manner that would do honor to the first people on earth: one of the avowed grounds of which was, that President Boyer neglected to secure general education to the people, a consideration that should make some of the states blush in comparison. After the expulsion of the tyrant they set about forming a more republican Constitution, admitting the whites who had participated in their dangers and successes, into all the rights of citizenship. If history be true, we owe to the Egyptians, said to be the modern Moorish race, the arts and sciences, and our early seeds of civilization. How many centuries did it take to bring them to perfection? When we reflect how little time the negro race has been under the influences of other civilized nations, and the rapid progress they have made in an upward direction, we have no reason to treat them with that absurd contempt, which, in both the eye of reason and religion, stands equally condemned. Why then, I am taunted by both pro-slavery and anti-slavery men, do I hold slaves? Uninfluenced by the opinions of the world, I intend in my own good time to act or not to act, as to me seems best in view of all the premises. Yet, I thus far pledge myself, that whenever Kentucky will join me in freeing ourselves from this curse, which weighs us down even unto death, the slaves I own, she shall dispose of as to her seems best. I shall ask nothing in return, but the enhanced value of my land which must ensue gradually from the day that we become indeed a free and independent state. I will go yet further, give me *free labor,* and I will not only give up my slaves, but I will agree to be taxed to buy the remainder from those who are unwilling or unable consistently, with a regard to pecuniary interest, to present them to the state, and then I shall deem myself and my posterity richer in dollars and cents even, than we were before. . . .

## NOTE

1. Clement Eaton, *A History of the Old South* (New York, 1949), p. 392.

# CHARLES SUMNER

## A Protest Against Segregation

In this letter, Charles Sumner (1811–1874), the great statesman and anti-slavery Senator from Massachusetts, protests against segregation by the New Bedford Lyceum. This event occurred several years before he entered the Senate on December 1, 1851. In 1845 he was a young lawyer who had already earned a reputation as scholar and reformer. Four years later, Sumner prepared the brief in *Roberts v. the City of Boston,* which demanded an end to the segregation of Negro school children in the city of Boston. Although the Massachusetts Supreme Court ruled against him, Boston ended school segregation in 1855. When the United States Supreme Court ruled against segregation in education in 1954 and 1955, much of its argument followed Sumner's. During the Civil War and Reconstruction, he was Senate leader of the Radical Republicans, and was instrumental in the passage of the Thirteenth, Fourteenth and Fifteenth Amendments as well as of much other civil rights legislation. The remarks preceding the letter to the Lyceum are in the original edition of his *Works* (Boston, 1874), Vol. I, p. 160, from which the letter is reprinted.

For a history of segregation in education in Massachusetts and the part played by the Abolitionists and other anti-slavery men and women, including Sumner, in eliminating it, see Louis Ruchames, "Race and Education in Massachusetts," *Negro History Bulletin* (December 1949), pp. 53–71.

## *Equal Rights in the Lecture-Room*

After accepting an invitation to lecture before the Lyceum at New Bedford, Mr. Sumner, learning that colored persons were denied membership and equal opportunities with white persons, refused to lecture, as appears in the following Letter, which was published in the papers of the time.

Shortly afterwards the obnoxious rule was rescinded, and Mr. Sumner lectured.

BOSTON, November 29, 1845.

*To the Chairman of the Committee*
  *of the New Bedford Lyceum.*

MY DEAR SIR,—I have received your favor of November 24, asking me to appoint an evening in February or March to lecture before the New Bedford Lyceum, in pursuance of my promise.

On receiving the invitation of your Lyceum, I felt flattered, and, in undertaking to deliver a lecture at some time, to be appointed afterwards, I promised myself peculiar pleasure in an occasion of visiting a town which I had never seen, but whose refined hospitality and liberal spirit, as described to me, awakened my warmest interest.

Since then I have read in the public prints a protest, purporting to be by gentlemen well known to me by reputation, who are members of the Lyceum, and some of them part of its government, from which it appears that in former years tickets of admission were freely sold to colored persons, as to white persons, and that no objection was made to them as members, but that at the present time tickets are refused to colored persons, and membership is also refused practically, though, by special vote recently adopted, they are allowed to attend the lectures without expense, provided they will sit in the north gallery.

From these facts it appears that the New Bedford Lyceum has undertaken within its jurisdiction to establish a distinction of *Caste* not recognized before.

One of the cardinal truths of religion and freedom is the *Equality and Brotherhood of Man.* In the sight of God and of all just institutions the white man can claim no precedence or exclusive privilege from his color. It is the accident of an accident that places a human soul beneath the dark shelter of an African countenance, rather than beneath our colder complexion. Nor can I conceive any application of the divine injunction, Do unto others as you would have them do unto you, more pertinent than to the man who founds a discrimination between his fellow-men on difference of skin.

It is well known that the prejudice of color, which is akin to the stern and selfish spirit that holds a fellow-man in slavery, is peculiar to our country. It does not exist in other civilized countries. In France colored youths at college have gained the highest honors, and been welcomed as if they were white. At the Law School there I have sat with them on the same benches. In Italy I have seen an Abyssinian mingling with monks, and there was no apparent suspicion on either side of anything open to question. All this was Christian: so it seemed to me.

In lecturing before a Lyceum which has introduced the prejudice of color among its laws, and thus formally reversed an injunction of highest morals and politics, I might seem to sanction what is most alien to my soul, and join in disobedience to that command which teaches that the children of earth are all of one blood. I cannot do this.

I beg, therefore, to be excused at present from appointing a day to lecture before your Lyceum; and I pray you to lay this letter before the Lyceum, that the ground may be understood on which I deem it my duty to decline the honor of appearing before them.

I hope you will pardon the frankness of this communication, and believe me, my dear Sir,

Very faithfully yours,<br>CHARLES SUMNER.

# HARRIET BEECHER STOWE

## ON RACIAL PREJUDICE

Harriet Beecher Stowe (1811–1896) wrote *A Key to Uncle Tom's Cabin* (Boston, 1853), a book of 260 double-column pages, in an effort to substantiate her view of slavery as portrayed in *Uncle Tom's Cabin*. She secured much of the material from Theodore Weld's volume, *American Slavery As It Is* (1839), supplemented by additional research of her own. Her knowledge of slavery was also based on personal contact with slavery and runaway slaves, gained during visits to Kentucky and while living in Cincinnati, Ohio, where her father, Dr. Lyman Beecher, was head of Lane Theological Seminary. *A Key to Uncle Tom's Cabin* contains valuable documentary evidence of the nature of Southern slavery, as well as material about prejudice and discrimination in the North. As the reader will notice, the burning of the homes of Negroes moving into white neighborhoods in the North did not originate in the twentieth century. The following selection is from Chapter VII, pp. 31 ff.

## *Miss Ophelia*

[Harriet Beecher Stowe represents Miss Ophelia as a type of Northerner who is pious and well-meaning yet is prejudiced toward the Negro and insensitive to his sufferings.]

. . . It is very easy to see that although slavery has been abolished in the New England States, it has left behind it the most baneful feature of the system—that which makes American worse than Roman slavery—the prejudice of caste and color. In the New England States the negro has been treated as belonging to an inferior race of beings;—forced to sit apart by himself in the place of worship; his children excluded from the schools; himself excluded from the railroad-car and the omnibus, and the peculiarities of his race made the subject of bitter contempt and ridicule.

This course of conduct has been justified by saying that they are a degraded race. But how came they degraded? Take any class of men, and shut them from the means of education, deprive them of hope and self-respect, close to them all avenues of honorable ambition, and you will make just such a race of them as the negroes have been among us.

So singular and so melancholy is the dominion of prejudice over the human mind, that professors of Christianity in our New England States have often, with very serious self-denial to themselves, sent the gospel to heathen as dark-complexioned as the Africans, when in their very neighborhood were persons of dark complexion, who, on that account, were forbidden to send their children to the schools, and discouraged from entering the churches. The effect of this has been directly to degrade and depress the race, and then this very degradation and depression has been pleaded as the reason for continuing this course.

Not long since the writer called upon a benevolent lady, and during the course of the call the conversation turned upon the incidents of a fire which had occurred the night before in the neighborhood. A deserted house had been burned to the ground. The lady said it was supposed it had been set on fire. "What could be any one's motive for setting it on fire?" said the writer.

"Well," replied the lady, "it was supposed that a colored family was about to move into it, and it was thought that the neighborhood wouldn't consent to that. So it was supposed that was the reason."

This was said with an air of innocence and much unconcern.

The writer inquired, "Was it a family of bad character?"

"No, not particularly, that I know of," said the lady; "but then they are negroes, you know."

Now, this lady is a very pious lady. She probably would deny herself to send the gospel to the heathen, and if she had ever thought of considering this family a heathen family, would have felt the deepest interest in their welfare; because on the subject of duty to the heathen she had been frequently instructed from the pulpit, and had all her religious and conscientious sensibilities awake. Probably she had never listened from the pulpit to a sermon which should exhibit the great truth, that "in Christ Jesus there is neither Jew nor Greek, barbarian, Scythian, bond nor free."

Supposing our Lord was now on earth, as he was once, what

course is it probable that he would pursue with regard to this unchristian prejudice of color? . . . And if Christ should enter, or some communion season, into a place of worship, and see the colored man sitting afar off by himself, would it not be just in his spirit to go there and sit with him, rather than to take the seats of his richer and more prosperous brethren?

It is, however, but just to our Northern Christians to say that this sin has been committed ignorantly and in unbelief, and that within a few years signs of a much better spirit have begun to manifest themselves. In some places, recently, the doors of school-houses have been thrown open to the children, and many a good Miss Ophelia has opened her eyes in astonishment to find that, while she has been devouring the *Missionary Herald,* and going without butter on her bread and sugar in her tea to send the gospel to the Sandwich Islands, there is a very thriving colony of heathen in her own neighborhood at home; and, true to her own good and honest heart, she has resolved, *not* to give up her prayers and efforts for the heathen abroad, but to add thereunto labors for the heathen at home.

Our safety and hope in this matter is this: that there are multitudes in all our churches who do most truly and sincerely love Christ above all things, and who, just so soon as a little reflection shall have made them sensible of their duty in this respect, will most earnestly perform it.

It is true that, if they do so, they may be called Abolitionists; but the true Miss Ophelia is not afraid of a hard name in a good cause, and has rather learned to consider "the reproach of Christ a greater treasure than the riches of Egypt."

That there is much already for Christians to do in enlightening the moral sense of the community on this subject, will appear if we consider that even so well-educated and gentlemanly a man as Frederick Douglass was recently obliged to pass the night on the deck of a steamer, when in delicate health, because this senseless prejudice deprived him of a place in the cabin; and that that very laborious and useful minister, Dr. Pennington, of New York, has, during the last season, been often obliged seriously to endanger his health, by walking to his pastoral labors, over his very extended parish, under a burning sun, because he could not be allowed the common privilege of the omnibus, which conveys

every class of white men, from the most refined to the lowest and
most disgusting. . . .

Those who are anxious to do something directly to improve
the condition of the slave, can do it in no way so directly as by
elevating the condition of the free colored people around them,
and taking every pains to give them equal rights and privileges.

This unchristian prejudice has doubtless stood in the way of
the emancipation of hundreds of slaves. The slave-holder, feeling
and acknowledging the evils of slavery, has come to the North,
and seen evidences of this unkindly and unchristian state of
feeling towards the slave, and has thus reflected within himself:

"If I keep my slave at the South, he is, it is true, under the
dominion of a very severe law; but then he enjoys the advantage
of my friendship and assistance, and derives, through his connection with me and my family, some kind of a position in the
community. As my servant he is allowed a seat in the car and a
place at the table. But if I emancipate and send him North, he
will encounter substantially all the disadvantages of slavery,
with no master to protect him."

This mode of reasoning has proved an apology to many a man
for keeping his slaves in a position which he confesses to be a bad
one; and it will be at once perceived that, should the position of
the negro be conspicuously reversed in our northern states, the
effect upon the emancipation of the slave would be very great.
They, then, who keep up this prejudice, may be said to be, in a
certain sense, slave-holders.

It is not meant by this that all distinctions of society should be
broken over, and that people should be obliged to choose their
intimate associates from a class unfitted by education and habits
to sympathize with them.

The negro should not be lifted out of his sphere of life because
he is a negro, but he should be treated with Christian courtesy *in*
his sphere. In the railroad car, in the omnibus and steamboat, all
ranks and degrees of white persons move with unquestioned
freedom side by side; and Christianity requires that the negro
have the same privilege.

That the dirtiest and most uneducated foreigner or American,
with breath redolent of whiskey and clothes foul and disordered,
should have an unquestioned right to take a seat next to any

person in a railroad car *or* steamboat, and that the respectable, decent and gentlemanly negro should be excluded simply because he is a negro, cannot be considered otherwise than as an irrational and unchristian thing: and any Christian who allows such things done in his presence without remonstrance, and the use of his Christian influence, will certainly be made deeply sensible of his error when he comes at last to direct and personal interview with his Lord. . . .

# THEODORE PARKER

## ON ANGLO-SAXON AND AFRICAN

Theodore Parker (1810–1860), pastor of the Twenty-eighth Congregational Society in Boston and an outstanding Unitarian minister, was one of the great American scholars of his day, an outspoken opponent of slavery and an active participant in organized efforts to prevent fugitive slaves from being dragged back into slavery. Parker was also one of John Brown's supporters in the attack on Harpers Ferry. In the first of the following selections, Parker offers his views on the nature of the Anglo-Saxon character. In the second, he compares the traits of various races in America. The first selection is from an address delivered at an anti-slavery convention in Boston on May 31, 1854 (printed in Parker's *Collected Works*, edited by Frances P. Cobbe, Vol. VI, pp. 1 ff.). The second is from an address delivered before the Massachusetts Anti-Slavery Convention, January 29, 1858 (*ibid.*, pp. 287 ff.).

## The Anglo-Saxon

. . . The Anglo-Saxon tribe is composite, and the mingling so recent, that we can still easily distinguish the main ingredients of the mixture. There are, first, the Saxons and Angles from North Germany; next, the Scandinavians from Denmark and Sweden; and, finally, the Normans, or Romanized Scandinavians, from France.

This tribe is now divided into two great political branches, namely, the Anglo-Saxon Briton, and the Anglo-Saxon American; but both are substantially the same people, though with different antecedents and surroundings. The same fundamental characteristics belong to the Briton and the American. . . .

1. There is a strong love of individual freedom. This belongs to the Anglo-Saxons in common with all the Teutonic family. But with them it seems eminently powerful. Circumstances have favoured its development. They care much for freedom, little for equality.

2. Connected with this, is a love of law and order, which continually shows itself on both sides of the ocean. Fast as we gain freedom, we secure it by law and constitution, trusting little to the caprice of magistrates.

3. Then there is a great federative power—a tendency to form combinations of persons, or of communities and states,—special partnerships on a small scale for mercantile business; on a large scale, like the American Union, or the Hanse towns, for the political business of a nation.

4. The Anglo-Saxons have eminent practical power to organize things into a mill, or men into a state, and then to administer the organization. This power is one which contributes greatly to both their commercial and political success. But this tribe is also most eminently material in its aims and means; it loves riches, works for riches, fights for riches. It is not warlike, as some other nations, who love war for its own sake, though a hard fighter when put to it.

5. We are the most aggressive, invasive, and exclusive people on the earth. The history of the Anglo-Saxon, for the last three hundred years, has been one of continual aggression, invasion, and extermination.

I cannot now stop to dwell on these traits of our tribal anthropology, but must yet say a word touching this national exclusiveness and tendency to exterminate.

Austria and Russia never treated a conquered nation so cruelly as England has treated Ireland. . . .

The same disposition to invade and exterminate showed itself on this side of the ocean.

In America, the Frenchman and the Spaniard came in contact with the red man; they converted him to what they called Christianity, and then associated with him on equal terms. The pale-face and the red-skin hunted in company; they fished from the same canoe in the Bay of Fundy and Lake Superior; they lodged in the same tent, slept on the same bear-skin; nay, they knelt together before the same God, who was "no respecter of persons," and had made of one blood all nations of men! The white man married the Indian's daughter; the red man wooed and won the pale child of the Caucasian. This took place in Canada, and in Mexico, in Peru, and Equador. In Brazil, the negro graduates at the college; he becomes a general in the army. But the Anglo-

Saxon disdains to mingle his proud blood in wedlock with the "inferior races of men." He puts away the savage—black, yellow, red. In New England, the Puritan converted the Indians to Christianity, as far as they could accept the theology of John Calvin; but made a careful separation between white and red, "my people and thy people." They must dwell in separate villages, worship in separate houses; they must not intermarry. The general court of Massachusetts once forbade all extra-matrimonial connection of white and red, on pain of death! The Anglo-Saxon has carefully sought to exterminate the savages from his territory. The Briton does so in Africa, in Van Diemen's Land, in New Zealand, in New Holland—wherever he meets them. The American does the same in the western world. In New England the Puritan found the wild woods, the wild beasts, and the wild men; he undertook to eradicate them all, and has succeeded best with the wild men. There are more bears than Indians in New England. The United States pursues the same destructive policy. In two hundred years more there will be few Indians left between the Lake of the Woods and the Gulf of Mexico, between the Atlantic and the Pacific Oceans.

Yet the Anglo-Saxons are not cruel; they are simply destructive. The Dutch, in New York, perpetrated the most wanton cruelties: the savages themselves shuddered at the white man's atrocity: "Our gods would be offended at such things," said they; "the white man's God must be different!" The cruelties of the French, and, still more, of the Spaniards in Mexico, in the West Indies, and South America, are too terrible to repeat, but too well known to need relating. The Spaniard put men to death with refinements of cruelty, luxuriating in destructiveness. The Anglo-Saxon simply shot down his foe, offered a reward for homicide, so much for a scalp, but tolerated no needless cruelty. If the problem is to destroy a race of men with the least expenditure of destructive force on one side, and the least suffering on the other, the Anglo-Saxon, Briton, or American, is the fittest instrument to be found on the whole globe.

## The Races of America

. . . It was left for America to begin a new experiment in the history of civilization—to bring divers races into closest contact.

The Catholic Spaniard began the experiment: he mixed his blood with the red man, whose country he subdued; he brought hither also the black man. Thus the African savage, the American barbarian, and the civilized Caucasian of Spain, became joint stockholders in this new coparcenary of races. The Protestant Briton continued what his Catholic predecessor had begun; and, while the Puritan was painfully voyaging to Plymouth, in the wilderness seeking an asylum where the Apocalyptic woman might bear her manchild to grow up in freedom, other Saxons were bringing a ship-load of negroes to the wilderness, to become slaves for ever. Thus the African came to British and Spanish America. Out of the 60,000,000 inhabitants of this continent, I take it about 9,000,000 are of this unfortunate race.

In the United States to-day, four of the five great races live side by side. There are some 60,000 or 80,000 Mongolian Chinese in California, I am told; there are 400,000 American Indians within our borders; perhaps 4,500,000 Africans; and 26,000,000 Caucasians. The union of such diverse ethnological elements makes our experiment of democracy more complex, and perhaps more difficult than it would otherwise be.

The Mongolians are few in numbers, and so transient in their stay that nothing more need now be said of them.

It is plain where the red man will go. In two hundred years, an Indian will be as rare in the United States as now in New England. Like the bear and the buffalo, he perishes with the forest, which to him and them was what cultivated fields, towns, and cities are to us. Our fathers tried to enslave the ferocious and unprogressive Indian; he would not work—for himself as a freeman, nor for others as a slave: he would fight. He would not be enslaved—he could not help being killed. He perishes before us. The sinewy Caucasian labourer lays hold on the phlegmatic Indian warrior; they struggle in deadly grasp—naked man to naked man, hand to shoulder, knee to knee, breast to breast; the white man bends the red man over, crushes him down, and chokes him dead. It is always so when the civilized meets the savage, or the barbarian—naked man to naked man: how much more fatal is the issue to the feeble when the white man shirted in iron has the smallpox for his ally, and rum for his tomahawk! In the long run of history, the race is always to the swift, and the battle to the strong. The Indian will perish—utterly and soon.

The African is the most docile and pliant of all the races of men; none has so little ferocity: vengeance, instantial with the Caucasian, is exceptional in his history. In his barbarous, savage, or even wild state, he is not much addicted to revenge; always prone to mercy. No  race is so strong in the affectional instinct which attaches man to man by tender ties; none so easy, indolent, confiding, so little warlike. Hence is it that the white men have kidnapped the black, and made him their prey.

This piece of individual biography tells us the sad history of the African race. Not long since, a fugitive slave told me his adventures. I will call him John—it is not his name. He is an entire negro—his grandfather was brought direct from the Congo coast to America. A stout man, thick-set, able-bodied, with great legs and mighty arms, he could take any man from this platform, and hurl him thrice his length. He was a slave—active, intelligent, and much confided in. He had a wife and children. One day his master, in a fit of rage, struck at him with a huge club, which broke both of his arms; they were awkwardly set, and grew out deformed. The master promised to sell the man to himself for a large sum, and take the money by installments, a little at a time. But when more than half of it was paid, he actually sold him to a trader, to be taken further South, and there disposed of. The appeals of the wife, the tears of the children, moved not the master whom justice had also failed to touch. As the boat which contained poor John shot by the point of land where he had lived, his wife stood upon the shore, and held her babies up for him to look upon for the last time. Descending the Mississippi, the captain of the boat had the river fever, lost his sight for the time, and John took the command. One night, far down the Mississippi, he found himself on board a boat with the three kidnappers who had him in their power, and intended to sell him. They were asleep below—the captain still blind with the disease—he watchful on deck. "I crept down barefoot," said John. "There they lay in their bunks, all fast asleep. They had money, and I none. I had done them no harm, but they had torn me from my wife, from my children, from my liberty. I stole up noiselessly, and came back again, the boat's axe in my hand. I lifted it up, and grit my teeth together, and was about to strike: and it came into my mind, 'No murderer hath eternal life.' I put the axe back in its place, and was sold into slavery. What would you have done in such a case?" I told him that I thought I should have sent the kidnappers to their own place first, and then trusted that the act would be imputed to me for righteousness by an all-righteous God! I need not ask what Mr. Garrison would do in like case. I think his Saxon blood would move swift enough to sweep off his non-resistant creed, and the three kidnappers would have started on their final journey before he asked, *Where shall I go?*"

John's story is also the story of Africa. The stroke of an axe would have settled the matter long ago. But the black man would not strike. One day, perhaps, he will do what yonder monument commends.

# WENDELL PHILLIPS

## ON CRISPUS ATTUCKS

Wendell Phillips (1811–1844), Boston-bred and Harvard-educated, abandoned a promising career at law to join the Abolitionists in 1837. He soon became Garrison's close friend and co-worker. One of America's greatest orators, his effectiveness as an anti-slavery leader was equalled only by that of Garrison. In this address, delivered before a Negro audience on March 5, 1858, in Faneuil Hall, at a festival commemorating the Boston Massacre, Phillips discourses on the significance of Crispus Attucks—the Negro who died in the Massacre—and takes issue with Theodore Parker on Negro character. It is reprinted from Wendell Phillips, *Speeches, Lectures and Letters,* Second Series (Boston, 1891), pp. 69–76.

## *Crispus Attucks*

LADIES AND GENTLEMEN: I am very glad to stand here in an hour when we come together to do honor to one of the first martyrs in our Revolution. I think we sometimes tell the story of what he did with too little appreciation of how much it takes to make the first move in the cold streets of a revolutionary epoch. It is a very easy thing to sit down and read the history; it is a very easy thing to imagine what we would have done,—it is a very different thing to strike the first blow. It is a very hard thing to spring out of the ranks of common, every-day life—submission to law, recognition of established government—and lift the first musket. The man or the dozen men who do it, deserve great, pre-eminent, indisputable places in the history of the Revolution. It is an easy thing to fight when the blood is hot; but this man whose memory we commemorate to-night stepped out of common life, every-day quiet, and lifted his arm among the very first against the government. It is only pre-eminent courage that can do this. To-day, in yonder capital of Paris, the whole government rests on a thin film of ice. A hundred men in arms in the streets would break it; that hundred men cannot be found,—a hundred men willing to risk their lives, with a cold, unmoved populace behind them. Those five men who were killed on that eventful night of the 5th of March, of whom Crispus Attucks was the leader,—they never have had their fair share of fame.

Our friend Theodore Parker said the Revolution was not born so early. I think him wrong there; it was. Emerson said the first gun heard round the world was that of Lexington. Who set the example of guns? Who taught the British soldier that he might be defeated? Who dared first to look into his eyes? Those five men! The 5th of March was the baptism of blood. The 5th of March was what made the Revolution something beside talk. Revolution always begins with the populace, never with the leaders. They argue, they resolve, they organize; it is the populace that, like the edge of the cloud, shows the lightning first. This was the lightning. I hail the 5th of March as the baptism of the Revolution into forcible resistance; without that it would have been simply a discussion of rights. I place, therefore, this Crispus Attucks in the foremost rank of the men that dared. When we talk of courage, he rises, with his dark face, in his clothes of the laborer, his head uncovered, his arm raised above him defying bayonets,—the emblem of Revolutionary violence in its dawn; and when the proper symbols are placed around the base of the statue of Washington, one corner will be filled by the colored man defying the British muskets. [Applause.]

I think it is right that we should come here and remember Crispus Attucks. It is right, because every colored man has but one thing to remember in life, and that is SLAVERY. All races are one—they are a unit. The white race is a unit, the Caucasian race is a unit, the black race is a unit—one. There is only one great, terrible fact in regard to the colored race at the present moment,—it is that millions of it wear the chain; there is nothing for the rest of the race decent to do but to devote themselves to the breaking of that chain. [Applause.] All literature, all wealth, all patriotism, all religion, should gravitate toward emancipation. I value the triumphs of the literary genius of Dumas solely as an argument thrown into the scale of the great balance, whether the colored man is worthy of liberty. Genius is worth nothing else now with the colored man, except as helping that argument. I would have you, as your friend Dr. Rock[1] suggested, thrifty, eloquent, industrious, successful, rich, able, only as an argument that the colored race has a right to a place side by side and equal with the white. I wish I could impress this truth on every colored man. His race to-day is on trial. The world says it merits only chains. The best thing he can do with his life, with his genius, with his wealth, with his character, is to throw them into the scale of the argument, and make pro-slavery prejudice kick the beam.

I want to say another thing. I do not believe in the argument which my learned and eloquent friend Theodore Parker has stated in regard even to the *courage* of colored blood. It is a hazardous thing to dare to differ with so profound a scholar, with so careful a thinker as Theodore Parker; but I cannot accept his argument and for this reason,—he says the Caucasian race, each man of it, would kill twenty men and enslave twenty more rather than be a slave; and thence he deduces that the colored race, which suffers slavery here, is not emphatically distinguished for courage. I take issue on that statement. There is no race in the world that has not been enslaved at one period. This very Saxon blood we boast, was enslaved for five centuries in Europe. We were slaves,—we *white* people. This very English blood of ours— Saxon—was the peculiar mark of slavery for five or six hundred years. The Slavonic race, of which we are a branch, is enslaved by millions to-day in Russia. The French race has been enslaved for centuries. Then add this fact,—no race, *not one,* ever vindicated its freedom from slavery by the sword; we did not win freedom by the sword; we did not resist, we Saxons. If you go to the catalogue of races that have actually abolished slavery by the sword, the colored race is the only one that has ever yet afforded an instance, and that is St. Domingo. [Applause.] This white race of ours did not vindicate its title to liberty by the sword. The villeins of England, who were slaves, did not get their own liberty; it was gotten for them. They did not even rise in insur-rection,—they were quiet; and if in 1200 or 1300 of the Christian era, a black man had landed on the soil of England and said: "This white race doesn't deserve freedom; don't you see the villeins scattered through Kent, Northumberland, and Sussex? Why don't they rise and cut their masters' throats?"—the Theo-dore Parkers of that age would have been like the Dr. Rocks of this,—they could not have answered. The only race in history that ever took the sword into their hands, and cut their chains, is the black race of St. Domingo. Let that fact go for what it is worth. The villeinage of France and England wore out by the progress of commerce, by the growth of free cities, by the education of the people, by the advancement of Christianity. So I think the slavery of the blacks will wear out. I think, therefore, that the simple and limited experiment of three centuries of black slavery is not basis enough for the argument. No; the black man may well scorn it, and say, "I summon before the jury, Africa, with her savage millions, that has maintained her independence for two or three thousand years; I summon Egypt with the arts; I summon St. Domingo with the sword,—and I choose to be tried in the great company of the millions, not alone!" And in that company, he may claim to have shown as much courage as any other race—full as much.

I, therefore, will never try the argument with the single illustration of American slavery. No; and yet if I did, I should be proud to have the same color with Margaret Garner;[2] for I know of no prouder name in the history of the nineteenth century than of that heroic mother, standing alone, defying the Democracy of thirty-one States, rising in the instinctive love of a mother superior to the low Christianity of the present age, and writing her religion and her heroism in the bloody right hand that gave her infant back to God for safe keeping. [Loud applause.] Any man might well be proud to share the color of that mother whose grave some future Plutarch or Tacitus will find, when he calls up the heroism of the nineteenth century.

My friend Mr. Nell[3] has gathered together, in a small volume, instances enough of the heroism of colored blood, and the share it took in our Revolution, and yet he has not told half the story. I commend his book to the care and patronage of every man who loves the colored race. And not only to buy it,—that is not enough. If there is any young man who has any literary ambition, let him fill up the sketch; let him complete the picture; let him go sounding along the untrodden fields of Revolutionary anecdote, and gather up every fact touching the share his race took in that struggle. Why, the wealthiest family in Boston,—

that of the Lawrences,—in their own family history, record the fact that the father of Abbott Lawrence was the captain of a company made up entirely of colored men; and when once, in the fierce and hot valor of a forgetful moment, he rushed too far into the ranks of the enemy, and was alone, ready to be made a prisoner, he looked back to his ranks of colored men, and they charged through two lines of the enemy, rescued their captain, and made it possible for the Lawrences to exist. [Applause.] They ought to be grateful—yes, that whole wealthy family ought to be grateful to colored courage that it saved their own father from a Jersey ship-of-war, and enabled him to take his share in the Revolutionary struggle, and to be buried in the old homestead at Groton. And doubtless, if your literary zeal shall follow up the path your friend Nell has opened, you will find scarcely any name on the whole roll of Revolutionary fame that does not owe more or less to colored courage and co-operation. I commend it to your care. Never forget the part your race took in the great struggle; cherish, preserve, illustrate it. Compel the white man to write your names, not as they have written them in Connecticut, at the bottom of the rest, with a line between, negro-pew fashion, but make them write them on the same marble and in the same line. The time will yet come when we will, as Caleb Cushing says, drag this Massachusetts Legislature at our heels, and *they* shall pay for a monument to Attucks. [Loud cheers, and cries of "Good."] It will be but the magnanimous atonement for the injury and forgetfulness of so many years. They owe it to him, and they shall yet pay it. You and I, faithful to our trust, will see to it. Our fathers were honest and grateful enough to bury him from beneath these very walls. John Hancock did himself the honor, from his own balcony in Beacon Street, to give that banner to colored men, recognizing them as citizens and as soldiers. The time shall come when the flavor of that good deed shall perfume Beacon Street, and make it worthier [cheers],—I always thought that I had a pride in being born in it; now I know the reason. [Renewed cheering.]

Yes, like "Old Mortality," we come here to-night to make the monument plainer, to scrape off the moss that has gathered over it. It is only "the beginning of the end." The time shall come, if you, young men, do your duty, when the part your ancestors played, when the laurels they won, when the deeds they performed in our Revolutionary era, shall be raked up from forgetfulness. I will tell you how. Do you know how great-grandfathers get remembered? I will tell you. The world is very forgetful,— Republics are proverbially ungrateful. You must not expect that the white men will wake up and do you justice. Oh, no! I will tell you how it is to be done. We are very fond of finding reasons for things and explaining them away. If we see a boy very bright, with great genius, we are fond of saying, "Well, we knew his father and mother, and they were very bright people." Or, if we see a grandson very famous, we say, "Well, he comes of a good stock; we remember his grandfather, he could do this thing or the other!" When Theodore Parker came into the city of Boston, and made the boldest pulpit in the city, men said, "It is all right. This is the blood that fired the first musket at Lexington, and it is only cropping out in a new place." Now, some of you colored men, Boston colored men, go you to-morrow and show your valor in the field, valor in life, valor in education, valor in making money, valor in making your mark in the world,—and instantly the papers will begin to say, "Oh, yes; they have always been a brave, gallant people! Was there not an Attucks in '70? By the by, let us build him a monument." You must remind us by instances. You must not come to us and argue; that is not the way to convince us. The common people do not stop to argue. You must convince us by a life. We want another Attucks; and I will conclude by showing you that you have another Attucks.[4] Here is a letter from Mr. Higginson, excusing himself for not coming; and with this, which is a very excellent speech in itself, I will finish mine.

## NOTES

1. Dr. John S. Rock, a prominent Boston Negro physician, lawyer and Abolitionist, was one of the speakers at the meeting addressed by Wendell Phillips. Dr. Rock's address at that meeting has been reprinted in Herbert Aptheker, ed., *A Documentary History of the Negro People in the United States* (New York, 1951) , pp. 402–405.
2. A colored woman who threw her child into the Ohio River rather than to have it carried into slavery. [Note in the original text.]

3. William C. Nell, Boston Negro Abolitionist, published his pioneering study, *The Colored Patriots of the American Revolution*, in Boston in 1855.

4. An allusion to the fact stated in Mr. Higginson's letter, "that the very first man to enter the court-house door, in the attempt to rescue Anthony Burns, was not, as has been commonly supposed, a white man, but a colored man." [Note in the original text. The reference is to Thomas Wentworth Higginson, anti-slavery minister and supporter of John Brown.]

# ABRAHAM LINCOLN

## NEGRO RIGHTS

In this address delivered on September 18, 1858, in Charleston, Illinois, in the course of his debates with Stephen Douglas, Abraham Lincoln affirms that his opposition to slavery does not extend to equal rights for the Negro. At this period in his life, Lincoln had not yet discarded some of the anti-Negro prejudices that he had imbibed as a youth in Kentucky, and that then prevailed in Illinois as well. During the course of the Civil War, his opinions on Negro rights changed markedly. Additional Lincoln material, with a more detailed discussion of his views on race, is presented in the second volume of this work.

The most comprehensive and perceptive statement of Lincoln's view of the Negro is to be found in Benjamin Quarles, *Lincoln and the Negro* (New York, 1962). For recent conflicting opinions of Lincoln's attitude toward the Negro, see Harold M. Hyman, "Lincoln and Equal Rights for Negroes: The Irrevelancy of the 'Wadsworth Letter,' " *Civil War History*, XII (September 1966), 258–266; Lerone Bennett, Jr., "Was Abe Lincoln a White Supremacist?" *Ebony*, February 1968, pp. 35–42, and Herbert Mitgang, "Was Lincoln Just a Honkie?" *The New York Times Magazine*, Feb. 11, 1968, pp. 35, 100–107, as well as the correspondence in subsequent issues.

LADIES AND GENTLEMEN:

It will be very difficult for an audience so large as this to hear distinctly what a speaker says, and consequently it is important that as profound silence be preserved as possible.

While I was at the hotel to-day an elderly gentleman called upon me to know whether I was really in favor of producing a perfect equality between the negroes and white people. [Great laughter.] While I had not proposed to myself on this occasion to say much on that subject, yet as the question was asked me I thought I would occupy perhaps five minutes in saying something in regard to it. I will say then that I am not, nor ever have been in favor of bringing about in any way the social and political equality of the white and black races, [applause]—that I am not nor ever have been in favor of making voters or jurors of negroes, nor of qualifying them to hold office, nor to intermarry with white people; and I will say in addition to this that there is a physical difference between the white and black races which I believe will for ever forbid the two races living together on terms of social and political equality. And inasmuch as they cannot so live, while they do remain together there must be the position of superior and inferior, and I as much as any other man am in favor of having the superior position assigned to the white race. I say upon this occasion I do not perceive that because the white man is to have the superior position the negro should be denied everything. I do not understand that because I do not want a negro woman for a slave I must necessarily want her for a wife. [Cheers and laughter.] My understanding is that I can just let her alone. I am now in my fiftieth year, and I certainly never have had a black woman for either a slave or a wife. So it seems to me quite possible for us to get along without making either slaves or wives of negroes. I will add to this that I have never seen to my knowledge a man, woman or child who was in favor of producing a perfect equality, social and political, between negroes and white men. I recollect of but one distinguished instance that I ever heard of so frequently as to be entirely satisfied of its correctness—and that is the case of Judge Douglas' old friend Col. Richard M. Johnson.[1] [Laughter] I will also add to the remarks I have made, (for I am not going to enter at large upon this subject,) that I have never had the least apprehension that I or my friends would marry negroes if there was no law to keep them from it, [laughter] but as Judge Douglas and his friends seem to be in great apprehension that they might, if there were no law to keep them from it, [roars of laughter] I give him the most solemn pledge that I will to the very last stand by the law of this state, which forbids the marrying of white people with negroes. [Continued laughter and applause.] I will add one further word, which is this, that I do not understand there is any place where an alteration of the social and political relations of the negro and the white man can be made except in the state legislature—not in the Congress of the United States—and as I do not really apprehend the approach of any such thing myself, and as Judge Douglas seems to be in constant horror that some such danger is rapidly approaching, I propose as the best means to prevent it that the Judge be kept at home and placed in the state legislature to fight the measure. [Uproarious laughter and applause.] I do not propose dwelling longer at this time on this subject.

## NOTE

1. Richard M. Johnson, Vice-President of the United States, 1837–41, never married, but had a Negro mistress, Julia Chinn, who bore him two daughters.

# CHAPTER 9

# *Pro-Slavery Thinkers*

## WILLIAM HARPER

### MEMOIR ON SLAVERY

Lawyer, judge and nullification leader, William Harper (1790–1847) was raised and educated in South Carolina. After moving to Missouri in 1818, he was appointed chancellor of the Missouri Territory during the following year and elected to that office after statehood was obtained. At various times thereafter, he served as United States Senator, as member and Speaker in the South Carolina legislature, Chancellor of the state and judge of its Court of Appeals. His *Memoir on Slavery,* written in 1837, "is regarded as one of the most important pro-slavery arguments in the history of the controversy," according to J. G. deR. Hamilton, in his essay on Harper in the *Dictionary of American Biography.* The following selection is reprinted from "the great classic of slavery defense,"[1] a volume entitled *The Pro-Slavery Argument; as Maintained by the Most Distinguished Writers of the Southern States, Containing the Several Essays, on the Subject, of Chancellor Harper, Governor Hammond, Dr. Simms, and Professor Dew* (Charleston, 1852), pp. 56 ff.

. . . That the African negro is an inferior variety of the human race, is, I think, now generally admitted, and his distinguishing characteristics are such as peculiarly mark him out for the situation which he occupies among us. And these are no less marked in their original country, than as we have daily occasion to observe them. The most remarkable is their indifference to personal liberty. In this they have followed their instincts since we have any knowledge of their continent, by enslaving each other; but contrary to the experience of every race, the possession of slaves has no material effect in raising the character, and promoting the civilization of the master. Another trait is the want of domestic affections, and insensibility to the ties of kindred. . . . They are, however, very submissive to authority, and seem to entertain great reverence for chiefs, priests, and masters. No greater indignity can be offered an individual, than to throw opprobrium on his parents. On this point of their character I think I have remarked, that, contrary to the instinct of nature in other races, they entertain less regard for children than for parents, to whose authority they have been accustomed to submit. . . . Let me ask if this people do not furnish the very material out of which slaves ought to be made, and whether it be not an improving of their condition to make them the slaves of civilized masters? There is a variety in the character of the tribes. Some are brutally and savagely ferocious and bloody, whom it would be mercy to enslave. From the travellers' account, it seems not unlikely that the negro race is tending to extermination, being daily encroached on and overrun by the superior Arab race. It may be, that when they shall have been lost from their native seats, they may be found numerous, and in no unhappy condition, on the continent to which they have been transplanted.

The opinion which connects form and features with character and intellectual power, is one so deeply impressed on the human mind, that perhaps there is scarcely any man who does not almost daily act upon it, and in some measure verify its truth. Yet in spite of this intimation of nature, and though the anatomist and physiologist may tell them that the races differ in every bone and muscle, and in the proportion of brain and nerves, yet there are some who, with a most bigoted and fanatical determination to free themselves from what they have prejudged to be prejudice, will still maintain that this physiognomy, evidently tending to that of the brute, when compared to that of the Caucasian race, may be enlightened by as much thought, and animated by as lofty sentiment. We who have the best opportunity of judging, are pronounced to be incompetent to do so, and to be blinded by our interest and prejudices—often by those who have no opportunity at all—and we are to be taught to distrust or disbelieve that which we daily observe, and familiarly know, on such authority. Our prejudices are spoken of. But the truth is, that, until very lately, since circumstances have compelled us to think for ourselves, we took our opinions on this subject, as on every other, ready formed from the country of our origin. And so deeply rooted were they, that we adhered to them, as most men will do to deeply rooted opinions, even against the evidence of our own observation, and our own senses. If the inferiority exists, it is attributed to the apathy and degradation produced by Slavery. Though of the hundreds of thousand scattered over other countries, where the laws impose no disability upon them, none has given evidence of an approach to even mediocrity of intellectual excellence; this, too, is attributed to the slavery of a portion of their race. They are regarded as a servile caste, and degraded by opinion, and thus every generous effort is repressed. Yet though this should be the general effect, this very estimation is calculated to produce the contrary effect in particular instances. It is observed by Bacon, with respect to deformed persons and eunuchs, that though in general there is something of perversity in the character, the disadvantage often leads to extraordinary displays of virtue and excellence. "Whoever hath any thing fixed in his person that doth induce contempt, hath also a perpetual spur in himself, to rescue and deliver himself from scorn." So it would be with them, if they were capable of European aspirations—genius, if they possessed it, would be doubly fired with noble rage to rescue itself from this scorn. Of course, I do not mean to say that there may not be found among them some of superior capacity to many white persons; but that great intellectual powers are, perhaps, never found among them, and that in general their capacity is very limited, and their feelings animal and coarse— fitting them peculiarly to discharge the lower, and merely mechanical offices of society.

And why should it not be so? We have among domestic animals infinite varieties, distinguished by various degrees of sagacity, courage, strength, swiftness, and other qualities. And it may be observed, that this is no objection to their being derived from a common origin, which we suppose them to have had. Yet these accidental qualities, as they may be termed, however acquired in the first instance, we know that they transmit unimpaired to their posterity for an indefinite succession of generations. It is most important that these varieties should be preserved, and that each should be applied to the purposes for which it is best adapted. No philo-zoost, I believe, has suggested it as desirable that these varieties should be melted down into one equal, undistinguished race of curs or road horses.

Slavery, as it is said in an eloquent article published in a Southern periodical work,[2] to which I am indebted for other ideas, "has done more to elevate a degraded race in the scale of humanity; to tame the savage; to civilize the barbarous; to soften the ferocious; to enlighten the ignorant, and to spread the blessings of Christianity among the heathen, than all the missionaries that philanthropy and religion have ever sent forth." Yet unquestionable as this is, and though human ingenuity and thought may be tasked in vain to devise any other means by which these blessings could have been conferred, yet a sort of sensibility which would be only mawkish and contemptible, if it were not mischievous, affects still to weep over the wrongs of "injured Africa." Can there be a doubt of the immense benefit which has been conferred on the race, by transplanting them from their native, dark, and barbarous regions, to the American continent and islands? There, three-fourths of the race are in a state of the most deplorable personal Slavery. And those who are not, are in a scarcely less deplorable condition of political Slavery, to barbarous chiefs—who value neither life nor any other human right, or enthralled by priests to the most abject and atrocious superstitions. Take the following testimony of one of the few disinterested observers, who has had an opportunity of observing them in both situations.[3] "The wild savage is the child of passion, unaided by one ray of religion or morality to direct his course, in consequence of which his existence is stained with every crime that can debase human nature to a level with the brute creation. Who can say that the slaves in our colonies are such? Are they not, by comparison with their still savage brethren, enlightened beings? Is not the West Indian negro, therefore, greatly indebted to his master for making him what he is—for having raised him from the state of debasement in which he was born, and placed him in a scale of civilized society? How can he repay him? He is possessed of nothing—the only return in his power is his servitude. The man who has seen the wild African, roaming in his native woods, and the well fed, happy looking negro of the West Indies, may, perhaps, be able to judge of their comparative happiness; the former, I strongly suspect, would be glad to change his state of boasted freedom, starvation, and disease, to become the slave of sinners, and the commiseration of saints." It was a useful and beneficent work, approaching the heroic, to tame the wild horse, and subdue him to the use of man; how much more to tame the nobler animal that is capable of reason, and subdue him to usefulness? . . .

## NOTES

1. Clement Eaton, *A History of the Old South* (New York, 1949), p. 385.
2. Southern Literary Messenger, for January, 1835. *Note to Blackstone's Commentaries.* [This and following note are from the original text.]
3. Journal of an officer employed in the expedition, under the command of Capt. Owen, on the West Coast of Africa, 1822.

# JOHN C. CALHOUN

## NEGROES AS SLAVES AND FREEDMEN

In 1844, Richard Pakenham, the British envoy to the United States, transmitted a letter from the British Foreign Office to the American Government disclaiming any desire to interfere with Texan independence or to dominate that territory. While admitting that Britain hoped for the abolition of slavery in Texas and elsewhere in the United States, it denied any intention of directly interfering with the institution or of stirring up "disaffection or excitement of any kind" in the South.

John C. Calhoun, then Secretary of State, replied on behalf of the United States. Perhaps most noteworthy was his defense of slavery as being in the best interests of the Negro, who, he claimed, was better off as a slave than as a free man. In support of his claim, he cited the statistics of the 1840 census, which indicated that the Northern states that had freed their Negroes had a far larger proportion of Negroes who were "deaf and dumb, blind, idiots, and insane, paupers, and in prison" than states that had maintained slavery.

A word about the 1840 census: though constituting the Sixth Census, it was the first to enumerate the mentally ill and feebleminded. A study of its statistics regarding the Negro indicates that it was probably the most inaccurate—fraudulent might be a better term for some of its figures—in American history. It recorded a total of 17,456 "insane and idiots" in the United States, out of a total population of about 17 million. While it showed relatively similar proportions of insanity for the white populations of the North and the South, one in 995 for the North and one in 945.3 for the South, it evidenced a striking difference between the regions in Negro insanity and feeblemindedness. For the South, the ratio was one in 1,558; for the North, one in 144.5. In effect, the rate of insanity or mental defectiveness among free Negroes was eleven times higher than among slaves.[1] The obvious conclusion, which pro-slavery men did not hesitate to publicize, was that slavery was far better for the Negro than freedom.

Fortunately, it was not long before the statistics were shown to be false by Dr. Edward Jarvis, at that time a physician of Concord, Massachusetts, a founder of the American Statistical Association in 1839, and a specialist in mental disorder. Dr. Jarvis, in an essay in the *Boston Medical and Surgical Journal* of September 21, 1842,[2] first pointed out some minor differences between the national statistics and those of the Overseers of the Poor in the various towns of Massachusetts in 1840, with the national census reporting far fewer "insane and idiotic paupers"; but in general, although questioning some of the statistics for other states as well, he did not hesitate to accept the variations between Northern and Southern Negroes and between Negroes and whites as valid. In a second essay in the same journal,[3] however, he reported amazing errors in the statistics. Examining the census reports for each town in Massachusetts, he found many instances of no Negro residents but several Negro insane. This was true for Massachusetts, as well as Connecticut, New Hampshire, New York, Michigan and others. In 1844, Dr. Jarvis again published his conclusions, in the *American Journal of Medical Sciences*,[4] and suggested that "no reliance whatever can be placed on what purport to be facts, respecting the prevalence of insanity among the free Negroes, set forth in that fallacious and self-condemning document, the Sixth Census of the United States."[5]

Although in February 1844, John Quincy Adams, then a Congressman, requested an impartial investigation of the census, Calhoun, then Secretary of State, asked the Superintendent of the Census, William A. Weaver, who had supervised the original count, to check the alleged errors. Weaver, as was to be expected, found the charges baseless. And for years, if not decades afterward, pro-slavery and segregationist writers continued to use the 1840 census to support their views.[6]

The following letter is from *The Works of John C. Calhoun* (New York, 1867), Vol. V, pp. 333–9.

## Mr. Calhoun to Mr. Pakenham

WASHINGTON, April 18th, 1844
DEPARTMENT OF STATE,

. . . A large number of the States has decided, that it is neither wise nor humane to change the relation which has existed, from their first settlement, between the two races; while others, where the African is less numerous, have adopted the opposite policy.

It belongs not to the Government to question whether the former have decided wisely or not; and if it did, the undersigned would not regard this as the proper occasion to discuss the subject. He does not, however, deem it irrelevant to state that, if the experience of more than half a century is to decide, it would be neither humane nor wise in them to change their policy. The census and other authentic documents show that, in all instances in which the States have changed the former relation between the two races, the condition of the African, instead of being improved, has become worse. They have been invariably sunk into vice and pauperism, accompanied by the bodily and mental inflictions incident thereto—deafness, blindness, insanity, and idiocy—to a degree without example; while, in all other States which have retained the ancient relation between them, they have improved greatly in every respect—in number, comfort, intelligence, and morals—as the following facts, taken from such sources, will serve to illustrate:

The number of deaf and dumb, blind, idiots, and insane, of the negroes in the States that have changed the ancient relation between the races, is one out of every ninety-six; while in the States adhering to it, it is one out of every six hundred and seventy-two—that is, seven to one in favor of the latter, as compared with the former.

The number of whites, deaf and dumb, blind, idiots, and insane, in the States that have changed the relation, is one in every five hundred and sixty-one; being nearly six to one against the free blacks in the same States.

The number of negroes who are deaf and dumb, blind, idiots, and insane, paupers, and in prison in the States that have changed, is one out of every six; and in the States that have not, one out of every one hundred and fifty-four; or twenty-two to one against the former, as compared with the latter.

Taking the two extremes of North and South—in the State of Maine, the number of negroes returned as deaf and dumb, blind, insane, and idiots, by the census of 1840, is one out of every twelve; and in Florida, by the same returns, is one out of every eleven hundred and five; or ninety-two to one in favor of the slaves of Florida, as compared with the free blacks of Maine.

In addition, it deserves to be remarked, that in Masssachusetts, where the change in the ancient relation of the two races was first made (now more than sixty years since) , where the greatest zeal has been exhibited in their behalf, and where their number is comparatively few (but little more than 8,000 in a population of upwards of 730,000) , the condition of the African is amongst the most wretched. By the latest authentic accounts, there was one out of every twenty-one of the black population in jails or houses of correction; and one out of every thirteen was either deaf and dumb, blind, idiot, insane, or in prison. On the other hand, the census and other authentic sources of information establish the fact that the condition of the African race throughout all the States, where the ancient relation between the two has been retained, enjoys a degree of health and comfort which may well compare with that of the laboring population of any country in Christendom; and it may be added, that in no other condition, or in any other age or country, has the negro race ever attained so high an elevation in morals, intelligence, or civilization.

If such be the wretched condition of the race in their changed relation, where their number is comparatively few, and where so much interest is manifested for their improvement, what would it be in those States where the two races are nearly equal in numbers, and where, in consequence, would necessarily spring up mutual fear, jealousy, and hatred, between them? It may, in truth, be assumed as a maxim, that two races differing so greatly and in so many respects, cannot possibly exist together in the same country, where their numbers are nearly equal, without the one being subjected to the other. Experience has proved that the existing relation, in which the one is subjected to the other, in the slaveholding States, is consistent with the peace and safety of both, with great improvement to the inferior; while the same experience proves that the relation which it is the desire and object of Great Britain to substitute in its stead in this and all other countries, under the plausible name of the abolition of slavery, would (if it did not destroy the inferior by conflicts, to which it would lead) reduce it to the extremes of vice and wretchedness. In this view of the subject it may be asserted, that what is called slavery is in reality a political institution, essential to the peace, safety, and prosperity of those States of the Union in which it exists. Without, then, controverting the wisdom and humanity of the policy of Great Britain, so far as her own possessions are concerned, it may be safely affirmed, without reference to the means by which it would be affected, that, could she succeed in accomplishing, in the United States, what she avows to be her desire and the object of her constant exertions to effect throughout the world, so far from being wise or humane, she would involve in the greatest calamity the whole country, and especially the race which it is the avowed object of her exertions to benefit.

The undersigned avails himself of this occasion to renew to the Right Honorable Mr. Pakenham the assurance of his distinguished consideration.

J. C. CALHOUN.

## NOTES

1. Albert Deutsch, "The First U.S. Census of the Insane (1840) and Its Use as Pro-Slavery Propaganda," *Bulletin of the History of Medicine,* XV (May 1944) , 472.
2. "Statistics of Insanity in the United States," Sept. 21, 1842, pp. 116–121.
3. "Statistics of Insanity in the United States," Nov. 30, 1842, pp. 271–2.
4. Philadelphia, 1844, VII, 74–75.
5. Quoted in Deutsch, "The First U.S. Census . . . ," p. 475.
6. *Ibid.,* pp. 478 ff.

# HENRY CLAY

## On Segregation

In this address on the subject of abolition petitions, delivered in the Senate on February 7, 1839, Henry Clay (1777–1852), lawyer, Congressman, Senator and Secretary of State, expresses his devotion to slavery and to the separation of the races. Yet Clay's views on slavery and the Negro were far more complex than those presented here. He was one of the large slaveholders of Kentucky, master of sixty slaves in 1846; but though accepting the institution in practice, he was opposed to it in theory. From time to time he emancipated slaves who had served him faithfully, yet he did not hesitate to try to recapture slaves who had run away. He regarded the Negro as an inferior and amalgamation of the races as an evil. He supported fugitive slave laws and approved of domestic slave traders, yet he favored gradual emancipation, with qualifications.[1] He was one of the founders of the American Colonization Society, presided over its first organization in Washington, in December 1816, and later served as its president. In his famous Pindell letter of February 17, 1849, he urged that Kentucky adopt a plan of gradual emancipation, at a constitutional convention which had been called for August of that year. His proposal was unpopular, however, and received no support at the convention. The address is reprinted from Calvin Cotton, ed., *Works of Henry Clay . . .* (New York, 1897), pp. 154–160.

. . . And now, Mr. President, if it were possible to overcome the insurmountable obstacles which lie in the way of immediate abolition, let us briefly contemplate some of the consequences which would inevitably ensue. One of these has been occasionally alluded to in the progress of these remarks. It is the struggle which would instantaneously arise between the two races in most of the Southern and Southwestern States. And what a dreadful struggle would it not be! Embittered by all the recollections of the past, by the unconquerable prejudices which would prevail between the two races, and stimulated by all the hopes and fears of the future, it would be a contest in which the extermination of the blacks, or their ascendancy over the whites, would be the sole alternative. Prior to the conclusion, or during the progress, of such a contest, vast numbers, probably, of the black race would migrate into the free States; and what effect would such a migration have upon the laboring classes in those States!

Now the distribution of labor in the United States is geographical; the free laborers occupying one side of the line, and the slave laborers the other; each class pursuing its own avocations almost altogether unmixed with the other. But, on the supposition of immediate abolition, the black class, migrating into the free States, would enter into competition with the white class, diminishing the wages of their labor, and augmenting the hardships of their condition.

This is not all. The abolitionists strenuously oppose all separation of the two races. I confess to you, Sir, that I have seen, with regret, grief, and astonishment, their resolute opposition to the project of colonization. No scheme was ever presented to the acceptance of man, which, whether it be entirely practicable or not, is characterized by more unmixed humanity and benevolence than that of transporting, with their own consent, the free people of color in the United States to the land of their ancestors. It has the powerful recommendation, that whatever it does is good; and, if it effects nothing, it inflicts no one evil or mischief upon any portion of our society. There is no necessary hostility between the objects of colonization and abolition. Colonization deals only with the free man of color, and that with his own free, voluntary consent. It has nothing to do with slavery. It disturbs no man's property, seeks to impair no power in the slave States, nor to attribute any to the general Government. All its action and all its ways and means are voluntary, depending upon the blessing of Providence, which hitherto has graciously smiled upon it. And yet, beneficent and harmless as colonization is, no portion of the people of the United States denounces it with so much persevering zeal, and such unmixed bitterness, as do the abolitionists.

They put themselves in direct opposition to any separation

whatever between the two races. They would keep them forever pent up together within the same limits, perpetuating their animosities, and constantly endangering the peace of the community. They proclaim, indeed, that color is nothing; that the organic and characteristic differences between the two races ought to be entirely overlooked and disregarded. And, elevating themselves to a sublime but impracticable philosophy, they would teach us to eradicate all the repugnances of our nature, and to take to our bosoms and our boards the black man as we do the white, on the same footing of equal social condition. Do they not perceive, that, in thus confounding all the distinctions which God himself has made, they arraign the wisdom and goodness of Providence itself? It has been His divine pleasure to make the black man black, and the white man white, and to distinguish them by other repulsive constitutional differences. It is not necessary for me to maintain, nor shall I endeavor to prove, that it was any part of His divine intention that the one race should be held in perpetual bondage by the other; but this I will say, that those whom He has created different, and has declared, by their physical structure and color, ought to be kept asunder, should not be brought together by any process whatever of unnatural amalgamation.

But if the dangers of the civil contest, which I have supposed, could be avoided, separation or amalgamation is the only peaceful alternative, if it were possible to effectuate the project of abolition. The abolitionists oppose all colonization, and it irresistibly follows, whatever they may protest or declare, that they are in favor of amalgamation. And who are to bring about this amalgamation? I have heard of none of these ultra-abolitionists furnishing in their own families or persons examples of intermarriage. Who is to begin it? Is it their purpose not only to create a pinching competition between black labor and white labor, but do they intend also to contaminate the industrious and laborious classes of society at the North by a revolting admixture of the black element?

It is frequently asked, What is to become of the African race among us? Are they forever to remain in bondage? That question was asked more than half a century ago. It has been answered by fifty years of prosperity but little checkered from this cause. It will be repeated fifty or a hundred years hence. The true answer is, that the same Providence who has hitherto guided and governed us, and averted all serious evils from the existing relation between the two races, will guide and govern our posterity. "Sufficient unto the day is the evil thereof." We have hitherto, with that blessing, taken care of ourselves. Posterity will find the means of its own preservation and prosperity. It is only in the most direful event which can befall this people, that this great interest, and all other of our greatest interests, would be put in jeopardy. Although in particular districts the black population is gaining upon the white, it only constitutes one fifth of the whole population of the United States. And taking the aggregate of the two races, the European is constantly, though slowly, gaining upon the African portion. This fact is demonstrated by the periodical returns of our population. Let us cease, then, to indulge in gloomy forebodings about the impenetrable future. But, if we may attempt to lift the veil, and contemplate what lies beyond it, I, too, have ventured on a speculative theory, with which I will not now trouble you, but which has been published to the world. According to that, in the progress of time, some one hundred and fifty or two hundred years hence, but few vestiges of the black race will remain among our posterity.

## NOTE

1. Clement Eaton, *Henry Clay and the Art of American Politics* (Boston and Toronto, 1957) , pp. 126–7.

# THE SUPREME COURT

## THE POLITICAL RIGHTS OF THE NEGRO IN 1857

In this selection from the Dred Scott Decision, delivered on March 6, 1857 by Chief Justice Roger Brooke Taney of Maryland, on behalf of the majority of the Supreme Court, we find an evaluation of the historical attitude of the English, at home and in the Colonies, toward the African Negro. Carrying his evaluation through the period of the Constitution, Justice Taney provided the basis for the Court's decision that the American Negro did not have the right of citizenship.

. . . The question is simply this: Can a negro, whose ancestors were imported into this country, and sold as slaves, become a member of the political community formed and brought into existence by the Constitution of the United States, and as such become entitled to all the rights, and privileges, and immunities, guarantied by that instrument to the citizen? One of which rights is the privilege of suing in a court of the United States in the cases specified in the Constitution.

It will be observed, that the plea applies to that class of persons only whose ancestors were negroes of the African race, and imported into this country, and sold and held as slaves. The only matter in issue before the court, therefore, is, whether the descendants of such slaves, when they shall be emancipated, or who are born of parents who had become free before their birth, are citizens of a State, in the sense in which the word citizen is used in the Constitution of the United States. And this being the only matter in dispute on the pleadings, the court must be understood as speaking in this opinion of that class only, that is, of those persons who are the descendants of Africans who were imported into this country, and sold as slaves. . . .

In the opinion of the court, the legislation and histories of the times, and the language used in the Declaration of Independence, show, that neither the class of persons who had been imported as slaves, nor their descendants, whether they had become free or not, were then acknowledged as a part of the people, nor intended to be included in the general words used in that memorable instrument.

It is difficult at this day to realize the state of public opinion in relation to that unfortunate race, which prevailed in the civilized and enlightened portions of the world at the time of the Declaration of Independence, and when the Constitution of the United States was framed and adopted. But the public history of every European nation displays it in a manner too plain to be mistaken.

They had for more than a century before been regarded as beings of an inferior order, and altogether unfit to associate with the white race, either in social or political relations; and so far inferior, that they had no rights which the white man was bound to respect; and that the negro might justly and lawfully be reduced to slavery for his benefit. He was bought and sold, and treated as an ordinary article of merchandise and traffic, whenever a profit could be made by it. This opinion was at that time fixed and universal in the civilized portion of the white race. It was regarded as an axiom in morals as well as in politics, which no one thought of disputing, or supposed to be open to dispute; and men in every grade and position in society daily and habitually acted upon it in their private pursuits, as well as in matters of public concern, without doubting for a moment the correctness of this opinion.

And in no nation was this opinion more firmly fixed or more uniformly acted upon than by the English Government and English people. They not only seized them on the coast of Africa, and sold them or held them in slavery for their own use; but they took them as ordinary articles of merchandise to every country where they could make a profit on them, and were far more extensively engaged in this commerce than any other nation in the world.

The opinion thus entertained and acted upon in England was naturally impressed upon the colonies they founded on this side of the Atlantic. And, accordingly, a negro of the African race was regarded by them as an article of property, and held, and bought and sold as such, in every one of the thirteen colonies which united in the Declaration of Independence, and afterward formed the Constitution of the United States. The slaves were more or less numerous in the different colonies, as slave labor was found more or less profitable. But no one seems to have doubted the correctness of the prevailing opinion of the time.

The legislation of the different colonies furnishes positive and indisputable proof of this fact. . . .

We refer to these historical facts for the purpose of showing the fixed opinions concerning that race, upon which the statesmen of that day spoke and acted. It is necessary to do this, in order to determine whether the general terms used in the Constitution of the United States, as to the rights of man and the rights of the people, was intended to include them, or to give to them or their posterity the benefit of any of its provisions.

It begins by declaring that "when in the course of human events it becomes necessary for one people to dissolve the political bands which have connected them with another, and to assume among the powers of the earth the separate and equal station to which the laws of nature and nature's God entitle them, a decent respect for the opinions of mankind requires that they should declare the causes which impel them to the separation."

It then proceeds to say: "We hold these truths to be self-evident: that all men are created equal; that they are endowed by their Creator with certain unalienable rights; that among them is life, liberty, and the pursuit of happiness; that to secure these rights, Governments are instituted, deriving their just powers from the consent of the governed."

The general words above quoted would seem to embrace the whole human family, and if they were used in a similar instrument at this day would be so understood. But it is too clear for dispute, that the enslaved African race were not intended to be included, and formed no part of the people who framed and adopted this declaration; for if the language, as understood in that day, would embrace them, the conduct of the distinguished men who framed the Declaration of Independence would have been utterly and flagrantly inconsistent with the principles they asserted; and instead of the sympathy of mankind, to which they so confidently appealed, they would have deserved and received universal rebuke and reprobation.

Yet the men who framed this declaration were great men—

high in literary acquirements—high in their sense of honor, and incapable of asserting principles inconsistent with those on which they were acting. They perfectly understood the meaning of the language they used, and how it would be understood by others; and they knew that it would not in any part of the civilized world be supposed to embrace the negro race, which, by common consent, had been excluded from civilized Governments and the family of nations, and doomed to slavery. They spoke and acted according to the then established doctrines and principles, and in the ordinary language of the day, and no one misunderstood them. The unhappy black race were separated from the white by indelible marks, and laws long before established, and were never thought of or spoken of except as property, and when the claims of the owner or the profit of the trader were supposed to need protection.

This state of public opinion had undergone no change when the Constitution was adopted, as is equally evident from its provisions and language.

The brief preamble sets forth by whom it was formed, for what purposes, and for whose benefit and protection. It declares that it is formed by the *people* of the United States; that is to say, by those who were members of the different political communities in the several States; and its great object is declared to be to secure the blessings of liberty to themselves and their posterity. It speaks in general terms of the *people* of the United States, and of *citizens* of the several States, when it is providing for the exercise of the powers granted or the privileges secured to the citizen. It does not define what description of persons are intended to be included under these terms, or who shall be regarded as a citizen and one of the people. It uses them as terms so well understood, that no further description or definition was necessary.

But there are two clauses in the Constitution which point directly and specifically to the negro race as a separate class of persons, and show clearly that they were not regarded as a portion of the people or citizens of the Government then formed.

One of these clauses reserves to each of the thirteen States the right to import slaves until the year 1808, if it thinks proper. And the importation which it thus sanctions was unquestionably of persons of the race of which we are speaking, as the traffic in slaves in the United States has always been confined to them. And by the other provision the States pledge themselves to each other to maintain the right of property of the master, by delivering up to him any slave who may have escaped from his service, and be found within their respective territories. By the first above-mentioned clause, therefore, the right to purchase and hold this property is directly sanctioned and authorized for twenty years by the people who framed the Constitution. And by the second, they pledge themselves to maintain and uphold the right of the master in the manner specified, as long as the Government they then formed should endure. And these two provisions show, conclusively, that neither the description of persons therein referred to, nor their descendants, were embraced in any of the other provisions of the Constitution; for certainly these two clauses were not intended to confer on them or their posterity the blessings of liberty, or any of the personal rights so carefully provided for the citizen.

No one of that race had ever migrated to the United States voluntarily; all of them had been brought here as articles of merchandise. The number that had been emancipated at that time were but few in comparison with those held in slavery; and they were identified in the public mind with the race to which they belonged, and regarded as a part of the slave population rather than the free. It is obvious that they were not even in the minds of the framers of the Constitution when they were conferring special rights and privileges upon the citizens of a State in every other part of the Union.

Indeed, when we look to the condition of this race in the several States at the time, it is impossible to believe that these rights and privileges were intended to be extended to them.

It is very true, that in that portion of the Union where the labor of the negro race was found to be unsuited to the climate and unprofitable to the master, but few slaves were held at the time of the Declaration of Independence; and when the Constitution was adopted, it had entirely worn out in one of them, and measures had been taken for its gradual abolition in several others. But this change had not been produced by any change of opinion in relation to this race; but because it was discovered, from experience, that slave labor was unsuited to the climate and productions of these States: for some of the States, where it had ceased or nearly ceased to exist, were actively engaged in the slave trade, procuring cargoes on the coast of Africa, and transporting them for sale to those parts of the Union where their labor was found to be profitable, and suited to the climate and productions. And this traffic was openly carried on, and fortunes accumulated by it, without reproach from the people of the States where they resided. And it can hardly be supposed that, in the States where it was then countenanced in its worst form—that is, in the seizure and transportation—the people could have regarded those who were emancipated as entitled to equal rights with themselves. . . .

It would be impossible to enumerate and compress in the space usually allotted to an opinion of a court, the various laws, marking the condition of this race, which were passed from time to time after the Revolution, and before and since the adoption of the Constitution of the United States. In addition to those already referred to, it is sufficient to say, that Chancellor Kent, whose accuracy and research no one will question, states in the sixth edition of his Commentaries, (published in 1848, 2 vol., 258, note *b,*) that in no part of the country except Maine, did the African race, in point of fact, participate equally with the whites in the exercise of civil and political rights.

The legislation of the States therefore shows, in a manner not to be mistaken, the inferior and subject condition of that race at the time the Constitution was adopted, and long afterwards, throughout the thirteen States by which that instrument was framed; and it is hardly consistent with the respect due to these States, to suppose that they regarded at that time, as fellow-citizens and members of the sovereignty, a class of beings whom they had thus stigmatized; whom, as we are bound, out of respect to the State sovereignties, to assume they had deemed it just and necessary thus to stigmatize, and upon whom they had impressed such deep and enduring marks of inferiority and degradation; or, that when they met in convention to form the Constitution, they looked upon them as a portion of their constituents, or designed to include them in the provisions so carefully inserted for the security and protection of the liberties and rights of their citizens. It cannot be supposed that they intended to secure to them rights, and privileges, and rank, in the new political body throughout the Union, which every one of them denied within the limits of its own dominion. More especially, it can not be believed that the large slaveholding States regarded them as included in the word citizens, or would have consented to a Constitution which might compel them to receive them in that character from another State. For if they were so received, and entitled to the privileges and immunities of citizens, it would exempt them from the operation of the special laws and from the police regulations which they considered to be necessary for their own safety. It would give to persons of the negro race, who were recognized as citizens in any one State of the Union, the right to enter every other State whenever they pleased, singly or in companies, without pass or passport, and without obstruction, to sojourn there as long as they pleased, to go where they pleased at every hour of the day or night without molestation, unless they committed some violation of law for which a white man would be punished; and it would give them the full liberty of speech in public and in private upon all subjects upon which its own citizens might speak; to hold public meetings upon political affairs, and to keep and carry arms wherever they went. And all of this would be done in the face of the subject race of the same color, both free and slaves, and inevitably producing discontent and insubordination among them, and endangering the peace and safety of the State.

# WILLIAM ANDREW SMITH

## Negro Ability: Slavery vs. Self-Government

Virginia-born William A. Smith (1802–1870) was at various times a clergyman, professor, college president and author. Elected president of Randolph-Macon College in 1846, he also served as professor of "Moral and Intellectual Philosophy." Although, in 1844, he admitted that "slavery is a great evil, but beyond our control; yet not necessarily a sin," in 1856 he was wholeheartedly in favor of the institution. He defended it in his volume, *Lectures on the Philosophy and Practice of Slavery, as Exhibited in the Institution of Domestic Slavery in the United States; with the Duties of Masters to Slaves,* edited by Thomas O. Summers (Nashville, Tenn., 1856). The following selection consists of pp. 176–191.

*Domestic Slavery, as a System of Government for the Africans in America, Examined and Defended on the Ground of Its Adaptation to the Present Condition of the Race*

There should be a separate and subordinate government for our African population—Objection answered—Africans are not competent to that measure of self-government which entitles a man to political sovereignty—They were not prepared for freedom when first brought into the country, hence they were placed under the domestic form of government—The humanity of this policy—In the opinion of Southern people they are still unprepared—The fanaticism and rashness of some, and the inexcusable wickedness of others, who oppose the South.

It having been proved that both the doctrine and the assumption of fact by Northern fanatics, in regard to the claim of the African to a republican form of government, are false, and that the presumption is in favor of the position of the South, that domestic slavery is the appropriate form of government for them, we are now left free to pursue our inquiry, without offset from these vagaries, into the merits of this system, and its appropriateness to the African race in this country.

The African is now here. Whether right or wrong originally, is not the question before us. He is here. What form of government is best suited to him, and those with whom he is necessarily associated? And,

I. Let it be observed, that they are a distinct race of people, separated by strongly marked lines of moral and physical condition from those amongst whom they reside. This difference is so strongly marked that there can be no spontaneous amalgamation by intermarriage, and consequently no reciprocity of social rights and privileges between the races. Their history in the whole country shows this to be the case. They must therefore continue to exist as a separate race. To this state of things the government over them should be adapted, unless we would violate a material condition of the problem to be solved. For if the law should not provide for this state of the case, the conventional usages of the superior race amongst whom they dwell will certainly do so. This is in proof from the example of all those States which have failed to provide for the African as a separate and distinct race; for the usages of society always supply the deficiency. This omission on the part of the law is evidently to the injury of the African. The history of the race in the Northern States will show this. Essential liberty is founded in, and is inseparable from, certain social rights and privileges. But in these respects, the African is a far more proscribed and degraded race in the Northern than in the Southern States.

A government, then, should be provided for the African, as a distinct and separate race, existing in the bosom of another and superior race. Of course this will be an *imperium in imperio*. And as they are confessedly the inferior race, who can never enjoy essential liberty or reciprocity of social condition with the whites, the government adapted to them must be inferior and subordinate to that of the whites amongst whom they dwell. It must be subordinate; for, in the nature of things, it must be an independent or a subordinate one. But two independent civil governments cannot coëxist, and control distinct races dwelling together in the same community. It follows that it must be subordinate. As subordinate, it must either assume some form of military government, or it must conform to the patriarchal species of government—a kind of family government—that is, the domestic form for which we contend. And as between a sub-ordinate military or patriarchal form of government, both as regards the expense and the comfort, there can be no controversy, we may consider the claims of the patriarchal form, or the system of domestic slavery, as established in this case.

But it may be supposed that the experiment in the Northern States invalidates the position, that this, being a distinct race of people, must be controlled by a separate and subordinate form of government. These States have a portion of this race, and it is said they find no difficulty to result from having placed them on a political footing with other citizens. But this is a mere assumption. It is not borne out by the facts of history.

As before stated, the conventional usages of society have denied them the social rights and privileges of free citizens! They have proscribed them as an inferior and degraded race.

The usage which forbids intermarriage is at once a bar to all social equality. The road to offices of trust, honor, and profit, is closed against them—nay, even the means of subsistence beyond a scanty supply of the necessaries of life. These facts are undeniable. Now, to talk of liberty when we effectually deny to a people all that essentially constitutes it, is idle in the extreme. It is a mere paper liberty!—liberty to submit to the crushing usages of society!—liberty to perish, in many instances, and that without sympathy from the State. In these respects the condition of the race is unquestionably better in the Southern States. If they must be a degraded race in the North as well as in the South, I hesitate not to affirm that our domestic system affords them a much better security for a competent and comfortable living. It makes better provision for them in old age and in youth, in sickness and in health, than is secured to them by their so-called liberty in the Northern States.

Of course, poor families (in the literal sense) in the South do not own slaves. They are usually held by those who at least enjoy the necessaries of life. Now, the progress of civilization has established the custom in all such families of sharing with their slaves the necessaries, and, not unfrequently, many of the comforts of life. The exceptions only make the rule general.

Again, the Southern system, by making the African a part of the family circle, brings him into more immediate contact with the habits of civilized life, and cultivates a high degree of sympathy between him and his owners. Hence, the well-known attachment of slaves to the families in which they were brought up; and their utter repugnance to being hired to a Northern family, whatever may be their reputation for piety. They are without practical sympathy for them. They often subject them to a degree of hard labor to which they are not accustomed. Many humane men in the South decline hiring their servants to such persons.

There are evils, it is true, inseparable from the presence of the race in this country, under any circumstances. By conferring on them a mere paper liberty, the Northern States have adroitly freed themselves of a portion of these evils; but then they have evidently accumulated them upon the African. The policy is marked by no sympathy for the blacks. There is much more of selfishness than of benevolence in the working of the system. We conclude that our position is true, that the Africans, being a separate and distinct race of people, who cannot spontaneously amalgamate with the whites, should be placed under a separate and subordinate form of government, if we consult either their welfare or our own. The examples referred to, as proof of the contrary, are strongly confirmatory of the position.

But to claim for the African political equality with the whites is subject to still stronger objections. We may further appeal to facts in support of our proposition.

II. They are not, in point of intellectual and moral development, in the condition for freedom: that is, they are not fitted for that measure of self-government which is necessary to political sovereignty. It cannot, therefore, be justly claimed for them. They have no right to it. It would not be to them an essential good, but an essential evil, a curse. To confer it on them, either by an act of direct or gradual emancipation, would be eminently productive of injury to the whole country, and utterly ruinous to them.

This proposition is capable of division. We will discuss the points in the order in which they stand.

First. They are not, in point of intellectual and moral development, fitted for that measure of self-government which is necessary to political sovereignty.

We have said they are an inferior race. That they are so in the original structure of their minds I pretend not to affirm—nay, I do not believe it. I believe in the unity of the races—that *God* *"hath made of one blood all nations of men."* Acts xvii. 26. But that the race in this country are inferior, in the general development of their intellectual and moral faculties, I am free to affirm. This I attribute to the crushing influence of the ages of barbarous and pagan life to which their forefathers in Africa were subjected. For, as, in the progress of civilization, each succeeding generation of civilized persons occupies a higher intellectual and moral platform, so, in the descending scale of barbarism, each succeeding generation of barbarians occupies a lower platform of intellectual and moral development. Hence, we can account for the exceedingly barbarous condition of the race when first brought into this country. It also follows, that a race of men whose intellects have been long stultified by ages of barbarism, cannot, by any contact with the principles and usages of civilized life, be speedily thrown up to an elevated platform.

This also accounts, in a good degree, for the slow progress which the race has made in civilization, since their introduction into the country.

To recur now to the fact, which cannot be controverted, that they were brought into this country in a state of extreme barbarism and Pagan ignorance: in the first place, were they then in a condition which fitted them for political sovereignty, and equality of social rights and privileges with the whites? If they were not for the latter, it is very plain that they were not for the former. It is quite certain that they were not prepared for either. If they were, why did not the Puritans of New England allow them this sovereignty and equality? By their consent and active coöperation, they were brought into the country. Shall we revilingly say, with some of their ungrateful descendants, that the good sense and love of liberty which had so lately driven them from their fatherland, to find an asylum here from the galling yoke of British oppression, had been so entirely absorbed in the passion for gain, as to cause them to be deaf to the claims of justice and humanity in behalf of the African! Shame on their graceless accusers! No: their good sense forbade that a race of barbarous Pagans, who could not be absorbed by intermarriage, but who must continue to exist amongst them as a separate and inferior race, should be placed on a common platform with free citizens! Their humanity, no less than their good sense, induced them to adopt the plan of domestic government, or slavery, sanctioned by the usages of all civilized nations in similar circumstances. If, for any cause, a horde of barbarians should be introduced into New England in the present day, in numbers too great to be absorbed without injury, and in a physical condition making it improper to permit their absorption by intermarriage with themselves, as in the case of the Africans, does any man in his senses pretend to believe that those States would confer on them either social equality or political freedom? They would certainly consider it due to themselves, no less than to the barbarians, to place them under a subordinate government of some kind. Well, this is precisely what their forefathers did in the case of the Pagan Africans; and what the Southern colonies did when the New Englanders brought them South. Thus the origin of domestic slavery, as a political institution, in the country, shows that it was founded in the humanity of our forefathers, no less than in their good sense. Hence the second position stated: Political equality cannot be justly claimed for them. They have no right to it. To them it would not be an essential good, but an essential evil—a curse.

On the basis of the doctrine of rights discussed in a preceding lecture, this proposition follows as a conclusion from the fact here established in regard to the Africans of this country.

But it may be said that the barbarous character of the race has greatly improved since their first introduction into this country. This is true—eminently so. And standing, as this fact evidently does, connected with the civilization and redemption of a whole continent of barbarians, upon whom the crushing sceptre of Pagan ignorance has lain for unnumbered ages, it fully vindicates both the wisdom and benevolence of the providence of God, which permitted their introduction in such vast numbers into civilized life, as affording the only means of accomplishing his humane design.

But the question of practical interest at this point is, Have they been so far raised in the scale of intellectual and moral elevation as to acquire for them the right in question? This point can be settled only by an appeal to facts. I hesitate not to allow, that if they are, it may be justly claimed for them, because they are in that moral condition which justly entitles them to it. It is also admitted that if at the same time, they are in a condition to be absorbed by a spontaneous amalgamation, they are entitled to it here; and much more so than a certain other class, who are flocking into the country, and to whom the right is accorded without scruple! This latter, however, is certainly not the case, as the facts before alluded to do clearly show. If, then, they be entitled to political freedom, they should be removed to another territory. Africa is the rightful home of the Africans. Thither they must go, if they should ever be fitted for self-government. Providence has wisely forecast this result, and is rapidly building up a free government on the coast of Africa, as their future home, and the centre of civilization and Christianity to that long-benighted continent.

But what of the question—Are they indeed fitted for political sovereignty? That many of the free colored population, and some among the slaves, may be so, I think is more than probably true. Of the former I would say, that it is a duty they owe themselves no less than the country to accept the offer of the Colonization Society, and remove to their native land. For, although it be allowed that they are in the moral condition of freedom, it is obvious that they never can be essentially free, in the bosom of a people with whom they can never amalgamate by marriage. And in regard to the latter, I have to say that such of their owners as give that play to their benevolent feelings which their circumstances admit, and, as far as they can do so with propriety, facilitate their removal to Africa by consent, entitle themselves to high commendation, and it is usually awarded them with great unanimity by Southern people.

But that the same admissions can be made in regard to the masses of this population in the country, I utterly deny. On the contrary, I affirm that duty to ourselves and humanity to them alike forbid that civil liberty be conferred on them in Africa, or elsewhere, and least of all in this country.

The assumption of Northern agitators, that the Southern people are not competent judges in this matter, because they are too much interested in their bondage, is as untrue in fact as it is offensive to our good sense and morals. No doubt there are many in the South capable of any form of wickedness; nor need it be denied that we are as liable to be misled in our judgments as other people. But it is equally true, that the good sense and integrity of the great mass of our population is a full counter-balance to the acknowledged cupidity of the few. And for a set of Northern agitators, who never resided at the South, and who know but little or nothing of the African character, to affect to understand it better than the intelligent communities of the South, is perhaps the coolest piece of impertinent self-conceit to be found on record!

The intelligent and honest portion of the country will scarcely fail to allow that the judgment of the Southern people as to the character and capabilities of the African is entitled to the highest confidence, and may be regarded as an authoritative settlement of this question. What, then, is the concurrent opinion of the Southern people? I think myself well and fully informed on this point. I hazard nothing in asserting, that it is the general and well-nigh the universal opinion of the intelligent and pious portion of our entire population, that our African subjects, taken as a whole, are not fitted for any form of political freedom of which we can conceive; that they are not in a condition to use it to their own advantage, or the peace of the communities in which they reside; and that to confer it upon them, in these circumstances, would in all probability lead to the extirpation of the race, as the only means of protecting civilization from the insufferable evils of so direct a contact with an unrestrained barbarism. It is also an opinion equally sanctioned, that if they were prepared for political freedom, it would be scarcely less disastrous to confer it upon them in this country. The reason is obvious. As they cannot spontaneously amalgamate with the whites, they could not, in the nature of things, enjoy freedom in their midst. Hence, if the masses should ever reach that point, in the progress of civilization, at which it might be proper to confer on them the rights of political freedom, another location would have to be sought for them.

The Southern people (using the term in the sense specified) constitute a large portion of the whole Union. They have pro-gressed as far in civilization, and, in many respects, much farther than any people in the whole country. A very large portion of them are confessedly pious, as well as intelligent. Taken as a whole, they are as eminently entitled to be regarded a religious people as any other people on the face of the globe. Now, that such a people, so obviously entitled to the highest consideration throughout the civilized world, should, in their circumstances of proximity to the African race, and long-continued personal acquaintance with their habits and character, their capabilities and their liabilities, be of the settled and almost undisputed opinion that they are not competent to self-government; and that, in their present circumstances, both the law of reciprocity and the law of benevolence to the African forbid that the rights of political freedom be accorded to them, does appear to me to afford the most conclusive settlement of this question of fact that the subject is capable of receiving. For, although a question of fact, it is capable of no more conclusive settlement than an enlightened public opinion can afford; and who are so well situated to form an opinion as the free and intelligent communities of the South? and who can be more honest in its expression?

As we cannot suppose the agitators of the country on this subject to be ignorant of the fact that such is the opinion of the Southern people, and as we cannot allow that they are incapable of appreciating the weight of this testimony, we reach the conclusion that they are the victims of a fanaticism resulting from a mistaken religious opinion and feeling, which hurries them madly forward, as regardless of the extent to which they implicate their own good sense as they are of the extent to which they are aspersing the reputation of their fellow-citizens, or the degree to which they are actually putting to hazard the lives of the very people for whom they piously persuade themselves they are laboring.

Those whose conduct does not admit of this apology are generally men who occupy the arena of political agitation. Their object, evidently, is to accumulate political power in the so-called free States, and to promote the ends of personal ambition. The fanatical excitement of the country may be turned to the account of these objects. Hence, they labor with a zeal worthy of a better cause. We of the South regard the agitators in Congress, for the most part, to be of this class. We consider them highly culpable,

if, indeed, they be not actually criminal. For we cannot suppose
them to be ignorant of the facts and reasonings here adduced.
And besides these, there are other facts of great and conclusive
authority in the settlement of this question, which we cannot
suppose have escaped the attention of men occupying their high
stations. I propose to notice some of them in the next lecture.

# WILLIAM J. GRAYSON

## COMMENTS ON SLAVERY AND FREE LABOR

In 1856, William Grayson (1788–1863), a South Carolina planter, after a long career in politics and public service, published a volume of poetry entitled *The Hireling and the Slave, Chicora, and Other Poems,* (Charleston, S.C.). In the first poem, "The Hireling and the Slave," he contrasted the lot of the slave to that of the free worker or hireling, to the advantage of the slave. In the preface to the volume, reprinted here in part, he sets forth his view that "slavery is the Negro system of labor," characterized by no greater evil than one might find in the system of free labor.

## *Preface*

The maligant abuse lavished on the slaveholders of America by writers in this country and England can be accounted for but in one way consistently with any degree of charitable consideration for the slanderers. They have no knowledge of the thing abused. They substitute an ideal of their own contriving for the reality. They regard slavery as a system of chains, whips, and tortures. They consider its abuses as its necessary condition, and a cruel master its fair representative. Mr. Clarkson took up the subject, originally, as a fit one for a college exercise in rhetoric, and it became a rhetorical exercise for life to himself and his followers. With these people the cruelty of slavery is an affair of tropes and figures. But they have dealt so long in metaphorical fetters and prisons, that they have brought themselves to believe that the Negroes work in chains and live in dungeons.

To prove the evils of slavery, they collect, from all quarters, its abuses, and show the same regard for fairness and common sense as they would do to gather all the atrocities of their own country committed by husbands and wives, parents and children, masters and servants, priest and people, and denounce these several relations in life in consequence of their abuses.

The laborer suffers wrong and cruelty in England, but they say it is against the law, against public opinion; he may apply to the courts for redress; these are open to him. Cruelty to the slave is equally against the law. It is equally condemned by public opinion; and as to the courts of law being open to the pauper hireling, we may remember the reply of Sheridan to a similar remark, Yes, and so are the London hotels: justice and a good dinner at a public house are equally within his reach. If, in consequence of the evils incident to hireling labor—because there are severe, heartless, grinding employers, and miserable, starving hirelings, it were proposed to abolish hireling labor, it would be quite as just and logical as the argument to abolish slavery because there are sufferings among slaves, and hard hearts among masters. The cruelty or suffering is no more a necessary part of the one system than of the other. Notwithstanding its abuses and miseries, the hireling system works beneficially with white laborers; and so also, notwithstanding hard masters, slavery, among a Christian people, is advantageous to the Negro. But to establish the hireling system with Africans would be as wise as to endeavor to bestow the constitutional government of England on Ashantee or Dahomey. In both cases there would be an equal amount of abstract truth and practical absurdity.

Slavery is that system of labor which exchanges subsistence for work, which secures a life-maintenance from the master to the slave, and gives a life-labor from the slave to the master. The slave is an apprentice for life, and owes his labor to his master; the master owes support, during life, to the slave. Slavery is the Negro system of labor. He is lazy and improvident. Slavery makes all work, and it insures homes, food, and clothing for all. It permits no idleness, and it provides for sickness, infancy, and old age. It allows no tramping or skulking, and it knows no pauperism.

This is the whole system substantially. All cruelty is an abuse; does not belong to the institution; is now punished, and may be in time prevented. The abuses of slavery are as open to all reforming influences as those of any other civil, social, or political condition. The improvement in the treatment of the slave is as marked as in that of any other laboring class in the world. If it be true of the English soldier or sailor that his condition has been ameliorated in the last fifty years, it is quite as true of the negro.

If slavery is subject to abuses, it has its advantages also. It establishes more permanent, and, therefore, kinder relations between capital and labor. It removes what Stuart Mill calls "the widening and imbittering feud between the class of labor and the class of capital." It draws the relation closer between master and servant. It is not an engagement for days or weeks, but for life. There is no such thing with slavery as a laborer for whom nobody cares or provides. The most wretched feature in hireling labor is the isolated, miserable creature who has no home, no work, no food, and in whom no one is particularly interested. *This is seen among hirelings only.*

The sale of slaves is thought to be a great evil to the slave. But what is it substantially more than a transfer of labor from one employer to another? Is this an evil to the laborer? Would it be considered an evil by the European hireling if the laws required every master, before he dismissed his workmen, to secure to them another employer? Would it be an evil to the hireling to be certain of obtaining work—to be safe from the misery of having no employer, no work, while he is starving for bread? The sale of the slave is the form in which the laws secure the slave from this misery of the hireling—secure to him a certainty of employment and a certainty of subsistence. The hireling has neither.

I do not say that slavery is the best system of labor, but only that it is the best for the Negro in this country. In a nation composed of the same race or similar races, where the laborer is intelligent, industrious, and provident, money-wages may be better than subsistence. Even under all advantages there are great defects in the hireling system, for which, hitherto, no states-man has discovered an adequate remedy. In hireling states there are thousands of idlers, trampers, poachers, smugglers, drunk-ards, and thieves, who make theft a profession. There are thou-sands who suffer for want of food and clothing, from inability to obtain them. For these two classes—those who will not work, and those who can not—there is no sufficient provision. Among slaves there are no trampers, idlers, smugglers, poachers, and none suffer from want. Every one is made to work, and no one is permitted to starve. Slavery does for the Negro what European schemers in vain attempt to do for the hireling. It secures work and subsistence for all. It secures more order and subordination also.[1] The master is a Commissioner of the Poor on every plantation, to provide food, clothing, medicine, houses, for his people. He is a police-officer to prevent idleness, drunkenness, theft, or disorder. I do not mean by formal appointment of law, but by virtue of his relation to his slaves. There is, therefore, no starvation among slaves. There are, comparatively, few crimes. If there are paupers in slave states, they are the hirelings of other countries, who have run away from their homes. Pauperism began with them when serfage was abolished.

But you must confess, it is said, that slavery is an evil. True enough; in the same sense in which the hireling's hard labor is an evil. But the poet tells us that there are worse things in the world than hard labor, "withouten that would come a heavier bale;" and so there are worse things for the Negro than slavery in a Christian land. Archbishop Hughes, in his late visit to Cuba, asked the Africans if they wished to return to their native country; the answer was always *no*. If the African is happier here than in his own country, can we say that, for him, the establishment of slavery is an evil? If the master is contented with his part in the system, with what reason can we regard it as an evil, so far as he is concerned? Slaves and masters are equally satisfied. The discontented are those who are neither.

What more can be required of slavery, in reference to the Negro, than has been done? It has made him, from a savage, an orderly and efficient laborer; it supports him in comfort and peace; it restrains his vices; it improves his mind, morals, and manners; it instructs him in Christian knowledge.

But the quarrel is with the master, and the design is to calumniate and injure him. And why this attack on the master? Who, among its pretended friends, will dare to say that they have done for the African race what the slaveholders of North America have done and are doing? What Abolitionist has bestowed on the Negro the same enduring patience, the same useful education, the same care and attendance? Who among them has done, or given, or sacrificed as much? Under the master's care, the miserable black savage has been fed, clothed, instructed in useful arts, and made an important contributor to the business and enjoyments of the world. What have the Abolitionists done, what have they given, for the Negro race? They use the slave for the purposes of self-glorification only, indifferent about his present or future condition. They are ambitious to bring about a great social revolution—what its effects may be they do not care to inquire.

All Christians believe that the affairs of the world are directed by Providence for wise and good purposes. The coming of the Negro to North America makes no exception to the rule. His transportation was a rude mode of emigration; the only practicable one in his case; not attended with more wretchedness than the emigrant ship often exhibits even now, notwithstanding the passenger law. What the purpose of his coming is we may not presume to judge. But we can see much good already resulting from it—good to the Negro in his improved condition; to the country whose rich fields he has cleared of the forest, and made productive in climates unfit for the labor of the white man; to the Continent of Africa in furnishing, as it may ultimately, the only means for civilizing its people.

The end of slavery, then, would seem to be, present good to the slave himself, to the country in which he labors and the world at large, and future good to his race. Whether Mr. Clarkson or Lord Carlisle approve or disapprove of the mode in which it has pleased divine Providence to bring all this about, the event will probably be the same. It may be doubted whether these gentlemen and their friends could have administered the affairs of the world more wisely, whatever our opinion may be of their wisdom or benevolence. As they will never have the power to try, this must remain among the other unsettled questions that perplex the ingenuity of mankind.

There is, however, a plain, practicable mode in which these anti-slavery zealots may confer freedom on thousands, year after year, without offense to any party. The plan is simple and easy. Let them show their sympathy for the Negro, not by eloquent speeches, but more eloquent acts; not with sentiment, but with sovereigns. They can buy any number of Negroes and carry them where they please. For such a purpose the government would not object. Efficient laborers are wanted in the West Indies. Here is a ready way to procure them. They may, in this manner, bestow freedom on many of the slaves of America, confer a benefit on their colonies, and gratify their own excited sensibilities with something more than unprofitable words. They feel profoundly for the Negro; let them feel to the amount of a million a year. This would be better than bringing Coolies from Asia and negroes from Africa by a system of very doubtful character. It would convince the world that their sympathy is an honest one, and not the offspring of vanity or arrogance. . . .

## Note [FROM THE ORIGINAL TEXT]

1. One of the best arrangements for the relief of the hireling laborer is the provision made in France of houses where the children of laborers are taken in when the laborers go to work in the morning, are carefully attended during the day, and restored to the parents on their return at night. A similar provision for the care of children is found on every plantation.

# EDMUND RUFFIN

## ON THE INFERIORITY OF THE NEGRO INTELLECT

An early advocate of Southern secession, prominent contributor to soil science, and defender of slavery, Edmund Ruffin (1794–1865) of Virginia published his well-known volume, *The Political Economy of Slavery; or, The Institution Considered in Regard to its Influence on Public Wealth and the General Welfare,* in Washington, in 1853. The following selection, pp. 15–17, 22, expresses Ruffin's belief in the intellectual inferiority of the Negro as a foundation-stone of his defense of slavery.


### *The Dogma of the Natural Mental Equality of the Black and White Races Considered*

When the anti-slavery doctrines were first taught, and for many years after, one of the main positions of the advocates was, the assumption of the natural equality and capacity for mental improvement of the black and white races, or the negro and Caucasian. This bold assumption of the one party was either tacitly admitted, or but rarely and faintly denied, by the other. It was then generally supposed that, with full opportunity and facilities, and sufficient time for improvement, the negro could be raised to be equal to the white man in mental acquirements—or, at least, to the capacity for self-government, and self-support and preservation. There had then been no sufficiently long and full practical trial or experiment of this doctrine. Since, there have been ample trials in practice which have served so fully to prove the contrary, that no unprejudiced mind can now admit the equality of intellect of the two races, or even the capacity of the black race either to become or remain industrious, civilized, when in a state of freedom and under self-government—or, indeed, in any other condition than when held enslaved and directed by white men. A few general statements and comments thereon will be here presented, on each of the several great and long continued experiments of freedom conferred on negroes, either as individuals, or in societies and communities, independent of the white race.

## The Intellectual Inferiority of the Black Race, Tested by Facts in the United States

Hundreds of thousands of individual cases of emancipated negro slaves, and their descendants, have existed in this country in the last two centuries. This class has now increased, in Virginia alone, to more than 50,000 in number. In the non-slaveholding States, also, there are numerous free negroes. It is true, that when thus interspersed among the much more numerous and dominant class of white inhabitants, the free negroes are subjected to some depressing and injurious influences, from which they would be relieved if forming a separate community. But, on the other hand, they have derived more than compensating benefits from their position, in the protection of government to person and property, and the security of both, and exemption from the evils of war, and from great oppression by any stronger power. Yet, in all this long time, and among such great numbers of free negroes, everywhere protected in person and property, and in the facilities to acquire property—and in some of the Northern States, endowed with political, as well as civil rights and power, equal with the white citizens—still to this day, and with but few individual exceptions, the free negroes in every State of this Confederacy, are noted for ignorance, indolence, improvidence, and poverty—and very generally, also, for vicious habits, and numerous violations of the criminal laws. In this plentiful country, where the only great want is for labor, and where every free laborer may easily earn a comfortable support, this free negro class is so little self-sustaining, that it now scarcely increases, in general, by procreation, and would annually decrease throughout the United States, if not continually recruited by new emancipations, and by fugitives from slavery. The free negroes fare best in the slaveholding States, and in them only is the whole increased by procreation. In the Northern or "free" States, if the free negroes were not continually added to by emancipated and fugitive slaves from the South, there would be seen a continued diminution of number, from the effects of suffering from want, and vicious habits. In all this long time of freedom, and with great facilities for improvement, there has not appeared among all these free negroes a single individual showing remarkable, or even more than ordinary, power of intellect—or any power of mind that would be deemed worth notice in any individual of the white race. Yet, in the Northern States, free schools are open to the children of the blacks as freely as to the whites—many have received collegiate education—and nothing but the immutable decree of God, fixing on them mental inferiority, has prevented high grades of intellect and of learning, being displayed in numerous cases. Further, the absence of industry is as general as the inferiority of mental powers. Some few free negroes are laborious, frugal, provident, and thrifty. A very few have acquired considerable amounts of property. But these rare qualities were not hereditary—and the children of these superior individuals would be as like as others to fall back to the ordinary condition of their class. In short, taken throughout, and with but few exceptions, the free negro class, in every part of this country, is a nuisance, and noted for ignorance, laziness, improvidence, and vicious habits.

## Experiment of Colonizing Freed Negroes in Liberia

But philanthropists, while admitting these facts, had associated the continued debasement of the free negroes in this country to their previous low condition, and to their still inferior position to the far more numerous and dominant white class. Relief from this alleged evil to the blacks, and, with it, every benefit of industry, thrift, and improvement, was expected to be obtained by the free negro when colonizing Liberia, in Africa. That colony has now been established forty years. It has been sustained, by funds raised by or for the Colonization Society, better than any colony ever before planted and settled by white people. It has wanted for nothing that the most benevolent and parental care of guardianship could provide. The settlers were generally of the best of the class of free negroes of this country, or of emancipated slaves, selected and provided for by their former owners, to enjoy the supposed benefits of freedom. The people and the government have had the protecting, beneficial, and always-desired guidance of white intellect; and there has been no injurious influence from white residents, or foreign interference. Besides all the money and commodities so liberally bestowed by benevolent individuals in this country to plant and support this colony, some of the State governments have afforded to it pecuniary or other aid, and the Federal Government has given much more important, though indirect aid and support, and also military and naval aid and protection. Further: since the so-called independence and ostensible self-government of Liberia, the higher officers of government have been mostly mulattoes, who are as much of the white as of the black blood and intellect. With all these advantages, and such long support by the money, and direction by the intellect, of the whites, the colony of Liberia is a complete (though a partly concealed and denied) failure. With a soil of exuberant fertility, and a climate no less bountiful for production, the inhabitants of Liberia do not yet produce sufficient food and other necessary means for subsistence. All the necessaries of life, including rice, sugar, and others of the most ready and plentiful products of the country, sell at such exorbitant prices as to show plainly their usual scarcity.[1] Lately the people were even menaced by actual famine, because of the great scarcity of articles of food, and the want of means to purchase food from abroad. Indolence and aversion to regular labor are universal. Agricultural operations and production are in the lowest condition. If the long-continued aid of the Colonization Society was even now withheld, and also the benevolent guidance and influence of the intellect of the white guardians and protection, this much boasted and falsely eulogised colony, and now "Republic of Liberia," would rapidly decline below its present low condition; and all the residents, who could not escape from it, to find shelter under the shadow of the white man's presence and government, would sink to the state of savage barbarism and heathen ignorance and vice, such as had formerly overspread the land. The only means by which negroes in Africa, as well as in America or elsewhere, can generally be made industrious and useful as laborers, and civilized, moral, and christian, will be when they are placed in the condition of domestic slaves to white masters. . . .

While so many whites in Europe, and even in America, blinded by prejudice, fanaticism, or ignorance of the negro characteristics, have argued to maintain the natural equality of the negro mind, the negroes themselves, including the most enlightened among them, have universally acknowledged the inferiority of their race. One of the results of this acknowledged inferiority is the well known general unwillingness of negroes to be governed by men of their own race, compared to their usual submissive obedience and docility to the government of white rulers. It is well known to every slaveholder, who has made an overseer of one of his slaves, that the greatest difficulty was because of the discontent of the negroes to be so governed. They will, in most cases, exhibit unwillingness to be commanded by the most worthy and respectable of their fellows, even if allied to them by ties of blood and friendship, and sometimes will proceed to disobedience, and even mutinous conduct, when they would have submissively obeyed and respected any white man as their overseer, even if, in truth, less respectable as a man, and less lenient and less intelligent in exercising the deputed authority of the master. This respect for white, and impatience of negro rule, extends no less through the class of free negroes. It is because of this general feeling that so few of this class have been or can be prevailed upon to emigrate voluntarily to Liberia. In these slaveholding States, the free negroes, in their usual degraded moral position, and inferior political rights, subject indirectly, if not legally, to the dominant white race, necessarily must suffer injustice and hardship from bad treatment in many cases. Yet it is rare that one of them, whether the most ignorant and degraded, or of the most worthy and intelligent, can be induced to accept the offered bounty of the Colonization Society, and of the State, to be sent to Liberia, and there be made a landholder, and an equal sharer of political rights. So strong is their repugnance to be governed by negroes, or to live where there are no white inhabitants, and, (as they say,) "no gentlemen," that if the free negroes of Virginia should be compelled to choose between being sent to Liberia, to be there free citizens, or to be made slaves, with their families, to white men in Virginia, it is probable that more than half of them would choose to become slaves, to secure white rulers and protectors. . . .

## Expediency of the Permanence of Negro Slavery,
## and of the Extension of the Area

Assuming as an indisputable fact that God has created and designed the negro race to be inferior in intellect to the white—that the negro possesses in a superior degree the qualities of docility and obedience, and of ability to endure the heat and miasmatic air of tropical climates, and that he only can safely labor in these most fruitful regions of the earth—while his feebleness of mind and indolence of body prevent his voluntary and sustained labor, even to preserve life—that the white man can and does direct, control, and compel the labors of the negro beneficially for both, and best for profitable production, for civilization, and for the general well-being of the world—I thence deduce the expediency and propriety of not only maintaining, and preserving inviolate, the existing condition of African slavery, but of its being extended to wherever the condition of the earth and its inhabitants would be manifestly improved thereby. Nearly all Spanish America has been degraded, and is now sunk below the hope for resuscitation, partly in consequence of the previous general mixture of blood of the inferior with the superior race—and still more because of the subsequent extinction of slavery, and the end of the former subordination of the African and native races to the European. With the throwing off the oppressive Spanish yoke, and declaring the political independence of all these extensive and fruitful colonies of Spain, it was universally expected that they would rapidly improve, and rise, in every attribute of worth and greatness. But all these sanguine and philanthropic hopes and expectations have been miserably and completely disappointed. By each of these revolutionary governments, miscalled free and republican, negro slavery was abolished by law, and equal political rights decreed to all classes of the population. The consequence was an immediate and progressive decline of industry and production; and now, after forty years of political independence, general security from foreign invaders, and with the possession of (their so-called) freedom and republican government, each and all of these republics are but anarchies, more degraded and wretched in every respect than when under the oppression and tyranny of their former colonial government. Of all tropical and South America, Brazil, which escaped civil war, and Cuba, which has continued a Spanish province, only, have retained the institution of African slavery. And these two countries only, and certainly for that cause, have greatly extended and exceeded their former production, notwithstanding all the evils of bad government in both these countries, and for Cuba, the most horrible political oppression by the mother country. From the mongrel races that occupy Mexico, Central America, the immense basins of the Orinoco, the upper Amazon, and the La Plata and its tributaries, and which are everywhere spreading and maintaining desolation over these fair and fertile regions of the earth, there is no hope for improvement under their present policy, and their miscalled free institutions. If any or all of these great countries had been subdued, or occupied, and governed by men of Anglo-Saxon race, and for even the last forty years of their free existence had been tilled by negro slaves, there would have been as much and as rapid improvement made in population, wealth, and greatness, as there has been of actual decline and degradation under the different existing conditions. And these countries, and their inhabitants, will still continue to decline, until the only present and sure remedy shall be in operation. No tropical country, or people, in any age, has ever greatly prospered, or been raised to a high grade of industry, production, refinement, and moral worth, except by the aid, and general diffusion of domestic slavery. And in modern times, the important and valuable products of sugar and cotton, have nowhere been great articles of exportation, except when obtained from the labor of domestic slaves. . . .

## Note [from the original text]

1. The following paragraph, not long since, appeared in the Richmond Dispatch, and various other papers, without comment, and has not been contradicted, and, therefore, is presumed to be correct, though the authority was not stated:

"A correspondent, at Liberia, writes that provisions are mostly imported from the United States. Flour ranges from $12 to $16 per barrel; hams and bacon from 20 to 25 cents per pound; hard bread $18 to $12 per 100 pounds; rice $5 per bushel; butter $62\frac{1}{2}$ cents per pound; salt fish from $12 to $14 per barrel; sugar 25 cents per pound; potatoes $1.25 per bushel; and everything for family use proportionately high."

# JAMES KIRKE PAULDING

## A NORTHERNER'S DEFENSE OF SEGREGATION

Not all defenses of slavery on racial lines were written by Southerners; there were Northerners who upheld the slaveholder's position with equal vigor. James Kirke Paulding (1779–1860), a prominent author, was born in New York and spent most of his life there, except for several years in Washington, D.C. under a political appointment by President Madison, and as Secretary of the Navy from 1839 to 1841. A friend and literary collaborator of Washington Irving, Paulding wrote comic history, verse stories, novels and essays. In the following selection from *Slavery in the United States* (New York, 1836), pp. 61–77, he defends slavery and segregation.

## Of Amalgamation, and a Community of Social and Political Rights

The advocates of immediate emancipation, aware of the consequences sketched in the preceding chapter, have sought to obviate them by recommending amalgamation; that is, indiscriminate marriages, between the whites and blacks, accompanied of course by a communion of social and civil rights, as a remedy for all the evils which must necessarily result from the adoption of their first principle. The remedy is rather worse than the disease.

The project of intermarrying with the blacks, is a project for debasing the whites by a mixture of that blood, which, wherever it flows, carries with it the seeds of deterioration. It is a scheme for lowering the standard of our nature, by approximating the highest grade of human beings to the lowest, and is equivalent to enhancing the happiness of mankind by a process of debasement.

That the negro should relish the idea of thus improving his breed at the expense of the white race is quite natural; that there should be found among the latter, men who recommend and enforce such a plan, even from the pulpit, appears somewhat remarkable, as an example of extraordinary disinterestedness. But that there should be white women, well educated and respectable females, supporting it by their money and their influence, their presence and co-operation; apparently willing, nay, anxious to barter their superiority for the badges of degradation; to become the mothers of mulattoes; voluntarily to entail upon their posterity a curse that seems coeval with the first existence of the negro, and cast away a portion of the divinity within them at the shrine of a mere abstract dogma, is one of the wonders which fanaticism alone can achieve.

That there are such men, and—shame on the sex—such women, is but too evident. But they are exceptions to the rest of their class, to the race to which they belong. They are traitors to the white skin, influenced by madbrained fanaticism, or the victims of licentious and ungovernable passions, perverted into an unnatural taste by their own indulgence. The proposition has been everywhere received with indignant scorn. Throughout the whole United States, with the single exception of little knots of raving fanatics in a few towns and villages, one chorus of disgust and abhorrence has met the odious project. In a country hitherto the most exemplary of any in the world for obedience to the laws, assemblages, not of idle and ignorant profligates, but of respectable citizens, have, in the absence of all statutes for repressing such outrageous attacks on the feelings of society and the established decorum of life, taken the law into their own hands, and dispersed or punished these aggressions. Nay, even the peaceable and orderly people of New-England, celebrated for their cool self-possession, their habitual devotion to the peace and harmony of society, have everywhere risen against the monstrous indignity, and infringed upon the laws of the land, in vindication of the purity of their blood. The universal sentiment of our race stands arrayed against the disgraceful alliance; and whether it be natural instinct, inspired reason, or long established prejudice, there exist no indications among us, to induce a belief that it will ever be eradicated from the hearts of the white people of the United States.

But, admitting it could, it is denied that such a consummation would be desirable, not only for the reasons just presented, but on the ground of other deep considerations. Such a mixture would at once destroy the homogeneous character of the people of the United States, on which is founded our union, and from which results nearly all those ties which constitute the cement of social life. A mongrel race would arise, of all shades and colours, each claiming under the new order of things equal social and civil rights, yet all enjoying real substantial consideration in proportion to the whiteness of their skin, and the absence of those indelible characteristics which mark the African race. It could never become the climax of dignity to wear the black skin. The law of the land might declare it equal to the white, and confer on it equal social and political rights; but the law of nature, or what is equivalent to it in this inquiry, the long habits, and feelings, and thinking, and acting, which have descended from generation to generation, and become a part of our being, would declare against it with a force that nothing could resist. Instead of two factions, we should have a dozen, arrayed against each other on every occasion, animated, not like the parties subsisting among us at present, by certain known principles of action, which may be said to ennoble such contests, but by petty malignant jealousies, arising from different shades of colour, different conformations of the nose or the chin, each carrying with it a claim to more or less consideration. Does not every truehearted American shrink and scoff, at sharing, or rather surrendering his rights to factions animated by such considerations, instead of his own lofty preferences or dislikes, founded on the love of liberty and the fear of despotism? Let it also be borne in mind that all these varieties of shades and colours would, by a natural instinct, unite against the whites as the highest grade, and thus, by outvoting, strip them of their dominion, and place them at the foot of the ladder of degradation.

The idea of educating the children of the free white citizens of the United States to consider the blacks their equals, is founded on a total ignorance of nature, its affinities and antipathies. These antipathies may be for a moment overcome or forgotten in the madness of sensuality, but they return again with the greater force from their temporary suspension. White and black children never associate together on terms of perfect equality, from the moment the former begin to reason. There exist physical incongruities which cannot be permanently reconciled; and let us add, that we have a right to conclude, from all history and experience,

that there is an equal disparity of mental organization. The
difference seems more than skin-deep. The experience of thousands of years stands arrayed against the principle of equality
between the white men and the blacks. Thousands, tens of
thousands, of the former, in all ages and nations, have triumphed
over every barrier of despotism and slavery; have overcome all
the obstacles of their situation, the deficiencies of education, the
prejudices of their age and country, the sense of degradation, the
laws, as it were, of fate itself, and become lights of the age,
leaders of their race. Has the black man ever exhibited similar
energies, or achieved such triumphs in his native land or anywhere else? All that he has ever done is to approach to the lowest
scale of intellectual eminence; and the world has demonstrated
its settled opinion of his inferiority, by pronouncing even this a
wonder. Within the last half century, the benefits of education,
and the means of acquiring property as well as respectability,
have been afforded to great numbers of free blacks, and every
means has been resorted to for the purpose of instilling into them
ideas of equality.

And what has been the result, ninety-nine times in a hundred?
Idleness, insolence, and profligacy. Instead of striving to approach the sphere of the white man by becoming expert in some
trade or business—some liberal pursuit or daring adventure—his
ambition is limited to aping his dress, imitating his follies,
caricaturing his manners. In the city of New-York are upward of
twenty thousand free blacks; and the right of suffrage is given by
the constitution to all who possess a freehold of one hundred
dollars, if we do not mistake the sum. Out of all these thousands,
not more than a hundred freeholders are found. What prevents
them from acquiring property? They have precisely the same
incentives as the white man; like him they have wants to supply
and families to maintain; they have civil rights like him to exercise their ambition; and though they may not successfully aspire
to high offices of state, there is no obstacle to their becoming of
consequence by acquiring an influence over their own colour,
which is assuredly a noble object of ambition.

There is nothing under heaven to prevent an industrious,
honest, prudent free negro from acquiring property here. On the
contrary, there is every disposition to encourage and foster his

efforts. He is looked upon as something remarkable; an exception to his kind—a minor miracle; and having once established a character, there is a feeling of kindness, mingled with a sentiment of pity, which operates highly in his favour. He meets men of business at least on equal terms; and though this may not be the case in his social relations, still, the advantages he derives from his integrity and talents, are such as in all ages have been found sufficient to stimulate the white man to the highest efforts of body and mind. Still less has the negro, whether free or a slave, in his own country or elsewhere, ever attained distinction in intellectual acquirements, in arts, science, or literature, although the means have been afforded in thousands of instances. He has scarcely reached the confines of mediocrity, and appears indifferent to almost every acquirement except dancing and music—one, the favorite accomplishment of weak and frivolous minds, the other, the divinity of worn-out nations. Even in these they do not arrive at originality, and have never been known to make any improvement on others. It cannot be said that they are depressed here by the consciousness that all their efforts would fail in acquiring those rewards that wait on genius. In the present state of public feeling, there can be no doubt that a tolerable African poet, novelist, artist, philosopher, or musician, would meet with a patronage and excite an admiration, beyond anything which a white man of equal talents could hope to receive.

It may be urged, in reply to this, that the negroes labour under the consciousness of being looked upon as an inferior race, and that their genius is repressed by the sense of degradation; that their minds are fettered, their intellects deadened and paralyzed by a conviction that, do what they will, they cannot overcome the disadvantages of their peculiar state, or rise to the level of the white man. But has not the latter, in every age and nation, been some time or other fettered by similar disadvantages? The time has been when the people of Europe were subjected to a state of hereditary vassalage, carrying with it all the attributes of slavery. They possessed no property—they enjoyed no political rights; and the distance between them and the feudal lords was as broad, and apparently as impassable, as that between the slave of the United States and his master. The distinction of colour alone was wanting to render the similitude complete. Yet the mind of the white man, gradually, by mighty efforts, and by a series of irresistible expansions, rose superior to all the disadvantages of his situation, and achieved victory after victory over what seemed invincible to human efforts. He never sunk to the level of the negro; his mind was not subjugated; he possessed within himself the principle of regeneration, and to this day continues marching steadily, resolutely, irresistibly forward to his destiny, which is to be free.

The mind of the African, not only in his native country, but through every change, and in all circumstances, seems in a great degree divested of this divine attribute of progressive improvement. In his own country he has, for a long series of ages, remained in the same state of barbarism. For aught we can gather from history, the woolly-headed race of Africans had the same opportunities for improvement that have fallen to the lot of the inhabitants of Asia and Europe. A portion of them lived contiguous to the Mediterranean—that famous sea along whose shores was concentrated the arts and literature of the world; the Carthaginians, rivals of Rome in war, in commerce, and in civilization, long flourished on their borders; the Romans established provinces among them; and the Saracens, then the most polished race of mankind, founded an empire at their doors. Yet they have never awakened from their long sleep of barbarism. They remained, and still remain, savages and pagans, destitute of the rudiments of civilization; three-fourths of them hereditary slaves, and the remainder subject to the will of little arbitrary despots, whose tyranny is proportioned to the insignificance of their dominions. Without the virtues of barbarians, they possess the vices of a corrupted race; and no one can peruse the travels of Mungo Park without receiving the conviction that they are a treacherous, inhospitable, and worthless breed. Even at this moment the news has arrived, that they have massacred a colony of their own colour, established for the most benevolent purposes, on their shores, and on a plan which, if ultimately successful, may free millions of their race from bondage, while it introduces, if any means are adequate to such a purpose, civilization and Christianity into the bosom of their country.

They seem, indeed, like their own native deserts, to be incapable of cultivation, destitute of the capacity of improvement.

The dews that would seem desirous to bless them produce no verdure; the rains only descend to sink into the barren insatiable soil, that gives back nothing in return. The sun, which in happier climes warms into maturity all the beneficent products of nature, here only scorches and consumes them; the breezes which are elsewhere the harbingers of health and pleasure, of coolness and refreshment, here come freighted with disease and death; the rivers, along whose borders alone man can exist, and only the black man, while they diffuse fertility, send forth exhalations fatal to all others; and the white traveller or missionary that comes hither to teach them the true religion, falls a martyr to his purpose. It may be said, indeed, with emphatic truth, that Africa is the region of desert sterility, of savage beasts and savage men, that cannot compare with the white race of Europe, or their descendants in the New World, who, under every disadvantage of situation, have attained to an elevated superiority which they now seem anxious to sacrifice in the desperate hope, that instead of sinking to the dead level of the African, they will be able to lift him to their own. Admitting, however, the theory, that the inferiority of the negro in the United States, and every other country in which he has been held in bondage, may be traced to that gradual debasement which is the natural result of successive generations of slavery, and that an equal succession of genera-tions of freemen will bring them up to the level of equality with ourselves, it seems somewhat unreasonable to call upon the South to pay the penalty, and bear all the consequences of the ex-periment.

. . . It remains then to inquire into the precise relations which alone can subsist between equal, or nearly equal numbers of white and black men, living together; the one possessing all the property, as well as all the political power, the other, of course, destitute of both; or on the other hand without property, yet admitted to all the rights of citizens.

In thus dissenting from the doctrine of entire equality between the white and black races of men, it is far from our design to insinuate that the latter are not justly entitled to a full partici-pation in whatever offices of benevolence may conduce to their welfare and happiness. The lower they may be in the scale of rational beings, the more they are entitled to our sympathies in their behalf. But it seems to us that these sympathies might be displayed to better purpose, in doing all we can to make them happy in their present state, than in desperate efforts to elevate them to another for which all past experience shows them to be greatly disqualified.

In making them believe themselves unhappy, we confer no benefit, unless we at the same time afford them the means of happiness. In giving them knowledge, we tempt them to that forbidden fruit, the taste of which banished our first parents from peace and content; for nothing is more certain than that knowledge, which disqualifies us for the enjoyment of the means of happiness we possess, without enabling us to obtain those we desire, is but a type of the gift of Satan in the garden of Eden. It is only when we possess a right to the exercise and enjoyment of every acquisition, that its attainment is at all desirable or salutary. A clear perception of the blessings of liberty, without the prospect of ever attaining to them, is equivalent to the tortures of Tantalus. To be chained to a rock, and hear the waters gurgling at our foot, to touch yet not be able to taste, adds tenfold to the miseries of thirst. To dream of freedom every night and awake every morning a slave, is to aggravate our impatience of all restraint; and never did inspiration give utterance to a truer axiom, than did the poet when he said—

"Where ignorance is bliss, 'tis folly to be wise."

One thing, however, is practicable, and will do more to pluck the sting from the heart of the slave than all the wild schemes of fanatical reformers. It is to treat them with a patriarchal kindness, "forbearing threatening," as the greatest of the apostles enjoins; making due allowances for their ignorance, and for the peculiarity of their tempers and disposition; giving them such food, raiment, and lodging, as their habits and necessities require; permitting them the free enjoyment of their holy-days and their hours of rest and relaxation; interchanging with them all those kind offices not incompatible with the relations that subsist between the master and slave; exacting from them nothing but a fair return for protection and maintenance; and taking special care that the sick, the children, and the aged who are past labour, are provided with everything essential to their comfort.

That such is the treatment, except in a few rare instances, of the slaves of the South, all who have resided in that quarter will bear testimony, if they speak the truth. Slavery is becoming gradually divested of all its harsh features, and is now only the bugbear of imagination. If the masters are not deterred from further concessions by the unwarrantable interference of the abolitionists, the period will soon come, if it has not already come, when the slave of the South will have little cause to envy the situation of the other labouring classes of the world. They will have nothing to desire but what is equally the object of pursuit to all mankind, namely, some fancied good beyond their reach, or which, if attained, either detracts from their happiness, or leaves them just where they were before.

It may possibly be objected to us, that these and similar sentiments scattered through this work, savour of optimism, and consequently tend to discourage all efforts in behalf of public or individual happiness. But if fairly scrutinized, such will not be found to be the case; for, though all mankind were optimists in theory, still there would be none in practice. Our abstract opinions have little, if any influence over our conduct. We are impelled to action by our wants or our passions, not by our metaphysical refinements; and the stoutest believer in the equal, unalterable happiness of all mankind, will not the less ardently labour to increase his own.

# JAMES FENIMORE COOPER

## THE NOVELIST AND THE SLAVE

James Fenimore Cooper (1789–1851), born in New Jersey, was raised among the landed gentry in New York. One of the most prominent writers of his day, a member of the New York group of authors, his novels included *The Pioneers* (1823), *The Last of the Mohicans* (1826), *The Prairie* (1827), *The Pathfinder* (1840), and *The Deerslayer* (1841) —the famous "Leatherstocking" series—as well as others dealing with the Revolution, sea and frontier life and the American Indian. In the following essay, Cooper describes American slavery as a racial arrangement and, although convinced of its inevitable demise, defends it by emphasizing its mildness, de-emphasizing the evil inherent in it, and stressing the horrors that would ensue from emancipation. It is reprinted from a volume of Cooper's essays, *The American Democrat, or Hints on the Social and Civil Relations of the United States of America,* published in Cooperstown in 1838.

## On American Slavery

American slavery is of the most unqualified kind, considering the slave as a chattel, that is transferable at will, and in full property. The slave, however, is protected in his person to a certain extent, the power of the master to chastise and punish, amounting to no more than the parental power.

American slavery is distinguished from that of most other parts of the world, by the circumstance that the slave is a variety of the human species, and is marked by physical peculiarities so different from his master, as to render future amalgamation improbable. In ancient Rome, in modern Europe generally, and, in most other countries, the slave not being thus distinguished, on obtaining his freedom, was soon lost in the mass around him; but nature has made a stamp on the American slave that is likely to prevent this consummation, and which menaces much future ill to the country. The time must come when American slavery shall cease, and when that day shall arrive, (unless early and effectual means are devised to obviate it,) two races will exist in the same region, whose feelings will be embittered by inextinguishable hatred, and who carry on their faces, the respective stamps of their factions. The struggle that will follow, will necessarily be a war of extermination. The evil day may be delayed, but can scarcely be averted.

American slavery is mild, in its general features, and physical suffering cannot properly be enumerated among its evils. Neither is it just to lay too heavy stress on the personal restraints of the system, as it is a question whether men feel very keenly, if at all, privations of the amount of which they know nothing. In these respects, the slavery of this country is but one modification of the restraints that are imposed on the majority, even, throughout most of Europe. It is an evil, certainly, but in a comparative sense, not as great an evil as it is usually imagined. There is scarcely a nation of Europe that does not possess institutions that inflict as gross personal privations and wrongs, as the slavery of America. Thus the subject is compelled to bear arms in a quarrel in which he has no real concern, and to incur the risks of demoralization and death in camps and fleets, without any crime or agency of his own. From all this, the slave is exempt, as well as from the more ordinary cares of life.

Slavery in America, is an institution purely of the states, and over which the United States has no absolute control. The pretence, however, that congress has no right to entertain the subject, is unsound, and cannot be maintained. Observing the prescribed forms, slavery can be legally abolished, by amending the constitution, and congress has power, by a vote of two thirds of both houses, to propose amendments to that instrument. Now, whatever congress has power to do, it has power to discuss; by the same rule, that it is a moral innovation on the rights of the states to discuss matters in congress, on which congress has no authority to legislate. A constitutional right, and expediency, however, are very different things. Congress has full power to declare war against all the nations of the earth, but it would be madness to declare war against even one of them, without sufficient cause. It would be equal madness for congress, in the present state of the country, to attempt to propose an amendment of the constitution, to abolish slavery altogether, as it would infallibly fail, thereby raising an irritating question without an object.

# NEHEMIAH ADAMS

## ON THE EVILS OF NEGRO EMANCIPATION

A Congregational minister in Cambridge and Boston from 1834 until his death, Nehemiah Adams (1806–1878) was also a prolific writer. He published sixteen volumes and many more essays and pamphlets, among them *A South-Side View of Slavery; or, Three Months at the South, in 1854* (Boston, 1854), based upon his visit to the South in the winter of that year. Frederick Persons, a biographer of Adams, suggests that "this was not a defense of slavery, but it recognized the better side of the institution and deplored the excesses of the Northern abolitionists."[1] However, despite Adams's claim to be "an ardent friend of the colored race," the book, based upon a belief in Negro inferiority, was generally taken to be a defense of slavery, as the reader may judge from the following selection. Thereafter, Dr. Adams came to be known in anti-slavery circles as "Southside Adams." The selection consists of pp. 119–122.

## *Results to be Expected from Emancipation*

The conviction forced itself upon my mind at the south, that t' ɔ most disastrous event to the colored people would be their emancipation to live on the same soil with the whites.

The two distinct races could not live together except by the entire subordination of one to the other. Protection is now extended to the blacks; their interests are the interests of the owners. But ceasing to be a protected class, they would fall a prey to avarice, suffer oppression and grievous wrongs, encounter the rivalry of white immigrants, which is an element in the question of emancipation here, and nowhere else. Antipathy to their color would not diminish, and being the feebler race, they would be subjected to great miseries.

All history shows that two races of men approaching in any considerable degree to equality in numbers can not live together unless intermarriages take place.[2] The Sabine women prepared the way for the admission of the Sabines to Rome, and gave them a place among the conscript fathers. Alexander, having conquered Persia, married the Persian Roxana, and thus lessened the social distance between the new provinces and the original empire. Alaric, Clovis, Henry I. of England, in Italy, Gaul, and among the Saxons, respectively, resorted to the same policy of intermarriage for the same purpose. The long dissensions between the Normans and Saxons under William Duke of Normandy and William Rufus disappeared when the two races followed the example of Henry. We know the happy results.

On the other hand, Egypt and Israel, the Hebrew people and the nations conquered by them, the Spaniards and Moors, many modern nations and the Jews, prove the impossibility of two races living together unless one race is dependent, or they intermarry. Like the Moors and the Jews, the blacks would eventually be driven out. Even now, in some places at the south the free blacks are prohibited by the laws of certain crafts, the stone cutter's for example, from lifting a tool in their work. White servants are exclusively employed in one of the largest hotels at the south.

The fighting propensity of the lower class of the Irish would expose the blacks to constant broils through the rivalry of labor. . . .

It would not be strange if, as the least evil, and to prevent their being exterminated, or driven out, as John Randolph's emancipated slaves and other companies of emancipated negroes have been, by one free State after another, or leading a wretched life like that of our New England Indians, it should be considered best for all concerned that they should enter again, after being emancipated, into some form of subordination to the whites. Their present bondage, with all its evils, real or supposed, it would then be seen, is by no means the worst condition into which they could fall.

Their women would be debased without measure if set free. So far from being surprised at any degree of looseness in morals among the slaves, one can only feel grateful for the influences of religion and so much of public sentiment as prevail among them to keep so large a proportion of them virtuous, as, considering their temperament and their place in society, it is believed exists. But let them be thrown wholly upon their own resources for subsistence, or subjected to the idle life which they would be tempted to lead, and the probable consequence to the blacks and whites, and to their posterity, would be fearful.

As an ardent friend of the colored race, I am compelled to believe that while they remain with us, subordination in some form to a stronger race is absolutely necessary for their protection and best welfare—a subordination, however, which shall be for the interests of the black man, as well as for his superiors, and from which every degree of oppression shall be purged away, the idea of their being doomed as a race or caste being abolished, and individual tendencies and aptitudes being regarded. If our southern brethren will protect and provide for them for this world and the next, we, as friends of man, should feel that we owe them a debt of gratitude and should be willing to assist, if necessary, in promoting their welfare.

Suppose, then, that we begin to take some new view of our duty with regard to slavery, having long enough, and uselessly, and injuriously enough beleaguered and battered it, only to find, in 1854, that, in spite of all our efforts and prayers, it is taking a stride more vast and astonishing than ever. A physician who had failed in his course of treatment, as we have with slavery, would ordinarily change it. Perhaps we are wrong. If our aim is good, perhaps we can effect it in a better way—a way in which the south itself will cooperate with us. Perhaps this whole continent can be pacified on this subject consistently with truth and righteousness, and to the increased happiness of all concerned.

## NOTES

1. Frederick Torrel Persons, "Nehemiah Adams," *Dictionary of American Biography*, Vol. I, p. 92.
2. Carey's *Domestic Slavery*. [Note in original text]

# CHAPTER 10

# *Anthropologists, Sociologists and Race*

## SAMUEL G. MORTON

### THE VARIETIES OF THE HUMAN SPECIES

A physician and naturalist, Samuel George Morton (1799–1851), of Philadelphia, the founder of invertebrate paleontology in America, did pioneering research in several areas of science. These included medicine, paleontology, anthropology, anatomy and zoology. His lifetime interest was the collection and comparative study of human skulls, the results of which were published in two separate volumes, *Crania Americana* and *Crania Aegyptiaca*. He was one of the leading proponents of the view that the races of mankind were of separate origin.

The following selection is from *Crania Americana; or, A Comparative View of the Skulls of Various Aboriginal Nations of North and South America: to which is Prefixed An Essay on the Varieties of the Human Species* (Philadelphia and London, 1839), pp. 1–7. The notes are in the original. For an excellent summary of Morton's life and work, see William Stanton, *The Leopard's Spots: Scientific Attitudes Toward Race in America, 1815–1859* (Chicago, 1960), pp. 25–35 and *passim*.

### *Crania Americana*

#### Introductory Essay
#### On the Varieties of the Human Species

The geographical distribution of the human race, is one of the most interesting problems in history. The oldest records seldom allude to an uninhabited country. The extremes of heat and cold, and the intervention of seas and mountains, have presented but trifling barriers to the peopling of the earth.

The condition of man, under these infinitely varied circumstances, is less the effect of coercion than of choice. Thus the Eskimau, surrounded by an atmosphere that freezes mercury, rejoices in his snowy deserts, and has pined in unhappiness when removed to more genial climes. On the other hand, the native of the torrid regions of Africa, oppressed by a vertical sun, and often delirious with thirst, thinks no part of the world so desirable and delightful as his own. The arid province of Chaco, in Paraguay, which the Spaniards stigmatise as a desert, is crowded by forty Indian nations, who regard it as an earthly paradise. It may be further remarked, in illustration of this subject, that extensive migrations have been mostly confined to the temperate zones: it is rare, for example, to find the Polar tribes wandering to the south, or the people of the torrid zones attempting to establish themselves in a colder climate. The exceptions to this rule are chiefly to be seen in the civilized communities of modern times, in which the spirit of migratory enterprise is without a limit.

From remote ages the inhabitants of every extended locality have been marked by certain physical and moral peculiarities, common among themselves, and serving to distinguish them from all other people. The Arabians are at this time precisely what they were in the days of the patriarchs: the Hindoos have altered in nothing since they were described by the earliest writers; nor have three thousand years made any difference in the skin and hair of the Negro. In like manner the characteristic features of the Jews may be recognised in the sculpture of the temples of Luxor and Karnak, in Egypt, where they have been depicted for nearly thirty centuries.[1]

This identity of physical characteristics, preserved through numberless generations, and often under very dissimilar circumstances, has occasioned various speculations in respect to the origin of the human family. The prevalent belief is derived from the sacred writings, which, in their literal and obvious interpretation, teach us that all men have originated from a single pair;[2] whence it has been hastily and unnecessarily inferred, that the differences now observable in mankind are owing solely to vicissitudes of climate, locality, habits of life, and various collateral circumstances.

Without attempting to pursue this intricate question in detail, we may inquire, whether it is not more consistent with the known government of the universe to suppose, that the same Omnipotence that created man, would adapt him at once to the physical, as well as to the moral[3] circumstances in which he was to dwell upon the earth? It is indeed difficult to imagine that an all-wise Providence, after having by the Deluge destroyed all mankind excepting the family of Noah, should leave these to combat, and with seemingly uncertain and inadequate means, the various external causes that tended to oppose the great object of their dispersion: and we are left to the reasonable conclusion, that each Race was adapted from the beginning to its peculiar local destination. In other words, it is assumed, that the physical characteristics which distinguish the different Races, are independent of external causes.

Such appear to have been the primitive distinctions among men: but hostile invasions, the migratory habits of some tribes, and the casual dispersion of others into remote localities, have a constant tendency to confound these peculiarities; and the proximity of two races has uniformly given rise to an intermediate variety, partaking of the characters of both, without being identical with either: these are called *mixed races.*

The grouping of mankind into Races, has occupied the ingenuity of many of the best naturalists of the past and present century; and here again we observe that diversity of opinion which is so frequent in human researches. Linnaeus referred all the human family to five races, viz: the American, the European, the Asiatic, and the African, and individuals of preternatural conformation. The Count de Buffon proposed six great divisions, viz: 1, The Hyperborean or Laplander, which embraces the Polar nations.—2, The Tartar, which includes the eastern and central nations of Asia.—3, The Southern Asiatic, which embraces the South Sea Islanders.—4, The European.—5, The Ethiopian.— And 6, The American. At a subsequent period Buffon reduced the races to five, by grouping the Laplanders with the Tartars, inasmuch as he regarded the one as a degenerate branch of the other.[4]

More recently Professor Blumenbach, of Gottingen, to whom

this department of science is under great obligations, has adopted the arrangement of Buffon; changing the names, however, of some of the divisions, and assigning, with much greater accuracy, their geographical distribution. Thus, the Laplander and Tartar of Buffon constitute the Mongolian variety of Blumenbach; the Southern Asiatic of the one corresponds to the Malay of the other; and the European and Caucasian represent the same people in both arrangements.

The system of the celebrated Cuvier is still more elementary, for it proposes three races only: the Caucasian, Mongolian, and Ethiopian; but the author hesitates to refer to either of these, the Malays, the Papuas, the Australians, and the South Sea Islanders.[5]

At the other extreme is Malte-Brun, the distinguished geographer, who enumerates sixteen races, of which the American nations form but one.[6]

Much has also been written in reference to the *unity* of the human species: the affirmative opinion is sustained by Linnaeus, Blumenbach, Cuvier, and many other distinguished naturalists; yet, on the contrary, Virey has divided mankind into two species, Dumoulin into eleven, and Bory into no less than fifteen.[7] Finally, a French professor, overstepping the barriers of reason and nature, has attempted to establish several subgenera.[8]

Such wide differences of opinion have led some persons to reject all classification in Anthropology; but the same objections would apply with equal force to the whole range of Natural Science, which, divested of arrangement, presents an uninviting chaos. As our means of comparing the races of men become more extended, our classification will of course improve; and meanwhile we must rest content with an approximation to accuracy. It may here be remarked, that two leading features constitute the basis of most of the attempted classifications of the human species: one of these is called the *physical*, the other the ethnographic method. In the former, mankind are grouped in great divisions characterised by similarity of exterior conformation; while on the last mentioned plan, the arrangement is based on analogies of language. Each of these systems has its advocates to the exclusion of the other; but it is reasonable to suppose that method most natural and comprehensive which is derived from both these sources, as well as from all others which tend to establish analogies among men. In order to combine, as far as possible, all these advantages, it is proposed in this place to consider the human species as consisting of *twenty-two families.*

It is necessary, however, to premise, that these families are not assumed as identical with races, but merely as groups of nations possessing, to a greater or less extent, similarity of physical and moral character, and language. Some of these families possess, it is true, the peculiarities of the aboriginal races to which they belong; but others are of mixed and very diverse extraction, and of comparatively recent origin.

Believing, however, as I do, in the primitive distribution of mankind into races in the sense already explained, yet being unprepared to offer any thing new on the subject, I shall, for the present at least, adopt the arrangement of Professor Blumenbach as respects these great divisions:[9] for although his system is obviously imperfect, yet it is, perhaps, the most complete that has hitherto been attempted.

## I. The Caucasian Race

The Caucasian Race is characterised by a naturally fair skin, susceptible of every tint; hair fine, long and curling, and of various colors. The skull is large and oval, and its anterior portion full and elevated. The face is small in proportion to the head, of an oval form, with well-proportioned features. The nasal bones are arched, the chin full, and the teeth vertical. This race is distinguished for the facility with which it attains the highest intellectual endowments.

1. The Caucasian Family.
2. The Germanic Family.
3. The Celtic Family.
4. The Arabian Family.
5. The Libyan Family.
6. The Nilotic Family.
7. The Indostanic Family.

## II. The Mongolian Race

This great division of the human species is characterised by a sallow or olive colored skin, which appears to be drawn tight over the bones of the face; long, black, straight hair, and thin beard. The nose is broad, and short; the eyes are small, black, and obliquely placed, and the eyebrows arched and linear: the lips are turned, the cheek bones broad and flat, and the zygomatic arches salient. The skull is oblong-oval, somewhat flattened at the sides, with a low forehead. In their intellectual character the Mongolians are ingenious, imitative, and highly susceptible of cultivation.

8. The Mongol-Tartar Family.
9. The Turkish Family.
10. The Chinese Family.
11. The Indo-Chinese Family.
12. The Polar Family.

### III. The Malay Race

The Malay Race is characterised by a dark complexion, varying from a tawny hue to a very dark brown. Their hair is black, coarse and lank, and their eye-lids drawn obliquely upwards at the outer angles. The mouth and lips are large, and the nose is short and broad, and apparently broken at its root. The face is flat and expanded, the upper jaw projecting, and the teeth salient. The skull is high and squared or rounded, and the forehead low and broad. This race is active and ingenious, and possesses all the habits of a migratory, predaceous and maritime people.

13. The Malay Family.
14. The Polynesian Family.

### IV. The American Race

The American Race is marked by a brown complexion, long, black, lank hair, and deficient beard. The eyes are black and deep set, the brow low, the cheek-bones high, the nose large and aquiline, the mouth large, and the lips tumid and compressed. The skull is small, wide between the parietal protuberances, prominent at the vertex, and flat on the occiput. In their mental character the Americans are averse to cultivation, and slow in acquiring knowledge; restless, revengeful, and fond of war, and wholly destitute of maritime adventure.

15. The American Family.
16. The Toltecan Family.

## V. The Ethiopian Race

Characterised by a black complexion, and black, woolly hair; the eyes are large and prominent, the nose broad and flat, the lips thick, and the mouth wide: the head is long and narrow, the forehead low, the cheek-bones prominent, the jaws projecting, and the chin small. In disposition the negro is joyous, flexible, and indolent; while the many nations which compose this race present a singular diversity of intellectual character, of which the far extreme is the lowest grade of humanity.

17. The Negro Family.
18. The Caffrarian Family.
19. The Hottentot Family.
20. The Oceanic-Negro Family.
21. The Australian Family.
22. The Alforian Family.

## NOTES [FROM THE ORIGINAL TEXT]

1. See Description de l'Egypte, Tome II, pl. 6, and Tome III, pl. 40.
2. "That the three sons of Noah overspread and peopled the whole earth, is so expressly stated in Scripture had, had we not to argue against those who unfortunately disbelieve such evidence, we might here stop: let us, however, inquire how far the truth of this declaration is substantiated by other considerations. Enough has been said to show that there is a curious, if not a remarkable analogy between the predictions of Noah on the future descendants of his three sons, and the actual state of those races which are generally supposed to have sprung from them. It may here be again remarked, that, to render the subject more clear, we have adopted the quinary arrangement of Professor Blumenbach; yet that Cuvier and other learned physiologists are of opinion that the *primary* varieties of the human form are more properly but *three*, viz: the Caucasian, Mongolian, and Ethiopian. This number corresponds with that of Noah's sons: assigning, therefore, the Mongolian race to Japheth, and the Ethiopian to Ham, the Caucasian, the noblest race, will belong to Shem, the third son of Noah, himself descended from Seth, the third son of Adam. That the primary distinctions of the human varieties are but *three*, has been further maintained by the erudite Prichard, who, while he rejects the nomenclature both of Blumenbach and Cuvier, as implying *absolute* divisions, arranges the leading varieties of the human skull under three sections, differing from those of Cuvier only by name. That the three sons of Noah who were to 'replenish the earth,' and on whose progeny very opposite destinies were pronounced, should give birth to

different races, is what might reasonably be conjectured. But that the observations of those who *do*, and of those who do *not* believe the Mosaic history, should tend to confirm its truth, by pointing out in what these three races do actually differ, both physically and morally, is, to say the least, a singular coincidence. It amounts, in short, to presumptive evidence, that a mysterious and very beautiful analogy pervades throughout, and teaches us to look beyond natural causes, in attempting to account for effects apparently interwoven in the plans of Omnipotence."—MURRAY, Encyc. of Geog. p. 255.

3. GENESIS, IX, 25, 26, 27.

4. SONNINI'S BUFFON, XX, p. 120, &c.

5. Regne Anim. I, 84.

6. See BORY DE ST. VINCENT, T. I, p. 95.—I have not been able to find this classification in Malte-Brun, ed. 1832.

7. *Ibid.* I, p. 83.

8. Broc, Essai sur les Races Humaines, 1836.

9. It will be observed, however, that the word *race* is substituted for *variety*, and the order in which these divisions follow each other in Blumenbach is somewhat changed. *Vide* BLUMENBACH, *De Gen. Humani Var. Nat.* p. 289.

# JOHN BACHMAN

## THE UNITY OF THE HUMAN RACE

Although born in New York, John Bachman (1790–1874), clergyman and naturalist, spent his adult years, from 1815 on, in Charleston, South Carolina, where he served as a Lutheran clergyman. The study of natural science, his lifetime avocation, attracted his interest in boyhood and was intensified by his association with the naturalists of the medical school of Charleston. Beginning in 1831, he collaborated with James Audubon, the ornithologist and painter, in various research projects; a collaboration which resulted in the well-known three-volume work, *The Viviparous Quadrupeds of North America* (1845–49). In addition to other essays and monographs, he wrote *The Doctrine of the Unity of the Human Race Examined on the Principles of Science* (Charleston, 1850), in which he defended the thesis that humanity consists of one species, a view which was then being challenged by many naturalists in the North as well as South. The following selections from Bachman's work consist of pp. 114–119, 147–151.

*Conclusions Deduced from the Infertility of Hybrids in All the Inferior Animals, and the Fertility in All the Races of Men*

We have now by the slow process of careful and laboured analysis, and with all the knowledge and experience we could bring to our aid, examined all the cases of hybridity that seem to require our notice in the paper of Dr. Morton. If we could recollect any others on record in favour of his theory, that he has omitted, we would not withhold them from our opponents; but he seems to have gleaned the field so industriously that he has left very little for his successors to gather. If we have taxed the patience of our readers by entering into details on subjects with which the majority of them are not expected to be familiar, we crave their indulgence, as the establishment of this point is one of the strong weapons that we intend to wield in defence of our theory, in regard to the unity of the races, and if possible in demolishing that of our opponents.

They are fully aware of the long established and undeniable fact that all the races of men in every age, and in every country produce prolific offspring in their association with each other. That the Caucasian, Mongolian, African, Malay, and the aboriginal American, all are affording us the most convincing evidences of this fact. That in this manner many new intermediate races have been produced on the confines of Asia, Africa and Europe, and that within the last two hundred years, a new race has sprung up in Mexico and South America, between one branch of the Caucasian and the native Indian, together with no small admixture of African blood. They are aware that in the United States, whose first permanent settlement commenced in Virginia in 1607, the two extremes of African and Caucasian have met and produced an intermediate race. We know them to be fully as prolific, if not more so, as the whites, where their constitutions have not been wasted by dissipation. We will not stop to inquire whether this race is equally as long lived as either of their originals; but even here we would find no difficulty, as no one will be disposed to deny the fact that some races of the pure Caucasian, the Mongolian and African families are more robust and longer lived than others. The facts, however, are undeniable that all these half breeds are prolific with each other, and we can point out at least the descendants of five generations, both in Carolina and New York, where there has been no intermixture with either of the original varieties; and they are to this day as prolific as any of the other races of men. We are aware that laboured articles have been written to show that the descendants of the two races, especially those between the Caucasian and African, in the process of time, become sterile. We have not, however, of late, heard this argument insisted on, and we believe it is virtually abandoned. The learned researches of Dr. Morton, (*Crania Americana*,) which is characterized by great knowledge and sound discrimination will, we think, set this matter forever at rest. We regard his "Essay on the varieties of the human species" as condensing in a hundred pages as much valuable information on this subject as is contained in any similar work to which we have had access. Although we are constrained to state that on an exami[n]ation of the valuable materials he has presented to us, we have arrived at different conclusions from those to which his mind seems to lean, and differ from him in our views of the origin of the Native American families, we must nevertheless admit that the world of science is greatly indebted to him for the faithful manner in which he has collected his materials, and the judgment he has in most cases evidenced in arranging them. The accounts scattered throughout his learned essay, of the many intermediate tribes of nations that have derived their origin from an admixture of Mongolian, Malayan, American, Caucasian and African blood, are calculated to convince all who have hitherto entertained any doubts on this subject that not only these widely separated, but all the varieties in the human species, produce in perpetuity an intermediate and fertile progeny. Malte Brun,[1] speaking of the Portuguese in Africa, says: "The Rio South branch is inhabited by the Maloes, a negro race, so completely mingled with the descendants of the original Portuguese as not to be distinguished from them. Several writers inform us that there is a large and growing tribe in South Africa called the Griqua, on Orange river, being a mixture of the original Dutch settlers and the Hottentots, composed of more than five thousand souls. These are referred to by Thompson and Lichtenstein, in their travels in South Africa. Several similar races, a mixture of the African and Spaniard or Portuguese, exist in South America, separated from other communities. The last calculation we have read of the population composed of the mixed races, in North and South America, amounted to upwards of five millions.

Inasmuch as all these facts were self-evident and undeniable, as could be testified by thousands of examples which presented themselves in every neighborhood, and in every land, so that it now has become a matter of difficulty among many bordering nations to designate the precise origin of millions of the inhabitants of the earth, our opponents have recently evidenced a disposition to rest their cause on a different foundation. The infertility of hybrids has always been a stumbling block in the way of their theory. If the races of men produced fertile offspring with each other, and the races of inferior animals did not, if the latter were found to be barren and unfruitful, and the former increased and multiplied, and replenished the earth, then they would be obliged to prove that man was an exception to this universal and invariable law that regulated the whole of the inferior creation. They possessed no evidences to prove this; for although man in his moral nature is endowed with high intellectual powers, yet in his physical nature he is an animal, coming into the world like other animals, and like them returning to the dust. In this dilemma they resorted to the desperate expedient of endeavouring to show that in respect to the fertility of hybrid offspring man was not peculiar; that many races of animals could be found possessing the same physical powers of producing intermediate and fertile races. Hence they have ransacked the almost forgotten tales of ancient travellers, and dragged from obscurity the vulgar errors long hidden beneath the dust of antiquity, and indulged themselves in conjectures and doubts, in order to weaken the faith of men in the long established views of naturalists in regard to the sterility of hybrids. Our object has been to show the frail tenure of the foundation on which they leaned for support, the many errors which they triumphantly paraded as facts, and the weakness of the arguments by which they sought to build up their theory.

We have shown from the examples of hybridity which they have so industriously collected that in nearly all the cases where a proximity of species permitted the production of hybrids they proved absolutely sterile; and that in the few remaining examples, nature was incessantly at work to restore the irregularity which art or accident had produced, and that these hybrids either died off, or if they continued for a short time, returned to one or the other of the original race.

They have not been able to point out in the whole range of animal creation a single example of a new race that was established and perpetuated by hybrids. They have not been able to bring a shadow of evidence in favor of their doctrine that varieties were in even a single case the result of any intermixture of species, since the most striking varieties exist in races where we can positively trace them to their original source—a single species far removed from any other. They made this new issue; it was required of them to produce such facts in support of their theory as would convince the inquiring student of nature of the truth of their theory. Would any jury of unbiassed men find a true bill on such surmises, conjectures, doubts and palpable errors as have here been arrayed as evidences against the doctrine of the unity of the human race?

We may then be permitted, in this stage of our argument to draw the following conclusions:

1. Nature, in all her operations, by the peculiar organization of each species—by their instinctive repugnance to an association—by the infertility of a hybrid production, when by art or accident this takes place,—and by the extinction of these hybrids in a very short period of time, gives us the most indubitable evidences that the creation of species is an act of Divine Power alone, and cannot be effected by any other means.

2. That no race of animals has ever sprung from a commingling of two or more species.

3. Domestication in every species that has been brought under subjection, produces striking and often permanent varieties, but has never evolved a faculty to produce fertile hybrids.

4. Since no two species of animals have ever been known to produce a prolific hybrid race, therefore hybridity is a test of specific character.

5. Consequently the fact that all the races of mankind produce with each other a fertile progeny, by which means new varieties have been produced in every country, constitutes one of the most powerful and undeniable arguments in favour of the unity of the races. . . .

We will now, in the conclusion of this chapter, sum up the evidence which we have produced in various parts of this Essay, or which are self-evident, and require no further proof in favour of the unity of the species.

1. There is but one true species in the genus homo.

In this he does not form an exception to the general law of nature. There are many of our genera which contain but a single species in the genus. Among American quadrupeds the musk ox, (*Ovibos moschutos*,) the beaver, (*Castor fiber*,) and the glutton or wolverine, (*Gulo luscus*,) and among birds, the wild turkey, (*Meleagris gallipavo*,) are familiar examples. The oscillated turkey, which was formerly regarded as a second species, has recently been discovered not to be a true turkey;—in addition to its different conformation, it makes its nest on trees, and lays only two eggs, possessing in this and other particulars the habits of the pigeon.

2. We have shown that all the varieties evidence a complete and minute correspondence in the number of the teeth and in the 208 additional bones contained in the body.

3. That in the peculiarity in the shedding of the teeth, so different from all other animals, they all correspond.

That they are perfectly alike in the following particulars:

4. In all possessing the same erect stature.

5. In the articulation of the head with the spinal column.

6. In the possession of two hands.

7. In the absence of the intermaxiliary bone.

8. In the teeth of equal length.

9. In a smooth skin of the body, and the head covered with hair.

10. In the number and arrangement of the muscles in every part of the body, the digestive and all the other organs.

11. In the organs of speech and the power of singing.

12. They all possess mental faculties, conscience, and entertain the hope of immortality. It is scarcely necessary to add that in these two last characteristics man is placed at such an immeasurable distance above the brute creation as to destroy every vestige of affinity to the monkey or any other genus or species.

13. They are all omnivorous and are capable of living on all kinds of food.

14. They are capable of inhabiting all climates.

15. They all possess a slower growth than any other animal, and are later in arriving at puberty.

16. A peculiarity in the physical constitution of the female, differing from all the other mammalians.

17. All the races have the same period of gestation, on an average produce the same number of young, and are subject to similar diseases.

If an objection is advanced against the rules by which we have been governed, and we are told that we have been blending specific and generic characters, we answer that in all the genera a species is selected and described as a type of the genus: hence there being but one species in the genus we have, in accordance with the rules by which naturalists are governed, selected the species as a type.

18. We have shown that man, as a domestic animal, is subject to the same changes which are effected in all domesticated animals; hence as species are taken in a different acceptation, in wild and domestic animals, our examinations of the varieties in men must be subjected to the same rules of examination. That these changes in men are constantly taking place, is evident, from the fact that great variations have occurred in several of the branches which we admit to be Caucasians, whilst wild animals with few exceptions have not undergone the slightest change. We have shown that from the many intermediate grades of form and color, in a being more subject to varieties than in any known species of animals, we can find no specific character so permanent as to warrant us in separating the varieties into distinct species. We insist on the right of applying the rules of classification to man as a domestic species. If our opponents urge the right of comparing him with wild animals, then they must first prove that men, like wild species are not subject to produce varieties. This is an experiment on which we think they will not venture. The human species cannot, therefore, be compared with wild animals that with few exceptions present a perfect uniformity. Place before you a hundred specimens of any wild species of quadruped or bird, with the few exceptions above alluded to, and there is scarcely a variation among any of the specimens. The descriptions of Aristotle are as applicable now as they were in his day. On the other hand, look at the countenances even of our neighbours and the members of our own families, gathered together around the social circle, and you see the most striking differences in the color of the eyes, the hair, and the complexion, in size, in form, in length of nose, shape of the head, volume of the brain, etc. These peculiarities are so striking that we can every where recognize those whom we have previously seen. On the other hand, the countenances of the individuals even in domestic animals can seldom be distinguished from each other. The eccentric poet, Hogg, or as he was proud to call himself the Ettric Shepherd, was able, as he stated, and no doubt correctly, to distinguish the individuals of the flock which he daily carried to the hills; but this talent even in distinguishing the countenances of

domesticated animals, is possessed by few others; on the contrary the very child learns to distinguish individuals of the human race by their countenances; no two individuals even in the same family, can be found possessing the same set of features. Man must, therefore, be compared and examined by the same rules that govern us in an examination of domesticated animals. Let us compare him with any of these species. Take those about whose origin no difficulty exists; the horse for instance, the only true species in the genus, for naturali[s]ts have now classed all the others under the asses and zebras; or take the hog, whose origin is admitted by all naturalists . . . apply the same rule first to the species and then to the varieties of men, and by these fair and legitimate rules of science, we are willing to enter into a comparison, and abide by the decision. The most eminent naturalists of all past ages, have with a unanimity almost unsurpassed, already decided the question, and those who are now entering into the field, about whose qualifications, as judges, the world as yet knows nothing, and is therefore, unprepared to pronounce an opinion, are bound to give some satisfactory reasons for their dissent.

19. That the varieties in men are not greater than are known to exist among domestic animals.

20. That all the varieties of men produce with each other a fertile offspring which is perpetuated, by which new races have been formed; and that this is not the case with any two species of animals.

21. That the insects which are found on the surface, and the vermes within the body, as far as they have been examined, are the same in all the varieties of men, and that where peculiar parasites infest men in particular countries they are equally found in all the races.

Until our opponents have proved that these propositions are not in accordance with the laws of science, or in violation of truth, we must regard their new theory as founded in error.

### NOTE [FROM THE ORIGINAL TEXT]

1. Universal Geog., vol. 4th, p. 227.

# LOUIS AGASSIZ

## THE VARIETIES OF RACES

When Jean Louis Rodolphe Agassiz (1807–1873), zoologist and geologist, came to the United States in 1846, he was already recognized as one of Europe's leading naturalists. He remained here until his death, teaching at Harvard and carrying on his scientific research with great diligence and industry.

In racial thought, he allied himself with the school which emphasized the diverse origins of the races of man and the fundamental nature of mental and physical racial differences. His belief in Negro inferiority helped to provide a rationale, not only for slavery, but also, after the Civil War, for those who sought to deprive the Negro of his newly-won political and economic opportunities. In the following selection, which consists of the final pages, 141–5, of his essay, "The Diversity of the Origin of the Human Race," which appeared in *The Christian Examiner and Religious Miscellany*, Vol. XLIX (Boston, July 1850), Agassiz stresses the idea of superior and inferior races.

## *The Diversity of the Origin of the Human Races*

. . . One consideration more, and we will close these remarks. Whether the different races have been from the beginning what they are now, or have been successively modified to their present condition (a view which we consider as utterly unsupported by facts), so much is plain,—that there are upon earth different races of men, inhabiting different parts of its surface, which have different physical characters; and this fact, as it stands, without reference to the time of its establishment and the cause of its appearance, requires farther investigation, and presses upon us the obligation to settle the relative rank among these races, the relative value of the characters peculiar to each, in a scientific point of view. It is a question of almost insuperable difficulty, but it is as unavoidable as it is difficult; and as philosophers it is our duty to look it in the face. It will not do to assume their equality and identity; it will not do to grant it, even if it were not questioned, so long as actual differences are observed. Giving up such an investigation would be as injurious as to give up an inquiry into the character of individual men whose appearance upon earth, at different times, has benefited mankind by their different abilities; it would be as improper as to deny the characteristic differences between the different nations of our own race upon the mere assertion that, because they belong to the same race, they must be equal. Such views would satisfy nobody, because they go directly against our every day's experience. And it seems to us to be mock-philanthropy and mock-philosophy to assume that all races have the same abilities, enjoy the same powers, and show the same natural dispositions, and that in consequence of this equality they are entitled to the same position in human society. History speaks here for itself. Ages have gone by, and the social developments which have arisen among the different races have at all times been different; and not only different from those of other races, but particularly characteristic in themselves, evincing peculiar dispositions, peculiar tendencies, peculiar adaptations in the different races. The Chinese and Japanese, being politically two distinct nations, but belonging to the same race, present perhaps the most striking evidence of the conformity between the civilizations in one and the same race; and the general contrast between those of distinct races is most apparent when we compare the state of Japan and China with that of the parts of Asia inhabited by Malays, or with the civilizations among the nations of the white race. New Holland, again, though, when first visited by Europeans, it was found to be already inhabited by populations differing in character from those of any other part of the world previously known, notwithstanding its proximity to Asia, with which it is almost connected by a series of islands not too far apart to have allowed early intercourse between those nations had it been in their nature to rise to a higher civilization,—New Holland, we say, presents, on the contrary, an example of a race entirely shut out from the rest of mankind, in which there has never been any indication of an advanced civilization. The same may be said of the Africans. And in their case we have a most forcible illustration of the fact that the races are essentially distinct, and can hardly be influenced even by a prolonged contact with others when the differences are particularly marked. This compact continent of Africa exhibits a population which has been in constant intercourse with the white race, which has enjoyed the benefit of the example of the Egyptian civilization, of the Phoenician civilization, of the Roman civilization, of the Arab civilization, and of all those nations that have successively flourished in Egypt and in the northern parts of Africa, and nevertheless there has never been a regulated society of black men developed on that continent, so particularly congenial to that race. Do we not find, on the contrary, that the African tribes are to-day what they were in the time of the Pharaohs, what they were at a later period, what they are probably to continue to be for a much longer time? And does not this indicate in this race a peculiar apathy, a peculiar indifference to the advantages afforded by civilized society? We speak, of course, of this race in its primitive condition at home, and not of the position of those who have been transported into other parts of the world to live there under new circumstances. Again, on the continent of America, have we not in the Indians evidence of another mode of existence, indications of other dispositions, of other feelings, of other appreciations of the advantages of life. The character of the Indian race has been so well sketched out by Dr. Morton, in his able works upon that subject, that we need not repeat what he has said. We would only ask, Does not that Indian race present the most striking contrast with the character of the negro race, or with the character of the Mongolian, especially the Chinese and Japanese? The indomitable, courageous, proud Indian,—in how very different a light he stands by the side of the submissive, obsequious, imitative negro, or by the side of the tricky, cunning, and cowardly Mongolian! Are not these facts indications that the different races do not rank upon one level in nature,—that the different tendencies which characterize man in his highest development are permanently brought out in various combinations, isolated in each of these races, in a manner similar to all the developments in physical nature, and, we may also say, similar to all the developments in the intellectual and moral world, where in the early stages of development we see some one side predominant, which in the highest degree of perfection is combined with all others, in wonderful harmony, even though the lower stages belong to the same sphere as the highest? So can we conceive, and so it seems to us to be indeed the fact, that those higher attributes which characterize man in his highest development are exhibited in the several races in very different proportions, giving, in the case of the inferior races, prominence to features which are more harmoniously combined in the white race, thus preserving the unity among them all, though the difference is made more prominent by the manner in which the different faculties are developed.

What would be the best education to be imparted to the different races in consequence of their primitive difference, if this difference is once granted, no reasonable man can expect to be prepared to say, so long as the principle itself is so generally opposed; but, for our own part, we entertain not the slightest doubt that human affairs with reference to the colored races would be far more judiciously conducted, if, in our intercourse with them, we were guided by a full consciousness of the real difference existing between us and them, and a desire to foster those dispositions that are eminently marked in them, rather than by treating them on terms of equality. We conceive it to be our duty to study these peculiarities, and to do all that is in our power to develop them to the greatest advantage of all parties. And the more we become acquainted with these dispositions, the better, doubtless, will be our course with reference to our own improvement, and with reference to the advance of the colored races. For our own part, we have always considered it as a most injudicious proceeding to attempt to force the peculiarities of our white civilization of the nineteenth century upon all nations of the world.

There are several other points bearing directly upon the question of the unity of mankind, and the diversity of origin of the human races, which we ought perhaps to have discussed here, such as the zoölogical characteristics of the individual races, and their special limitation, their transitions, and their mixture, and the question of hybrids in general; but these are subjects extensive enough to themselves to require to be discussed separately. We have no intention for the present to enter upon the discussion of facts not strictly connected with the philosophy of the question, and we leave this subject with the hope of having removed many doubts and much hesitation.

# JOSIAH NOTT

## TYPES OF MANKIND

Josiah Clark Nott (1804–1873) was a leading Southern surgeon and physician as well as a devoted student of ethnology. In collaboration with George R. Gliddon (1809–1857), U.S. Consul at Cairo and lecturer on Egyptology, he published a volume of more than seven hundred pages entitled *Types of Mankind: or, Ethnological Researches, Based upon the Ancient Monuments, Paintings, Sculptures, and Crania of Races, and upon Their Natural, Geographical, Philological, and Biblical History: Illustrated by Selections from the Inedited Papers of Samuel George Morton, M.D. (Late President of the Academy of Natural Sciences at Philadelphia,) and by Additional Contributions from Prof. L. Agassiz LL. D.; W. Usher, M.D.; and Prof. H. S. Patterson, M.D.* (Philadelphia, 1854). The selection which follows is from Chapter I, pp. 62–80, written by Nott, in which he argues for the diversity of origin and the permanence of existing races.

## Geographical Distribution of Animals, and the Races of Men

Have all the living creatures of our globe been created at one common point in Asia, and thence been disseminated over its wide surface by degrees, and adapted to the varied conditions in which they have been found in historical times? or, on the other hand, have different genera and species been created at points far distant from each other, with organizations suited to the circumstances in which they were originally placed?

Two schools have long existed, diametrically opposed to each other, on this question. The *first* may be termed that of the Theological Naturalists, who still look to the Book of Genesis, or what they conceive to be the inspired word of God, as a text-book of Natural History, as they formerly reputed it to be a manual of Astronomy and Geology. The *second* embraces the Naturalists proper, whose conclusions are derived from facts, and from the laws of God as revealed in his works, which are immutable. . . .

It has been a popularly-received error, from time immemorial, that degrees of latitude, or in other words, temperature of countries, were to be regarded as a sure index of the color and of certain other physical characters in races of men. This opinion has been supported by many able writers of the present century, and even in the last few years by no less authority than that of the distinguished Dr. Prichard, in the *"Physical History of Mankind."* A rapid change, however, is now going on in the public mind in this respect, and so conclusive is the recent evidence drawn from the monuments of Egypt and other sources, in support of the permanence of distinctly marked types of mankind, such as the Egyptians, Jews, Negroes, Mongols, American Indians, etc., that we presume no really well-informed naturalist will again be found advocating such philosophic heresies. Indeed, it is difficult to conceive how any one, with the facts before him, (recorded by Prichard himself,) in connection with an Ethnographical Map, should believe that climate could account for the endless diversity of races seen scattered over the earth from the earliest dawn of history.

It is true that most of the black races are found in Africa; but, on the other hand, many equally black are met with in the temperate climates of India, Australia, and Oceanica, though differing in every attribute except color. A black skin would seem to be the best suited to hot climates, and for this reason we may suppose that a special creation of black races took place in Africa. The strictly white races lie mostly in the Temperate Zone, where they flourish best; and they certainly deteriorate physically, if not intellectually, when removed to hot climates. Their type is not in reality changed or obliterated, but they undergo a degradation from their primitive state, analogous to the operation of disease. The dark-skinned Hyperboreans are found in the Frigid Zone; regions most congenial to their nature, and from which they cannot be enticed by more temperate climes. The Mongols of Asia, and the aborigines of America, with their peculiar types, are spread over almost all degrees of latitude. . . . Does not the same physical adaptation, the same instinct, which binds animals to their primitive localities, bind the races of Men also? Those races inhabiting the Temperate Zones, as, for example, the white races of Europe, have a certain degree of pliability, that enables them to bear climates to a great extent hotter or colder than their native one; but there is a limit beyond which they cannot go with impunity—they cannot live in the Arctic with the Esquimaux, nor in the Tropic of Africa with the Negro. The Negro, too, (like the Elephant, the Lion, the Camel, &c.,) possesses a certain pliability of constitution, which enables him to enter the Temperate Zone; but his Northern limit stops far short of that of natives of this Zone. The higher castes of what are termed Caucasian races, are influenced by several causes in a greater degree than other races. To them have been assigned, in all ages, the largest brains and the most powerful intellect; *theirs* is the mission of extending and perfecting civilization—they are by nature ambitious, daring, domineering, and reckless of danger—impelled by an irresistible instinct, they visit all climes, regardless of difficulties; but how many thousands are sacrificed annually to climates foreign to their nature!

It should also be borne in mind, that what we term Caucasian races are not of one origin: they are, on the contrary, an amalgamation of an infinite number of primitive stocks, of different instincts, temperaments, and mental and physical characters. Egyptians, Jews, Arabs, Teutons, Celts, Sclavonians, Pelasgians, Romans, Iberians, etc., etc., are all mingled in blood; and it is impossible now to go back and unravel this heterogeneous mixture, and say precisely what each type originally was. Such commingling of blood, through migrations, wars, captivities, and amalgamations, is doubtless one means by which Providence carries out great ends. This mixed stock of many primitive races is the only one which can really be considered cosmopolite. Their infinite diversity of characteristics contrasts strongly with the immutable instincts of other human types.

How stands the case with those races which have been less subjected to disturbing causes, and whose moral and intellectual structure is less complex? The Greenlander, in his icy region, amidst poverty, hardship, and want, clings with instinctive pertinacity to his birthplace, in spite of all apparent temptations—the Temperate Zone, with its luxuries, has no charm for him. The Africans of the Tropic, the Aborigines of America, the Mongols of Asia, the inhabitants of Polynesia, have remained for thousands of years where history first found them; and nothing but absolute want, or self-preservation, can drive them from the countries where the Creator placed them. These races have been least adulterated, and consequently preserve their original instincts and love of home. This truth is illustrated in a most remarkable degree by the Indians of America. We still behold the small remnants of scattered tribes fighting and dying to preserve the lands and graves of their ancestors.

We shall have more to say, in another chapter, on the amalgamation of races, but may here remark, that the infusion of even a minute proportion of the blood of one race into another, produces a most decided modification of moral and physical character. A small trace of white blood in the negro improves him in intelligence and morality; and an equally small trace of negro blood, as in the quadroon, will protect such individual against the deadly influence of climates which the pure white-man cannot endure. For example, if the population of New England, Germany, France, England, or other northern climates, come to Mobile, or to New Orleans, a large proportion dies of yellow fever: and of one hundred such individuals landed in the latter city at the commencement of an epidemic of yellow fever, probably half would fall victims to it. On the contrary, negroes, under all circumstances, enjoy an almost perfect exemption from this disease, even though brought in from our Northern States; and, what is still more remarkable, the mulattoes (under which term we include all mixed grades) are almost equally exempt. The writer (J. C. Nott) has witnessed many hundred deaths from yellow fever, but never more than three or four cases of mulattoes, although hundreds are exposed to this epidemic in Mobile. The fact is certain, and shows how difficult is the problem of these amalgamations.

That negroes die out and would become extinct in New England, if cut off from immigration, is clearly shown by published statistics.

It may even be a question whether the strictly-white races of Europe are perfectly adapted to any one climate in America. We do not generally find in the United States a population constitutionally equal to that of Great Britain or Germany; and we recollect once hearing this remark strongly endorsed by HENRY CLAY, although dwelling in Kentucky, amid the best agricultural population in the country. KNOX holds that the Anglo-Saxon race would become extinct in America, if cut off from immigration. Now, we are not prepared to endorse this assertion; but inasmuch as nature works not through a few generations, but through thousands of years, it is impossible to conjecture what time may effect. It would be a curious inquiry to investigate the physiological causes which have led to the destruction of ancient empires, and the disappearance of populations, like Egypt, Assyria, Greece, and Rome. Many ancient nations were colonies from distant climes, and may have wasted away under the operation of laws that have acted slowly but surely. The commingling of different bloods, too, under the law of hybridity, may also have played an important part. Mr. LAYARD tells us that a few wandering tribes only now stalk around the sites of the once-mighty Nineveh and Babylon, and that, but for the sculptures of SARGAN AND SENNACHERIB, no one could now say what race constructed those stupendous cities. But let us return from this digression.

To this inherent love of primitive locality, and instinctive dislike to foreign lands, and repugnance towards other people, must we mainly attribute the fixedness of the unhistoric types of men. The greater portion of the globe is still under the influence of this law. In America, the aboriginal barbarous tribes cannot be forced to change their habits, or even persuaded to successful emigration: they are melting away from year to year; and of the millions which once inhabited that portion of the United States east of the Mississippi river, all have vanished, but a few scattered families; and their representatives, removed by our Government to the Western frontier, are reduced to less than one hundred thousand. It is as clear as the sun at noon-day, that in a few generations more the last of these Red men will be numbered with the dead. We constantly read glowing accounts, from interested missionaries, of the civilization of these tribes; but a civilized *full-blooded* Indian does not exist among them. We see every day, in the suburbs of Mobile, and wandering through our streets, the remnant of the Choctaw race, covered with nothing but blankets, and living in bark tents, scarcely a degree advanced above brutes of the field, quietly abiding their time. No human ingenuity can induce them to become educated, or to do an honest day's work: they are supported entirely by begging, besides a little traffic of the squaws in wood. To one who has lived among American Indians, it is in vain to talk of civilizing them. You might as well attempt to change the nature of the buffalo. . . .

Now, it is worthy of remark, that since the discovery of America, and during several centuries, the fair races have inhabited North America extensively, while the dark races, as the Spaniards, have occupied South and Central America, and Mexico; both have displaced the Aboriginal races, and yet neither has made approximation in type to the latter, nor does any person suppose they could in a hundred generations. And so with the Negroes, who have lived here through eight or ten generations. We have no more reason to suppose that an Anglo-Saxon will turn into an Indian, than imported cattle into buffaloes. We shall show, in another chapter, that the oldest Indian crania from the Mounds, some of which are probably several thousand years old, bear no resemblance to those of any race of the old continent. . . .

History, traditions, monuments, osteological remains, every literary record and scientific induction, all show that races have occupied substantially the same zones or provinces from time immemorial. Since the discovery of the mariner's compass, mankind have been more disturbed in their primitive seats; and, with the increasing facilities of communication by land and sea, it is impossible to predict what changes coming ages may bring forth. The Caucasian races, which have always been the representatives of civilization, are those alone that have extended over and colonized all parts of the globe; and much of this is the work of the last three hundred years. The Creator has implanted in this group of races an instinct that, in spite of themselves, drives them through all difficulties, to carry out their great mission of civilizing the earth. It is not reason, or philanthropy, which urges them on; but it is destiny. When we see great divisions of the human family increasing in numbers, spreading in all directions, encroaching by degrees upon all other races wherever they can live and prosper, and gradually supplanting inferior types, is it not reasonable to conclude that they are fulfilling a law of nature?

We have always maintained *diversity* of origin for the whole range of organized beings. If it be granted, as it is on all hands, that there have been many centres of creation, instead of one, what reason is there to suppose that any one race of animals has sprung from a single pair, instead of being the natural production of many pairs? And, as was written by us many years ago, "if it be conceded that there were two primitive pairs of human beings, no reason can be assigned why there may not have been hundreds." . . .

Zoologically, the races or species of mankind obey the same organic laws which govern other animals: they have their geographical points of origin, and are adapted to certain external conditions that cannot be changed with impunity. The natives of one zone cannot always be transferred to another without deteriorating physically and mentally. Races, too, are governed by certain psychological influences, which differ among the species of mankind as instincts vary among the species of lower animals. These psychological characteristics form part of the great mysteries of human nature. They seem often to work in opposition to the physical necessities of races, and to drive individuals and nations beyond the confines of human reason. We see around us, daily, individuals obeying blindly their psychological instincts; and one nation reads of the causes which have led to the decline and fall of other empires without profiting by the lesson.

The laws of God operate not through a few thousand years, but throughout eternity, and we cannot always perceive the why or wherefore of what passes in our brief day. Nations and races, like individuals, have each an especial destiny: some are born to rule, and others to be ruled. And such has ever been the history of mankind. No two distinctly-marked races can dwell together on equal terms. Some races, moreover, appear destined to live and prosper for a time, until the destroying race comes, which is to exterminate and supplant them. Observe how the aborigines of America are fading away before the exotic races of Europe.

Those groups of races heretofore comprehended under the generic term Caucasian, have in all ages been the rulers; and it requires no prophet's eye to see that they are destined eventually to conquer and hold every foot of the globe where climate does not interpose an impenetrable barrier. No philanthropy, no legislation, no missionary labors, can change this law: it is written in man's nature by the hand of his Creator.

While the mind thus speculates on the physical history of races and the more or less speedy extermination of some of them, other problems start up in the distance, of which the solution is far beyond the reach of human foresight. We have already hinted at the mysterious disappearance of many great races and nations of antiquity.

When the inferior types of mankind shall have fulfilled their destinies and passed away, and the superior, becoming intermingled in blood, have wandered from their primitive zoological provinces, and overspread the world, what will be the ultimate result? May not that Law of nature, which so often forbids the commingling of species, complete its work of destruction, and at some future day leave the fossil remains alone of man to tell the tale of his past existence upon earth?

# SAMUEL A. CARTWRIGHT

## SLAVERY AND ETHNOLOGY

Samuel A. Cartwright (1793–1862) has been referred to as "the brutal Louisiana physician and publicist . . . with his banana-skin humor."[1] Cartwright believed in the essential and unalterable inferiority of the Negro, who had presumably been created with characteristics suited for slavery, as contrasted with the white man whose racial characteristics made him a natural master. The following selection is from his essay entitled "Slavery in the Light of Ethnology," which appeared in E. N. Elliott, *Cotton is King, and Pro-Slavery Arguments* (Augusta, 1860), pp. 717 ff. It was originally published under the title, "Natural History of the Prognathous Species of Mankind," in the New York *Day-Book*, November 10, 1857, and was reprinted as an appendix to *The Dred Scott Decision: Opinion of Chief Justice Taney* . . . , J. H. Van Evrie, ed. (New York: Van Evrie, Horton & Co., 1859).[2]

## On the Caucasians and the Africans

The Nilotic monuments furnish numerous portaits of the negro races, represented as slaves, sixteen hundred years before the Christian era. Although repeatedly drawn from their native barbarism and carried among civilized nations, they soon forget what they learn and relapse into barbarism. If the inherent potency of the prognathous type of mankind had been greater than it actually is, sufficiently great to give it the independence of character that the American Indian possesses, the world would have been in a great measure deprived of cotton and sugar. The red man is unavailable as a laborer in the cane or cotton field, or any where else, owing to the unalterable ethnical laws of his character. The white man can not endure toil under the burning sun of the cane and cotton field, and live to enjoy the fruits of his labor. The African will starve rather than engage in a regular system of agricultural labor, unless impelled by the stronger will of the white man. When thus impelled, experience proves that he is much happier, during the hours of labor in the sunny fields, than when dozing in his native woods and jungles. He is also eminently qualified for a number of employments, which the instincts of the white man regard as degrading. If the white man be forced by necessity into employments abhorrent to his instincts, it tends to weaken or destroy that sentiment or principle of honor or duty, which is the mainspring of heroic actions, from the beginning of historical times to the present, and is the basis of every thing great and noble in all grades of white society.

The importance of having these particular employments, regarded as servile and degrading by the white man, attended to by the black race, whose instincts are not repugnant to them, will be at once apparent to all those who deem the sentiment of honor or duty as worth cultivating in the human breast. It is utterly unknown to the prognathous race of mankind, and has no place in their language. When the language is given to them they can not comprehend its meaning, or form a conception of what is meant by it. Every white man, who has not been degraded, had rather be engaged in the most laborious employments, than to serve as a lacquey or body servant to another white man or being like himself. Whereas, there is no office which the negro or mulatto covets more than that of being a body servant to a real gentleman. There is no office which gives him such a high opinion of himself, and it is utterly impossible for him to attach the idea of degradation to it. Those identical offices which the white man instinctively abhors, are the most greedily sought for by negroes and mulattoes, whether slave or free, in preference to all other employments. North or South, free or slave, they are ever at the elbow, behind the table, in hotels and steamboats; ever ready, with brush in hand, to brush the coat or black the shoes, or to perform any menial service which may be required, and to hold out the open palm for the dime. The innate love to act as body servant or lacquey is too strongly developed in the negro race to be concealed. It admirably qualifies them for waiters and house servants, as their strong muscles, hardy frames, and the positive pleasure that labor in a hot sun confers on them, abundantly qualify them for agricultural employment in a hot climate.

Hence, the primordial cell germ of the Nigritians has no more potency than what is sufficient to form a being with physical power, when its dynamism becomes exhausted, dropping the creature in the wilderness with the mental organization too imperfect to enable him to extricate himself from barbarism. If Nature had intended the prognathous race for barbarism as the end and object of their creation, they would have been like lions and tigers, fierce and untamable. So far from being like ferocious beasts, they are endowed with a will so weak, passions so easily subdued, and dispositions so gentle and affectionate, as readily to fall under subjection to the wild Arab, or any other race of men. Hence they are led about in gangs of an hundred or more by a single individual, even by an old man, or a cripple, if he be of the white race and possessed of a strong will. The Nigritian has such little command over his own muscles, from the weakness of his will, as almost to starve, when a little exertion and forethought would procure him an abundance. Although he has exaggerated appetites and exaggerated senses, calling loudly for their gratification, his will is too weak to command his muscles to engage in such kinds of labor as would readily procure the fruits to gratify them. Like an animal in a state of hibernation, waiting for the external aid of spring to warm it into life and power, so does the negro continue to doze out a vegeto-animal existence in the wilderness, unable to extricate himself therefrom—his own will being too feeble to call forth the requisite muscular exertion. His muscles not being exercised, the respiration is imperfect, and the blood is imperfectly vitalized. Torpidity of body and hebetude of mind are the effects thereof, which disappear under bodily labor, because that expands the lungs, vitalizes the blood, and wakes him up to a sense of pleasure and happiness unknown to him in the vegeto-animal or hibernating state. Nothing but will is wanting to transform the torpid, unhappy tenant of the wilderness into a rational and happy thing—the happiest being on earth, as far as sensual pleasures are concerned.

The white man has an exaggerated will, more than he has use for; because it frequently drives his own muscles beyond their physical capacity of endurance. The will is not a faculty confined within the periphery of the body. It can not, like the imagination, travel to immeasurable distances from the body, and in an instant of time go and return from Aldabran, or beyond the boundaries of the solar system. Its flight is confined to the world and to limits more or less restricted—the less restricted in some than in others. The will has two powers—direct and indirect. It is the direct motive power of the muscular system. It indirectly exerts a dynamic force upon surrounding objects when associated with knowledge. It gives to knowledge its power. Every thing that is made was made by the Infinite Will associated with infinite knowledge. The will of man is but a spark of the Infinite Will, and its power is only circumscribed by his knowledge. A man possessing a knowledge of the negro character can govern an hundred, a thousand, or ten thousand of the prognathous race by his will alone, easier than one ignorant of that character can govern a single individual of that race by the whip or a club. However disinclined to labor the negroes may be, they can not help themselves; they are obliged to move and to exercise their muscles when the white man, acquainted with their character, *wills* that they should do so. They can not resist that will, so far as labor of body is concerned. If they resist, it is from some other cause than that connected with their daily labor. They have an instinctive feeling of obedience to the stronger will of the white man, requiring nothing more than moderate labor. So far, their instincts compel obedience to will as one of his rights. Beyond that, they will resist his will and be refractory, if he encroaches on what they regard as their rights, viz: the right to hold property in him as he does in them, and to disburse that property to them in the shape of meat, bread and vegetables, clothing, fuel and house-room, and attention to their comforts when sick, old, infirm, and unable to labor; to hold property in him as a con-servator of the peace among themselves, and a protector against trespassers from abroad, whether black or white; to hold property in him as impartial judge and an honest jury to try them for offenses, and a merciful executioner to punish them for viola-tions of the usages of the plantation or locality.

With those rights acceded to them, no other compulsion is necessary to make them perform their daily tasks than *his will be done*. It is not the whip, as many suppose, which calls forth those muscular exertions, the result of which is sugar, cotton, bread-stuffs, rice, and tobacco. These are products of the white man's will, acting through the muscles of the prognathous race in our Southern States. If that will were withdrawn, and the plantations handed over as a gracious gift to the laborers, agricultural labor would cease for the want of that spiritual power called the will, to move those machines—the muscles. They would cease to move here, as they have in Hayti. If the prognathous race were expelled [from] the land, and their place supplied with double their number of white men, agricultural labor in the south would also cease, as far as sugar and cotton are concerned, for the want of muscles that could endure exercise in the smothering heat of a cane or cotton field. Half the white laborers of Illinois are prostrated with fevers from a few days' work in stripping blades in a Northern corn field, owing to the confinement of the air by the close proximity of the plants. Cane and cotton plants form a denser foliage than corn—a thick jungle, where the white man pants for breath, and is overpowered by the heat of the sun at one time of day, and chilled by the dews and moisture of the plants at another. Negroes glory in a close, hot atmosphere; they instinctively cover their head and faces with a blanket at night, and prefer laying with their heads to the fire, instead of their feet. This ethnical peculiarity is in harmony with their efficiency as laborers in hot, damp, close, suffocating atmosphere—where instead of suffering and dying, as the white man would, they are healthier, happier, and more prolific than in their native Africa —producing, under the white man's will, a great variety of agricultural products, besides upward of three millions of bales of cotton, and three hundred thousand hogsheads of sugar. Thus proving that subjection to his will is normal to them, because, under the influence of his will, they enjoy life more than in any other condition, rapidly increase in numbers, and steadily rise in the scale of humanity.

The power of a stronger will over a weaker, or the power of one living creature to act on and influence another, is an ordinance of nature, which has its parallel in the inorganic kingdom, where ponderous bodies, widely separated in space, influence one another so much as to keep up a constant interplay of action and reaction throughout nature's vast realms. The same ordinance which keeps the spheres in their orbits and holds the satellites in subordination to the planets, is the ordinance that subjects the negro race to the empire of the white man's will. From that ordinance the snake derives its power to charm the bird, and the magician his power to amuse the curious, to astonish the vulgar, and to confound the wisdom of the wise. Under that ordinance, our four millions of negroes are as un- alterably bound to obey the white man's will, as the four satellites of Jupiter the superior magnetism of that planet. . . . The subjugation of equals by artifice or force is tyranny or slav- ery; but there is no such thing in the United States, because equals are on a perfect equality here. The subordination of the Nigri- tian to the Caucasian would never have been imagined to be a condition similar to European slavery, if any regard had been paid to ethnology. Subordination of the inferior race to the superior is a normal, and not a forced condition. Chains and standing armies are the implements used to force the obedience of equals to equals—of one white man to another. Whereas, the obedience of the Nigritian to the Caucasian is *spontaneous* be- cause it is normal for the weaker will to yield obedience to the stronger. The ordinance which subjects the negro to the empire of the white man's will, was plainly written on the heavens during our Revolutionary war. It was then that the power of the united will of the American people rose to its highest degree of intensity.

Every colony was a slaveholding colony excepting one; yet the people, particularly that portion of them residing in districts where the black population was greatest, hastened to meet in the battle-field the powerful British armies in front of them, and the interminable hosts of Indian warriors in the wilderness behind them, leaving their wives and children, their old men and crip- ples, for seven long years, *to their negroes to take care of.* Did the slaves, many of whom were savages recently imported from Africa, butcher them, as white or Indian slaves surely would have done, and fly to the enemy's standard for the liberty, land, money, rum, savage luxuries and ample protection so abundantly promised and secured to all who would desert their master's families? History answers that not one in a thousand joined their masters' enemies; but, on the contrary, they continued quietly their daily labors, even in those districts where they outnum- bered the white population ten to one. They not only produced sufficient breadstuffs to supply the families of their masters, but a surplus of flour, pork, and beef was sent up from the slaveholding districts of Virginia to Washington's starving army in Pennsylvania. . . . These agricultural products were created by savages, naturally so indolent in their native Africa, as to prefer to live on ant eggs and caterpillars rather than labor for a subsistence; but for years in succession they continued to labor in the midst of their masters' enemies—dropping their hoes when they saw the red coats, running to tell their mistress, and to conduct her and the children through by-paths to avoid the British troopers, and when the enemy were out of sight returning to their work again. The sole cause of their industry and fidelity is due to the spiritual influence of the white race over the black.

The empire of the white man's will over the prognathous race is not absolute, however. It can not force exercise beyond a certain speed; neither the will nor physical force can drive negroes, for a number of days in succession, beyond a very moderate daily labor—about one-third less than the white man voluntarily imposes on himself. If force be used to make them do more, they invariably do less and less, until they fall into a state of impassivity, in which they are more plague than profit—worthless as laborers, insensible and indifferent to punishment, or even to life; or, in other words, they fall into the disease which I have named Dysesthaesia Ethiopica, characterized by hebetude of mind and insensibility of body, caused by over working and bad treatment. Some knowledge of the ethnology of the prognathous race is absolutely necessary for the prevention and cure of this malady in all its various forms and stages. Dirt eating, or Cachexia Africana, is another disease, like Dysesthaesia Ethiopica, growing out of ethnical elements peculiar to the prognathous race. The ethnical elements assimilating the negro to the mule, although giving rise to the last named disease, are of vast importance to the prognathous race, because they guarantee to that race an ample protection against the abuses of arbitrary power. A white man, like a blooded horse, can be worked to death. Not so the negro, whose ethnical elements, like the mule, restricts the limits of arbitrary power over him.

Among the four millions of the prognathous race in the United States, it will be difficult, if not impossible, to find a single individual negro, whom the white man, armed with arbitrary power, has ever been able to make hurt himself at work. It is beyond the power of the white man to drive the negro into those long continued and excessive muscular exertions such as the white laborers of Europe often impose upon themselves to satisfy a greedy boss, under fear of losing their places, and thereby starving themselves and families. Throughout England, nothing is more common than decrepitude, premature old age, and a frightful list of diseases, caused by long continued and excessive muscular exertion. Whereas, all America can scarcely furnish an example of the kind among the prognathous race. The white men of America have performed many prodigies, but they have never yet been able to make a negro overwork himself. . . .

## NOTES

1. William Stanton, *The Leopard's Spots*, p. vii.
2. Eric L. McKitrick, ed., *Slavery Defended: the Views of the Old South* (Englewood Cliffs, New Jersey, 1963) , p. 139n.

# FREDERICK DOUGLASS

## AN EVALUATION OF RACIAL ANTHROPOLOGY

Frederick Douglass (1817?–1895), the great Negro Abolitionist, journalist and orator, delivered the following address, "The Claims of the Negro Ethnologically Considered," at Western Reserve College on July 12, 1854. It is one of the most perceptive pre–Civil War evaluations of Negro racial characteristics, and a devastating critique of the so-called scientific attempts of the time to prove the inferiority of the Negro. It was originally printed as a pamphlet in Rochester in 1854, and has been reprinted in *The Life and Writings of Frederick Douglass*, Philip S. Foner, ed. (International Publishers, New York), Vol. II, pp. 289–309.

## *The Claims of the Negro Ethnologically Considered*

Gentlemen, in selecting the Claims of the Negro as the subject of my remarks to-day, I am animated by a desire to bring before you a matter of living importance—a matter upon which action, as well as thought is required. The relation subsisting between the white and black people of this country is the vital question of the age. In the solution of this question, the scholars of America will have to take an important and controlling part. This is the moral battle field to which their country and their God now call them. In the eye of both, the neutral scholar is an ignoble man. Here, a man must be hot, or be accounted cold, or, perchance, something worse than hot or cold. The lukewarm and the cowardly, will be rejected by earnest men on either side of the controversy. The cunning man who avoids it, to gain the favor of both parties, will be rewarded with scorn; and the timid man who shrinks from it, for fear of offending either party, will be despised. To the lawyer, the preacher, the politician, and to the man of letters, there is no neutral ground. He that is not for us, is against us. Gentlemen, I assume at the start, that wherever else I may be required to speak with bated breath, here, at least, I may speak with freedom the thought nearest my heart. This liberty is implied, by the call I have received to be here; and yet

I hope to present the subject so that no man can reasonably say, that an outrage has been committed, or that I have abused the privilege with which you have honored me. I shall aim to discuss the claims of the Negro, general and special, in a manner, though not scientific, still sufficiently clear and definite to enable my hearers to form an intelligent judgment respecting them.

The first general claim which may here be set up, respects the manhood of the Negro. This is an elementary claim, simple enough, but not without question. It is fiercely opposed. A respectable public journal, published in Richmond, Va., bases its whole defence of the slave system upon a denial of the Negro's manhood.

"The white peasant is free, and if he is a man of will and intellect, can rise in the scale of society; or at least his offspring may. He is not deprived by law of those 'inalienable rights,' 'liberty and the pursuit of happiness,' by the use of it. But here is the essence of slavery—that we do declare the Negro destitute of these powers. We bind him by law to the condition of the laboring peasant for ever, without his consent, and we bind his posterity after him. Now, the true question is, have we a right to do this? If we have not, all discussions about his comfortable situation, and the actual condition of free laborers elsewhere, are quite beside the point. If the Negro has the same right to his liberty and the pursuit of his own happiness that the white man has, then we commit the greatest wrong and robbery to hold him a slave—an act at which the sentiment of justice must revolt in every heart and Negro slavery is an institution which that sentiment must sooner or later blot from the face of the earth."—*Richmond Examiner.*

After stating the question thus, the *Examiner* boldly asserts that the Negro has no such right—BECAUSE HE IS NOT A MAN!

There are three ways to answer this denial. One is by ridicule; a second is by denunciation; and a third is by argument. I hardly know under which of these modes my answer to-day will fall. I feel myself somewhat on trial; and that this is just the point where there is hesitation, if not serious doubt. I cannot, however, argue; I must assert. To know whether a Negro is a man, it must first be known what constitutes a man. Here, as well as elsewhere, I take it, that the "coat must be cut according to the cloth." . . .

Man is distinguished from all other animals, by the possession of certain definite faculties and powers, as well as by physical organization and proportions. He is the only two-handed animal on the earth—the only one that laughs, and nearly the only one that weeps. Men instinctively distinguish between men and brutes. Common sense itself is scarcely needed to detect the absence of manhood in a monkey, or to recognize its presence in a Negro. His speech, his reason, his power to acquire and to retain knowledge, his heaven-erected face, his habitudes, his hopes, his fears, his aspirations, his prophecies, plant between him and the brute creation, a distinction as eternal as it is palpable. Away, therefore, with all the scientific moonshine that would connect men with monkeys; that would have the world believe that humanity, instead of resting on its own characteristic pedestal—gloriously independent—is a sort of sliding scale, making one extreme brother to the ourang-ou-tang, and the other to angels, and all the rest intermediates! Tried by all the usual, and all the *un*usual tests, whether mental, moral, physical, or psychological, the Negro is a MAN—considering him as possessing knowledge, or needing knowledge, his elevation or his degradation, his virtues, or his vices—whichever road you take, you reach the same conclusion, the Negro is a MAN. His good and his bad, his innocence and his guilt, his joys and his sorrows, proclaim his manhood in speech that all mankind practically and readily understand.

A very recondite author says, that "man is distinguished from all other animals, in that he resists as well as adapts himself to his circumstances." He does not take things as he finds them, but goes to work to improve them. Tried by this test, too, the Negro is a man. You may see him yoke the oxen, harness the horse, and hold the plow. He can swim the river; but he prefers to fling over it a bridge. The horse bears him on his back—admits his mastery and dominion. The barnyard fowl know his step, and flock around to receive their morning meal from his sable hand. The dog dances when he comes home, and whines piteously when he is absent. All these know that the Negro is a MAN. Now, presuming that what is evident to beast and to bird, cannot need elaborate argument to be made plain to men, I assume, with this brief statement, that the Negro is a man.

The first claim conceded and settled, let us attend to the

second, which is beset with some difficulties, giving rise to many opinions, different from my own, and which opinions I propose to combat.

There was a time when, if you established the point that a particular being is a man, it was considered that such a being, of course, had a common ancestry with the rest of mankind. But it is not so now. This is, you know, an age of science, and science is favorable to division. It must explore and analyze, until all doubt is set at rest. There is, therefore, another proposition to be stated and maintained, separately, which, in other days, (the days before the Notts, the Gliddens, the Agassiz, and Mortons, made their profound discoveries in ethnological science,) might have been included in the first.

It is somewhat remarkable, that, at a time when knowledge is so generally diffused, when the geography of the world is so well understood—when time and space, in the intercourse of nations, are almost annihilated—when oceans have become bridges—the earth a magnificent hall—the hollow sky a dome—under which a common humanity can meet in friendly conclave—when nationalities are being swallowed up—and the ends of the earth brought together—I say it is remarkable—nay, it is strange that there should arise a phalanx of learned men—speaking in the name of *science*—to forbid the magnificent reunion of mankind in one brotherhood. A mortifying proof is here given, that the moral growth of a nation, or an age, does not always keep pace with the increase of knowledge, and suggests the necessity of means to increase human love with human learning.

The proposition to which I allude, and which I mean next to assert, is this, that what are technically called the Negro race, are a part of the human family, and are descended from a common ancestry, with the rest of mankind. The discussion of this point opens a comprehensive field of inquiry. It involves the question of the unity of the human race. Much has and can be said on both sides of that question.

Looking out upon the surface of the Globe, with its varieties of climate, soil, and formations, its elevations and depressions, its rivers, lakes, oceans, islands, continents, and the vast and striking differences which mark and diversify its multitudinous inhabitants, the question has been raised, and pressed with increasing ardor and pertinacity (especially in modern times,) can all these various tribes, nations, tongues, kindreds, so widely separated, and so strangely dissimilar, have descended from a common ancestry? That is the question, and it has been answered variously by men of learning. Different modes of reasoning have been adopted, but the conclusions reached may be divided into two—the one YES, and the other NO. *Which* of these answers is most in accordance with facts, with reason, with the welfare of the world, and reflects most glory upon the wisdom, power, and goodness of the Author of all existence, is the question for consideration with us? On which side is the weight of the argument, rather than which side is absolutely proved?

It must be admitted at the beginning, that, viewed apart from the authority of the Bible, neither the unity, nor diversity of origin of the human family, can be demonstrated. To use the terse expression of the Rev. Dr. Anderson, who speaking on this point, says; "It is impossible to get far enough back for that." This much, however, can be done. The evidence on both sides, can be accurately weighed, and the truth arrived at with almost absolute certainty.

It would be interesting, did time permit, to give here, some of the most striking features of the various theories, which have, of late, gained attention and respect in many quarters of our country—touching the origin of mankind—but I must pass this by. The argument to-day, is to the unity, as against that theory, which affirms the diversity of human origin.

## The Bearings of the Question

A moment's reflection must impress all, that few questions have more important and solemn bearings, than the one now under consideration. It is connected with eternal as well as with terrestrial interests. It covers the earth and reaches heaven. The unity of the human race—the brotherhood of man—the reciprocal duties of all to each, and of each to all, are too plainly taught in the Bible to admit of cavil.—The credit of the Bible is at stake—and if it be too much to say, that it must stand or fall, by the decision of this question, *it is* proper to say, that the value of that sacred Book—as a record of the early history of mankind—must be materially affected, by the decision of the question.

For myself I can say, my reason (not less than my feeling, and my faith) welcomes with joy, the declaration of the Inspired Apostle, "that God has made of one blood all nations of men for to dwell upon all the face of the earth." But this grand affirmation of the unity of the human race, and many others like unto it, together with the whole account of the creation, given in the early scriptures, must all get a new interpretation or be overthrown altogether, if a diversity of human origin can be maintained.—Most evidently, this aspect of the question makes it important to those, who rely upon the Bible, as the sheet anchor of their hopes—and the frame work of all religious truth. The young minister must look into this subject and settle it for himself, before he ascends the pulpit, to preach redemption to a fallen race.

The bearing of the question upon Revelation, is not more marked and decided than its relation to the situation of things in our country, at this moment. *One seventh* part of the population of this country is of Negro descent. The land is peopled by what may be called the most dissimilar races on the globe. The black and the white—the Negro and the European—these constitute the American people—and, in all the likelihoods of the case, they will ever remain the principal inhabitants of the United States, in some form or other. The European population are greatly in the ascendant in numbers, wealth and power. They are the rulers of the country—the masters—the Africans, are the slaves—the proscribed portion of the people—and precisely in proportion as the truth of human brotherhood gets recognition, will be the freedom and elevation, in this country, of persons of African descent. In truth, this question is at the bottom of the whole controversy, now going on between the slaveholders on the *one* hand, and the abolitionists on the other. It is the same old question which has divided the selfish, from the philanthropic part of mankind in all ages. It is the question whether the rights, privileges, and immunities enjoyed by some ought not to be shared and enjoyed by all.

It is not quite two hundred years ago, when such was the simplicity (I will not now say the pride and depravity) of the

Anglo Saxon inhabitants of the British West Indies, that the learned and pious Godwin, a missionary to the West Indies, deemed it necessary to write a book, to remove what he conceived to be the injurious belief that it was sinful in the sight of God to baptize Negroes and Indians. The West Indies have made progress since that time.—God's emancipating angel has broken the fetters of slavery in those islands, and the praises of the Almighty are now sung by the sable lips of eight hundred thousand freemen, before deemed only fit for slaves, and to whom even baptismal and burial rights were denied.

The unassuming work of *Godwin* may have had some agency in producing this glorious result. One other remark before entering upon the argument. It may be said, that views and opinions, favoring the unity of the human family, coming from one of lowly condition, are open to the suspicion, that *"the wish is father to the thought,"* and so, indeed, it may be.—But let it be also remembered, that this deduction from the weight of the argument on the one side, is more than counter-balanced by the pride of race and position arrayed on the other. Indeed, ninety-nine out of every hundred of the advocates of a diverse origin of the human family in this country, are among those who hold it to be the privilege of the *Anglo-Saxon* to enslave and oppress the African—and slaveholders, not a few, like the Richmond Examiner to which I have referred, have admitted, that the whole argument in defence of slavery, becomes utterly worthless the moment the African is proved to be equally a man with the Anglo-Saxon. The temptation therefore, to read the Negro out of the human family is exceedingly strong, and may account somewhat for the repeated attempts on the part of Southern pretenders to science, to cast a doubt over the Scriptural account of the origin of mankind. If the origin and motives of most works, opposing the doctrine of the unity of the human race, could be ascertained, it may be doubted whether *one* such work could boast an honest parentage. Pride and selfishness, combined with mental power, never want for a theory to justify them—and when men oppress their fellowmen, the oppressor ever finds, in the character of the oppressed, a full justification for his oppression. Ignorance and depravity, and the inability to rise from degradation to civilization and respectability, are the most usual allegations against the oppressed. The evils most fostered by slavery and oppression, are precisely those which slaveholders and oppressors would transfer from their system to the inherent character of their victims. Thus the very crimes of slavery become slavery's best defence. By making the enslaved a character fit only for slavery, they excuse themselves for refusing to make the slave a freeman. A wholesale method of accomplishing this result, is to overthrow the instinctive consciousness of the common brotherhood of man. For, let it be once granted that the human race are of multitudinous origin, naturally different in their moral, physical, and intellectual capacities, and at once you make plausible a demand for classes, grades and conditions, for different methods of culture, different moral, political, and religious institutions, and a chance is left for slavery, as a necessary institution. The debates in Congress on the Nebraska Bill during the past winter, will show how slaveholders have availed themselves of this doctrine in support of slaveholding. There is no doubt that Messrs. Nott, Glidden, Morton, Smith and Agassiz were duly consulted by our slavery propagating statesmen. . . .

## Superficial Objections

Let us now glance again at the opposition. A volume, on the Natural History of the Human Species, by Charles Hamilton Smith, quite false in many of its facts, and as mischievous as false, has been published recently in this country, and will, doubtless, be widely circulated, especially by those to whom the thought of human brotherhood is abhorrent. This writer says, after mentioning sundry facts touching the dense and spherical structure of the Negro head:

"This very structure may influence the erect gait, which occasions the practice common also to the Ethiopian, or mixed nations, of carrying burdens and light weights, even to a tumbler full of water, upon the head."

No doubt this seemed a very sage remark to Mr. Smith, and quite important in fixing a character to the Negro skull, although different to that of Europeans. But if the learned Mr. Smith had stood, previous to writing it, at our door (a few days in succession), he might have seen hundreds of Germans and of

Irish people, not bearing burdens of *"light* weight," but of *heavy* weight, upon the same vertical extremity. The carrying of burdens upon the head is as old as Oriental Society; and the man writes himself a blockhead, who attempts to find in the custom a proof of original difference. On page 227, the same writer says:

"The voice of the Negroes is feeble and hoarse in the male sex."

The explanation of this mistake in our author, is found in the fact, that an oppressed people, in addressing their superiors—perhaps I ought to say, their oppressors—usually assume a minor tone, as less likely to provoke the charge of intrusiveness. But it is ridiculous to pronounce the voice of the Negro feeble; and the learned ethnologist must be hard pushed, to establish differences, when he refers to this as one. Mr. Smith further declares, that

"The typical woolly haired races have never discovered an alphabet, framed a grammatical language, nor made the least step in science or art."

Now, the man is still living (or was but a few years since), among the Mandingoes of the Western coast of Africa, who has framed an alphabet; and while Mr. Smith may be pardoned for his ignorance of that fact, as an ethnologist, he is inexcusable for not knowing that the Mpongwe language, spoken on both sides of the Gaboon River, at Cape Lopez, Cape St. Catharine, and in the interior, to the distance of two or three hundred miles, is as truly a grammatically framed language as any extant. I am indebted, for this fact, to Rev. Dr. *M. B. Anderson,* President of the Rochester University; and by his leave, here is the Grammar—[holding up the Grammar.] Perhaps, of all the attempts ever made to disprove the unity of the human family, and to brand the Negro with natural inferiority, the most compendious and barefaced is the book, entitled *"Types of Mankind,"* by Nott and Glidden. One would be well employed, in a series of Lectures, directed to an exposure of the unsoundness, if not the wickedness of this work.

## The African Race But One People

But I must hasten. Having shown that the people of Africa are, probably, one people; that each tribe bears an intimate relation to other tribes and nations in that quarter of the globe, and that the Egyptians may have flung off the different tribes seen there at different times, as implied by the evident relations of their language, and by other similarities; it can hardly be deemed unreasonable to suppose, that the African branch of the human species—from the once highly civilized Egyptian to the barbarians on the banks of the Niger—may claim brotherhood with the great family of Noah, spreading over the more Northern and Eastern parts of the globe. I will now proceed to consider those physical peculiarities of form, features, hair and color, which are supposed by some men to mark the African, not only as an inferior race, but as a distinct species, naturally and originally different from the rest of mankind, and as really to place him nearer to the brute than to man.

## The Effect of Circumstances Upon the Physical Man

I may remark, just here, that it is impossible, even were it desirable, in a discourse like this, to attend to the anatomical and physiological argument connected with this part of the subject. I am not equal to that, and if I were, the occasion does not require it. The form of the *Negro*—[I use the term *Negro,* precisely in the sense that you use the term Anglo Saxon; and I believe, too, that the former will one day be as illustrious as the latter]—has often been the subject of remark. His flat feet, long arms, high cheek bones and retreating forehead, are especially dwelt upon, to his disparagement, and just as if there were no white people with precisely the same peculiarities. I think it will ever be found, that the *well* or *ill* condition of any part of mankind, will leave its mark on the physical as well as on the intellectual part of man. A hundred instances might be cited, of whole families who have degenerated, and others who have improved in personal appearance, by a change of circumstances. A man is worked upon by what *he* works on. He may carve out his circumstances, but his circumstances will carve him out as well. I told a boot maker, in New Castle upon Tyne, that I had been a plantation slave. He said I must pardon him; but he could not believe it; no plantation laborer ever had a high instep. He said he had noticed, that the coal heavers and work people in low condition, had, for the most part, flat feet, and that he could tell, by the shape of the feet, whether a man's parents were in high or low condition. The thing was worth a thought, and I have thought of it, and have looked around me for facts. There is some truth in it; though there are exceptions, in individual cases. . . .

I am stating facts. If you go into Southern Indiana, you will see what climate and habit can do, even in one generation. The man may have come from New England, but his hard features, sallow complexion, have left little of New England on his brow. The right arm of the blacksmith is said to be larger and stronger than his left. The ship carpenter is at forty round shouldered. The shoemaker carries the marks of his trade. One locality becomes famous for one thing, another for another. Manchester and Lowell, in America, Manchester and Sheffield, in England, attest this. But what does it all prove? Why, nothing positively, as to the main point; still it raises the inquiry—May not the condition of men explain their various appearances? Need we go behind the vicissitudes of barbarism for an explanation of the gaunt, wiry, ape like appearance of some of the genuine Negroes? Need we look higher than a vertical sun, or lower than the damp, black soil of the Niger, the Gambia, the Senegal, with their heavy and enervating miasma, rising ever from the rank growing and decaying vegetation, for an explanation of the Negro's color? If a cause, full and adequate, can be found here, *why seek further?*

The Eminent Dr. *Latham,* already quoted, says that nine tenths of the white population of the globe are found between 30 and 65 degrees North latitude. Only about one fifth of all the inhabitants of the globe are white; and they are as far from the Adamic complexion as is the Negro. The remainder are—*what?* Ranging all the way from the brunette to jet black. There are the red, the reddish copper color, the yellowish, the dark brown, the chocolate color, and so on, to the jet black. On the mountains on the North of Africa, where water freezes in winter at times, branches of the same people who are *black* in the valley are *white* on the mountains. The Nubian, with his beautiful curly hair, finds it becoming frizzled, crisped, and even wooly, as he approaches the great Sahara. The Portuguese, white in Europe, is brown in Asia. The Jews, who are to be found in all countries, never intermarrying, are white in Europe, brown in Asia, and

black in Africa. Again, what does it all prove? Nothing, absolutely; nothing which places the question beyond dispute; but it
*does* justify the conjecture before referred to, that outward circumstances *may* have something to do with modifying the various phases of humanity; and that color itself is at the control of
the world's climate and its various concomitants. It is the sun
that paints the peach—and may it not be, that he paints the *man*
as well? My reading, on this point, however, as well as my own
observation, have convinced me, that from the beginning the
Almighty, within certain limits, endowed mankind with organizations capable of countless variations in form, feature and
color, without having it necessary to begin a new creation for
every new variety.

A powerful argument in the favor of the oneness of the human
family, is afforded in the fact that nations, however dissimilar,
may be united in one social state, not only without detriment to
each other, but, most clearly, to the advancement of human welfare, happiness and perfection. While it is clearly proved, on the
other hand, that those nations freest from foreign elements,
present the most evident marks of deterioration. Dr. JAMES MC-
CUNE SMITH, himself a colored man, a gentleman and scholar, al-
leges—and not without excellent reason—that this, our own great
nation, so distinguished for industry and enterprise, is largely indebted to its composite character. . . . The Medes and Persians
constituted one of the mightiest empires that ever rocked the
globe. The most terrible nation which now threatens the peace of
the world, to make its will the law of Europe, is a grand piece of
Mosaic work, in which almost every nation has its characteristic
feature, from the wild Tartar to the refined Pole.

But, gentlemen, the time fails me, and I must bring these
remarks to a close. My argument has swelled beyond its appointed measure. What I intended to make special, has become,
in its progress, somewhat general. I meant to speak here to-day,
for the lonely and the despised ones, with whom I was cradled,
and with whom I have suffered; and now, gentlemen, in conclusion, what if all this reasoning be unsound? What if the Negro
may not be able to prove his relationship to Nubians, Abys-
sinians and Egyptians? What if ingenious men are able to find
plausible objections to all arguments maintaining the oneness of

the human race? What, after all, if they are able to show very good reasons for believing the Negro to have been created precisely as we find him on the Gold Coast—along the Senegal and the Niger—I say, what of all this?—"*A man's a man for a' that.*" I sincerely believe, that the weight of the argument is in favor of the unity of origin of the human race, or species—that the arguments on the other side are partial, superficial, utterly subversive of the happiness of man, and insulting to the wisdom of God. Yet, what if we grant they are not so? What, if we grant that the case, on our part, is not made out? Does it follow, that the Negro should be held in contempt? Does it follow, that to enslave and imbrute him is either *just* or *wise?* I think not. Human rights stand upon a common basis; and by all the reason that they are supported, maintained and defended, for one variety of the human family, they are supported, maintained and defended for *all* the human family; because all mankind have the same wants, arising out of a common nature. A diverse origin does not disprove a common nature, nor does it disprove a united destiny. The essential characteristics of humanity are everywhere the same. In the language of the eloquent *Curran,* "No matter what complexion, whether an Indian or an African sun has burnt upon him," his title deed to freedom, his claim to life and to liberty, to knowledge and to civilization, to society and to Christianity, are just and perfect. It is registered in the Courts of Heaven, and is enforced by the eloquence of the God of all the earth.

I have said that the Negro and white man are likely ever to remain the principal inhabitants of this country. I repeat the statement now, to submit the reasons that support it. The blacks can disappear from the face of the country by three ways. They may be colonized,—they may be exterminated,—or, they may die out. Colonization is out of the question; for I know not what hardships the laws of the land can impose, which can induce the colored citizen to leave his native soil. He was here in its infancy; he is here in its age. Two hundred years have passed over him, his tears and blood have been mixed with the soil, and his attachment to the place of his birth is stronger than iron. It is not probable that he will be exterminated; two considerations must prevent a crime so stupendous as that—the influence of Christianity on the one hand, and the power of self interest on the other; and, in regard to their dying out, the statistics of the country afford no encouragement for such a conjecture. The history of the Negro race proves them to be wonderfully adapted to all countries, all climates, and all conditions. Their tenacity of life, their powers of endurance, their malleable toughness, would almost imply especial interposition on their behalf. The ten thousand horrors of slavery, striking hard upon the sensitive soul, have bruised, and battered, and stung, but have not killed. The poor bondman lifts a smiling face above the surface of a sea of agonies, *hoping on, hoping ever.* His tawny brother, the Indian, dies, under the flashing glance of the Anglo Saxon. *Not* so the Negro; civilization cannot kill him. He accepts it—becomes a part of it. In the Church, he is an Uncle Tom, in the State, he is the most abused and least offensive. All the facts in his history mark out for him a destiny, united to America and Americans. Now, whether this population shall, by *Freedom, Industry, Virtue and Intelligence,* be made a blessing to the country and the world, or whether their multiplied wrongs shall kindle the vengeance of an offended God, will depend upon the conduct of no class of men so much as upon the Scholars of the country. The future public opinion of the land, whether anti-slavery or pro-slavery, whether just or unjust, whether magnanimous or mean, must redound to the honor of the scholars of the country or cover them with shame. There is but one safe road for nations or for individuals. The fate of a wicked man and of a wicked nation is the same. The flaming sword of offended justice falls as certainly upon  the nation as upon the man. God has no children whose rights may be safely trampled upon. The sparrow may not fall to the ground without the notice of His eye, and men are more than sparrows.

Now, gentlemen, I have done. The subject is before you. I shall not undertake to make the application. I speak as unto wise men. I stand in the presence of Scholars. We have met here to-day from vastly different points in the world's condition. I have reached here—if you will pardon the egotism—by little short of a miracle; at any rate, by dint of some application and perseverance. Born, as I was, in obscurity, a stranger to the halls of learning, environed by ignorance, degradation, and their con-

comitants, from birth to manhood, I do not feel at liberty to
mark out, with any degree of confidence, or dogmatism, what is
the precise vocation of the Scholar. Yet, this I *can* say, as a
denizen of the world, and as a citizen of a country rolling in the
sin and shame of Slavery, the most flagrant and scandalous that
ever saw the sun, "Whatsoever things are true, whatsoever things
are honest, whatsoever things are just, whatsoever things are
pure, whatsoever things are lovely, whatsoever things are of good
report, if there be any virtue, and if there be any praise, think on
these things."

## GEORGE FITZHUGH

### SOCIOLOGY FOR THE SOUTH

George Fitzhugh (1806–1881) was a Southern lawyer and writer who contributed to the New York *Day Book*, the *Richmond* (Virginia) *Examiner* and *DeBow's Review*. His best known works are *Sociology for the South; or the Failure of Free Society* (Richmond, Va., 1854) and *Cannibals All! or, Slaves without Masters* (1857). The following selection is from pp. 81 ff. of the former work, in which he argues that slavery is best suited to the nature of the Negro.

## *Negro Slavery*

We have already stated that we should not attempt to introduce any new theories of government and of society, but merely try to justify old ones, so far as we could deduce such theories from ancient and almost universal practices. Now it has been the practice in all countries and in all ages, in some degree, to accommodate the amount and character of government control to the wants, intelligence, and moral capacities of the nations or individuals to be governed. A highly moral and intellectual people, like the free citizens of ancient Athens, are best governed by a democracy. For a less moral and intellectual one, a limited and constitutional monarchy will answer. For a people either very ignorant or very wicked, nothing short of military despotism will suffice. So among individuals, the most moral and well-informed members of society require no other government than law. They are capable of reading and understanding the law, and have sufficient self-control and virtuous disposition to obey it. Children cannot be governed by mere law; first, because they do not understand it, and secondly, because they are so much under the influence of impulse, passion and appetite, that they want sufficient self-control to be deterred or governed by the distant and doubtful penalties of the law. They must be constantly controlled by parents or guardians, whose will and orders shall stand in the place of law for them. Very wicked men must be put into penitentiaries; lunatics into asylums, and the most wild of them into strait-jackets, just as the most wicked of the sane are manacled with irons; and idiots must have committees to govern and take care of them. Now, it is clear the Athenian democracy would not suit a negro nation, nor will the government of mere law suffice for the individual negro. He is but a grown up child, and must be governed as a child, not as a lunatic or criminal. The master occupies towards him the place of parent or guardian. We shall not dwell on this view, for no one will differ from us who thinks as we do of the negro's capacity, and we might argue till dooms-day, in vain, with those who have a high opinion of the negro's moral and intellectual capacity.

Secondly. The negro is improvident; will not lay up in summer for the wants of winter; will not accumulate in youth for the exigencies of age. He would become an insufferable burden to society. Society has the right to prevent this, and can only do so by subjecting him to domestic slavery. In the last place, the negro race is inferior to the white race, and living in their midst, they would be far outstripped or outwitted in the chase of free competition. Gradual but certain extermination would be their fate. We presume the maddest abolitionist does not think the negro's providence of habits and money-making capacity at all to compare to those of the whites. This defect of character would alone justify enslaving him, if he is to remain here. In Africa or the West Indies, he would become idolatrous, savage and cannibal, or be devoured by savages and cannibals. At the North he would freeze or starve.

We would remind those who deprecate and sympathize with negro slavery, that his slavery here relieves him from a far more cruel slavery in Africa, or from idolatry and cannibalism, and every brutal vice and crime that can disgrace humanity; and that it christianizes, protects, supports and civilizes him; that it governs him far better than free laborers at the North are governed. There, wife-murder has become a mere holiday pastime; and where so many wives are murdered, almost all must be brutally treated. Nay, more: men who kill their wives or treat them brutally, must be ready for all kinds of crime, and the calendar of crime at the North proves the inference to be correct. Negroes never kill their wives. If it be objected that legally they have no wives, then we reply, that in an experience of more than forty years, we never yet heard of a negro man killing a negro woman. Our negroes are not only better off as to physical comfort than free laborers, but their moral condition is better.

But abolish negro slavery, and how much of slavery still remains. Soldiers and sailors in Europe enlist for life; here, for five years. Are they not slaves who have not only sold their liberties, but their lives also? And they are worse treated than domestic slaves. No domestic affection and self-interest extend their aegis over them. No kind mistress, like a guardian angel, provides for them in health, tends them in sickness, and soothes their dying pillow. Wellington at Waterloo was a slave. He was bound to obey, or would, like admiral Bying, have been shot for gross misconduct, and might not, like a common laborer, quit his work at any moment. He had sold his liberty, and might not resign without the consent of his master, the king. The common laborer may quit his work at any moment, whatever his contract; declare that liberty is an inalienable right, and leave his employer to redress by a useless suit for damages. The highest and most honorable position on earth was that of the slave Wellington; the lowest, that of the free man who cleaned his boots and fed his hounds. The African cannibal, caught, christianized and enslaved, is as much elevated by slavery as was Wellington. The kind of slavery is adapted to the men enslaved. Wives and apprentices are slaves; not in theory only, but often in fact. Children are slaves to their parents, guardians and teachers. Imprisoned culprits are slaves. Lunatics and idiots are slaves also. Three-fourths of free society are slaves, no better treated, when their wants and capacities are estimated, than negro slaves. The masters in free society, or slave society, if they perform properly their duties, have more cares and less liberty than the slaves themselves. "In the sweat of thy face shalt thou earn thy bread!" made all men slaves, and such all *good men* continue to be.

Negro slavery would be changed immediately to some form of peonage, serfdom or villienage, if the negroes were sufficiently intelligent and provident to manage a farm. No one would have the labor and trouble of management, if his negroes would pay in hires and rents one-half what free tenants pay in rent in Europe. Every negro in the South would be soon liberated, if he would take liberty on the terms that white tenants hold it. The fact that he cannot enjoy liberty on such terms, seems conclusive that he is only fit to be a slave.

But for the assaults of the abolitionists, much would have been done ere this to regulate and improve Southern slavery. Our negro mechanics do not work so hard, have many more privileges and holidays, and are better fed and clothed than field hands, and are yet more valuable to their masters. The slaves of the South are cheated of their rights by the purchase of Northern manufactures which they could produce. Besides, if we would employ our slaves in the coarser processes of the mechanic arts and manufacturers, such as brick making, getting and hewing timber for ships and houses, iron mining and smelting, coal mining, grading railroads and plank roads, in the manufacture of cotton, tobacco, &c., we would find a vent in new employments for their increase, more humane and more profitable than the vent afforded by new states and territories. The nice and finishing processes of manufactures and mechanics should be reserved for the whites, who only are fitted for them, and thus, by diversifying pursuits and cutting off dependence on the North, we might benefit and advance the interests of our whole population. Exclusive agriculture has depressed and impoverished the South. We will not here dilate on this topic, because we intend to make it the subject of a separate essay. Free trade doctrines, not slavery, have made the South agricultural and dependent, given her a sparse and ignorant population, ruined her cities, and expelled her people.

Would the abolitionists approve of a system of society that set white children free, and remitted them at the age of fourteen, males and females, to all the rights, both as to person and property, which belong to adults? Would it be criminal or praiseworthy to do so? Criminal, of course. Now, are the average of negroes equal in formation, in native intelligence, in prudence or providence, to well-informed white children of fourteen? We who have lived with them for forty years, think not. The competition of the world would be too much for the children. They would be cheated out of their property and debased in their morals. Yet they would meet every where with sympathizing friends of their own color, ready to aid, advise and assist them. The negro would be exposed to the same competition and greater temptations, with no greater ability to contend with them, with these additional difficulties. He would be welcome nowhere; meet with thousands of enemies and no friends. If he went North, the white laborers would kick him and cuff him, and drive him out of employment. If he went to Africa, the savages would cook him and eat him. If he went to the West Indies, they would not let him in, or if they did, they would soon make of him a savage and idolater.

We have a further question to ask. If it be right and incumbent to subject children to the authority of parents and guardians, and idiots and lunatics to committees, would it not be equally right and incumbent to give the free negroes masters, until at least they arrive at years of discretion, which very few ever did or will attain? What is the difference between the authority of a parent and of a master? Neither pay wages and each is entitled to the services of those subject to him. The father may not sell his child forever, but may hire him out till he is twenty-one. The free negro's master may also be restrained from selling. Let him stand in *loco parentis,* and call him papa instead of master. Look closely into slavery, and you will see nothing so hideous in it; or if you do, you will find plenty of it at home in its most hideous form.

The earliest civilization of which history gives account is that of Egypt. The negro was always in contact with that civilization. For four thousand years he has had opportunities of becoming civilized. Like the wild horse, he must be caught, tamed and domesticated. When his subjugation ceases he again runs wild, like the cattle on the Pampas of the South, or the horses on the prairies of the West. His condition in the West Indies proves this. . . .

# INDEX

INDEX

# Index